Sylvia J. Makowski

Integrating

Reengineering with

Total Quality

Also available from ASQC Quality Press

A History of Managing for Quality: The Evolution, Trends, and Future Directions of Managing for Quality
J. M. Juran, editor-in-chief

Total Quality Service: A Simplified Approach to Using the Baldrige Award Criteria
Sheila Kessler

The Reward and Recognition Process in Total Quality Management
Stephen B. Knouse

Actual Experiences of a CEO: How to Make Continuous Improvement in Manufacturing Succeed in Your Company
Hank McHale

Managing the Four Stages of TQM: How to Achieve World-Class Performance
Charles N. Weaver

Reengineering the Organization: A Step-by-Step Approach to Corporate Revitalization
Jeffrey N. Lowenthal

Process Reengineering: The Key to Achieving Breakthrough Success
Lon Roberts

To request a complimentary catalog of publications, call 800-248-1946.

INTEGRATING

REENGINEERING WITH

TOTAL QUALITY

Joseph N. Kelada

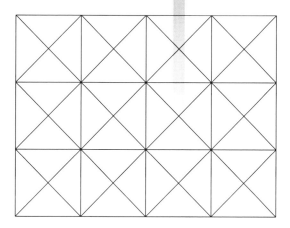

ASQC Quality Press
Milwaukee, Wisconsin

Integrating Reengineering with Total Quality
Joseph N. Kelada

Library of Congress Cataloging-in-Publication Data

Kelada, Joseph N., 1934–
    Integrating reengineering with total quality / Joseph N. Kelada.
        p.   cm.
    Includes bibliographical references and index.
    ISBN 0-87389-339-5
    1. Total quality management.   2. Organizational change—
Management.   3. Corporate reorganizations.   I. Title.
    HD62.15.K45   1995
    658.5'62—dc20   95-23859
                                                              CIP

© 1996 by ASQC

Although not a translation of "Comprendre et réaliser la qualité totale," 2nd ed., by the same author (Dollard-des-Ormeaux, Quebec, Canada: Quafec Inc., 1992), this work reproduces large copyrighted segments of that book. This reproduction has been duly authorized. Except for figures and illustrations, specifically identifying those segments would have been impractical.

10 9 8 7 6 5 4 3 2

ISBN 0-87389-339-5

Acquisitions Editor: Susan Westergard
Project Editor: Kelley Cardinal

ASQC Mission: To facilitate continuous improvement and increase customer satisfaction by identifying, communicating, and promoting the use of quality principles, concepts, and technologies; and thereby be recognized throughout the world as the leading authority on, and champion for, quality.

Attention: Schools and Corporations
ASQC Quality Press books, audio, video, and software are available at quantity discounts with bulk purchases for business, educational, or instructional use. For information, please contact ASQC Quality Press at 800-248-1946, or write to ASQC Quality Press, P. O. Box 3005, Milwaukee, WI 53201-3005.

For a free copy of the ASQC Quality Press Publications Catalog, including ASQC membership information, call 800-248-1946.

Printed in the United States of America

 Printed on acid-free paper

 ASQC
Quality Press
611 East Wisconsin Avenue
Milwaukee, Wisconsin 53202

To my mother,
with deep love
and affection.

Contents

Chapter 6   How to Implement Total Quality Management   121

PART II   Practicing TQM

Chapter 7   The Human Aspect of Total Quality   151

Chapter 8   Planning for Total Quality   185

Chapter 9   Organizing for Total Quality   211

Chapter 10   Total Quality Assessment and Control   239

Chapter 11   Total Quality Assurance and Standardization   273

Foreword

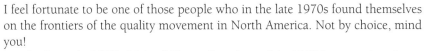

I feel fortunate to be one of those people who in the late 1970s found themselves on the frontiers of the quality movement in North America. Not by choice, mind you!

In the early 1970s I joined Xerox Canada, and in 1976 I was assigned to a post in Rochester, New York as head of multinational business planning for my company. Among my most important challenges was finding product for the Japanese market. By then, many of Xerox's original patents had expired, and our Japanese affiliate, Fuji Xerox, was being eaten alive by a horde of new competitors based in Japan. Not only were these new entrants making acceptable products, they were doing so at about half of our cost!

What we gradually began to appreciate was that we had not encountered just a new class of competition but a whole new management technique that was so powerful that the only response possible was to emulate it. We were fortunate to have a very strong ally in Fuji Xerox, or the outcome of the battle might have been very different indeed.

Despite their lack of experience in product development and their somewhat limited manufacturing expertise, Fuji Xerox was able to turn the situation around without much help from us. Simply put, they did it by fully embracing the quality imperative—so much so that, in 1980, they won the Deming Prize for quality leadership.

This was a potent lesson for all of us at Xerox, and, with the leadership of David Kearns, president of Xerox Corporation, we quickly redirected our efforts. By 1978, we had determined the product designs for the 1980s and there were many attempts to implement the now infamous quality circles.

When I took over as president of Xerox Canada in 1982, there was still a lot of struggle going on with our attempts to integrate this flood of new concepts in management. Fortunately, our manufacturing people showed the way. Their natural bent for statistical quality control and their focus on process enabled them to more readily adapt to this new environment. As a result, our new product line, now called the "10 Series," was an unqualified success, and it literally saved our company.

We were far from satisfied, however. We now knew how powerful these precepts were, and we wanted to apply them broadly throughout the company. Our goal was to outperform our competition by applying quality principles in every aspect of our business.

Our strategy was straightforward. Superior quality is the most devastating competitive strategy possible. Why? Because best quality always wins, but only when the sole arbiter of quality is the customer.

Thus it was that, in 1983, a team representing all of the functions in Xerox Corporation developed what came to be called "Leadership Through Quality." This was a "bet the company" approach that committed everyone to an all-out effort to make total quality the centerpiece in every aspect of the business.

Our aim was to move from a company that was bureaucratic and slow to one that was customer focused and change driven. We wanted to become a company that led the way in high response and high performance for customers.

The active ingredient in our approach was our quality improvement process. Drawn largely from Deming's work, this process was built on team problem-solving skills. It focused on process improvement as the key to continuously creating superior quality. Absolutely everyone in the company, starting at the top, was trained in this new language and method.

Anyone who has made the same journey of discovery that we did can readily understand that it takes a lot longer in the doing than in the telling. However, despite many false starts and restarts along the way, we did it. We transformed the company, and, in the process, we not only saved Xerox, we set it on a new, higher trajectory into the future.

What intrigues me about Joseph Kelada's book is that he identifies many of the tough issues we faced in implementing total quality and offers some common-sense approaches. Obviously, we all have to adapt these ideas to our own organizations, but Kelada lays out a framework that will help guide readers through this critical transition.

I am particularly interested in the debate that surrounds the term *business reengineering*. Is this a new approach that ultimately supplants TQM, or is it, in fact, an important extension of the quality imperative? Based on our experience, I strongly believe the latter.

In our work at Xerox, we ultimately concluded that it was essential to overlay the continuous quality process that existed at all levels with a series of councils responsible for the long chain systems that wind their way through the entire company. Improving these systems was absolutely vital to creating the kind of quantum change needed to achieve our goals. The problem we had was that no one person or organization had the capability or the mandate to manage these critical systems from start to finish. As a result, we had lost the cause-and-effect relationships essential to sustaining systems that are self-monitoring, with the result that we appeared to be constantly "shooting behind the duck."

What we needed were highly integrated, dynamic systems capable of meeting customer requirements on a long-term basis. We applied exactly the same principles found in leadership through quality at this higher level of implementation, and we were able to produce some astounding results. This approach was a major contributor both to Xerox Corporation's winning the Malcolm Baldrige National Quality Award and to Xerox Canada's winning the Gold Award for Quality.

As I said at that time, I can summarize my feelings on the subject of total quality by saying, simply, "it works." Unfortunately, total quality is very difficult to accomplish, and many organizations will fail to achieve it. Those who do, however, will find that the world is their marketplace and that they will have a brilliant future.

I believe that this book will reinforce its readers' resolve to lead the charge toward change in their organizations. I also believe it will clarify their understanding of the issues and give them fresh ideas for overcoming the barriers to achieving total quality.

In order to achieve its full economic potential, every country must have a broadly based approach to the use of these new management techniques—at all levels and in all institutions. Books such as this one by Joseph Kelada are making an invaluable contribution toward this end.

David R. McCamus
Former President
Xerox Canada

Preface

This is a book about quality, total quality, and total quality management; how they relate to each other; and how they relate to and integrate with reengineering. Why another book on total quality? Since the expression *quality control* appeared in the early years of this century, and since the expressions *total quality* and *total quality management* surfaced more than 10 years ago, thousands and thousands of publications—books and articles—have been produced on these topics. So what is there to say that has not been said before, over and over again?

Since the early 1980s, when total quality and total quality management began to be talked about and attract the attention of business leaders internationally, the world has changed drastically. The Berlin Wall has crumbled; the Soviet Union is dissolved; most of Europe has united into one huge market; communist countries have or are trying to become capitalistic; and the Americas have initiated a huge, free-trade market, which started with the United States and Canada and has recently been joined by Mexico.

As *Fortune* puts it, "Since 1985, thousands of organizations have adopted and applied the principles of total quality management (TQM). It has proven to be a highly adaptive management tool that is here to stay. It has passed the fad test. TQM has delivered on its promise, but has not reached its potential."[1]

Today, people talk much less about TQM; however, they practice it, applying its concepts and principles to their work. TQM has become a way of thinking, of being, and of doing that does not really need to be called anything. As Rahul Jacob puts it, "Many companies that have successfully adopted TQM don't even use the phrase *total quality* anymore; it has simply become a way of doing business."[2]

So, why write a book about TQM now? When people first talked and authors first wrote about total quality or total quality management, they presented it as a new global approach to management, based on their experience with quality control and their views of the future. Now the future has become present—or even past. What was utopia then is reality now. Companies have practiced—or have attempted to practice—total quality management. We have witnessed successes and failures, though, unfortunately, more failures than successes. If we are to progress, we have to profit from these experiences and learn the lessons that will help us to avoid failures and achieve success.

On January 1, 1993, the world woke up to a new, unified European market, the European Union (EU). Borders disappeared and customs personnel were sent home. A new buzzword spread rapidly across Europe, then around the world: *ISO 9000*. It represented a series of quality standards, developed and published by the International Organization for Standardization and recommended by the EU to govern trade among its member countries and with other countries around the world.

Then another wave began—that of registration to one of the ISO standards. This added to the confusion in the total quality field; various authors and specialists had given it different definitions and suggested different approaches, each claiming that theirs was the only way to achieve total quality. Some authors and consultants wrongly equated total quality with ISO 9000, whose attraction is an internationally recognized status that has become a good marketing asset.

At the same time, the concept of *reengineering* became popular. Some experts claim that reengineering has replaced total quality which, they explain, is nothing but an incremental, limited, and continuous improvement of existing processes. In contrast, reengineering is a radical change in business processes. This is the most effective approach to dealing with the drastic changes the world is undergoing.

However, reengineering is nothing but innovations or breakthroughs that, together with continuous improvement, are means to achieve and maintain total quality. Reengineering and total quality are not two different approaches; they are two parts of the same approach. Reeengineering is the means, total quality the objective. This is what this book is all about.

Since the late 1970s, I have written about quality and total quality; taught these subjects at the undergraduate, graduate, and postgraduate levels; spoken about them in North America, Europe, Asia, and Africa; read about, met, and listened to quality specialists such as W. Edwards Deming (Mr. Deming invited me to witness an intervention at a General Motors plant in 1989), J. M. Juran, Armand V. Feigenbaum, Philip Crosby, and Kaoru Ishikawa; and consulted with private companies as well as public organizations. Thus, having observed more than a decade of total quality and a couple of years of reinvented reengineering, I now have a mature and revised view of these subjects. This book presents a number of new concepts that I have either developed or that have been developed by others and that I have applied or have seen applied by successful organizations, although often intuitively. Among these are the *total quality triad, QVALITY* and *ACE, introversive* and *extraversive* management, and the *market-in* concept. Internal customers have become *internal partners* or *teammates*.

Moreover, the book integrates the numerous practices that these organizations have adopted, though often in an unrelated fashion. It also shows how total quality is achieved through a balanced combination of continuous improvement and reengineering.

The book has been organized in two parts. The first part deals with the objectives of embarking on a total quality process and the definitions of and relationships between quality, total quality, total quality management, and business reengineering. It also discusses how these concepts operate in a service environment. Part I ends with step-by-step instructions for implementing TQM.

Chapter 1 introduces the importance of the subject and presents the reasons for failure and the conditions for success of the total quality approach. Chapter 2 defines the terms *quality* and *total quality* in objective, concrete, and measurable characteristics, introducing the total quality triad and the QVALITY and ACE concepts, describing the customer's needs. Chapter 3 discusses the principles of total quality management and introduces a new concept that I call *extraversive management* as opposed to the traditional *introversive* approach. Chapter 4 develops the notions of continuous improvement and reengineering or innovation, showing that total quality is achieved through both. Chapter 5 deals with total quality in a service environment, and chapter 6 presents a step-by-step approach to implementing TQM in an organization.

Part II takes the reader through the management activities and practices required to achieve and maintain total quality. Chapter 7 concentrates on the essential human aspects of total quality. Indeed, nothing significant can be achieved and maintained without the continuous contribution of all of the people in the organization, at all levels, all the time. Chapter 8 presents the activities related to planning for total quality. The total quality diagnosis is the starting point of any total quality process. Then, objectives have to be set that will satisfy both the shareholder and the customer. A strategy is then prepared and a plan of action worked out to implement the strategy successfully.

Chapter 9 deals with organizing for total quality. Traditional pyramid-shaped organizations do not work as efficiently as before. Instead of managing by function, the trend now is *managing by process.* Teams do not work within the boundaries of a functional department but around processes. GE Medical Systems has a "vice president of order to remittance" in charge of activities ranging from procurement and production to marketing and sales, shipping, accounting, and so on.

Chapter 10 deals with total quality assessment and control. One has to stop, from time to time, and observe what is being achieved. One has to collect information to detect and correct errors and limit their consequences, as well as to feed the diagnosis activity required for planning and replanning.

Chapter 11 is on quality assurance and standardization. Rather than detecting and correcting errors, systems are designed to prevent their occurrence. This applies to the organization's suppliers (*external quality assurance*) as well as to the organization itself (*internal quality assurance*).

Chapter 12 presents the ISO 9000 series standards. With the globalization of the economy and trade, internationally recognized quality systems standards had to be developed and applied, replacing former national standards, if and where they existed. Although it offers no guarantee that quality will result, the ISO 9000 series is a very useful tool in helping to produce quality.

Chapter 13 summarizes the main practices related to TQM—even if some of them were not developed with total quality in mind—and it shows how these should be integrated into a global approach such as the one presented in this book.

An epilogue closes the book, and a glossary is added to eliminate the confusion that most terms in the total quality field present.

The uniqueness of this book is the fact that it offers a global framework within which to integrate the basic concepts and practices required to successfully implement, achieve, and maintain total quality, in which the reengineering concept has been integrated.

Notes

1. "Quality: The Next Decade of Progress," *Fortune,* 19 September 1994, 158.

2. Rahul Jacob, "TQM: More than a Dying Fad?" *Fortune,* 18 October 1993, 66.

Acknowledgments

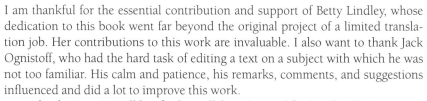

I am thankful for the essential contribution and support of Betty Lindley, whose dedication to this book went far beyond the original project of a limited translation job. Her contributions to this work are invaluable. I also want to thank Jack Ognistoff, who had the hard task of editing a text on a subject with which he was not too familiar. His calm and patience, his remarks, comments, and suggestions influenced and did a lot to improve this work.

I thank Pierre F. Caillibot for his collaboration and for kindly allowing me to use his material on ISO 9000, as well as Maureen Breitenberg from the National Institute of Standards and Technology of the U.S. Department of Commerce, the International Organization for Standardization, Josiane Désilets from the Standards Council of Canada, and the Canadian General Standards Board for their help and information about standardization and the ISO 9000 series standards, and for their contribution of material for the two chapters on standardization and ISO 9000. Because many parts of this material were blended with other material in the two chapters, not all of it has been referenced at the end of these chapters.

I owe to professor Mattio O. Diorio special debt, because he was instrumental in my joining the Production and Operations Management (POM) Department of the HEC Business School and in my specializing in quality and later in total quality. His moral support and his collaboration throughout these years have helped me develop, teach, and apply a number of concepts and practices presented in this work. He also kindly volunteered to review part of the book. I also thank Professor Jean Nollet, the Department Chair, and my colleagues at the POM department for their constant support and collaboration. I thank Sheila King, who has assisted me for many years in an effort that culminated in the production of this book. My thanks to Serge Godin (Group CGI), Dave McCamus and Rémi Lacasse (Xerox Canada), and Gordon Levering (Armstrong Canada) for their collaboration and support.

I am also thankful to HEC Business School for their financial support while I prepared the material for this book. My special thanks to Susan Westergard, Kelley Cardinal, Annette Wall, Cathy Christine, Mark Olson, the reviewers, and all of the people at ASQC Quality Press for their collaboration and support. They provided helpful comments and recommendations and helped in the creation of this work as presented in its final format.

PART I
THE FOUNDATION
OF TOTAL QUALITY

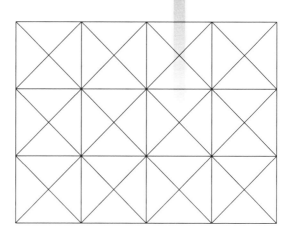

Total quality is here to stay. Since the concept took fire in the early 1980s, a large number of companies have attempted to implement it in order to regain and/or maintain their competitiveness in a drastically changing business world. A few of these organizations have succeeded, while a great number have failed and abandoned their attempt, claiming that total quality is a passing fad or that it is not applicable in this part of the world, in their industry, or in their specific cases.

Some organizations embarked on a total quality process because they saw the light, others because they felt the heat. Why is it, then, that some have succeeded while most have failed?

Part I consists of six chapters. It will answer this question, presenting the conditions of the success or causes of the failure of such companies. It goes on to lay down the foundations of the total quality approach, defining concretely the terms *quality* and *total quality*. It then defines *total quality management*.

The advent of the reengineering movement has created some confusion concerning its connection, if any, with the total quality approach. Should organizations stop their total quality process and switch now to reengineering? I show here that total quality and reengineering are not two different or conflicting approaches. They are two aspects of the same approach.

Total quality is not limited to the manufacturing sector. It is also applicable to the ever-expanding service sector. Part I presents an overview of the application of total quality in this sector, pointing out its similarity with the manufacturing sector and the difference between the two sectors.

Finally, Part I outlines a step-by-step program to implement total quality and to evaluate the implementation process.

Chapter 1

*Some do it because they've seen the light,
others because they feel the heat.*

The Management Revolution

Winds of Change

Winds of change are sweeping across the globe, and as they pass, they are shifting political boundaries, destroying the barriers to trade, and drastically rearranging the face of the political landscape.

The transformations they have ushered in would have been undreamed of only 20, 10, or even 5 years ago: the Berlin Wall has crumbled, and Germany has unified; Czechoslovakia and Yugoslavia have both broken up; the Soviet Union has collapsed and, with it, the Iron Curtain; in South Africa, apartheid is history; there are breakthroughs in the Middle East peace initiative. Everywhere borders have been relaxed, tariffs and trade barriers eased; Eastern Europe has joined the free world; 15 countries of Western Europe are moving toward greater economic unity and have created a unified market—the European Union; other European countries are participating in free trade agreements. The United States, Canada, Mexico, and others have discussed or are discussing the formation of a free trade zone, despite the efforts of the protectionist lobbies in these countries. We are already living in a world economy with international markets where companies face global competition. As one company's slogan says, "We do business in only one market: Planet Earth." And who knows, in the future even that market may expand!

The world is also undergoing radical technological and social changes. All of these changes are significantly affecting the way business is conducted in not only international markets but also in all local markets, which are now increasingly exposed to worldwide competition. No organization, big or small, private or public, in the manufacturing or the service sector, can afford to ignore these changes.

And what changes they are, indeed! Not so long ago, chances were that the rose you gave to your sweetheart had been grown in a nearby greenhouse. Not today! That rose may well have been flown in only a few hours ago from Chile, Singapore, or some other place thousands of miles away. Time was when we talked of owning an American car. But does such a thing as an American car even exist nowadays? We see Chrysler, Ford, and General Motors cars manufactured in Canada, Mexico, or Taiwan; Toyotas, Hondas, and Nissans are manufactured in the United States and Canada. In reality, cars no longer have a "nationality." Until recently, one of the most popular imported "foreign" cars in Japan was a Honda, manufactured in the United States! According to a Toyota advertisement, the Camry model, manufactured in Georgetown, Kentucky, is made with U.S. parts purchased from 174 American suppliers scattered through many states. The advertisement indicated that these American suppliers are not really all American. Actually, most of them are either owned by Toyota itself, by subsidiaries of other Japanese firms, or by joint American–Japanese companies.

Not since the Industrial Revolution have organizations been faced with the absolute necessity of changing the way they are managed and operated. However, despite all the changes in the world, a great number of organizations have not adjusted their way of thinking and doing things. They persist in using antiquated approaches to management and still apply concepts developed a century ago, when Henri Fayol suggested a pyramid-shaped organizational structure, inspired by the military, with big bosses at the top and smaller bosses at the bottom, and Frederick W. Taylor advocated increased productivity by improving the management-developed methods that workers used. Not that these concepts were wrong; productivity did increase dramatically, and most companies organized along those lines have indeed performed well through the years. However, as one manager put it, these companies are applying yesterday's methods today and still hope to be in business tomorrow.

Fortune magazine has called IBM and General Motors dinosaurs, suggesting that the decline of these giants is the biggest "what-went-wrong" story in U.S. business history.[1] Gone are the days when powerful organizations like these could develop and manufacture products under the assumption that they, better than anyone else in the world—their own customers included—knew what was good for the customer. They are now being taught a few lessons by nations such as Japan, which, from its status a half century ago as a small, resourceless country, has grown into a giant economic power. Similarly, Korea and other Asian nations—until recently considered Third World countries—have moved to an impressive position on the world scene, with products that can compete with those from Japan, Germany, and the United States.

Not only are things changing, but the rate of change is accelerating. The progress of technology-based change is more geometric than linear. An increasing number of organizations are reacting to these changes; they are introducing new ways of thinking, adopting new attitudes and behaviors, and implementing new management approaches. Some of these companies adopt new approaches because they realize that the new ways are the ways of the future: these are the companies that have seen the light. Other companies adopt such approaches only as a last resort when they are feeling the heat of global competition and, perhaps, facing bankruptcy.

However, a disappointingly high percentage of these organizations have failed to make any significant improvements to their overall performance in the marketplace. Discouraged, they have abandoned their attempts, then blamed their failures on the various new management approaches which, they claim, are either too theoretical, too faddish, or, as in the case of Japanese techniques, too culturally alien to integrate into our social fabric.

These setbacks notwithstanding, there is a management revolution afoot. Amidst the string of recently emerged management approaches, practices, and techniques—many of which seem to make good sense and yield concrete results—the total quality approach, or *total quality management* (TQM), has attracted a great deal of attention. Although all of its techniques do not work for every circumstance, the significant number of its success stories indicates that, if properly applied, TQM does produce excellent results in a majority of cases.

More recently, the reengineering approach or concept has emerged. Most authors make a distinction between this approach and TQM. Some go so far as to suggest that the two are totally dissimilar, while others suggest that they complement each other. In my opinion, reengineering and TQM are both part of the same approach.

The supporters of each of the various management approaches, including TQM, would claim that their approach is based on revolutionary ways of thinking that render all other management theories obsolete. In fact, all of these approaches make use of management principles and practices that have been known, taught, and applied for a long time. Customer satisfaction; process management for improvement or innovation; flowcharting techniques (newly dubbed *mapping*); elimination, modification, or combination of activities aimed at streamlining processes and optimizing outputs; participative management; teamwork; problem-solving techniques—all of these are well-known buzzwords that have circulated in the business world for almost a century. The missing secret ingredient is the *integration* of all these concepts and practices into a single, global approach that will allow organizations to meet the expanded competition of a world market.

The Total Quality Approach

The worldwide emphasis on quality followed on the heels of the oil crises and the subsequent economic recessions of the 1970s. Interest rates and inflation climbed to record heights. Western organizations started to lose their traditional markets to imports as customers looked for more energy-efficient, durable, and reliable products.

This made companies realize that product quality was a critical factor for success or even mere survival. The case of the American automotive industry is the first to come to mind. In the 1970s, it lost a third of its domestic North American market to imports, mainly Japanese but also German; and only through gigantic efforts has it been able to recover some of that loss.

It was imperative to improve quality; therefore, companies started introducing new concepts and techniques—such as the quality circles used in Japan—and at the same time revived old techniques like quality assurance and statistical process control (SPC). Quality experts W. Edwards Deming and J. M. Juran, who had worked with the Japanese in the 1950s and were credited with their success in producing top-quality products, finally began to be discovered in their own country 20 years later. The Western world was swept by a tidal wave of books, seminars, and conferences on quality. Quality did improve, but, by the early 1980s, the quality circles programs faded out, and the results of quality programs were not as dramatic as companies had hoped for. Furthermore, as the quality of Western products improved, that of Japanese and other Asian nations' products improved even more.

In the 1980s, a new approach was born: the total quality approach, better known now as TQM. This approach advocates that

- The concept of quality extends well beyond the quality of the product
- Everyone in an organization participates in the quality improvement process
- Top management, starting with the chief executive officer and chief operations officer, demonstrates strong involvement and leadership
- The emphasis is laid on attaining and surpassing customer satisfaction
- External partners also participate in the total quality effort

At this point, the quality movement has made further progress, entering the service sector, including government agencies and publicly owned organizations.

Why Do Attempts to Implement TQM Fail?

Having observed a number of organizations around the world, I note that the majority of those who attempt to introduce the total quality approach fail. In fact, I estimate that about 80 percent of them fail, no matter how much money and time they have spent on the TQM effort. I attribute this high rate of failure to the fact that total quality is perceived by many as a philosophy rather than as a practical approach. Actually, most so-called total quality experts have suggested *what* to do, but they have not placed enough emphasis on *how* to do it. However, this is not the only reason for TQM failures. Based on my observations, there are five main causes of these failures, that is, five conditions that must be met if attempts to implement TQM are to succeed (see Figure 1.1). Weakness in either

1. Top management's will to change and capability of changing
2. An accurate definition of both *quality* and *total quality*
3. Knowing how to implement total quality
4. Knowing how to achieve total quality
5. Knowing how to maintain total quality

Figure 1.1. Five conditions for the successful implementation of TQM.

Source: J. N. Kelada, *Technologie de la qualité totale, reengineering et autres techniques* (Dollard-des-Ormeaux, Quebec, Canada: Editions Quafec, 1994), 1–5.

one or several of these conditions have caused the failure of the TQM implementation attempts.

The very first condition for success in the implementation of TQM is the existence of a sense of urgency to change things around, a conviction of the absolute necessity to modify a long-standing way of thinking. In successful organizations, top managers themselves are both convinced and convincing. In other words, they are committed to the changes that TQM requires, and they are able to convince the rest of their organization that these changes are essential. In fact, they convince not only their own managers and personnel, but also their outside partners—suppliers, distributors, and so on—who are key collaborators in the achievement of total quality. We have observed that, where companies succeed in achieving and maintaining total quality, this conviction runs high—close to obsession, in fact.

The second condition for success is understanding the difference between *quality* and *total quality* and being able to define both in concrete and measurable terms. I got a call once from the president of a well-known consulting firm who informed me that he had just landed an important contract with a big customer to implement total quality. He was wondering if I would be interested in meeting his staff to explain what total quality was all about! No one can achieve something that is not clearly defined and measured. One must know not only what both quality and total quality are, but also what to do in order to achieve and maintain them. Business leaders are not totally to blame for this lack of knowledge. In fact, their confusion about these concepts is exacerbated by this very proliferation of quality gurus, consultants, and so-called total quality experts. Each of these experts preaches a different gospel, a different approach, and gives his or her own definition and interpretation of total quality. With the sweeping demand for total quality expertise, experts have sprung up everywhere, out of nowhere, and have invaded the business world. Definitions of quality and total quality abound. However, the definitions are mostly too vague and sometimes even contradictory.

The third condition of success concerns the implementation process. A step-by-step methodology is required to successfully introduce, achieve, and maintain total quality, and it should be rigorously applied. Systematic evaluation of each step is essential to success. In other words, to practice TQM successfully, one must know *why* it is so important to adopt TQM, *what* quality and total quality are all about, and *how* to achieve, maintain, and implement them.

The fourth condition of success is knowing how to *achieve* total quality. Wanting to change, and knowing what quality and total quality mean, are not enough to guarantee success. One must understand how to do it. Conversely, understanding how to achieve quality will not likely lead to success unless accompanied by the will to do it and a clear definition of what the ultimate goal is. To give an illustration, some companies neither attempt to convince people of the importance of total quality nor define quality and total quality in concrete, measurable terms. They embark right away on massive training programs for all employees on quality improvement techniques and expect to reach some tangible and significant results in the short term or, at most, medium term. On quite a number of occasions, I have had calls from companies that had spent significant amounts of money on training but were disappointed because none of their employees seemed to understand how to use the techniques they had just learned. Typically, the representatives of these companies expressed their need as a revivifying "shot in the arm." They had not understood that they could not expect to make a significant change in culture, habits, attitudes, and behavior by simply teaching people new techniques; they had not explained why the techniques had to be used nor what they were meant to achieve.

However, once people are convinced that they have to achieve total quality and know how to define and measure it, they, of course, have to be taught how to achieve it. Over the years, a total quality *technology* has emerged that includes step-by-step processes, methodologies, and techniques such as policy deployment, quality function deployment, process management and reengineering, problem identification, and problem solving.

The fifth condition is knowing how to *maintain* total quality. After the first rush of enthusiasm, there seems to be a cool-down period; people are observed to be losing steam, tailing off, slowing down; old habits reappear while posters and charts start collecting dust. Companies view it as a normal phenomenon and do not know how to revive the initial enthusiasm and keep it going. As the process slows down, skepticism replaces enthusiasm. These organizations had learned how to achieve total quality, they had convinced their personnel that change was imperative, they had defined quality and total quality, they had even trained everybody to achieve it—but they did not know how to maintain it, year after year.

The solution to maintaining effort and interest in total quality lies in strong leadership on the part of management. The behavior of top managers must reflect not only their attitudes toward total quality but also their recognition of their employees' successes. Visible recognition of success in the form of celebrations and rewards for employees is a particularly effective means of maintaining interest in total quality.

In this book, we shall systematically present ways and means to fulfill these five conditions for success. However, let us first explore the evolution in the world of quality.

The Importance of Quality

A popular saying goes, "If it ain't broke, don't fix it"; however, in the business world, it is changing to, "If it's broke, fix it. If it ain't broke, improve it." I would say, "Right the wrongs and improve the rights." North Americans, having evolved immediately following World War II into an affluent society, developed a tolerance toward products and services of poor quality. At that time, the rest of the world was repairing the massive destruction suffered during the conflict, whereas the North American industrial base was intact. The world was a market where demand surpassed the supply of goods and services. Companies had little to fear from competition, and anything produced could be sold.

North Americans accepted a certain amount of waste as a fact of life, and they tolerated delays, defects, and sometimes mediocrity. They even created a demand for short-lived products. The craving for newer models or ever more fashionable products produced a continuous need for replacement as, for example, in the automobile industry, where models were changed each year.

However, in today's marketplace, the business community, faced with increasing international competition and reeling from the hardships of economic recession, unemployment, and high interest rates, now recognizes that quality is an important factor to be considered. Articles in magazines like *Business Week, Fortune,* and *Harvard Business Review,* as well as numerous best-sellers, all underline management's increasing awareness of the importance of quality. The number of conferences on quality continues to increase, and, each year in North America, governments dedicate the month of October to quality. Companies such as Xerox, Motorola, Harley Davidson, AT&T, and others have significantly improved their performance by rigorously following the quality path.

However, even though they have witnessed the astonishing results obtained by countries that practice quality almost as a national philosophy—Germany, Japan, and more recently Korea and other Asian countries—top management in North America very often merely gives lip service to the quest for quality. It seems only to be a vague wish or hopeful thinking. While quality has indeed improved in our part of the world, it is mainly due to the pressure of better quality imports, and, in many instances, the rate of improvement is slower than that of foreign competition.

One study[2] shows that quality directly affects profits. A company with a small market share that produces low-quality products makes, on the average, a 7 percent return on investment (ROI), while a similar company producing high-quality products makes a 20 percent ROI. If we make the obvious assumption that quality increases the market share, then ROI can jump from a mere 7 percent to as high as 29 percent! In Japan, it is estimated that companies that were awarded the highly coveted Deming Prize have consistently made, on the average, twice as much profit as the industry average.

Effects of Quality and Consequences of Unquality

Although no one produces a substandard product or poorly performs a service intentionally, we nevertheless tend to accept it as part of human nature. Indeed, we even say, "To err is human and to forgive is divine." This human error, added to the tolerance of North Americans for errors, is among the reasons that unquality products persist in the marketplace. Numerous examples exist to illustrate this point. While popular belief may blame terrorist activities for fatal airplane accidents, one study showed that 67 percent of these accidents were due to human error on the part of pilots, crew members, or air controllers.[3] The explosion of the space shuttle Challenger seems to have resulted from defective design in O-ring joints—a defect known to the operating personnel but never corrected. In the former Soviet Union, the infamous 1986 Chernobyl nuclear plant accident and its catastrophic side effects were also caused by human error. When plant technicians decided to bypass some safety procedures, their error resulted in a reactor meltdown, an explosion, and, to our day, ongoing consequences: malformed children are born, animals suffer from mysterious diseases, and agriculture will be affected for many more years to come.

In France, the Perrier water incident was also due to human error. Traces of benzene (oil) were found in a few bottles, and, as a result, millions of bottles of this product were destroyed and important markets were lost for a significant period of time. A joke at the time declared that when the price of oil went up, so did the price of Perrier water. Another study showed there to be a 15 percent error rate in hospital medications. They were being given either at the wrong time, or in the wrong quantity, or to the wrong patient.[4] In one instance, a nurse gave 600 milligrams of Xylocaine to a patient instead of 60; the patient died 45 minutes later from a heart attack. In another study, 2000 autopsies revealed that 34 percent of the doctors' diagnoses contained "human" errors and that one third of those errors resulted in the patient's death.

Other reasons account for the unquality of products and services. One is the gross underestimation of quality costs,[5] and a second is the complexity of defining and measuring quality. Both activities are much more complex than measuring a quantity or ensuring that deadlines are met. In manufacturing, defining and measuring quality requires specialists (engineers, technicians, chemists, biologists), laboratories, sophisticated instruments, and apparatus with which to estimate costs. In a service environment, the situation is even more complex. There, quality is still more difficult to define, let alone evaluate or measure objectively.

Even where there exists a profound and genuine conviction, quality is not necessarily achieved. In reality, for a product to be marketable not only does it have to be produced at the right or required level of quality, but it has to be produced and delivered on time ("We need it right away!"), in the right quantity ("We have to install 634 units, repair 32 vehicles, serve 456 customers"), at the right place ("We have to have it delivered to a specific neighborhood, city, country, market"), and at a minimum cost ("We can't go over budget. We have to reduce costs to be competitive"). In short, this whole set of conditions—including all the customer specifications and the required quality level—must be fulfilled simultaneously with quality. Management, as well as practically everyone else, struggles with many simultaneous objectives—quality, quantity, schedule, costs—and often quality is sacrificed or compromised to meet the other objectives.

Quality is indeed everybody's business. A company can be likened to a chain that is only as strong as its weakest link. Every department and every individual may affect the final quality of a product or service. A buyer may order substandard materials or parts, a storekeeper might damage a part or product, an engineer may provide faulty specifications, a draftsperson might make an error in a drawing, an operator may not follow a manufacturing procedure, a shipper may ship the wrong product, or an installer might do a shoddy job. And if all of these processes go well, still a rude employee (receptionist, delivery person, sales representative) can alienate a customer, who will stop buying the product regardless of its high quality, punctual delivery, or minimum cost. So many people, both inside and outside an organization, may affect the final quality that the slightest error committed by anyone along the chain may undermine everyone else's efforts to achieve and improve quality.

Recognizing the importance of quality and its impact on their economy and on their companies' profitability, countries have initiated national efforts to promote quality. Since the early 1950s, the Union of Japanese Scientists and Engineers (JUSE) has awarded the Deming Prize to companies successful in achieving significant results in their quality efforts. Since 1988, the Malcolm Baldrige National Quality Award has become a highly regarded award in the United States. The president of the United States presents it annually to organizations (large and small, from the manufacturing and the service sectors) that have demonstrated the will to achieve quality products and services by setting up formal and effective quality systems. The measure of customer satisfaction they have achieved attests to their success.[6] Companies or divisions of companies such as Motorola, Xerox, IBM, General Motors, Federal Express, and Milliken are among the select few chosen to be recipients of the Malcolm Baldrige Award. The year 1992 saw the establishment of a similar award in Europe, where King Juan Carlos presented the European Quality Award for the first time to Rank Xerox for its achievement in quality.

Management Attitude

Top managers may recognize the importance of quality and talk about it at every opportunity they have, inside and outside their company, but they still pass the responsibility for quality actions and programs down to someone from upper or middle management. Top managers do not generally become personally involved in these actions or programs, yet they are willing to approve sizable budgets for them and support their lower echelons' efforts to carry them out. Ironically, they delegate lower-level managers to go to conferences, seminars, and public meetings on quality management originally aimed at top management and, because they are generally looking for visibility and exposure, top managers show up at such events only when these are highly publicized and frequented by journalists and political figures. In reality, despite all the attention paid to it, top management still considers the subject of quality to be a technical matter, similar to production or engineering. Management must realize that quality is not a technical responsibility that can be left to specialists.

The Cost of Unquality

The cost of unquality is grossly underestimated. Top management in many organizations estimate it to be less than 5 percent of gross sales revenues. Experts on industrial firms put it at more than 20 percent (that is, three to four times the profit expressed as a percentage return on sales). In service firms, the loss due to poor quality is much higher still. Traditional accounting systems cannot compute the cost of unquality, most of it being considered the cost of doing business. Defects are tolerated and attributed to unavoidable human error. As Juran and Gryna put it, "chronic quality problems are the ones which have been occurring for a long time, and are accepted as inevitable."[7] For example, a 2 percent level of poor quality in the form of defective products translates into the habit of producing 2 percent more product than is actually required, buying 2 percent more raw materials, increasing the level of inventories by 2 percent, hiring 2 percent more workers—and eventually a point is reached where these levels are considered normal and they go unnoticed. A chain reaction sets in. Demand for these products drops and is diverted to the competition; the producer attributes the drop in sales to recession, economic conditions, or to unfair practices by local or foreign competition; and ultimately the producer seeks government help and subsidies to save jobs.

Overquality incurs still higher costs, and therefore care should be taken to avoid it. Overquality is insidious, for it is not generally detected from customer complaints and so goes unnoticed. Yet it affects and reduces competitiveness because it adds to cost without yielding any benefits to either the producer of goods or services or to the customer; it is a waste and total loss.

If the costs of unquality and overquality are indisputable, can we then presume that quality really bears no cost? Philip B. Crosby, in his best-seller *Quality Is Free,* argues that unquality is the factor that entails cost; it results in doing the same thing over and over again and in costly scrap and rework.[8] If all employees do their work right the first time, these costs are eliminated. While this is true, one cannot say that quality is free. It is profitable but not free, for an organization must invest in prevention, training, and improving design and processes to achieve quality. If it makes this investment, then it can expect to see a significant return on investment over a medium and long range.

Management must understand that quality is not expensive—but unquality is. In a bank, a money transfer done correctly costs $10, but if done incorrectly it costs up to $400 to correct the consequences. In this example unquality costs 4000 percent more than quality! Finally, management should not blame unquality on workers because—according to some estimates—they are responsible for no more than 20 percent of all errors and defects. The remaining 80 percent are attributable to buyers, design engineers, process engineers, or errors in production and inventory control activities, order entries, and so forth.

Therefore, organizations have no choice. They must improve on the quality of products and services if they are to survive and if jobs are to be saved. Managers and workers must be able to feel pride in a job done well and a sense of belonging to a successful team and organization. Whatever competition the organization faces, it can still perform effectively if it consistently produces quality goods and services.

TQM Training and Education in the United States

In Morgantown, West Virginia, in July 1990, a group of academicians met to consider the role of academia in the development of TQM and competitiveness. This conference, the first ever of its kind, raised a number of crucial points.[9]

Industry and government leaders, it noted, have been linking the decline in competitiveness with a corresponding decline in the quality of today's college graduates. These leaders' message to academicians is that universities have dragged their feet long enough in implementing and teaching total quality management. David Kearns—who, as chairman, led the Xerox Corporation when it won the 1989 Malcolm Baldrige National Quality Award—suggested that "For all of the frailties and problems that we have in higher education in the U.S., it is the best in the world." And he added, "That asset now has to be leveraged . . . to regain our competitive advantage in the world."[10]

Implementing TQM in America's universities is no small order, however. In fact, after three days of discussion in the aforementioned meeting, it became apparent that academia has a long way to go before it can effect the changes that industry and government insist are paramount to maintaining the nation's well-being. "We're still at the awareness development stage," conceded Curt Tompkins, dean of engineering at West Virginia University.[11] "In order to address TQM curriculum needs, it is critical that all engineering and management undergraduate students be exposed to statistical thinking and human resource management techniques," according to Rashpal Ahluwalia, a West Virginia University industrial engineering professor. Ahluwalia's survey of engineering schools revealed a number of areas where TQM-related instruction would be appropriate. In terms of management issues, he suggested that engineering schools should integrate instruction in the TQM philosophy, team building, organizational behavior, and basic management.[12]

"Business school graduates are ill-prepared to help our companies plan and take necessary quality improvement steps in the years ahead," said the then U.S. assistant secretary of commerce, Thomas Murrin. "The subject of quality has been considered a domain belonging solely to our university's statistical experts. Corporate quality improvement and TQM require a much broader view to be effective. Our universities and business schools must expand their faculties' horizons accordingly."[13] Jack Evans, business professor at the University of North Carolina, stated that about 75 percent of 85 business schools surveyed offer "something on quality." "That's the good news," he said. "The bad news is how much and what's being offered. All too often, what you find in the 'typical university' syllabus is a week on control charts, not very much on notions like quality as a competitive force." Evans suggested a number of teaching opportunities in business schools: "In accounting, business schools can offer instruction on measurement systems linked to TQM; in finance, they can develop a better understanding of the cost of quality; in marketing, customer satisfaction and quality as a competitive issue; in operations, the problem-solving process, the role of variation, teamwork and continuous improvement as a way of life; and in organizational behavior, issues of motivation, recognition, and job security."[14]

To those educators not tempted by the carrot of encouragement, the Commerce Department's Murrin held out a stick of coercion. "No quality improvement movement can succeed without the active involvement of an educated and trained workforce," he admonished. "It's way past time for action when it comes to improving our education and our quality improvement systems. The competition is not waiting for us to wake up."[15]

In August 1991, American Express, Ford, IBM, Motorola, Procter & Gamble, and Xerox sponsored the Total Quality Forum, an annual gathering of academic leaders. By the end of the conference, Forum participants had agreed to work towards an agenda for action. The chairmen of these six companies wrote an open letter, published in the *Harvard Business Review,* that called for broader participation in the campaign for change. In it, they declared their belief that "business and academia have a shared responsibility to learn, to teach, and to practice total quality management. If the United States expects to improve its global competitive performance, business and academic leaders must close ranks behind an agenda that stresses the importance and value of TQM. . . . Academic institutions that are slow to embrace TQM, at best, miss the opportunity to lead change and, at worst, run the risk of becoming less relevant to the business world."[16]

Since these comments by both the Total Quality Forum and the Morgantown conference, a greater number of universities and colleges across North America have been offering courses in quality and in total quality management.

Amidst the volley of explanations and subtle distinctions, one thing is obvious: authors do not define total quality the same way. They tend to call different things by the same name or the same things by different names. Not only is the business world confused, but so are the institutions that have the responsibility to teach these approaches and/or assist in their implementation.

Conclusion

The intent of this book is not to prove anyone right or wrong, nor is it meant to provide mere definitions of words and expressions. Its aim, rather, is to put together a basic collection of concepts and techniques that will form a step-by-step methodology for achieving and maintaining high business performance and that is based on diversified experience, readings, teaching, research, and consulting.

It is clear that, faced with rapid, momentous, evolving changes, organizations have to significantly modify their way of thinking and acting. This holds true for all organizations, large and small, private and public, manufacturing and service. In order to survive and progress, companies must put greater emphasis on striving to consistently achieve not only high levels of quality, but, indeed, total quality. Total quality is not a fad or fashion that will disappear next season. It is a revolutionary concept that is taking root and fundamentally altering the way organizations do business and are managed.

Facing drastic changes, businesses must first take a long, hard look at themselves and come up with a frank, unembellished appraisal of their present situation. They have to fully understand what the implications of implementing the total quality concept are: why they should implement it; how they should implement it; and how they will achieve and maintain it. They have to improve on their products and processes.

Review Questions

1. Most of the quality control approaches and techniques used by the Japanese, such as statistical process control and participative management, were developed in the United States as early as the 1920s. Recently, an increasing number of North American organizations, inspired by Japanese success, have been implementing these techniques. Explain why our organizations have waited so long to implement these techniques.

2. Unquality plagues our products and services. There is positive and unequivocal proof that quality pays, not only on a national level, but also on a company level. Why then are so many unquality products produced?

3. Crosby writes that quality is free, yet a number of managers think that it is expensive and they cannot afford it. Besides, they argue, it is inevitable that a company will produce some defective products. Please comment.

Notes

1. Carole J. Loomis, "Dinosaurs?" *Fortune,* 3 May 1993, 36–42.

2. R. D. Buzzell and Bradley T. Gale, *The PIMS Principles* (New York: Free Press, 1987), 109.

3. Anthony Ramirez, "How Safe Are You in the Air?" *Fortune,* 22 May 1989, 75–88.

4. J. M. Juran and Frank M. Gryna, *Quality Control Handbook* (New York: McGraw-Hill, 1988), 33–60.

5. Quality cost includes the cost of unquality (waste, scrap, refunds, rework, repairs under guarantee, etc.) as well as the cost of quality (prevention and control).

6. Measuring customer satisfaction will be explained in chapter 6, "Planning for Total Quality."

7. J. M. Juran and Frank M. Gryna, *Quality Planning and Analysis* (New York: McGraw-Hill, 1980), 99.

8. Philip B. Crosby, *Quality Is Free* (New York: McGraw-Hill, 1979).

9. Alan Chapple, "Colleges Get the Word: Make TQM a Staple of Engineering and Business Education," *Engineering Times* 12, no. 9 (September 1990): 1–2.

10. Ibid.

11. Ibid.

12. Ibid.

13. Ibid.

14. Ibid.

15. Ibid.

16. John F. Akers, IBM Corporation; Paul Allaire, Xerox Corporation; Edwin L. Artzt, Procter & Gamble; Robert W. Galvin, Motorola; Harold A. Poling, Ford Motor Company; and James D. Robinson III, American Express Corporation, "An Open Letter: TQM on the Campus," *Harvard Business Review* 69, no. 4 (November–December 1991): 94–95.

Chapter 2

Total quality is a win–win–win game.
If all the players follow the rules, no one loses.

Total Quality in 3-D

Defining *Quality* and *Total Quality*

As indicated in chapter 1, one of the five reasons organizations fail to implement the total quality approach is that they do not know what quality and total quality are. In order to achieve quality and total quality, we have to define them in concrete, objective, and measurable terms. What we cannot measure, we cannot achieve.

People confuse the concepts of quality and total quality. I once asked the vice president in charge of total quality for a large organization what, in his expert opinion, total quality was. For a few seconds, he hesitated and seemed embarrassed. Then he suggested that it means top management showing some leadership as far as quality is concerned. He added that, in his opinion, total quality is a continuous quality improvement program (CQI). I then asked what the difference was between total quality, quality, and CQI. He shrugged and said that all these expressions amounted to the same thing and he wondered why the company had put *total* in his title anyway. I was not surprised to hear, a few months later, that this organization had terminated its quality program after having spent half a million hard-earned dollars on it. Not only had the vice president lost the "total" in his title, he had lost his entire title—and his job. As he looked for a new position, he vowed that he would never have anything more to do with quality, be it total or not!

Some experts say that both quality and total quality mean doing it right the first time. Juran asks, with good reason, doing *what* right the first time? In Deming's opinion, "This is just another meaningless slogan, a cousin of zero defect."[1] Others variously define the quality/total quality approach as being either mainly teamwork, employee empowerment, participative management, or customer driven. Other popular definitions equate quality and total quality with continuous improvement or process management. Then there are the zero definitions: zero defect, zero inventory, zero paper, zero this, and zero that.

What complicates the issue is that neither the original, world-renowned quality gurus—Deming and Juran—nor their successor, Crosby, used the expressions *total quality* or *total quality management,* at least not until recently. Moreover, these gurus and other quality experts have not been in perfect accord on a common method of achieving quality. While there is consensus among quality scholars and practitioners that top management leadership and customer satisfaction are crucial in any quality project, they offer significantly different definitions of total quality and total quality management.

Rather than trying to find definitions that suit everyone, I set about observing a number of successful organizations from all over the world to see what they were doing and what name they gave to it. Those observations brought home to me the fact that there is a significant difference between what people say they do, what they write about what they do, and what they actually do. In 1976, as a new professor in a business school, after working for 20 years in technical as well as managerial positions in various organizations (the textile industry, the merchant navy, the electronic industry, and a public utility), I was asked to develop and, in 1978, teach a course on quality management for students specializing in production and operations management. I had then to participate in all known quality organizations of the time, starting with the local section of the American Society for Quality Control (ASQC). Later, in 1985, I was off on a sabbatical leave which took me to several continents around the world, including Europe (France and Great Britain), Asia (Japan and, later, Korea), and North America (Canada and the United States).

Based upon my observations and upon the teachings of Deming, Juran, Crosby, Feigenbaum, and Ishikawa—all of whom I met on many occasions—I came to the conclusion that, first, the concept of *quality* has to be defined, then *total quality* must be tackled, in a precise, concrete way. This was an indispensable prerequisite if I wanted to be able to teach the subject with credibility or use and test these concepts in my consulting activities with industry, services, and government organizations. This book is the result of these efforts and experiences.

What the Quality Gurus Think

Quality has become almost a religion and, as with any religion, has its high priests and gurus. Four gurus, all Americans, have long dominated the quality field: W. Edwards Deming, Joseph M. Juran, Armand V. Feigenbaum, and Philip B. Crosby. In an article published in *Fortune,* Jeremy Main wrote that all of these men seemed to be possessed by a sense of messianic mission, convinced that America has a paramount need for their advice.[2] Deming and Juran respected each other, although, according to Juran, Deming had an insufficient grasp of the various aspects of management. As an example of their differences, Deming proposed that managers "eliminate fear," whereas Juran felt that fear has positive effects that can bring out the best in people. For Juran, Crosby is simply a public relations expert. While both Deming and Juran conceded that Crosby is a great motivator and an excellent speaker, they saw him as lacking substance and being unable to offer a concrete methodology for achieving quality.

Deming and Juran are known above all for their work in Japan in the 1950s. Deming, the most admired among the four, has been called the "Prophet of Quality." Feigenbaum is well-known for the concept he coined: *total quality control*. Indeed, he is the only one of the four to have used the word *total* from the outset. When I met him in Tokyo, I asked him if the word *total* in his expression referred to *control* or to *quality*. He replied, very diplomatically, "To both!" In my opinion, and according to what he has written, the word *total* applied at the time to *control* and not to *quality*. Crosby, who has the preacher's gift of persuasion, knows how to charm business managers with speeches full of anecdotes on incidents illustrating poor quality. He has had the greatest commercial success among the four. Over the years, his Quality College in Florida has attracted an impressive number of managers and business executives.

These four quality experts do agree on a number of things, one of which is that, among all of the factors affecting a company's competitiveness, quality is the principal one. They also all underline the necessity of giving quality primary strategic importance and of investing top management with its responsibility. The notion that all people must participate in the achievement of quality is common to them all as well. However, they do not all define quality in the same way. Main observes that the realm of quality is nebulous, being packed with slogans, statistics, and complicated jargon. This, according to him, explains why the quality message is not understood. However, he adds, when the message is understood and put into practice, it produces remarkable results.

Kathawala[3] compared the four approaches, noting the following definitions. For Deming, quality resided in satisfying customer or consumer needs. In these needs, he included the characteristics of the product itself, its availability in the market, and its price. For Juran, quality is *fitness for use*. Crosby says that quality is conformance to requirements. Feigenbaum underlines the changing and elusive nature of quality, which he sees as an ever-moving target. As he says, "The word *quality* does not have the popular meaning of 'best' in any absolute sense. To industry, it means 'best for certain customer conditions.'"

Deming's 14 Points

Deming presented his approach to achieving quality in 14 points, which, he stated, are the responsibilities of top management. He summarized them as follows:[4]

1. Create constancy of purpose toward improvement of product and service. Innovate, allocate resources to long-term planning. Put resources into research and education.

2. Adopt the new philosophy. Do not tolerate commonly accepted levels of errors and defects.

An anecdote goes this way: Americans have invented the concept of acceptable quality level (AQL). For a buyer, this would be the maximum tolerated level of unquality. For example, when a buyer orders, say, 10,000 electric bulbs, he or she specifies on the purchase order an AQL of 2 percent. That means that the buyer will not accept any lot containing over 2 percent of defective bulbs.

However, one day, a Japanese supplier receives a purchase order for 20,000 units of a certain item with the mention, AQL 1 percent. He is astonished, asking himself why his customer would want to purchase 200 defective units. In order to satisfy his customer, he manufactures 18,800 good units and 200 defective ones and ships the order to his customer with a note explaining that he did not understand the reason for ordering the defectives, but he packed them separately so that they could be easily identified.

3. Cease dependence on mass inspection to achieve quality. Inspection does not improve quality. Quality is built into a product and cannot be inspected into it.

4. End the practice of awarding business on the basis of price tag alone. Minimize total cost by working with a single supplier.

5. Improve constantly and forever every process for planning, production, and service. Continually improve test methods and identify problems, from the very first planning stages right up to distribution to customers.

6. Institute training on the job. In Japan, managers start their careers with a long internship. They work in procurement, accounting, distribution, and sales.

7. Adopt and institute leadership. The job of management is not supervision, but leadership.

8. Drive out fear. No one can perform unless he or she feels secure.

While visiting the manager of a personnel department, I asked what would happen to someone in his company who makes an error. He smiled confidently and showed me a big red binder on a shelf behind him. "It is all here," he said. "First notice, second notice, third notice, then first suspension, second suspension, third suspension, and so on." (I suspect the procedure goes all the way to the death penalty!) Then I asked what happens to people who never make mistakes. There was a long moment of silence; then he said that there was nothing is his binder about that. "Besides," he added, "aren't they paid for that?"

Anyone who makes an error would understandably either hide it out of fear of the red book or, if noticed, would blame it on someone else. Anyway, the red book did not seem to stop people from making mistakes.

9. Break down barriers between staff areas. Create teams of members coming from all areas and sectors of the business to prevent and solve problems.
10. Eliminate slogans, exhortations, and targets for the workforce. Posters and slogans have never helped anyone to do a better job.
11. Eliminate numerical quotas for the workforce and numerical goals for management.
12. Remove barriers that rob people of the pride of workmanship. Eliminate the annual rating or merit system.

I suggested to the personnel manager that he scrap his red binder and replace it with a green one. Rather than punishing the guilty, he would reward the ones who make no errors. Errors then become opportunities for improvement without being a threat to whoever makes a mistake.

13. Institute a vigorous program of education and self-improvement for everyone.
14. Put everybody in the company to work to accomplish the transformation.

Crosby's Four Absolutes

For Philip B. Crosby, achieving quality is based on four fundamental principles that he calls *absolutes*.[5]

1. The definition of quality is *conformance to requirements*.

Quality is wrongly used to signify the relative worth of things in such phrases as *good quality* and *bad quality*. Goodness is something that cannot be measured, whereas conformance to requirements is precisely measurable. Requirements must be clearly stated so that they cannot be misunderstood. Measurements are then taken continually to determine whether those requirements are being conformed to.

2. The system of quality is prevention.

The most visible of the expenses of conventional quality practice lie in the area of appraisal. Appraisal is always done after the fact; it is an expensive and unreliable way of ensuring quality. What has to happen is prevention. Prevention involves monitoring advertising claims, taking affirmative action in providing customer information, and establishing early warning systems to detect any potential problems.

3. The performance standard is zero defects.

Setting requirements is a process that is readily understood. This is not the case of the need for meeting those requirements each and every time. Establishing a *shipped-product quality level* means that a certain number of errors are planned. Established *acceptable quality levels* represent the number of nonconforming items that can occur in an acceptable lot. These performance standards, however, convince people that the determination to get things done right just is not there. The performance standard must be zero defects, not "That's close enough."

4. The measurement of quality is the price of nonconformance.

Quality is considered not a management function, but rather a technical one. Quality is never looked at in financial terms the way everything else is. It is measured by indexes and defects, or in other terms management cannot understand. The best measurement for quality is money. Quality should be measured by the price of nonconformance, that is, by all the expenses involved in doing things wrong.

Crosby's "Do it right the first time" summarizes his notion of the three main principles. *It* corresponds to the requirements, *right* means zero defects, and *the first time* targets prevention.

Juran's Trilogy

For Juran, quality is synonymous with fitness for use, a definition that includes the features that lead to product satisfaction and absence of defects. He suggests a conceptual approach to managing quality—a trilogy of processes through which quality is managed. Quality should be planned, controlled, and improved.[6]

Feigenbaum's Total Quality Control

Feigenbaum discusses quality in the manufacturing sector. His book, *Total Quality Control* (read *total control of quality,* not *control of total quality*) recommends *extended* management of quality, applied at all stages, from design to delivery of product, and thus it departs from the traditional practice of limiting quality control to the manufacturing stage.[7] The Japanese, especially Kaoru Ishikawa, have extended the notion of quality management to include all activities inside the business as well as those of external partners. Ishikawa called this broadened notion *companywide quality control.*[8]

Redefining *Quality* and *Total Quality*

Before discussing quality management, let us try to define the concept of quality. Most of the upper managers with whom I have had the opportunity to discuss the matter seem to base their evaluation of the quality of their products and services on the number and nature of customer complaints. The extent of this approach has been confirmed in an ASQC/Gallup survey.[9] From this, then, are we to assume that a business that has lost all its customers, and therefore has no complaints, has achieved quality? A ridiculous notion, indeed! Yet it is one that clearly illustrates the kind of near-sighted, compartmentalized vision of quality that can be arrived at when trying to define quality from too limited a vantage point.

With the help of a research assistant, I once conducted an informal in-house survey on what managers of different departments in a small number of companies defined as a quality product. The following summarizes the conclusions we reached.

- For the *marketing* manager, the quality of the product is what makes it sell well. This attitude towards quality brings to mind a study I conducted on the quality of construction materials in a Third World country. I observed that a brick maker was not putting enough cement in his product—his bricks were quite brittle. However, he felt that the quality he produced was acceptable and saw no need to change it. He had enough orders to keep him busy for more than a year ahead, so he did not understand why he should bother to make them any better. I should add that all of the quality bricks sold in that market were imported, and their cost was prohibitive to people who wanted to build a small dwelling by themselves.

- In the *finance* department, a quality product is one that is profitable for the company. Of course, the marketing people do not always agree with this definition, since there are instances where a company uses a loss leader (that is, a product sold at a loss) as a lure to help market other, more lucrative products.

- For *production* personnel, quality means conformance to specifications, standards, drawings, blueprints, or other technical documents. By the same token, quality control department employees equate poor quality with nonconformance.

- *Workers* know that they have produced quality when their line supervisors do not complain about their work. This is rather dangerous because if mistakes are not pointed out they cannot be avoided in the future. Also, if the boss believes that poor quality is unavoidable—error being human and forgiveness divine—he or she will tend to have the errors corrected after the fact, without giving workers any feedback on the poor quality of their work. Consequently, error or defect detection will prevail over prevention.

- For *purchasing* personnel, quality is perceived as a lower limit. For example, if purchasing had to find a five-ton crane, they would buy a six-ton crane if one was found at a really good price or if a five-ton crane could not be found.

- For the *research and development* people, quality is defined as the state of the art, that is, developing the best possible products. Generally, this leads to what has been termed *gold plating,* or overquality, as defined later in the chapter.

- For representatives of certain *government* organizations, a quality product is one that presents no threat to public safety and security.

- For *top managers,* a quality product is one that enables them to satisfy the needs of the stockholders and the owners of the company.

• For the *customer* of the product—whether a consumer or a company— quality represents the product's ability to satisfy a certain number of specific needs.

Given that business cannot exist without customers, and because customers are the ones who decide to buy or not to buy, this last definition must logically prevail over all others. But then the notion of *needs* has to be defined, as well as the concepts of *unquality* and *overquality*. Let us briefly consider these two last terms before undertaking an in-depth look at the idea of needs.

Unquality is what causes customer dissatisfaction. This dissatisfaction can be very costly to producers; indeed, they might have to replace or repair the product, ship and reinspect it at their own expense, or even get entangled in related lawsuits. What is more, they can lose orders, customers, and even entire markets, as has happened in a number of North American industries and firms. An overquality product does not result in customer dissatisfaction and, therefore, according to the customer's definition, could be considered a quality product. However, it generally incurs needless costs that reduce the company's profitability if the product is sold at the same price as the competition's product. In addition, it can affect the company's competitiveness because other competitors can sell simpler products that cost customers less and still satisfy their needs.

Defining *Product Quality*

The international quality standard ISO 8402 defines *quality* as the totality of characteristics of a product, process, organization, person, activity, or system that bear on its ability to satisfy stated and implicit needs.[10] What are these characteristics?

First and foremost is the product's *suitability* for an intended use.[11] In other words, we must know what the product is supposed to do. Is it intended to transport; cut or weigh; or measure time, temperature, thickness, or hardness? Is it meant to provide protection against material risk or injury, as insurance does? Is it to be used in health care services? Is it designed to provide entertainment? Is it aimed at getting a return on an investment?

Suitability can be either *functional* or *nonfunctional*. It is said to be functional if the product performs the function for which it was conceived and designed. For example, a sword is made to cut; if it is serving as a weapon, its use is functional. But when it is used as a wall ornament, its use is nonfunctional. A famous industrialist once said that he manufactured cosmetics but sold dreams. As we know, cosmetics are much more nonfunctional than functional. Advertisements suggest that they can give their users beauty and youth, whereas what they really give them are illusions of beauty and youth.

Yacht clubs are established to offer their members a variety of services that allow them to sail or enjoy their motorboats, clearly a functional use. However, people can join an exclusive yacht club simply to enjoy the social status that goes with it—a nonfunctional use—using its bar, lounge, and dining room facilities much more than its docks. People do not go to restaurants only to eat (a functional use); some go to conduct business meetings, others to enjoy an intimate dinner, still others for social gatherings (all nonfunctional uses).

It is vital to know what the consumer wants to do with the product, that is, what the intended use of a product is. For example, if a sword is intended as a wall decoration, its ability to cut is not important; on the contrary, it is imperative that it *not* if an accident is to be avoided. The nonfunctional uses of a restaurant influence its floor design, decoration, and location, even more than the food it serves. The projected use of a product influences all stages of its design, development, manufacture, and packing. Moreover, the projected use affects most promotion, advertising, distribution, display, and pricing decisions related to the product.

Functional use can include both a *main function* and *secondary functions*. Cars are manufactured to provide transportation (the main function). An automatic transmission enables drivers to change gears automatically. In terms of the product's use, this is a nonessential secondary function that, for a great number of users, improves the product's performance. Eyeglasses may have corrective lenses (the main function) that automatically darken in sunlight (the secondary function) and thereby become sunglasses.

While companies continue to concentrate on improving and perfecting main product function, some of them are also now endeavoring to innovate and develop secondary functions. We should note that certain secondary functions are sometimes as important as the main function. For example, a car is meant primarily to provide transportation (the main function), but it has become a given that the car should do so comfortably and safely (secondary functions), hence the importance of seat belts, shock absorbers, airbags, and so forth.

To satisfy a need, a product not only has to be able to perform and achieve its intended objective, it has to be able to do so for a reasonable length of time. This is called product *durability*. A car, for example, not only should be able to transport goods or passengers, but it must do so for certain periods of time, say 5 to 10 years, before it falls into a condition in which repair is no longer economically feasible. In some countries, where repairing a car is cheaper than buying a new one, cars last more than 20 years.

Not only should products be durable and last a reasonable length of time, they should also be reliable. In general, *reliability* can be considered synonymous with *availability for use*. Technically speaking, reliability is defined as the probability of a product operating without breakdown or failure for a given period of time under normal operating conditions. An electric razor is said to be 99 percent reliable in the first three years if the probability of its breaking down is 1 percent for that period of time. When one buys a printer for a computer, the technical specifications indicate an MTBF value, such as 2000 or 5000 hours. This value, which stands for *mean time between failures*, is another measure of reliability and gives an indication of the time the printer can run before it has to be repaired.

In the service industries, reliability is measured by the percentage of time a service is available for use over a period of time. For example, if a highway is 99.9

percent reliable for the first year after it is constructed, it means that it can be used 99.9 percent of the time in that year under normal conditions—wars, earthquakes, accidents, and avalanches being excluded.

For some products, *uniformity* is a key ingredient of quality. Uniformity can be defined as a level of quality that is constant from one unit, shipment, or batch to another. Some canned-goods manufacturers add color to products—such as strawberry jam—to maintain a consistent appearance. A change in appearance could be construed as a change in the level of quality, even when this is not the case. In the service industries, customers expect the same level of quality each time they use the service, whether the service is car repairs, haircuts, or eating out. When travelling abroad to exotic countries, I sometimes look for food with a familiar taste and, hence, go to a McDonald's restaurant, because the uniformity of their products—including their names (Big Mac, McNuggets)—is well-known around the world.

Maintainability is another characteristic of quality. Maintainability includes the ease of maintenance and the availability of spare parts and service for the product once it starts being used. Many foreign car manufacturers wishing to penetrate a new market, such as the North American market, first make sure that they establish an extensive network of dealers and service centers. And they see to it that spare parts are readily available, that is, that most parts are stocked in that market or can be flown in on relatively short notice. However, many European car manufacturers have failed to penetrate the North American market because the local American mechanic at the corner service station would not dare touch a European car, hence reducing their maintainability.

The international quality standards series known as the ISO 9000 series and ISO 8402[12] adds another characteristic, namely *dependability*. Dependability is defined as the collective term describing the available performance of a product. This performance is influenced by the reliability, the maintainability, and the maintenance support performance of the product.

Other characteristics suggested in this standard are *compatibility,* which is the ability of entities to be used together under specific conditions to fulfill relevant requirements; *interchangeability,* or the ability of an entity to be used in place of another, without modification, to fulfill the same requirements; *safety,* the state in which the risk of harm to persons or damage to the product is limited to an acceptable level; and, finally, *product liability,* a generic term used to describe the onus on a producer or others to make restitution for loss related to personal injury, property damage, or other harm caused by a product.

There are other characteristics associated with quality that depend on the nature of the product: toxicity (for a paint), stability (for a drug or chemical), appearance, and so on.

Quantifiable absolute or relative parameters must be associated with all of the aforementioned quality characteristics. For example, a five-passenger car capacity, a two-inch steel-cutting capacity, a 50-pound weighing capacity, a five-year product-life, a 95 percent reliability. In banking services, quality can be measured by the variety of services offered—savings, loans, mortgages, investment—or by the number of errors made in transactions.

Intrinsic and Extrinsic Quality

The characteristics of a product—suitability, durability, reliability, uniformity, maintainability—determine its *intrinsic* quality, namely all of the qualities that its producer planned and built into it (such as design, materials, manufacturing process, and workmanship). Another aspect of quality is the *extrinsic* quality of a product, or its perceived quality—which is not necessarily directly related to specific efforts made by producers of quality goods or services. For example, French wines were traditionally considered superior to California wines, until producers from California entered their wines for a wine tasting in France. In a blind test, where judges could not identify the origin of the wine, a particular California wine was rated higher than certain French wines. Following this, there was a spectacular increase in the sales of California wines. Suddenly, consumers perceived these wines to be better than before, even though the producers had not changed their product in any way!

Extrinsic quality depends on the buyer's perception of quality and includes a strong psychological element. Recently, a party guest was impressed by the delicious taste of a Camembert cheese, until she noticed its label, which showed that it came from a Third World country. Suddenly she found it had an "aftertaste" that she couldn't quite put her finger on. Some time ago, a Swiss watch manufacturer, Omega, conducted a study concerning their production costs for a proposed electronic quartz watch similar to a Japanese model. The Swiss company found that it could not manufacture a watch of equivalent quality at a competitive price. However, a market study showed that because of its international reputation, Omega could sell its watch at a higher price than the Japanese watch and, therefore, make a profit. The watch was manufactured, and it sold very well. What was surprising was the multitude of Japanese who flocked to buy it!

Extrinsic quality is a concept of particular interest to marketing personnel. This was illustrated some time ago when Pepsi-Cola launched a campaign against its powerful rival, Coca-Cola, by having the general public conduct blind taste tests on both beverages. The tests proved that some people could not distinguish one soft drink from another and others even preferred Pepsi. Pepsi-Cola sales subsequently grew to such an extent that Coca-Cola changed its 100-year-old formula. However, after suffering losses with the new taste, Coca-Cola reverted to its original "Classic" formula.

Clearly, if one product is truly of lower quality than another, the extrinsic dimension will not play such an important role. A few years ago, Canada imported from the then Soviet Union a low-priced car, the Lada, which could not compete with the quality of domestic cars or with other imports. Similarly, the former Yugoslavia exported the Yugo, an inexpensive, substandard small car, to the United

States. In spite of their much-below-average price, neither car sold well. No marketing effort could have possibly raised their extrinsic quality.

What is more, it often takes a long time to establish an extrinsic quality, which usually comes from having sustained a level of quality superior to competitive products through the years. The Omega watch case mentioned above is a good example. Over the years, the Swiss company had earned and established an excellent reputation for the quality of its products before it launched its electronic watch. The same applies to a bad reputation, which is very difficult to reverse. Remember when the *Made in Japan* label was associated with mediocrity? It took just as much, if not more, effort for Japan to improve the extrinsic quality of their products as it did for them to improve their intrinsic quality.

From Quality to Total Quality

Product quality is defined by the customer and the customer alone. In the 1970s, Western companies started putting more emphasis on quality to keep their markets or recapture lost shares of these markets. However, in the 1980s, the concept of total quality appeared. This hot new topic—some would even call it faddish—has been defined in different ways over the years, thus creating a great deal of confusion. Moreover, most of the definitions have been philosophical in nature. Some will say that total quality is a business strategy. Others consider it to be a new management philosophy. Still others say, "It's more than a program, it's a state of mind," or "It's not a program, it's a process." Even if they are correct, these definitions do not get us very far. As stated at the beginning of this chapter, if we want to achieve total quality—or anything else, for that matter—we must define it in concrete and measurable terms.

Rather than trying to find an academic definition for total quality, we started by identifying the factors that guide and influence a customer's decision to buy or not to buy a certain product. My research—not strictly scientific but based on a number of observations—led me to conclude that the seven attributes that customers look for are as follows:

1. *Quality*. As we have defined it, this means quality in the product (goods or services) and in the accompanying ancillary services. These comprise presale services (that is, demonstration, free use, information about the various products offered, and so on); services provided during the acquisition process (help in selecting the proper product); and services provided after acquisition (installation, servicing, maintenance, warranties).

2. *Volume*. Volume means delivery of an item in its required quantity or size, or delivery of service to a certain number of customers.

3. *Administration*. Systems and procedures that a customer experiences are streamlined, rapid, and free of errors. These encompass all the customer's dealings with a company, covering everything from ordering a product to receiving

the invoice and paying for the product or service; from customer credit evaluation and order confirmation procedures or modifications to requests for technical or commercial information, complaint procedures, and processing.

4. *Location.* Customers—existing or potential, possible or probable—want the product to be available or delivered at the desired location.

5. *Interrelationships and Image.* Customers want to be treated well, promptly, and courteously, and they want to have good relationships with company personnel or representatives. They also like to do business with a company that has a good image, respects the environment, and is community minded.

6. *Timely* delivery of the required product or service.

7. A maximum *yield* from the product. For the customer, this concept of yield involves more than paying the lowest price possible. Actually, customers are ready to pay more for a product if its benefits—such as reduced operating costs, or high resale value—are higher. Yield also entails getting maximum value for the money, not only in the short term but in the long term as well. Some people call this the cost–benefit ratio.

In an initial survey, we found an eighth characteristic pertaining to economic and, possibly, nationalistic aspects (the "buy-local" approach). But this characteristic was dropped when the international free trade and GATT agreements in North America and Europe were adopted. Serendipitously, the first letters of these seven attributes—*quality, volume, administration, location, interrelationships* and *image, timely* delivery, and maximum *yield*—form the acronym QVALITY, which, by coincidence, resembles the word *quality.*

In a test, I asked a number of my students—none of whom knew about these seven customer–total quality indicators—to go out, find a store, and order four television sets for our audiovisual department, to be received within a week. We began with a meeting to determine which TV sets to buy. We studied a number of advertisements in various catalogs, and the students discussed their personal experiences with various TV sets. Together with the audiovisual department's specialists, we reached the decision to buy a certain model, say the ABC-12. The students went out to order the sets, and, when they came back, they were asked how they had decided from which store to order the sets.

The students explained their decision-making process this way. At each store, they found a salesperson from whom they could get the information they required (interrelationships–I). They started by asking the salesperson if the store had ABC-12 TV sets in stock, and if it was able to offer after-sales service (quality–Q). The second question was to inquire if the store had four TV sets on hand (volume–V). The students then asked the vendor (though not always in this order):

- If he would deliver the sets (location–L)
- If he would bill them or accept a credit card (administrative system–A)

- What his price would be for four TV sets, and what free-service warranty they would get (yield–Y)
- If the sets could be delivered by the following week (time–T)

In short, the customer's needs can be expressed and defined by the acronym QVALITY, which represents the seven indicators listed above. This is the customer dimension of total quality, which is a notion much broader in scope than mere quality of products. It means meeting the customer's needs according to the terms of the QVALITY factors (see Figure 2.1).

Of these seven factors, five were identified as *turn-on factors.* These are QVLTY, which, when they are present, attract a customer. We call them the PTO, or *present turn-on factors* (positive). The other two factors, A and I, do not attract customers per se but, if absent, could repel them. We call these the ATO or *absent turn-off factors* (nonnegative). For example, a courteous salesperson may not be able to convince a customer to buy a certain item, but once the customer has decided to buy it, a rude salesperson could make him forego the purchase and decide to buy from another merchant.

If we want to measure *customer total quality,* we have to measure each of these seven factors. Obviously, the customer does not give the same weight to each of

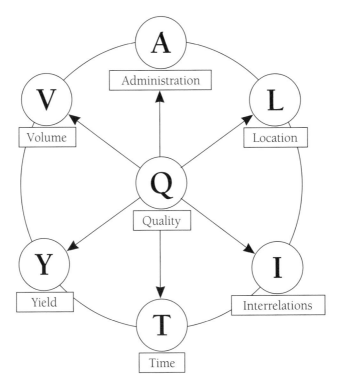

Figure 2.1. The customer's seven total quality indicators.

these characteristics; therefore, a weighting factor has to be sought for each customer or group of customers, or else for a majority of customers.

Let us take a closer look at the seven factors that customers look for and expand upon their definitions.

Quality

Quality has already been defined as the suitability of a product—its durability, reliability, maintainability, uniformity, and so on. Suitability is generally expressed by a verb and a measure, as in "transports 5 passengers," "cuts 3 inches of steel," "measures up to 3 feet," "weighs up to 10 pounds."

Volume

Volume represents the quantity required, or sometimes the size desired, as, for instance, in the case of a 2-story home or a 50-story building, or of a computer payroll system for 50 or 50,000 employees. It can also be expressed in terms of the number of customers to be served, as in the case of a bank or a beauty parlor, or in terms of a particular amount, say, the amount of money available for a mortgage at a financial institution.

Administration

Administration comprises all systems and administrative procedures that the customer has to go through in order to get information, place an order, complain, pay a bill, get credit, and so on. These systems are distinct from the internal systems and procedures of the company. They should cause the least possible inconvenience to the present or potential customer; customers should find them easy, uncomplicated, rapid, and error-free. The administration factor covers any procedures and documents and should include the possibility of performing these procedures by the customer's preferred method, whether that be by mail, by phone, in person only, or at the seller's premises or elsewhere. In fact, we find that customers will pay an extra point on a mortgage to the financial institution that will quickly process their requests by a phone call or fax, rather than go to a competitor who insists on their presence and obliges them to wait in line for cumbersome and lengthy procedures. Where billing systems are concerned, customers may feel it important to get a bill that they can easily understand rather than an incomprehensible, computer-designed bill.

When customers find procedures to be too complicated to wade through, serious problems arise. For example, in France, the high-tech, high-speed train known as the TGV (*train à grande vitesse*) is one of the fastest, if not the fastest, in the world. However, a number of people shy away from using it because of the administrative complications they have to go through to purchase a ticket.

A bill I recently received from a company miles away is another case in point. All I could read on it were mysterious items identified by some lengthy computer codes. When I called the company for information, I was kept waiting while a radio station played music, gave me a traffic report on their city (not mine), a weather report, and the world and local news. Then a person, obviously in a great hurry, asked the reason for my call and proceeded to pass me on to three or four employees before I got the right one. Once I had my information, I asked why the items were not indicated on the bill in plain English, so that the customer could easily understand. I was told those codes were used internally. The engineering department used them to pick up the right parts, the purchasing department used them for ordering, the stockroom for inventory control, production for assembly purposes, and accounting for sending out bills to customers. "What about me?" I ventured. I was politely informed that all I had to do was pay the bill.

Most companies do not realize the effect that a billing system can have on a customer. The following instance shows just how important it can be. An office supplies company captured most of its main competitor's customers simply by changing the composition and format of its bill. The billing department manager designed a form that clearly identified items. Ten red pencils read just like that: 10 red pencils. In addition, right beside the total, a thought for the day was nicely printed, offering customers an upbeat aphorism on happiness, love, friendship, or positive thinking so they would pay their bills with a smile. Moreover, the traditional, dreaded two-liner threats (indicating the penalties incurred by those who do not pay within a given deadline) were removed. In their place was a note on how to save up to 20 percent on the items purchased or to be purchased. (For example, the bill suggested buying 12 pencils rather than 10, as it was cheaper to order by the dozen.)

Administrative procedures must produce some tangible result for the customer, as illustrated in a sarcastic joke about a Third World country where food had to be rationed. A young man arrives at the cooperative grocery store to buy a couple of pounds of sugar. He notices that the usual crowd blocking all entrances has disappeared. A poster instructs him to go to wicket 5. There, a clerk fills in a form with the customer's request, then asks him to take it to the second floor. The second-floor clerk neatly registers the request in a big book and gives the customer a token he has to present at counter 7, where sugar is sold. At the counter, the clerk takes the token and politely says to the customer, "Sorry, we are out of sugar, but don't you think we now have a well-organized system?"

In another instance, in a small country, an older man waits in line to pay a telephone bill that the government-owned utility has sent him. He seems very upset, so a young man next to him in line inquires about the reason for his concern.

"This is unfair," the man claims. "They are charging me for a huge number of long-distance calls that I never made, and I still have to pay my bill, just in case. You know how fussy government people are."

The young man trying to comfort him suggests, "Maybe somebody else in your family made those calls."

"Son," says the man, "I have no family. I don't even have a telephone!"

Location

The location factor has numerous aspects: product availability, easy delivery, transportation facilities, after-sale services, warehousing, and physical layout. The product has to be available and delivered easily wherever it is required, without undue inconvenience to the customer. Transportation facilities come into play in the product's delivery—air, land, or sea transportation from producer to customer. Available after-sale services—maintenance, repairs, and servicing—should be readily accessible. Warehousing may be needed for the customer who has no space to store purchased materials; the seller may offer to store these materials in a location convenient to the customer, at little or no additional cost.

Another factor related to location is the physical layout, that is, the comfortable arrangement and attractive decor of the facilities that the customer visits to obtain a product or a service. Customer-service areas should be set up in locations convenient for customers, and great care should be taken to make their visit as pleasant as possible (coffee and cookies, recent magazines made available, a telephone and a fax machine to allow waiting customers to keep in touch with the rest of the world, perhaps even a TV room so that waiting customers can keep up with the news). The layout of banks, car dealerships, clinics, shopping centers, and distributors' outlets should be designed with efficiency, effectiveness, and customer reception in mind. Every detail in a company's physical layout tells customers that the company cares about them.

We must take note, however, of a new trend that has recently started to develop, a trend that seemingly contradicts some of these tenets about customer service and that would have been unthinkable only a few years ago. Warehouse-type outlets are spreading fast. Their wares—everything from food staples to tires, office supplies, and TV sets—are piled up on racks. Some of these have to be purchased in large, predetermined quantities (packs of 12 or boxes of 6). No service, or limited service, is available, and customers have to wait in long lines to pay for their purchases. Nevertheless, all products are accessible in one shopping stop, and customers realize substantial savings which offset the lack of decor and ambiance.

Interrelationships

Interrelationships involve the communication between producer and customer. Customers are faced with certain communication processes when they inquire about a product or a service, place or modify an order, pay (or refuse to pay) a bill, or complain. Whether customers exchange faxes and correspondence with company personnel or encounter them face to face, they should be treated with courtesy at all times. For example, in many shops, salesclerks are requested to address customers paying with a credit card by their names (which the clerks can read from the card) rather than calling them "sir" or "madam." Actually, this trend is expanding to all instances where the person dealing with the customer has access to his or her name (checking airline boarding passes, and so on). To facilitate producer–customer communication, many companies are installing more toll-free telephone lines.

Interrelations are not limited to company personnel; they extend to its external partners as well. I heard of an unfortunate experience when I discussed this topic with one of my clients. They had just lost their biggest customer. I inquired if it was because they had delivered defective products. Surprisingly, I was told the loss had nothing to do with the quality of their product. Actually, the incident happened while a shipment was being delivered to their customer's premises. The delivery truck hit a car near the receiving dock. Accidents like this do, indeed, happen. However, this was the president's car, and he happened to be in it. Moreover, the truck driver was so angry, he got out of his truck and attacked the president! The purchasing manager of the affronted company was instructed never to do business with "those people" again. When he heard of this incident, the president of the supplier company immediately contacted his client. In his telephone conversation with the other president, he added more fuel to the fire by saying that he was calling to explain the situation, not to offer any apologies, because the truck driver did not work for his company! But when asked who had selected this carrier, he had to admit that it was his company. He had lost this customer forever.

Business often depends on the quality of interrelations between company and customer, as witnessed in the case of the president of a small company who wanted to buy a machine tool worth a quarter of a million dollars. Four suppliers were available in his area. He called the first one. After telling the receptionist why he was calling, he was politely asked to hold the line and assured that it would not be long. But he was put on hold and totally forgotten. He hung up, purchased his machine from another supplier, and went on to tell everybody he knew not to deal with that "totally unreliable" company. Although this company had the best engineers in the country and produced one of the best machines, it had just lost many possible orders and customers because of a seemingly insignificant incident.

In still another scenario, a would-be customer calls a financial institution to inquire about savings programs. While being put on hold, the institution's telephone airs music transmitted by a local radio station, but during a pause in the music, the station plays a commercial urging listeners to deal with a competitor for savings and investment services.

In an increasing number of organizations, managers tell their employees that, if they want to keep their jobs, they had better treat the customer like a king. They forget a tiny detail. Most of their employees are more like those anti-royalist patriots who thought kings were good only for the guillotine.

On many occasions (too numerous to describe), I, as customer, have indeed felt like a king—albeit a king during the French Revolution! Walking away, I have often thanked God that my head and neck were still attached. The executioner's block is hardly what one has in mind when receiving the royal treatment. Once, standing under a huge banner that said "The customer is king," I ventured to plead to the person behind the counter, "Please, don't treat me like a king, just like a human being!"

Visiting a car manufacturer in Japan, I was welcomed at the door by a sign displaying my name and my country's flag. I was embarrassed and timidly indicated to my host that I was not a prime minister or a president; I was just a modest university professor. With a very polite smile, he suggested that presidents do not usually drive their small-sized cars, but I might. How's that for interrelations with a potential customer!

Image

Image is another condition that might entice a customer to buy a certain product. It is the respect for the physical and social environment that the producer shows in the conduct of his or her business. Although a product might satisfy the QVALITY characteristics, some potential customers would refuse to buy it if the producer is known to pollute the environment or uses materials—especially in packing—that are not biodegradable or recyclable. At one point, the McDonald's restaurant chain started changing its styrofoam packing because styrofoam is a nonbiodegradable, nonrecyclable material. Some customers had actually stopped patronizing McDonald's restaurants, not because of the hamburgers, but because of the styrofoam packing in which they were sold. Some large corporations look for recycled paper even though it is more expensive than nonrecycled paper. More and more consumer organizations are publicizing incidents of pollution caused by manufacturing companies and urging people to boycott such companies.

Finally, some consumers are socially conscious and put pressure on companies and countries to refrain from unethical practices by refusing to buy products from companies that exploit women, children, or minorities, or from countries that do not respect human rights. This is another part of the seller's image.

Time

Obviously, the time component has to do with timing and timeliness, with deadlines and schedules. It includes cutting waiting time in line-ups and eliminating backorders. In a restaurant, it can entail quick service if one is in a hurry (lunch time); but it can also call for service that is relaxed and slow, when one has time to enjoy the outing and the company (evening wining and dining, for example). Indeed, in some countries I have visited, the waiter will not present the bill until the customer asks for it.

In a branch of a well-known financial institution, a task force was instructed to try to improve customer service. The team members thought cutting the waiting time and shortening the waiting lines for their customers would be a good beginning. After a six-month effort, this time was significantly reduced, but the branch had lost most of its customers. The majority of these customers were retired workers who considered their biweekly trip to cash their pension checks a social event to look forward to. They actually enjoyed the waiting. When the waiting time was cut, they transferred their dealings to another institution where they could take their time.

Yield

The yield component goes beyond the cost of the product. It takes into consideration the long-term economics of a specific purchase. The purchase price may be high, but long-term benefits (or yield) could justify such a high price. For instance, it made sense for one paint manufacturer to sell its product at twice the competitors' price because it was much more durable and, therefore, cheaper in the long run.

The customer-driven QVALITY definition of total quality has several advantages. First of all, it is a definition that includes seven characteristics, each of which is measurable. Moreover, in contrast to those that portray quality as merely a technical aspect of a product, this definition shows the need to involve all people, at all levels and in all sectors of an enterprise. Traditionally, the only people in a company who feel concerned about quality are the ones directly involved with the product itself, that is, those who propose or design the product, design the process to manufacture it, purchase materials or equipment to produce it, ship it, and answer complaints about it. All the rest—the personnel department, the computer systems department, public relations, accounting, and so on—are certain that quality is none of their business.

During a presentation on total quality to the upper management of one company, an opulent-looking, well-built, cigar-smoking gentleman informed me that he was sitting at this meeting as an observer only. I assumed then that he did not work for the company, but he was quick to inform me that he was the vice president of finance and, as such, had nothing whatsoever to do either with quality or with customers. However, after I had presented the customer total quality indicators—QVALITY—he seemed intrigued and admitted that he had never imagined that the billing system could be of any interest to the customer.

When he later asked some major customers what they thought about the billing system, they were very surprised; they considered invoices a necessary evil. Indeed, as I mentioned before, bills can be threatening documents, containing cautions, albeit in small print, about the consequences to the client if he or she fails to pay within the deadline that the vendor deems reasonable. One of the customers told the vice president that he employed a clerk full time for the sole purpose of compiling statistics based on invoices paid: the frequency of certain purchases, quantity and price fluctuations, and so on. On learning of this, the company offered to include all the necessary data on this particular customer's invoices. The customer was very pleasantly surprised, and the vice president of finance no longer claimed that he had nothing to do with quality or customers. He had finally understood.

Total Quality: Delighting the Customer

For customers, total quality goes still further. In fact, with competition now on a worldwide scale, it is no longer sufficient for a product to satisfy a customer. Keeping and developing a market means going beyond that. At an international conference on quality in Korea, I attended a presentation on the ACE concept. The lecturer's topic had nothing to do with either blackjack strategy or developing a devastating tennis serve, but rather with the *above customer expectations* (ACE) principle, also sometimes referred to as *beyond customer satisfaction*. This concept proposes exceeding the expectations of customers and surpassing the feeling of mere satisfaction. Customers must be excited and enthused by a product, delighted by a service. Customers must be more than satisfied—they must be surprised, swayed, and won over! That's what stops the competition dead in their tracks. Customers are hard to find nowadays, so it is crucial to hang on to the old ones. It has been estimated that attracting a new customer costs five times more than keeping an old one.

For example, a Japanese automobile manufacturer set a precedent by offering its customers 24-hour assistance in case they should inadvertently lock themselves out of their car, run out of gas, fail to start their car after accidentally leaving their headlights on, or even have a flat tire. Although most of these problems are caused by the drivers themselves, the car manufacturer took the responsibility for them, going well beyond the call of duty to offer a solution at no cost to the owner–customer. The vice president of finance who offered his clients customized bills is yet another example of exceeding customer expectations.

Recently I was an outpatient in a hospital, waiting my turn to have some X-rays taken. There I was, patiently sitting in a drafty corridor waiting for my name to be called, with no clothes except the typical ill-fitting hospital gown that I couldn't close at the back, and seriously wondering whether this waiting was doing my health any good. I was called, and, to my surprise, the radiologist addressed me by my name, asked me to sit down, and went on to explain what he was going to do, why he was going to do it, what he would do with the results, and how long the whole process would take. What's more, he asked me if I had any comments to make about patient admission procedures and the service I had received before seeing him. I was delighted!

In a store where customers usually took a number when they arrived and then waited their turn, I was surprised when the owner changed the number system to letters. He explained that he didn't want his customers to feel like numbers any more. Because he didn't know their names, he had decided to use a letter system. Another store I know of uses flower names: orchid, rose, lily, daisy. It's not ideal, but it's better than numbers. On the tag, there is a short description of that particular flower, along with a picture of it. Customers seem amused; most of them appreciate the system.

We go beyond customer satisfaction when we offer services that the customer needs but doesn't expect. This happens in some service centers where customers who bring in their cars for repairs find that not only are the repairs done but, in addition, the car is washed and vacuumed, and they are themselves greeted with courtesy, treated with respect, and provided with a comfortable waiting room. They see that great efforts have been made to alleviate the inconvenience of being deprived of their means of transportation. On the other side of the coin, there are many repair shops who simply make the necessary repairs and leave it at that, along with all the traces of oil and grease. What's more, some shops don't even repair the car properly, or else do repairs that the car doesn't need!

This courting of the customer has created a new trend. We are moving from mass production to mass customization; from providing a customer with a car of "any color he chooses, provided it is black" to offering the customer so many choices and options that the product is almost tailor made to his or her specifications. Mass customization has been defined as mass production of individually customized goods and services.[13]

The ACE concept is not to be confused with overquality, which consists of offering products that exceed the customer's specific needs, as in the case of the purchase of a 10-ton capacity crane when never more than 1 ton has to be lifted, or in the case of a watch being designed with the precision of 1/1000 of a second per year when it is intended only for normal use by a teenager. ACE is exemplified by the service mechanic who, having heard of this concept, not only repaired his client's car but also washed and vacuumed it. Basically it means satisfying a customer's *need* (for instance, cleaning the car) when he does not *expect* this service. In our last example, the customer was so pleasantly surprised that he wrote a letter of congratulations to the mechanic's boss.

A particular car rental company provides another example of ACE. This company has eliminated all administrative procedures for its airport customers, for example, waiting at the counter, signing a contract, taking possession of the keys, and so on. On leaving the airport, passengers are driven in a comfortable bus to a parking lot where their names are displayed (no flags though, for now, but who knows?). Their rented car awaits them with the engine already running. If the weather is very hot, the air conditioning has already cooled the interior; if it is very cold, the car is already warmed up. The only thing left for the customer to do is to get in and drive away.

Everybody knows that it is not always easy to anticipate the exact nature of customer needs. This is one of the greatest challenges of defining quality. To illustrate the point: a telephone is used primarily for verbal and electronic communication between two customers; nevertheless, for a telephone company, total quality goes much further than ensuring the quality of communication. It means providing customers with directory assistance and information (delivered with a pleasant tone of voice, courtesy, speed, exactness, and so on); billing (invoice format and content); information of interest to customers; unpaid-bill reminders; prompt correction of billing errors; and various directories and services that are unsolicited but nevertheless useful. An American bank initiated its quality improvement process by drawing up—with the help of its customers—a list of 700 customer-defined total quality indicators.[14] These indicators can be given absolute values (such as number of errors and waiting time), or relative values (degree of satisfaction, courtesy of staff) on scales from 0 to 10.

The Total Quality Triad

Total quality does not stop at satisfying or even delighting the customer—that is only one dimension of total quality. Indeed, it is often forgotten—or insufficiently repeated—that a for-profit organization primarily exists as a result of efforts and investments on the part of its owners, entrepreneurs, or shareholders. They invest in a company and legitimately expect *quality return* on their investment, that is, dividends and capital gains. Moreover, in order to achieve its objectives, survive, and progress, an organization must be able to rely on its people continuously. While it is true that a company cannot exist without customers, it is also true that it can't exist without people. What these people seek from their work in an organization is a *quality of life*.

At the center of this shareholder–customer–people adventure is the CEO, who has to orchestrate these players into a partnership that must also include the active and ongoing participation of the upstream and downstream partners (suppliers, distributors, carriers, and so on). I call this the total quality triad (see Figure 2.2). It is a win–win–win game in which all participants actively and constantly contribute mutually to each other's satisfaction. Total quality thus involves three dimensions, or, if you will, three qualities: a quality return for the shareholder, QVALITY and ACE for the customer, and a quality life for the people in the organization.

The shareholders' needs lie in a quality return on their invested capital (that is, a return that exceeds other sources of return, such as bank deposits). They also include other nonfinancial needs, such as pride in owning a company, social

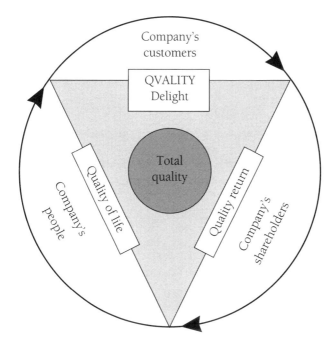

Figure 2.2.   The total quality triad.

status, and so on. Customers' needs are products and services that exceed their expectations in terms of QVALITY. People needs reside in the quality of life in the workplace and at home. Indeed, some organizations look after the well-being of their people outside the work environment. They set up counseling services to help their people and any member of their immediate families fight alcoholism; they provide families with health care, help them educate their children, and so on.

These are the three dimensions of total quality. Of course, in addition to contributing to the well-being of society at large, all of this activity must take place within an environmentally conscious framework. The triangle represents the triad. It is inverted to represent change. The customer is at the top because he or she is the source of satisfaction for both the shareholder (quality return) and the people in the organization (quality of life).

In terms of the priority that these needs take, it is important to distinguish between the private and public sectors. In the private sector, the shareholders of a for-profit company take top priority. As we said before, firms exist primarily to satisfy their owners, shareholders, and investors. Satisfying customer needs enables the business to accumulate income (when the business is profitable, and that is after all its purpose, its raison d'être), which translates into profit for the business and dividends for its shareholders; whereas, in the public sector, customers, who are the beneficiaries or recipients of the services, get top priority. There, the taxpayers—or the government they have elected—replace the private sector's shareholders. Their heavy tax load represents the economic factor that public organizations, who rely on public funding, must consider. It constitutes the restraint that curbs their budgets and spending (see Figure 2.3).

I was invited to attend a meeting where the CEO of a medium-size corporation was speaking to his people, trying to convince them to adopt total quality and apply its concepts at all levels. For a whole hour, he spoke about customer importance and customer satisfaction. He warned the people—employees and managers alike—that unsatisfied customers meant bankruptcy, loss of jobs, unemployment. He concluded by stressing the need to constantly think about the customer and nobody else. At the end of his speech, the CEO asked for my opinion on his mobilization-minded speech. First, I pointed out that, at a similar meeting, a CEO frightened his people by talking about bankruptcy and doom to such a point that, after the meeting, a great number of the attendees were so worried they started looking for other jobs. Six months later, the company had lost most of its best people. I asked him if he knew what his audience was thinking about during his speech about the customer. I suggested that every single one of them was rightfully thinking, "What's in it for me?" No one in his right mind would take a job with the objective of satisfying a customer or even a boss; people want to satisfy themselves. Even volunteers working in Third World countries to help their populations fight sickness or hunger do it to satisfy themselves; they get their satisfaction by saving a life, feeding the hungry, or protecting an orphan.

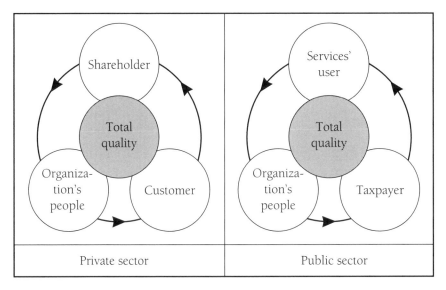

Figure 2.3. The total quality triad in the public and private sectors.

Source: Adapted from J. N. Kelada, *Comprendre et réaliser la qualité totale,* 2nd ed. (Dollard-des-Ormeaux, Quebec, Canada: Quafec Publications, 1992), 26. Reprinted with permission.

Stressing the total quality triad shows the shareholders, the customers, and the people in the organization that every one of them has to give in order to receive. Each one of them does it for his or her own ultimate benefit. The people must understand and believe that, for them, satisfying a customer is but a means to satisfy themselves because it will earn them a salary, provide them with challenges, bring them recognition and rewards, and satisfy their need for belonging to a winning team.

We should point out that some companies take exception to the expression "total quality." For them, it seems to suggest targeting perfection in products, that is, goods or services. We do not live in a perfect world, so they consider total quality to be utopian. Total quality does not mean perfect quality in a product or a service. As we have seen, it reaches beyond the notion of product quality and extends to

- The needs of all customers, whether near or far, directly or indirectly connected with the acquisition, use, and maintenance of the product
- All the possible services preceding, accompanying, or following these stages
- Shareholders' and organization's people needs

Rather than talking about total quality, some companies and authors prefer to speak about *continuous improvement*. In our opinion, this phrase does not convey the underlying notion of total quality. It is too vague and incomplete. It is vague because it does not specify what is to be improved. Some say it means the improvement of processes, others indicate it means improvement of products, while still others insist it is the improvement of both (see chapter 4 for more on continuous improvement).

Total Quality and Traditional Marketing

Marketing specialists have been talking about satisfying, attracting, and retaining customers forever and a day. They offer their customers after-sales guarantees and frequently woo them with very costly promotional and advertising campaigns. This makes us question whether the total quality concept is any different from that old way of thinking because it still leads companies to envelop their customers in a kinglike aura. The Japanese even talk about a "customer–god." Obviously a similarity remains: customer focus. But—and here is the important and inevitable "but"—after that similarity, the total quality approach differs significantly.

In the traditional context, the marketing and sales specialists determine or surmise what customers need. Then they channel this information to the experts in product development, design, and production. In effect, it is the marketing and sales specialists who are in the driver's seat. They dictate the price to invoice, the conditions of payment, and the percentage of discount to be granted.

But this is not so in the total quality approach, which advocates that all the organization members, from the president atop his or her hierarchical pyramid to the worker on the assembly line, must share the common concern for the customer and the customer's total satisfaction. Executives and department heads—comfortably ensconced in well-appointed offices surrounded by armies of secretaries and support staff and enjoying various privileges, like parking, private dining rooms, and well-equipped meeting rooms—are no longer the bosses. The real and only bosses are the shareholders who invest in the company and the customers who buy its products. It is the customers who, in effect, pay the rent and people's salaries, generate the profits that become dividends for the shareholders, and ensure the company's survival. Exceeding customer expectations is becoming the common objective of top management and employees alike. For executives, it is the means par excellence of making profits and, for employees, the challenge through which they satisfy their personal needs.

The total quality approach proposes that the notion of customer focus be introduced everywhere in the business. As we shall see later, this is the *market-in* concept rather than traditional *marketing*. Some business executives, having started to adopt this philosophy, invite their customers to visit their premises and, above all, meet their staff—their whole staff. Others organize occasions for their own personnel to visit their major customers' premises. They ask their people to keep their ears open and report to the company what the public and the present and potential customers are saying about the business, its products, services, and competitors. Each individual in the company is expected to be a marketing agent and a representative of the company.

As indicated before, total quality aims at satisfying the shareholder, but this is dependent on having first satisfied customer needs by providing total quality. An essential part of the customer satisfaction equation is satisfying a company's employees' needs. The whole equation amounts to the total quality triad and underscores the importance of the human factor as a main factor in this triad.

Conclusion

The total quality approach advocates the simultaneous and mutual satisfaction of shareholders, customers, and company's people needs. It is not a passing fad, contrary to the opinions of some executives. It is a revolution in business management that organizations can afford neither to ignore nor to delay. Their survival and progress depend on it.

The principles of total quality can be applied to both private and public organizations in the industrial and service sectors. In order to achieve total quality, it is important to define it in simple, concrete, and measurable terms. We have identified its three dimensions. Shareholders view it as a means of getting a quality return on their investment. They also find in it more subjective benefits, such as pride of part-ownership in a highly successful company, perhaps one with an international reputation. This holds true even more so for owners, entrepreneurs, or founders of companies for whom financial considerations are sometimes less important than the satisfaction they draw from the company they own.

The seven components of QVALITY, the customer dimension of total quality, must be used constantly and consistently to satisfy the greatest possible number of the customer's implicit or explicit needs. Moreover, merely satisfying customers is no longer enough. Companies have to delight them, go beyond their satisfaction and above their expectations. Companies must elicit their customers' enthusiasm through the products and services they can offer.

For individuals in the company, satisfaction has to be reflected in their quality of life as a whole. In the workplace, this means, of course, a salary, fringe benefits, and challenges, but it also means receiving recognition and rewards that crown their efforts and promote their feelings of belonging to a winning team— the company they call their own. In addition, that satisfaction must extend to their quality of life outside the company and promote their own well-being as well as that of their families.

Review Questions

1. Total quality includes, but goes far beyond, simple product quality. Explain and give examples.

2. How would you reply to a top manager in the finance department who stated that he or she had absolutely nothing to do with quality, and even less with customers, and therefore had no interest in getting involved in activities related to total quality?

3. Some people believe that surpassing customers' expectations and going beyond their satisfaction are synonymous with overquality. What are your comments on this?

4. Why is it important for a company wishing to achieve total quality to define the concept clearly? Define total quality in the context of a car manufacturer and an insurance company.

Notes

1. W. Edwards Deming, *Out of the Crisis* (Cambridge, Mass.: MIT CAES, 1986), p. 66.

2. Jeremy Main, "Under the Spell of the Quality Gurus," *Fortune,* 18 August 1986, 30–34.

3. Yunus Kathawala, "A Comparative Analysis of Selected Approaches to Quality," *International Journal for Quality and Reliability Management* (June 1989).

4. W. Edwards Deming, *Quality, Productivity, and Competitive Position* (Cambridge, Mass.: MIT CAES, 1982), 16–17.

5. Philip B. Crosby, *Quality Without Tears* (New York: McGraw-Hill, 1984), 59, 66, 85, 86, 89.

6. Joseph M. Juran, *Juran's Quality Control Handbook* (New York: McGraw-Hill, 1988).

7. A. V. Feigenbaum, *Total Quality Control* (New York: McGraw-Hill, 1961). This is a revised edition of the book *Quality Control* (New York: McGraw-Hill, 1951).

8. Kaoru Ishikawa, *What Is Total Quality Control? The Japanese Way* (Englewood Cliffs, N.J.: Prentice Hall, 1985), 91.

9. "Gallup Survey: Top Executives Talk About Quality," *Quality Progress* 19, no. 12 (December 1986): 48–55

10. ISO 8402, part of the *ISO 9000 Compendium: International Standards for Quality Management* (Geneva: International Organization for Standardization, 1994).

11. Juran equates suitability with fitness for use. His definition has provided a great deal of the inspiration for my own work on the subject.

12. ISO 8402 and the *ISO 9000 Compendium.*

13. Joseph Pine II, *Mass Customization—The New Frontier in Business Competition* (Boston: Harvard Business School Press, 1993).

14. Richard Thomas, "Bank on Quality," *Quality Progress* 20, no. 2 (February 1987): 27–29.

Chapter 3

Total quality is a voyage, not a destination.

Traditional Management and TQM

Traditional Management and Total Quality

Japan's phenomenal economic success has roused the interest of all industrialized nations and developing countries as well. Western business management specialists, particularly in North America, intent on examining the possibility of importing it for their own use, have studied the Japanese phenomenon intensely. They have tried to discover its underlying secrets and thereby determine the basic business model behind its success. These business administration specialists, theorists, and practitioners unearthed two surprising facts. First, the majority of the techniques and concepts used in Japan had been developed in the United States. Second, when used in the West, these techniques either never produced satisfactory results or else failed completely. From these observations one might draw the hasty conclusion that the success of the Japanese is linked to their culture and traditions, which are so vastly different from ours.

However, many examples can be found to illustrate that this is not quite true. Many Western companies that have been acquired by the Japanese get the same results as those established in Japan, yet, apart from a few Japanese in upper management, they are staffed by Western personnel. As indicated in chapter 1, some businesses fail in their attempt to implement total quality even though they use Japanese business techniques in general and total quality management techniques in particular. One of the reasons is that they do not know what TQM is all about. The objective of this chapter is to present a clear and concrete definition of TQM, showing how it differs from traditional management.

Japanese Total Quality Control

During a visit to Japan, I asked my interpreter to contact a company in the suburbs of Tokyo to request an appointment with the person responsible for quality. He lost no time in phoning the business in question and was promptly asked if I wanted to meet the president. When he explained that I had no wish to disturb the president and would be happy just to meet the person in charge of quality, my interpreter was immediately informed that the person in charge of quality was, indeed, the president. A meeting was therefore arranged for me, along with my interpreter, to interview the president. During our interview, the president repeatedly used the expression, "Tic-you-shee." This piqued my curiosity, but when my interpreter deciphered what the president had said, this term was not translated but merely repeated. I therefore asked him to be good enough to translate the term, as I had the impression that it was fundamental to the president's answers. He seemed very surprised and told me that this was no Japanese term, but a very well-known English expression: "Tic-you-shee" turned out to be none other than TQC—total quality control. The Japanese had adopted it without bothering to translate it.

This president added that, for him, the T in TQC stood for *top,* and because he was the top of his company he felt that he had ultimate responsibility for quality. The expression TQC occurred constantly in all my interviews and made me decide to unlock whatever magical meaning it held for those I met. I received various documents written completely in Japanese with these three letters being the only ones from our alphabet to appear, and they were used repeatedly. On several occasions I was made aware that, in Japan, TQC did not have the meaning given to it by its American originator, Armand V. Feigenbaum. My research showed that each company, each Japanese organization, interpreted TQC in its own fashion. Meanwhile, today, in the United States and just about everywhere else in the world, TQM (total quality management) has replaced TQC.

In the end, TQM is, above all, a philosophy of management. While all the operational policies of a company emanate from this philosophy, the particular techniques used, whether in Japan or elsewhere, are but its external manifestations and are less significant than the spirit that underlies them. When Westerners import, reclaim, and introduce these techniques into their own businesses without making any prior change to their company culture or philosophy, they should not be amazed to find out that the techniques do not yield the same results as they do in Japan.

From Quality Control to Total Quality Management

In a number of organizations, top managers aiming to achieve total quality recognize the importance of the organization's members—the internal partners—and place emphasis almost exclusively on sensitizing their personnel to the constant need to pursue quality. This consciousness-raising process has given birth to a whole new jargon—one talks of empowerment, dramatization, mobilization, sensitization. Other organizations, just as exclusively, use techniques to control and ensure quality by detecting errors, defects, and anomalies, or, even better, by trying to prevent them. The people in each sector of the business are thus trained to use techniques to improve quality and solve problems in their particular sectors. Neither of these two orientations, the one exclusively technical and the other exclusively human, have yielded the results expected; the ensuing improvements in quality have been modest and, in many cases, short-lived. They are still a far cry from total quality.

Although there are numerous approaches to quality management, we will choose two completely opposite approaches to illustrate our point: approach A and approach Z. In practice, people usually lean toward one or the other of these approaches. In approach A, or the quality control approach, quality is limited to the product offered. Here the quality function is perceived as a technical function, much as engineering, maintenance, or production would be. Even though it touches everyone's domain, responsibility for it is generally left to specialists at a middle-management level, who monitor quality only on the factory floor, on the materials and parts receiving dock, or at the shipping stage of the finished product. These specialists work in laboratories filled with complicated apparatus or in offices papered with strange graphs. They have their own technical jargon that no one else even ventures to understand. They talk of defects, defectives, rejects, deviations, substandards, downgrades, internal and external failures, customer returns, exchanges, repairs, reimbursements, complaints, discards, demerits, inspection, destructive and nondestructive tests, control, assurance, statistics, and design of experiments.

In approach A, quality specialists often play the role of watchdogs or police, constantly on the alert to catch those who are guilty of infractions against the procedures, standards, or specifications set up by zealous engineers. Seated atop their ivory tower, the latter are obsessed by the quest for technical and technological perfection. For these engineers and designers, quality is nothing less than *the state of the art!* In this pecking order, the *doers* are systematically separated from the *inspectors.* Those in charge of production, precisely because they have to keep putting out certain quantities of product on time and at the lowest cost, spend more time and effort trying not to get caught by these quality specialists than trying to achieve or improve the quality of their products.

Admittedly this is an exaggerated, even satirical, caricature of the quality control setup in these businesses. However, as with all caricatures, it stretches the facts in order to underline the truth—in this case, the everyday absurdities of life in some organizations. In fact, I have presented this caricature frequently to audiences in all kinds of organizations, always insisting on its wild exaggeration of reality. Surprisingly, I have often received the comment that I was describing their organization to the hilt, as if I had worked there all my life!

On the other end of the spectrum, the company taking approach Z considers total quality to be its global objective. It is top management's primary responsibility. Here authentic participatory management and teamwork are advocated, individuals are responsible for their own quality control, and the quality department, if one exists, acts as a support and assists the other departments. In this case *quality* certainly includes the finished product but goes well beyond it. As we have seen in chapter 2, it means satisfying the needs of the stockholders (or taxpayers in the public sector), the customers, the company people, and society as a whole. It is sought after in every segment of the organization, not exclusively in production or inspection departments. In contrast to the narrowly circumscribed quality of approach A, we are thus speaking of a quality that is *total* and all-encompassing in nature.

Note that total quality is achieved with the collaboration of external upstream and downstream partners. Upstream partners include

- The suppliers of human, physical, and financial resources, whether they be
  - Financial or banking institutions that provide financial or accounting services
  - Institutions of education and higher learning (universities, colleges, schools) that provide the necessary work force
  - Suppliers of raw materials and equipment
- Organizations providing various services, such as consulting, computer services, and so on
- Organizations and various associations providing companies with technical or other assistance

The downstream partners are the distributors, wholesalers, retailers, carriers, installers, salespeople, after-sales service representatives, and so on.

Total quality is attained by using a distinctive type of management. Companies simultaneously target satisfaction for each section of the total quality triad (see Figure 2.2)—that is to say, for their stockholders, their customers, and their people, or, in the public sector, for taxpayers, recipients of benefits, and people in the organization. This type of management is total quality management.

In short, total quality is achieved through total quality management, practiced everywhere, by everyone, and at all times.

My definition of TQM was inspired by the work of the great thinkers on the subject—W. Edwards Deming (who, in 1988, invited me to participate in one of his consulting sessions with General Motors in Detroit), Joseph M. Juran, Armand V. Feigenbaum, Philip B. Crosby, and Kaoru Ishikawa—all of whom I have met on various occasions. It is also based on numerous observations I have made about the practices of many companies, both local and foreign, that have had a remarkable degree of financial success. Total quality management can be applied in all sectors of a business producing goods or services and is in no way limited to workers on the shop floor.

Historical Evolution

Before tracing the evolution of total quality from inspection on the factory floor at the beginning of the century to total quality management at the dawn of the twenty-first century (see Figure 3.1), we should note that artisans have traditionally always been responsible for the quality of work they produced. It was only when workers found themselves grouped together in factories that the responsibility for checking the quality of their work devolved to the line supervisor.

As the line supervisor's duties expanded into hiring workers, training them on the job, paying them at the end of the day or of the week, and sometimes even settling their personal conflicts, a new discipline was created: inspection. In North American factories, inspectors checked all products before they were dispatched to customers. This activity eventually came to include the raw materials received (thus, incoming inspections). Subsequently, inspection was further extended to work-in-process.

In turn, inspection gave way to control. Tests were designed, control systems established, laboratories built. Toward the end of the 1920s, statistical techniques were developed and applied to quality control (statistical quality control, including acceptance sampling and statistical process control, SPC).

Control is an activity whose objective is to *detect* errors and defects for their eventual correction. However, *prevention* being more efficient and economical

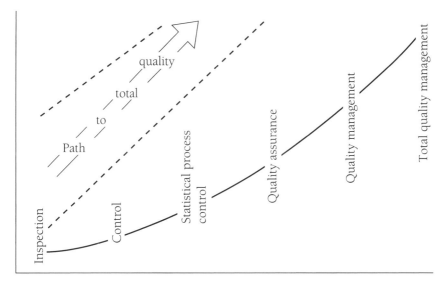

Figure 3.1.   From inspection to TQM.

Source: J. N. Kelada, *Comprendre et réaliser la qualité totale,* 1st ed. (Dollard-des-Ormeaux, Quebec, Canada: Editions Quafec, 1991), 40. Reprinted with permission.

than correction, *quality assurance* was introduced and encouraged. Suppliers were required to provide their customers with an assurance that the products ordered would be designed, manufactured, and delivered to the level of quality ordered. But to ensure quality, it was found that one had to plan it, back it up with adequate organization (structures and systems), and manage one's personnel with an eye to obtaining and controlling the required quality. In short, one had to manage quality. Therefore, from quality assurance, interest turned to *quality management.*

With the appearance of the notion of *total quality* came the realization that to achieve it one had to adopt a new style of management: total quality management or TQM. The stages of this evolution are described in Table 3.1.

1. Inspection of finished products in manufacturing.	2. Quality control of manufactured products (tests, labs, etc.).	3. Quality control of incoming materials, work-in-process, and finished products. Statistical quality control techniques.	4. Quality planning and control in product design, incoming materials, work-in-process, and finished products.
5. Quality planning, control, and assurance in product design, supplier evaluation, incoming materials, work-in-process, finished goods, and after-sale service. ISO 9000 standards applied.	6. Quality planning, control, and assurance in goods and services design, supplier evaluation, incoming materials, work-in-process, finished products, after-sale service in manufacturing and service industries. ISO 9000 standards applied.	7. Quality management in goods and services design, supplier evaluation, incoming materials, work-in-process, finished goods and services, after-sale service in manufacturing and service industries, partnerships up- and downstream.	
8. Objective: Customer satisfaction, meeting customer's requirements. Means: partnership with outside partners (up- and downstream), participation by all. Applied in manufacturing and services, in private and public sectors. Total quality control.	9. Objective: Beyond customer satisfaction, above customer expectations. Means: Leadership in quality, internal and external partnerships, teamwork, people empowerment, top management involvement, continuous improvement, total quality management.	10. Objective: Shareholder–customer–people satisfaction. Means: Leadership in quality, internal and external partnerships, top management involvement, continuous improvement and innovation, total quality management, business reengineering.	

Table 3.1. From inspection to total quality management.

Source: Adapted from J. N. Kelada, *Comprendre et réaliser la qualité totale,* 2nd ed. (Dollard-des-Ormeaux, Quebec, Canada: Editions Quafec, 1992), 51. Reprinted with permission.

Total Quality Management

Quality does not happen by chance; it has to be managed. Like business management in general, quality management is a group of activities whose aim is to define a certain number of objectives and achieve them through the optimum use of the resources available. It includes all the activities involving planning, organization, direction, control, and assurance that the manager has to perform in order to achieve the requisite quality, on time, and at the best possible cost.

Planning involves defining—for each individual, service, sector, or division of the business—what quality consists of, and then determining the means to do it. This means identifying the internal partner downstream and the end customer, establishing their needs, and determining what to do in order to meet or exceed their expectations.

Organization involves determining the administrative structures and allocating the resources, as well as establishing the systems and methods necessary to achieve the quality defined and specified in the planning phase.

Direction concerns all the human aspects of management: motivating and mobilizing personnel, providing support, exercising enlightened leadership, adopting a management style conducive to the attainment of the established objectives, resolving conflicts in the workplace, and so on.

The purpose of *control* is to *detect* errors or defects. Results are measured, then compared with the stated objectives in order to spot and correct any deviation.

Quality *assurance* is achieved through a group of *preventive* activities intended to ensure the quality of the results. These activities systematically ensure that planning, organization, direction, and control are executed correctly. Quality assurance consists of verifying that these activities have been carried out efficiently, thereby guaranteeing that an optimum level of quality is reached. It is the same concept that accounting auditors use in internal and external auditing. Quality assurance consists of periodically auditing existing systems and procedures, manufacturing and administrative processes, and finally materials and products (goods and services) received, as well as finished products and work-in-process.

A clear distinction must be made between management, control, and assurance, for they are still often confused just as much in theory as in practice.

Through quality management, the required quality can be attained. Through total quality management, total quality can be achieved and maintained. In fact, every business has a number of strategic objectives—economic, social, technical, commercial—that are achieved by reaching the company's operational objectives. As already mentioned, the underlying aim of TQM is to procure profitability for the company by providing products and services targeted at fulfilling customers' needs, which are expressed in terms of the seven characteristics of customer total quality, QVALITY. Profitability is achieved by satisfying people's needs, collaborating closely with external upstream and downstream partners, and at the same time respecting the environment that we leave as a legacy to our descendants.

The success of TQM will therefore lie in accepting the challenge to simultaneously satisfy the three stakeholders of the total quality triad: stockholders, customers, and people (see Figure 3.2). In one of my recent seminars, a participant asked which of these three should take priority. Another participant offered a surprising analogy that I had never thought of: just as with color television, where the three elementary colors must constantly be juggled and adjusted to obtain an image with the full spectrum of colors, the trick of TQM is to judiciously divide and shift one's attention between all three elements in order to create the most perfectly balanced picture possible. For example, in the public sector, should one be primarily concerned about the taxpayers and their tax load, the customer (in this case the beneficiary of services), or the public servant? The challenge for those responsible is to find a happy balance between these three concerns, especially since the three occasionally happen to be rolled up into one and the same person.

TQM is consequently one of the most important aspects of business management, and its importance is increasing. For an organization to reach its strategic

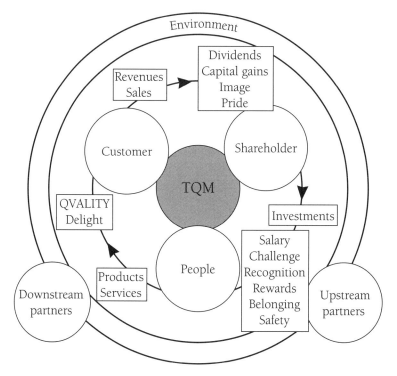

Figure 3.2. TQM and the total quality triad.

Source: J. N. Kelada, *Comprendre et réaliser la qualité totale,* 2nd ed., (Dollard-des-Ormeaux, Quebec, Canada: Editions Quafec, 1992), 25. Reprinted with permission.

objectives, everyone in charge of a function within the company must participate in achieving total quality. Total quality management is thus a matter that concerns both top management and anyone in charge of a company operation. It should not be considered as purely technical and consequently left to technicians, however competent they may be. This in no way diminishes the importance of the technical elements of quality management, such as statistical quality control, process analysis, or design of experiments; but, all the same, TQM is not limited to these elements. In the following chapters, we shall examine the various activities involved in TQM.

How can the notion of total quality be applied to a function such as personnel? Take the example of the corporation that wanted to recruit university graduates with average marks of 85 percent or more from five different geographic regions. The recruiting campaign results showed that applications had been received from only two regions and that the candidates' average marks were 78 percent. Hiring department staff found some explanations for these results by employing techniques used in TQM, such as Pareto analysis and Ishikawa's cause-and-effect diagram (which we shall look at in chapter 13). The new recruiting campaign took heed of these findings and, as a result, found candidates from five regions with average marks of 83 percent.

The number of corporations and organizations interested in the total quality approach is slowly but surely increasing, and, surprisingly, this phenomenon is not limited only to the industrial and private sectors but extends into service and public sectors.

Defining *Total Quality Management*

Based on the total quality approach, TQM has three dimensions (see Figure 3.3): (1) the human dimension: psychological and political; (2) a logical dimension: rational and systematic; and (3) a technology or technological dimension: mechanical and systematic. In our opinion, the first is the most important; yet it is the least visible aspect of TQM.

TQM is principally based on a management *philosophy*, a way of thinking from which emanates a way of doing that is assumed by all persons in the organization as well as by its external partners. This represents the *why* of total quality. This philosophy is profit oriented, customer focused, people centered, partner assisted, and environmentally conscious (concerned with the community as well as with pollution, garbage, noise, the ozone layer, and so on). Everybody works as a team headed by the CEO, who assumes responsibility for the total quality objective and communicates it, not only to all the personnel in the corporation, but also to the external upstream and downstream partners. Managers work in a team *with* internal partners or associates.

The first dimension of TQM is its *human aspect.* A great actor once attributed 99 percent of his success to effort (sweat) and 1 percent to talent. Similarly, TQM

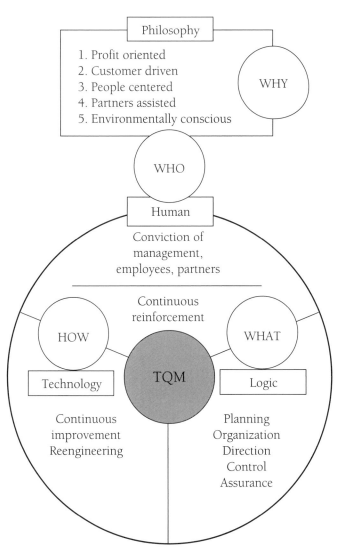

Figure 3.3. Total quality management's three dimensions.

Source: J. N. Kelada, *Comprendre et réaliser la qualité totale,* 2nd ed. (Dollard-des-Ormeaux, Quebec, Canada: Editions Quafec, 1992), 55. Reprinted with permission.

is triggered and maintained mainly by the will to do it (the *will* as distinct from the *wish*) rather than the knowledge of how to do it. TQM advocates quality everywhere, in all sectors of the company, by everyone, at all times. It is practiced at all levels of the hierarchy; it has to start at the top and go right down to the worker who completes the order.

Customer satisfaction comes through true participation on the part of all people in the company—management and nonmanagement, supervisory or nonsupervisory staff, bosses and employees—as well as the company's external partners.

The human aspect is of utmost importance and has two objectives: to start and to maintain a total quality process in any organization. Indeed, top managers must be convinced that they have to change their ways of doing business; they have to exercise strong leadership inside the organization with their people and outside with their external partners, both of whom they have to mobilize. They have to "walk their talk," practice what they preach, be committed and involved. Then, once the total quality process is underway, they have to continuously reinforce it by their attitude and behavior, by rewards and recognition, by participation and teamwork.

This aspect includes the mobilization effort required at the launching phase, which triggers the interest for total quality among all of the organization's members and creates the enthusiasm and motivation to embark on such a process. It also includes reinforcement activities to continuously maintain motivation, interest, and enthusiasm for total quality day after day, year after year.

The second dimension relates to what TQM is. This is its *logical* aspect, where

- The customer must be identified.
- Total quality has to be defined, along with the role each individual has to play in order to achieve it.
- Total quality must be managed using procedures and approaches that are global, rational, logical, and well organized.
- Mechanisms to facilitate teamwork must be developed and established.
- The business process has to be improved or redesigned, reengineered.
- The decision-making process must be periodically reviewed.
- Procedures for problem identifying, solving, and preventing (PISP) are adopted.

Remember that no logic can work unless you are really convinced it will. That foundation having been laid, you must know what you have to do, you have to do it well, and you must always improve on it. Without a deep conviction, the irrational reigns over the rational and faulty reasoning replaces logic. The quality circles spin around, producing nothing. Time is wasted on resolving imaginary problems and rationalizing the causes of the ensuing failures.

TQM's logic is based on the fact that nothing is perfect, that everything can and must be improved by everyone's participation in all parts of the organization. This is the *total quality chain,* where each link is just as important as the next. All departments, every manager or employee, every line supervisor or operator, represents a link in a chain that is only as strong as its weakest link (see Figure 3.4). Moreover, total quality does not come about haphazardly; it is not achieved by

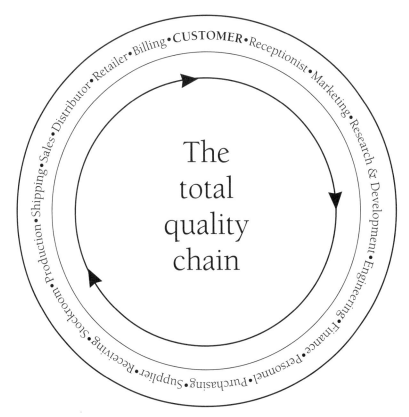

Figure 3.4. The total quality chain.

Source: Adapted from J. N. Kelada, *Comprendre et réaliser la qualité totale*, 2nd ed. (Dollard-des-Ormeaux, Quebec, Canada: Editions Quafec, 1992), 57. Reprinted with permission.

luck or accident. It must be managed, that is to say, planned, organized, directed, controlled, and assured.

Note that, because of the confusion that the term *internal customer* can bring about, I prefer to use the expression *internal partner*. The notion of partnership tends to reinforce, and even create, team spirit in the company. Sometimes, the qualifiers *upstream* or *downstream* are added to *partners* only to indicate the partners' relative position on the total quality chain.

The third dimension of TQM represents the *how*. An elaborate technology has been developed in the field of total quality, for it is not sufficient to be convinced that we have to change and work together in order to succeed; nor is it enough to know that we have to plan and organize. We must also know, specifically, *how* to achieve total quality. The total quality technology includes a number of methodologies, tools, and techniques used at either or both of the strategic and the operational levels. To name but a few, let us mention business reengineering (BR), or business process reengineering (BPR), process management, quality function deployment (QFD), policy deployment, statistical process control (SPC), the seven quality control (QC) tools, the seven quality management tools, design of experiments (DOE), problem-solving techniques, ISO 9000, quality assurance (QA) systems, and the Baldrige Award guide to evaluating quality systems. Hundreds of articles and books have been published on each of these topics. Chapter 13 deals with this aspect in more detail.

The Objective and the Means

We have to stress the fact that TQM is often considered a *program*. Actually, it is not a program with a beginning and an end; it is a *process* that never ends. Moreover, total quality management is often confused with total quality itself. It should be emphasized that TQM is only a means; total quality is its objective and its result (see Figure 3.5).

The PDCA Cycle

The quality improvement cycle illustrates the notion of continuous improvement as it is linked to the achievement of total quality. This cycle is called the plan-do-check-act (PDCA) cycle or circle. The Japanese call it the Deming cycle, or the

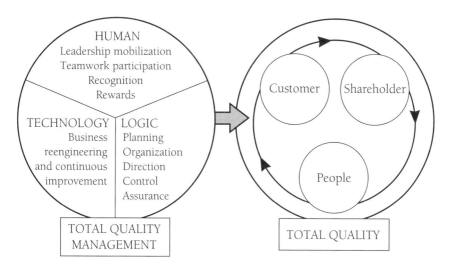

Figure 3.5. Total quality an objective, TQM a means, continuous improvement and reengineering a tool.

Source: Adapted from J. N. Kelada, *Comprendre et réaliser la qualité totale,* 2nd ed. (Dollard-des-Ormeaux, Quebec, Canada: Editions Quafec, 1992), 58. Reprinted with permission.

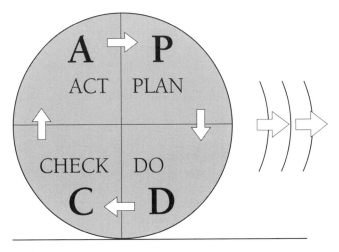

Figure 3.6. The PDCA cycle.

Deming wheel. Deming called it the Shewhart cycle, after Walter A. Shewhart, the famous quality statistician.

The cycle starts with thinking and planning (*plan*), for example, determining who the customers are, what they want, and how to satisfy them. The task is then performed, and the service rendered or the product manufactured (*do*). Next, in the control phase (*check*), the product or service is checked for quality. Lastly, if it does not meet the customer requirements it is corrected, or if it does, it is further improved (*act*). Before you undertake any action or perform any activity, you should practice getting a mental picture of the revolving motion of this cycle. Figure 3.6 shows that, each time the wheel turns, it moves ahead little by little, step by step. This advance symbolizes quality's step-by-step continuous improvement. If you repeat a task a hundred times or more and apply this cycle each time, by the hundredth time you will obviously reach near-perfection.

People who use this cycle avoid repeating the same error. In fact, once they start to think and plan, they review what they did the last time they went around. If they previously made a mistake, then they can avoid repeating it. And if the result was good, as is often the case, they can improve on it or go a step further, reengineer it. I have observed that this cycle is just as effective for the person working on the shop floor as for the upper manager, and it works as well for producing goods as it does for offering a service.

Introversive and Extraversive Management

The following incident took place in the emergency room of a well-known hospital. A patient who had been injured while working on the roof of his house went to the receptionist on duty. She asked him for his hospital card, but he apologized because he could not find it. That didn't matter; she would make him another one. "You can't get anything done in the hospital without a card," she explained. She asked him for information which she conscientiously entered on specially prepared forms. The patient suffered in silence while all the boxes on the form were meticulously completed, one after the other.

When later asked what, in her mind, her mission in that hospital was, the receptionist had no hesitation in replying that it was to make sure that the forms were filled in correctly. But what about the patient? She maintained that he was the medical staff's responsibility. What about his well-being, his comfort? What about easing his pain? She explained, very rationally, that her superiors judged her solely on the accuracy of the information she collected and entered into the form. When she had been appointed to the position, her superiors had been very specific about her responsibilities. For her, the patient was merely a source of information. She was evaluated on the work she had to do—accurately filling in forms. No one evaluated her on courtesy, welcoming attitude, or patient satisfaction. She did what she had been asked to do, carefully and efficiently. And for that she was irreproachable.

In another instance, I was asked to meet the top management team at a hospital to discuss the possibility and relevance of introducing total quality into their organization. Before starting my presentation, I asked participants to introduce themselves and briefly describe their roles in the hospital. The first participant explained he was responsible for accounting, financial statements, and budgets. The second stated that her role was to manage the human resources, that is, hire and fire, train personnel and assist in their evaluation, negotiate collective agreements, and discuss and settle grievances with the various unions. The third participant was in charge of purchasing. He talked at length about suppliers, stockrooms, and purchase orders, about making sure no one went over budget except for extreme situations.

The head of the nursing department indicated clearly that she was there to make sure procedures were religiously followed by all of her staff. Most of her time was spent in preparing and modifying her huge staff's work schedule (shifts, vacations, holidays) and in fighting to reduce absenteeism. The manager of the computer systems department explained that, clearly, everything that had to do with computers and systems was his business. He endeavored to explain how complex his job was, given the technological revolution going on in the medical world, as practically everywhere else. The chief doctor insisted he always made sure that operation rooms were clean and tight and their personnel well-disciplined.

The introductions went on, and at one point I felt I had to stop them. I asked my puzzled audience, "Are there any patients or sick people in this hospital?" If there were any, so far no one among these senior managers had appeared to have noticed them!

Actually, in any organization, people react in the same way when queried about how they perceive their roles. Accountants count, buyers buy, personnel departments hire and fire, inspectors inspect, welders weld, painters paint. If they all do their jobs right and the company still goes bankrupt, obviously it is not their fault, not their doing. This in fact is how managers traditionally manage— and, in so doing, they miss the forest for all the trees. Where is the customer in this myopic vision? While some people may define the total quality approach in very philosophical terms and others may define it in more technical terms, in the end, what they all want is to regain the overall picture—the whole forest, as it were, not just the trees. In an age of increasing specialization and compartmentalization, where work tasks turn inward on themselves to form ever-diminishing, concentric circles, the total quality approach simply advocates a return to a very fundamental, even primitive, concept: every organization—be it for-profit or nonprofit, private or public, industrial or service, small, medium, or large—exists only because it has customers whose needs it has to meet. In the private sector, this leads to the principal objective of satisfying the organization's investors, the shareholders, and, in the public sector, this has to be done while trying to ease the burden of taxes on taxpayers.

This larger picture would have been nearly impossible to lose sight of in another era. In the good old days, artisans personally conducted their business directly with their customers and suppliers. The special bonds created between customer, artisan, and supplier held advantages for each one of them. Today, the artisan has disappeared into a sea of other artisans, all employees or workers under the command of an army of big, medium, and little bosses. They know neither the company's customers nor its suppliers. A bank cashier was required to file checks and various documents and enter data into a computer whenever she had no customers at her wicket. When I visited the bank, I noticed that every time a customer came to her station, she looked annoyed, and she made no bones about showing it. When I asked her why, she declared, "Well, sir, these customers are a nuisance. They stop me from working!"

The main purpose of total quality is to keep reminding us of our primary mission: profitability through customer satisfaction. If individual employees do not have direct contact with customers, then their obligation is to assist an internal partner in satisfying the needs of the customer. In any organization, this must be every person's objective, every person's challenge. To respond to that challenge, everyone in the organization must work as a team, forgetting the traditional roles of managers and workers, of supervisors and supervised, bosses and subordinates. Everyone must participate in the decision-making process and always remember that he or she is there for the customer. The buyer has to stop thinking that his mission is to buy, the computer specialist to program computers, and the accountant to count. In a sector as sensitive as health and social services, this holds true even more and takes on greater consequence. This area deals with something of supreme importance—human life. There, the mission is so high and noble that it cannot be replaced by filling in a form, buying supplies, organizing a pharmacy, or preparing financial statements. Therein lies total quality, and there is nothing specifically Japanese about that!

I have had occasion to observe that some companies are baffled when faced with all these new ideas. They try to combine the more traditional ideas with those of today, but this mix-and-match approach to management techniques comes to no avail because of the fundamentally opposed natures of the old and new management practices.

Traditionally, management practices what I call *introversive management*. This consists of evaluating the efficiency of the company by looking within the company, or within a sector of the company, and scrutinizing its internal procedures (introvision) (see Figure 3.7). Thus when top management evaluates the performance of a given department, it does so by measuring its output in terms of its *mission:* number of employees hired, hired at the right time, and at a minimal cost; number of purchase orders processed; number of computer systems installed or updated; number of error-free internal financial transactions. Plans of action include objectives such as improving the working conditions, introducing new technology, updating systems and procedures, reviewing the organizational structure and job descriptions, implementing a new project management approach, and modifying the planning process. One again wonders, where are the customers? What about the shareholders?

In fact, the marketing and sales departments provide the only point of contact with the customer. They act as the official liaison between the customer and the company. In fact, however, they do not even talk about the *customer* but, instead, about the *market.* For them, often, the customer has long been an intangible notion—a 30- to 35-year-old male, making on the average $41,000, having 0.75 of a wife, 1.1 children, and 0.45 of a dog! As far as I am concerned, I have

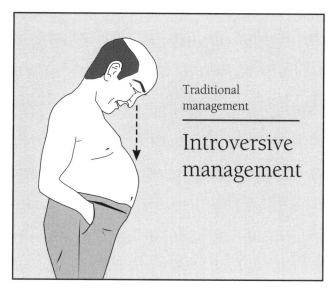

Figure 3.7.   Introversive management.

never met anyone in my life with three quarters of a wife or with half a dog. More-over, the marketing people, rather than directly connecting the company to the customer, act more as a filter of information received from the customer. The de-partment interprets the information and, in turn, transmits that interpretation to whichever company members it deems are fit to receive it. The link to the cus-tomer becomes even more tenuous when one considers that the company's gaze is turned inward. Will the people who receive that information be receptive to it when they most likely define their mission in the company in the narrow terms of their own internal departmental mission? Maybe I somewhat exaggerate here, but there is definitely some truth in all this.

Achieving total quality requires what I describe as *extraversive management,* that is, measuring performance by looking not only outside a given department but outside the organization, rather than inside (see Figure 3.8). Every depart-ment and every individual within a department must view his or her role as con-tributing to the *customers'* needs. Fulfillment of these needs, in turn, translates into revenues, profits for the company, and finally dividends for shareholders. Through their appointed representatives (that is, top management), shareholders then contribute to providing the organization's people with a quality life. A qual-ity life includes a quality of work life, that is, a salary, challenging work, a sense of belonging to a winning team, and rewards and recognition for challenges met. It also includes quality of personal and family life, when, as previously mentioned,

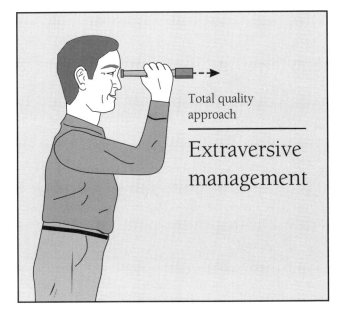

Figure 3.8. Extraversive management.

the organization helps individuals or groups with their personal and social lives (for example, help with alcoholism, community services, general education for employees, education for children, and services for employees' aged relatives).

Productivity and Total Quality

The traditional concept of productivity is a good illustration of introversive management. Technically, productivity can be defined as the relationship between the output (production) and the input (resources).

$$\text{Productivity} = \frac{\text{Output}}{\text{Input}} = \frac{\text{Production}}{\text{Resources}}$$

Output can be expressed in units produced or units sold. To determine productivity, we divide output by the resources needed to produce that output. For example, we divide the number of units produced by the number of people required to produce them. However, the productivity equation above does not explicitly mention either the customer or the shareholder (profitability), and the vision is inward.

Obviously, productivity directly affects the profitability of a company. Raising productivity in an organization often means reducing operating costs. Thanks to increases in productivity, our society enjoys a much better standard of living than that of our forefathers. But this quest for productivity has negative effects because it pushes managers to concentrate their attention on internal or departmental objectives. When productivity is set as an objective, people perceive it as meaning either increased production or reduced resources—which translates for them into either working harder or losing their jobs, both of which are negative perceptions.

In order to achieve those internal or departmental objectives, managers emphasize productivity rates and optimal use of resources. In contrast to this traditional approach, the total quality approach emphasizes specifically shareholder and customer satisfaction. Managers and personnel are urged to look outward, share common objectives, and exceed customer expectations. But the company's profitability and the stockholders' or taxpayers' satisfaction are always kept foremost in mind. Consideration is given to the needs of society and the environment as well as to the strategies used by the competition to satisfy customers. Collaboration is sought with both upstream and downstream partners, suppliers, carriers, distributors, and so on who, for too long, have been considered almost adversaries. The whole approach is centered on satisfying the people—the internal partners—who are called upon to be active participants at all times in the quest for total customer satisfaction. The people's satisfaction, in effect, ensures the company's profitability and competitiveness.

Even though TQM is extraversive, productivity is not ignored, for it is an important element of consideration in total quality management. We find in it the notion of productivity, since the other material and financial resources are considered.

However, these resources are not on the same level as the company's *people.* You find, too, the three aspects of total quality management: the human, the logic, and the technology. The style of management and leadership used by the managers represents the human aspect; the full gamut of management activities constitute the logic; the management techniques embody the technology. All in all, it is a win–win–win situation. Customers are won over and delighted to see their expectations exceeded; stockholders are satisfied and happy to get a higher return on their investment; and the people in the company are happy and proud to work as members of a team and participate regularly in the decision-making process of *their* company.

Conclusion

In spite of the major changes taking place in the world—economic, social, political, and technological—our managers continue to manage just as they did more than a century ago. With the exception of marketing and sales managers, all other managers fail to see past the proverbial tips of their noses—in this case, their own narrowly circumscribed mission to hire, train, and pay personnel, produce financial statements, buy goods and services for all of the departments in the company, manufacture products, manage inventories, develop and design computerized systems, prepare or supervise the application of procedures, motivate the staff, and so on. To evaluate the performance of a company or a department within the company, they measure absenteeism and inventory levels, determine whether or not they are on budget, and gauge how well personnel are motivated. This all amounts to introversive management.

Today's generation is witness to the globalization of economies, competition on a worldwide scale, and momentous changes in hitherto established political systems and societal values. Some companies have realized that it is time to change. Faced with the new demands of our era, they have shifted their strategies and orientations. They have chosen *total quality.* To achieve total quality, they have adopted a new style of management, total quality management, where all those responsible—managers *and* workers—are fully aware that they have common objectives and that they must reach them together. Total quality can be a source of pride and satisfaction for all people in the company. It is important to allow and encourage people—both managers and workers, upper management and executives, line and staff—to work together in unison as a team to improve the company's performance in all their activities.

The first requisite for achieving total quality is to convince everyone of its importance. Without this conviction, all efforts and initiatives, no matter how rational and sophisticated they are, are doomed to certain failure. Each person must know why he or she has to target total quality and achieve it. The second requisite is the logical component of quality. You have to know what quality is and what to do to improve it. Only when these two preliminary requirements are satisfied can you go on to the technology. Quality improvement teams use a rational methodology and particular techniques for preventing, identifying, and solving problems. Then, using the appropriate methods, they measure improvement against the customers' requirements.

It should be noted that, if the basic philosophy is not accepted and shared by all the personnel in the organization wishing to introduce TQM, it is futile to launch into the technical aspects of improving quality. On the other hand, though, wholeheartedly accepting this philosophy will in itself go a long way toward instigating change. The mere conviction that one has to do better and better counts for more than 80 percent in the process of total quality management. This makes simple conviction an excellent means for achieving total quality in a company. And instilling that conviction should not be a hard sell, because with quality, everybody wins. The staff is proud, stockholders achieve their objectives, and customers are more than satisfied. One has to be completely convinced; the rest will come almost of its own accord.

In short, we can say that total quality management is based on a profit oriented, customer focused, people centered, partner assisted, and environmentally conscious philosophy. It consists of a human aspect, a logic (a rational aspect), and an elaborate technology.

Review Questions

1. What difference is there between quality management, quality control, and quality assurance?

2. Total quality management, TQM, is a global approach to achieving total quality. Some perceive TQM as a utopian approach, others as a cultural approach valid for some Asiatic countries, but not for North American organizations. Still others see it as a transitory fad. Discuss.

3. TQM claims to be extraversive management. In concrete terms, how does it differ from traditional, introversive management? Explain this to a company CEO, giving clear examples.

4. Some management theoreticians and practitioners are surprised by the extent of the total quality movement in the world. They claim that this approach does not present anything new, that the concepts are old, some dating back to Taylor, and have been simply rehashed and then dubbed avant-garde and revolutionary. Here are some examples. Total quality advocates customer orientation. Traditional marketing specialists claim that this is exactly what they have been suggesting for almost half a century. Similarly, human science scholars equate total quality with participative management, which they advocated many years ago. How, then, does the total quality approach differ from the traditional marketing approach? How does TQM differ from the customer-focused, participative management approaches suggested previously?

Chapter 4

Continuous Improvement and Reengineering

Total Quality or Business Reengineering?

While visiting a European country, I was asked to give a talk at the local quality association on total quality and business reengineering. Due to the short notice given to the participants, it was estimated that the meeting would attract only a dozen or so interested people. The organizers were astonished to get 200 requests to attend the meeting. Because the room available could hold only 60 participants, the organizers had to apologize to the remaining 140 people. It was obvious that the subject was a hot one.

Out of curiosity, I asked the participants to tell me the reasons that they had decided to attend the meeting. Approximately one third of the participants said that they had been asked by their management to start implementing business reengineering as soon as possible, and having read a book or two on the subject, they were there to ask questions. The second third of the participants seemed more troubled. Their organizations had already implemented a total quality approach, and they wondered if they had to drop it and start on reengineering, as many articles in the business press suggested. The remaining third were there to see what the concept was all about, to keep informed.

I meet these three concerns wherever I go. Indeed, since 1993, business reengineering (BR) is everywhere. Books and articles are published regularly on the subject, stressing the importance of this approach, calling it a *must,* the *only* way to go if an organization is to survive. At one point, even the president of the United States was talking about "reinventing government." *Business Week* featured an article called "Rethinking IBM."[1] Management theoreticians as well as practitioners suggest that we must redesign, reconstruct, or recreate our organizations. They insist on the fact that, faced with the urgency to remain competitive, organizations have to rethink the way they operate.

According to a number of BR activists, major, radical changes must be made to *business processes,* instead of using the total quality approach which, they say, advocates incremental improvement of existing *work processes.* They suggest that these radical changes are required to produce the significant improvement—the breakthrough—essential to survival in the present condition of world economics and fierce global competition. Some say that BR is completely unrelated to total quality, while others view it as a complement to it. Top managers are wondering whether they should abandon total quality and rush to reengineer their organizations. Before jumping to conclusions, let us review the situation.

So-called BR specialists, as well as a number of total quality experts, wrongly associate total quality exclusively with continuous improvement. In reality, a company cannot always improve, because at a given point improvement is either impossible, unfeasible, or extremely expensive. One then has to innovate or reengineer. On the other hand, we cannot always reengineer, either. Generally, after reengineering we have to debug, improve, polish up, refine, and fine-tune.

In fact, contrary to what the proponents of continuous improvement think, this improvement is not linear; it tapers off (see Figure 4.1). In fact, improvement can go from 80 percent to 90 percent, and from 90 percent to 99 percent, even from 99 percent to 99.9 percent, but after that no significant improvement is really possible, feasible, or often even desirable. After a certain level of improvement, the value to the customer of an incremental increase in the quality level, relative to its cost to the producer, rarely warrants such an improvement.

At a given point, then, continuous improvement has to be stopped and replaced with reengineering, if a company wants to be, and remain, competitive.

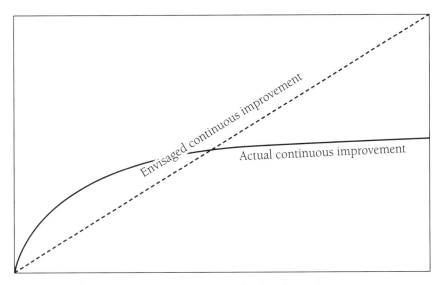

Figure 4.1. Continuous improvement: perceived and actual.

This pattern applies both to products and processes. In my understanding, both continuous improvement and innovation are essential: one should innovate, then improve, innovate, then improve again, and so on and so forth (see Figure 4.2).

In this model, then, the total quality approach and reengineering neither contradict nor complement each other; they are but two parts of the same approach. This is well illustrated at AT&T, whose *Reengineering Handbook* posits that BR is a fundamental component of the total quality approach.[2]

In my view, total quality is an *objective,* TQM is the *means* to achieve it, and the techniques used for continuous improvement and reengineering are important *tools* in the TQM technology.

Note that the definition of continuous improvement indicated here is what the Japanese call *kaizen.* It is also the definition given to it by many so-called quality specialists as well as a number of business reengineering experts. This is incremental, gradual, and continuous. In his book, *Kaizen,* Masaaki Imai, who coined the term, states that "kaizen means improvement. It means continuing improvement involving everyone—managers and workers alike." He also indicates that "a

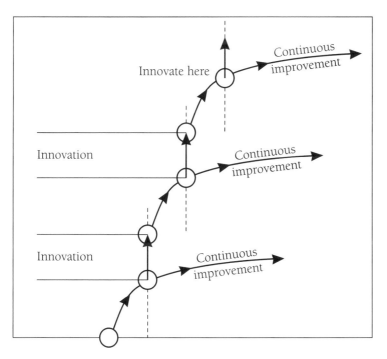

Figure 4.2. Continuous improvement and innovation (reengineering).

Source: J. N. Kelada, *Technologie de la qualité totale, reengineering et autres techniques* (Dollard-des-Ormeaux, Quebec, Canada: Quafec Publications, 1994), 1–9. Reprinted with permission.

kaizen strategy maintains and improves the working standard through small, gradual improvements." He adds that "improvement can be defined as kaizen and innovation, where . . . innovation calls forth radical improvements as a result of large investments in technology and/or equipment."[3] Therefore, a difference is made here between improvement and continuous improvement.

Actually, more and more total quality theoreticians and practitioners now insist that continuous improvement does include innovation, reengineering, or breakthroughs. The 1995 Malcolm Baldrige National Quality Award criteria booklet states that "achieving the highest levels of performance requires a well-executed approach to continuous improvement. The term 'continuous improvement' refers to both incremental and 'breakthrough' improvement."[4] In this book, we have adopted Imai's view that improvement consists of continuous improvement (small and incremental) and reengineering (radical improvement, although not necessarily always resulting from large investments in technology or equipment).

Defining *Business Reengineering*

In general terms, BR means *radically* changing an organization's way of thinking and, consequently, of doing things. More specifically, it involves changing processes, organizational structures, management style and behavior, compensation and reward systems, as well as relationships with shareholders, customers, suppliers, and other external partners.

BR is thus different from continuous improvement, which is considered to be gradual and incremental and is simply doing better what is already being done. Reengineering is synonymous with innovation. It is more than automating or computerizing existing operations or processes. Progressing from handwritten to typed to computer-generated checks or bank drafts is not reengineering; eliminating the necessity of a check altogether—as in the case of direct deposits or withdrawals—is.

An Example of Reengineering at Work

When visiting a manufacturer some time ago, I witnessed a most impressive reengineering feat. Prior to the reengineering, delivery schedules to customers were not being met and operating costs were running high, affecting either the price to the customer or the company profits and the shareholders' dividends. By tracing these problems back to their originating operations, it became apparent that the main cause lay with the company's dealings with its principal parts supplier. This included ordering from the supplier—that is, issuing purchase orders, receiving parts, checking the incoming parts against the purchase orders, notifying accounts payable, issuing a check, and checking with production control's master schedule. At the supplier's end, each purchase generated a work order, a shipping order, a delivery slip, an invoice, the receipt of a check, and the deposit of the check at a bank. Transactions didn't stop there, however, because when the bank received the check it had to credit the supplier's account, debit the customer's account, send statements to both, and then file the check. These processes required the intervention, at the customer's end, of the manufacturing, production control, materials control, receiving, and accounting departments. At the supplier's end, various departments involved in order entry, manufacturing, materials control, production control, shipping, and accounts receivable came into play. At the bank, too, actions were required by many departments.

Teams using a continuous improvement approach to reduce time, cost, and errors would have analyzed and improved on each of these processes separately. As it was, one reengineering team—with representatives from each of the departments involved, the supplier, and the bank—had used the reengineering approach to group these activities into one all-encompassing process.

In the newly reengineered process, the supplier's delivery person delivers a number of pallets containing parts, then collects the pallets that have been emptied. Attached to each empty pallet is a plastic card bearing a magnetic band showing the part number and the quantity of parts initially transported on the pallet. The delivery person takes the cards, slides them one by one through a computer slot, and takes away the empty pallets.

This simple process of using cards for inventory control triggers an automatic cascading effect. An order for new parts is placed; a work order is issued at the supplier's end; feedback is provided to the materials control and the production control departments (so that they can synchronize the ordering of parts and the production schedules); accounts payable are updated; the bank gets a notice to pay the supplier; the bank credits the supplier's account, debits the customer's account, and updates the balance for both the customer and the supplier. Errors have been drastically reduced, time and costs have been saved, and the customer pays only when the parts are used rather than when they are received—an additional, welcomed saving.

No attempt was made to improve the ordering, billing, accounts payable, or check-issuing systems; these were simply eliminated altogether. That's reengineering!

Total Quality–Oriented Reengineering

When reengineering is implemented, the objectives of total quality must always be foremost if success is to be ensured. Otherwise, implementation can be costly and still not yield acceptable or long-term results. BR emphasizes radically changing the existing processes under the assumption that those changes will definitely improve the company's global performance or the performance of one of its specific processes. However, to be effective, the company's internal organization and processes should be directly and formally linked to enhancing profitability through the fulfillment of its customers' needs. Provided that this relationship is correctly and explicitly established right from the start, then reengineering can be one of the best tools to achieve total quality, and it will significantly improve a company's performance. The following example illustrates this point.

In a large company, people were complaining about the purchasing system. The purchase requisition process was too lengthy, and the whole purchasing process was cumbersome and prone to error. Many managers attributed the organization's declining performance to the inefficiency of this process. So a BR team was set up. The team worked hard to rethink the process from scratch. Cycle time was shortened, some procedures were totally eliminated, more sensible uses of computer systems were introduced, and errors were avoided. However, the general performance of the organization deteriorated still further. It was then revealed that errors made outside of the purchasing department were now processed even faster and more efficiently than before. This reengineering project failed because it had been assumed that changes in the purchasing process would significantly improve the company's performance; there had been no prior effort to specifically link this process to the company's profitability and customer satisfaction. Everyone had been working under an assumption rather than on facts.

In no way does this mean that reengineering is inefficient or even dangerous; neither does it mean that partial reengineering should be rejected or even that only companywide projects are successful. It merely points out that, in the absence of a global diagnosis, it is possible to make the erroneous assumption that a given process adversely affects the performance of an organization. Any reengineering effort based on such an assumption will obviously lead to failure.

Levels of Reengineering

Authors as well as organizations use the terms *work process reengineering, business process reengineering,* and *business reengineering* interchangeably, as synonyms. Because of the confusion of these terms and expressions, I suggest different levels of reengineering. By so doing, confusion is avoided when discussing reengineering; not only is each term more clearly understood, but implementation of any of the types is also made easier.

Work process reengineering (WPR) deals with any process in a company that describes the sequence of activities through which a major function is achieved, such as packing a finished product, processing an order or a purchase requisition, picking up and delivering internal mail, treating a customer complaint, hiring a new employee, and so on.

Business process reengineering (BPR) concerns the whole process of a company. It describes the entire sequence of activities directly or indirectly connected to satisfying the needs of a company's customers while generating a quality return on investment for the shareholders. The business process is made up of all the work processes in the company. With the new relationship with suppliers and other external partners, up- and downstream, it is wise to include in the company's business process the partners' process as well, be it a supplier of materials or services upstream or a distributor downstream.

Business reengineering (BR) goes beyond BPR. It deals with all aspects of running the business. It includes the management style, the organizational structures, the business philosophy and strategies in marketing, production and operations, personnel management, purchasing, organizational structures, accounting concepts, information systems, and global business strategy. As such, business *process* reengineering is but one aspect of business reengineering.

Total reengineering (TR) is synonymous to global reengineering or total quality–oriented business reengineering.

So the difference between business reengineering and total reengineering is that, in the latter, reengineering activities are formally, directly, and explicitly linked to the realization of the triple objective of total quality—achieved through constant collaboration with the external partners, and with respect for the organization's environment. Therefore, total reengineering starts with identifying the needs of all stakeholders of the total quality triad and links them with every aspect of running the business, as shown in Figure 4.3. As indicated before, total reengineering is applied only when continuous improvement is no longer effective.

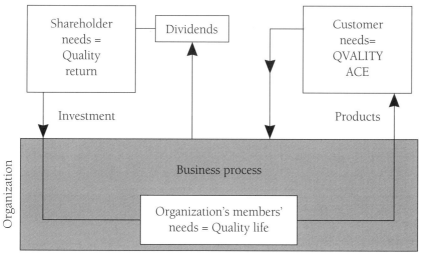

Figure 4.3. The business process and the total quality triad.

Anatomy of a Business Process

Most authors talk about business processes while, in fact, I consider that there is only one business process (see Figure 4.4). It comprises what I call the *mainstream process* and a number of *support processes.*

The mainstream process includes

- All *operations* undertaken, extending from the instant that the organization perceives a customer need that it can fulfill to the moment the final bill is paid, through the guarantee period and through the point at which the customer is ready for a replacement (process A–Z, see Figure 4.4). It ends with the organization's profit or loss translated into dividends, or lack thereof, for the shareholders.

- All *management activities* required to ensure the operations are carried out effectively, on time, and at minimum cost. These include planning, organizing, directing, control, and assurance.

- The *information systems* essential to ensuring that operations and management activities are carried out and completed effectively.

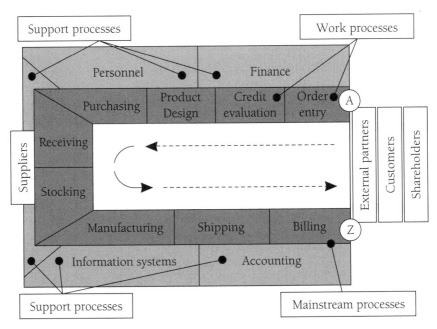

Figure 4.4. The business process.

Source: J. N. Kelada, *Technologie de la qualité totale, reengineering et autres techniques* (Dollard-des-Ormeaux, Quebec, Canada: Quafec Publications, 1994), 2–4. Reprinted with permission.

The support processes are those processes that allow the mainstream process to function effectively by supplying it with necessary information, personnel or training, capital and expenditures, and so on. These processes either do not require direct contact with customers or else are not directly aimed at satisfying them. They include most of the personnel management, finance, and accounting responsibilities. However, they exclude such functions of these processes as the personnel department's customer training activities, and bank loans or credit lines that the finance department negotiates for customers. These are part of the mainstream process.

In no way does this mean that personnel management, accounting, or finance activities are not as important as, or are less important than, those in the mainstream process. Indeed, these support processes can directly affect the profitability of the organization because they use and manage a sizable portion of its funds. Moreover, they affect the Y (yield) component of QVALITY, for, by reducing costs, they allow their organization to offer its customers better prices and more advantageous financial terms and conditions.

Reinventing the Organization

In order to cope with the changes they now face, companies are being advised to reinvent their organizations, redesign their business processes, and recreate their corporations. In their effort to drive home the urgency of these notions, authors lace their writing with a plethora of *re-* words. For example, authors such as Morris & Brandon variously suggest reassessing, repositioning, reconfiguring, restructuring, and revitalizing the business. This can be done by adopting new approaches, applying new methodologies, and using new techniques already developed or in the process of development. For example, the new concept of extraversive management (see chapter 3) is replacing traditional introversive management; activity-based costing (ABC) is replacing traditional accounting systems; and activity-based management (ABM) is helping to optimize the use of resources by identifying and managing the most critical value-adding activities in the organization (see chapter 13).

In order to reengineer the business successfully, one has to examine all of the elements of the total quality concept—that is, the needs of the shareholders, customers, and organization's members—then identify the mainstream process operations and the management of these activities (planning, organization, direction, and control) as well as the support processes, such as finance and personnel management. The business process can thus be broken down into work processes, activities, tasks, and elements. This examination should show that each facet of the business process contributes to the achievement of the global objectives of the organization and to the well-being of its people.

In fact, the major feature of this global approach, as compared with the traditional one, is its shift from a *microvision* to a *macrovision* of the organization, its systems, its structures, and its work methods. Macrovision nevertheless includes microvision within its larger scope. Instead of assigning individual departmental or sector-based objectives, all departments and sectors in the organization have the common, explicit (rather than traditionally implicit) objective of contributing to the company's shareholder and customer-driven global objectives. That is what the concept of extraversive management is all about.

This approach may appear simple, possibly even simplistic, but it is based strictly on common sense. Nonetheless, there is no denying that integrating all activities within an organization, in addition to taking into account the external upstream and downstream partners' activities, presents a serious challenge.

The Company: A Set of Processes

A company is in reality a set of processes involving persons, departments, sectors, or divisions that have upstream or downstream internal or external partners. In effect, producing a financial statement, writing a report, and hiring an employee are all work processes very similar to those required to produce goods of any sort. As shown, the customer is outside the company, but inside we have partners (for example, the persons who work with the financial statement, the report, or the newly hired employee), to whom some people still refer as *internal customers,* an expression that has to be avoided, as we will see later on, since it destroys team spirit and forces people to work *for* each other rather than *with* each other.

As a means of seeking personal satisfaction and well-being, everyone has to contribute to the company's profitability for the sake of its shareholders. This is accomplished by satisfying the customers and exceeding their expectations, that is to say, offering customers quality goods and services by meeting their requirements in terms of quantity, on-time delivery, location, and cost; by maintaining an excellent relationship with them; and by simplifying to the utmost the administrative aspects—in all, our famous QVALITY. And all this must be done in collaboration with internal and external partners.

Details of the Mainstream Process

The Product Quality Cycle and the A–I Cycle

The *quality* of a product—goods or services—is its ability to satisfy specific customer needs. Besides, as we have seen, from the customer's (or potential customer's) perspective, total quality covers, among other things, interrelations with the company, its people, and its representatives, as well as the entire administrative process that customers face—the delivery schedule, billing procedure, and so on. Therefore, in order to achieve total quality, we must first identify the mainstream process comprising all of those activities that enable businesses to fulfill or go beyond customer satisfaction. The two main components of this process are the *product quality process,* also known as the *product quality cycle,* since it is a loop which has to be closed, and the A–I cycle (the *administrative* and *interrelations—* that is, customer interrelations—cycle).

The first of these, the product quality process, comprises all of the activities regarding the product itself and constitutes what we call the product-quality cycle (see Figure 4.5). This cycle includes four phases: quality creation, preparation, realization, and maintenance.

In this section, we shall examine the product quality cycle in a manufacturing environment. The functioning of this cycle in a service environment will be dealt with in chapter 5.

Quality Creation. Quality creation includes needs definition or requirements identification, and the development of the product concept and the product itself, all of which leads to the design and determination of the specifications of both the product and the manufacturing process. At the *product design* stage, the *nature* and *type* of product to be manufactured are determined. You can have airplanes (nature) to provide transportation, but they can be jet or propeller (type); furniture (nature) can be manufactured from wood, metal, or bamboo

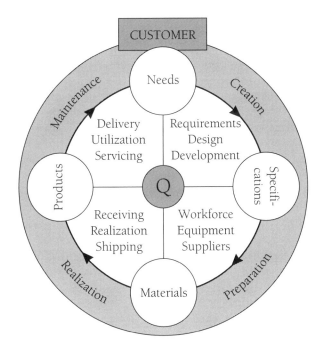

Figure 4.5. The product quality cycle.

Source: J. N. Kelada, *Comprendre et réaliser la qualité totale,* 2nd ed. (Dollard-des-Ormeaux, Quebec, Canada: Quafec Publications, 1992), 28.

(type); restaurants (nature) can be cafeteria-, fast food-, or dining room-style (type).

An aspect to consider at the design stage is the yield or, in other words, the value for money, or cost–benefit ratio. Sometimes customers are looking for what they call the best quality possible. For example, certain customers may say that they want a watch with the "highest possible degree of precision."

It has been observed that, in general, upgrading from bad to fair quality is less costly for the manufacturer but more valued by the customer than upgrading from fair to good. The value is measured here by the price the customer is ready to pay for the increase in quality level. The increase in perceived value dwindles even further when we go from good to excellent quality, in which case the increase in production costs largely surpasses the added value for the customer. For example, reducing a 20-minute waiting period in a bank by half is much more valuable to a customer than reducing a 1-minute wait by half. Nevertheless, the half-minute reduction generally costs the bank much more than the 10.

Once the product concept has been selected, the next stage is *product development*. The design phase of large construction projects is called *preliminary engineering* and the development phase *detailed engineering*. In the development phase, all the necessary preparatory calculations are made: plans, drawings, and technical specifications detailing product dimensions; materials and parts involved in the manufacturing process; and the necessary manufacturing and assembly processes. The quality creation phase ends by establishing product specifications, tolerance range, manufacturing process and procedures and the raw materials, components, subassemblies, and parts to be used in manufacturing the product.

Quality Preparation.   Quality preparation has to do with preparing the workforce, equipment, work methods, and supplies. *Qualification* is the procedure that evaluates a worker's ability to achieve the required quality levels. It takes place when new workers are recruited and hired, but it can also be used to qualify existing staff. In the latter case, the possibility of recycling and retraining is examined before any unqualified individuals are dismissed and new people recruited. But training is not enough. Workers must also be informed and motivated to create quality. Consequently, it is in the company's interests to make sure that there is a motivating work climate and that personnel have been fully sensitized to the importance of doing the *right* job right the first time, all the time.

Production and maintenance equipment and storage facilities, as well as work methods and procedures, must also all be qualified. That is to say, they must be checked to ensure that they are capable of producing the required levels of quality. *Capability* studies show whether or not equipment can sustain the required tolerance range. If the equipment is proven to lack that capability, these studies make it possible to calculate the probable percentage of defective units that would be produced with the existing equipment.

Work methods must be clear, easy to understand, achievable, readily accessible to workers, and regularly updated. Work instructions and quality control procedures are often set out in a *quality manual,* made available to production and quality personnel. One of the most important aspects in this phase is the supply of raw materials, parts, and various components. Unquality materials affect the quality of the finished product, increase cost, and delay delivery. A chain reaction can then set in: the finished product, with its defects undetected, is shipped, stored, installed, and then replaced or fixed, often at great expense to the manufacturer. This can cause undesired and sometimes catastrophic consequences, such as the loss of an order, a customer, or even an entire market. Only by searching for and evaluating potential suppliers can you ensure that you are dealing with reliable suppliers.

The introduction of the *just-in-time* (JIT) philosophy into companies makes the purchasing management aspect even more critical. This approach—aimed at reducing, if not entirely eliminating, waste such as high-cost inventories—requires that parts and various raw materials be delivered just in time for production. If they are delivered on time, but defective, the entire production process comes to a standstill. In the purchasing area, this has led to the adoption of a new practice that contributes to quality—and an increasing number of manufacturing companies are using it. In an effort to reduce their own incoming inspection costs, they require that suppliers introduce effective quality control and quality assurance systems into their own organizations.

Quality Realization. The quality realization phase includes receiving the materials, components, and parts ordered; using various processes to transform them into a finished product; temporarily storing work in process; and packing and shipping the finished product. This is the stage at which we find most of the formal quality control activities and systems, and often they are the only ones in place. In fact, quality control came into being on the shop floor, and that is where it is still talked about the most. Clearly, quality management activities have to be extended to all phases of the quality cycle. Presently, there is increasing use of a whole range of statistical techniques for quality control of manufactured products. These techniques are called *statistical process control* (SPC). They make it possible to monitor the level of quality produced and detect, in advance, any trend (or tendency) to significantly deviate from the established specifications. The capability of a process is evaluated by these techniques.

Quality Maintenance. Close attention to quality must not stop once the finished product has been shipped. In fact, its quality must be maintained until it has satisfied the need for which it was produced and is then disposed of. This is the quality maintenance phase, in which the finished product is generally transported, stored, installed, and distributed before use. There is a risk of product quality deterioration at each step of the way. Adequate means of transportation must be ensured. For example, refrigerated trucks must be used to transport perishable goods; there must be adequate storage facilities to protect product quality. Many manufacturers, like paint or food producers, make sure that distributors and retailers move their products out of storage according to their order of arrival (FIFO—first in, first out). Otherwise, some items would remain in storage longer than others, and their quality would be seriously affected. Manufacturers recommend storing only small quantities of such products to avoid any danger of quality deterioration. In many cases, the product must be correctly installed, so many manufacturers insist that either their own personnel, or qualified people whom they recommend, be in charge of the installation. In any case, producers should generally provide clear and precise installation instructions for their products.

Furthermore, the way a product is used can greatly affect its quality, operation, durability, and reliability. Using a product for an activity that exceeds its designed capacity can be dangerous. Lifting a six-ton weight with a five-ton-capacity crane may cause serious accidents, apart from permanently damaging the crane. A product used (or misused) for a job that it was not designed for can deteriorate in quality and become less effective, not to say outright dangerous for the health and safety of its user or for the environment. For example, metal should not be cut with a saw made for cutting wood, or water boiled in a plastic container. Therefore, manufacturers must provide clear operating instructions along with their products. Manufacturers must also alert users to the possible dangers resulting from the use and/or misuse of the product and instruct them on how to protect themselves when using it.

Many products require regular maintenance and occasional repairs. Manufacturers must offer adequate after-sales service and clear instructions to help users carry out some maintenance themselves. They must make sure that spare parts are available for the whole lifetime of the product they sell. In fact, there are laws requiring manufacturers to stock spare parts for a certain period of time, even after they no longer manufacture the product.

Finally, the manufacturers should also consider the disposal of used products. For example, the parts of some products could emit radiation and should be disposed of with care. Special instructions for disposal should be included with these products. Environmentally conscious companies would indicate nonpolluting methods of disposal. Furthermore, they would design nonpolluting products and packing materials.

Quality management is practiced throughout the entire quality cycle. During each phase of every stage, it targets the following objectives.

Phase 1: Specifications = needs, that is, the product developed will indeed meet the needs for which it was designed

Phase 2: Qualification of the workforce, equipment, methods, and suppliers

Phase 3: Product = specifications, that is, the product conforms to specifications

Phase 4: Product = needs, that is, the product is suitable for its intended use

Other intangible factors, which may be subjective but very real, such as a customer's personal tastes or loyalty toward certain products or manufacturers, must also receive full consideration all along the four phases of the quality cycle.

Companies often find that preparing a product quality cycle is a very useful exercise. Participants, with little regular contact on a day-to-day basis, get an overview of the entire quality-producing process. Often this is the first time that they realize how closely interrelated their own jobs are and how intimately they are tied in to the overall results of all other sectors. When a well-known company in Montreal, Canada, was preparing its quality cycle, the research and development personnel met the plant manufacturing people for the first time. At that point, they realized how important certain little details were in the way they prepared their drawings, details they had previously felt were superfluous. The quality cycle can be applied just as easily to a service as to the manufacture of goods. As a preventive measure, one must ensure that all activities in a cycle are performed correctly and that all errors are promptly detected, analyzed, and corrected to stop future repetition. I will come back to this point in chapter 5 on total quality in services.

Causes of Unquality

Let us bear in mind that it is much easier and cheaper to prevent or correct an error at the beginning of the product quality cycle than in its last stages. Obviously, it is easier to correct an error at the design stage than to recall several million cars to correct it. In an industrial company manufacturing power transformers, a preliminary study revealed that more than half the production errors could be attributed to the drawings used in the factory. Many costly errors were avoided by simply changing the size of certain drawings that had proven to be too small and not clear enough. Similarly, it usually does not cost anything to stop using a supplier incapable of supplying adequate materials or services. Defective raw materials and components can seriously affect the quality of a finished product, especially if the defects are not discovered until after the product has been shipped and is in the customer's hands. Errors detected in the factory are still relatively easy to correct compared with errors discovered after a product has been transported, stored, and installed. The difficulty of remedying these errors is compounded if the product has been shipped to a distant location.

Generally, it has been observed that, in their quest for quality, companies focus their efforts on the quality realization stage and on their operations. Manufacturing companies emphasize inspection of incoming materials, of work in process, and of finished products prior to shipping. However, after examining the causes of poor quality, I would say that, in general,

- About 40 percent of unquality is caused by errors during Phase 1, that is to say, due to incorrect interpretation of customer requirements, design errors, and errors in the drawings or specifications.

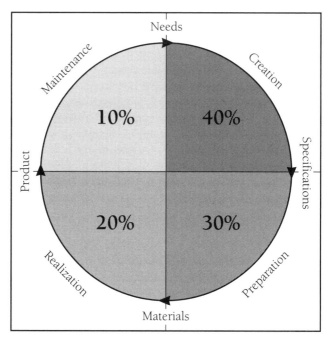

Figure 4.6. Causes of unquality.

Source: J. N. Kelada, *Comprendre et réaliser la qualité totale,* 2nd ed. (Dollard-des-Ormeaux, Quebec, Canada: Quafec Publications, 1992), 34.

- Thirty percent of the causes of unquality occur in the preparation phase. They are the result of an untrained or poorly informed workforce, inadequate equipment, or suppliers incapable of delivering quality raw materials, components, or services.
- Twenty percent of the causes of unquality are found at the realization, manufacturing, or execution phase.
- The remaining 10 percent are found in Phase 4—delivery, transportation, retail storage, and use or maintenance of the final product.

Though these percentages are only approximate, they still demonstrate clearly that the emphasis should be placed on the quality creation phase rather than on the manufacturing or product-use phase (see Figure 4.6).

The A–I Cycle

As far as total quality is concerned, customer satisfaction does not stop at the product itself (that is, product quality, quantity, on-time delivery at the desired location, and at minimum cost to the customer). It also covers the administrative

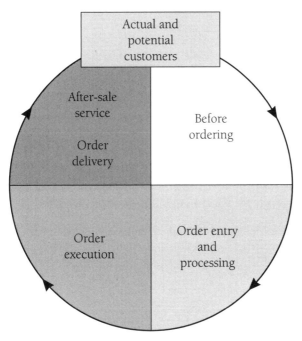

Figure 4.7.   The A–I cycle.

Source: J. N. Kelada, *Comprendre et réaliser la qualité totale,* 2nd ed. (Dollard-des-Ormeaux, Quebec, Canada: Quafec Publications, 1992), 35.

procedures imposed on customers, actual or potential, and the interrelationship of customers with the enterprise, its staff, and its representatives. In the A–I cycle we can follow all activities related to its administrative (A) and customer interrelations (I) aspects (see Figure 4.7). These activities can be carried out throughout each of the four following stages.

1. *Activities preceding the customer's final decision to buy a product or use a service.* At this stage, the potential customer is getting information or is being solicited. There has to be an ongoing goal to retain customers, turn possible customers into probable ones, and then turn probable customers into actual customers. The whole of the verbal, written, and electronic information communications system has to be examined and its effectiveness guaranteed. All procedures must be carried out with perceptible courtesy so that the enterprise can woo, charm, surprise, and delight potential customers. The administrative system must also be analyzed to ensure that procedures (such as requests for information) at this stage are minor, speedy, and free of error.

2. *Activities related to order entry.* In this area, verbal, written, or computerized communication procedures associated with order entry are carefully examined. In addition, the buyers seek out suppliers equipped to use electronic data

interchange systems in order to reduce paperwork, costs, delays, and risk of errors when orders are entered.

3. *Activities that take place during order completion.* For example, a customer may look for some flexibility on the part of a supplier when modifications must be made to an order in the process of completion. At this point the supplier can either adopt a legalistic, just-going-by-the-book attitude or, in an effort to establish or maintain good business relations, show some understanding toward the customer by accommodating the changes.

4. *Activities related to order delivery and after-sales service.* Many companies establish mechanisms to facilitate contact with the client users to help them solve problems related to the product's use or reconditioning. They install toll-free service lines for their clients, for example.

Ever-increasing competition and higher customer expectations are driving companies seeking to achieve total quality to put just as much effort into the administrative procedures and their customer interrelationships as into product design and production.

Shareholders and People's Satisfaction Processes

Two other processes that are important to analyze are the finance process and the organization's personnel management process. These will not be detailed here, for there are a number of specialized publications dealing with them.

In brief, the finance process is shareholder oriented. It has to manage the funds in the organization in order to optimize the return for the shareholders. These funds include the shareholders' investments, the long- and short-term debts, the revenues from sales, the financial policies regarding payments to suppliers (for example, 2/10, N/30), investment of the surplus funds available, liquidity policies, government subsidies solicitation, mergers and alliances, and so on. The result is, generally, materialized by the dividends per share paid to the shareholders and by return on equity, return on investment, and other well-known financial ratios.

The people management process is usually called the human resources management process. We prefer the term *personnel* or, even better, *people management* because the persons in an organization are more than a resource (which means a source of supply) that can be used as the financial and physical resources are. This process has to help achieve a quality of life for all the people, at work and outside work. It has to develop an organization where people work as teams, are paid equitably, have challenging jobs, are mobilized, recognized, and rewarded for what they do, and helped with their problems at work as well as in their family and personal lives.

It is the *integration* of these four processes—product quality, A–I, finance, and people management—that allows an organization to achieve and maintain total quality. Quite a challenge indeed, but this is the only way to accomplish it.

Conclusion

Failure to see the interrelation between total quality and reengineering has led many organizations to consider them two different approaches. Moreover, a number of organizations are setting aside their total quality activities and are replacing them with business reengineering projects. What one must realize is that reengineering is synonymous with innovation. It is rethinking the way things have always been done. It goes beyond incremental continuous improvement. However, contrary to what is sometimes thought, the total quality objective of simultaneously satisfying the company's shareholders, customers, and people, with the collaboration of external partners, is achieved through both continuous improvement and innovation, that is, both incremental improvement and reengineering.

Another area of confusion results from the proliferation of expressions concerning reengineering. One must differentiate between work process reengineering, business process reengineering, business reengineering, and total reengineering. These are different levels of reengineering, each being a part of the subsequent one, with the last one including all others.

The business process consists of a mainstream process and support processes. The mainstream process comprises all activities, or group activities that I call work processes, required to design, realize, and deliver the product or service meant to satisfy the customer's needs, as well as the activities required to invoice and collect amounts owed, while it also generates the company's revenues and profits which turn into dividends for the shareholders. This is all done through the company's people management processes, along with the collaboration of outside partners and respect for the environment.

The three main support processes—finance, accounting, and personnel management—and the secondary ones, such as computer systems development, operations, and others, are essential in helping the mainstream process to operate. These support processes maintain, develop, and protect the human, financial, and informational resources required to achieve the company's goals.

Each activity in the mainstream and support processes should always contribute to the company's goals. Total reengineering signifies rethinking and/or improving the complete business process—mainstream and support processes alike. It also includes rethinking the organization's people management approach, the production and operations philosophies, and the marketing strategy. It demands nothing short of reinventing the company.

Review Questions

1. Total reengineering goes far beyond business process reengineering. Explain.
2. Some specialists suggest that business reengineering consists of identifying all processes in a company and reengineering them one by one, starting with the most critical one. Please comment.

3. Explain how total reengineering fits into the total quality approach.
4. What is the product quality cycle useful for? Give an example.

Notes

1. *Business Week,* 4 October 1993, 86.

2. AT&T Quality Steering Committee, *Reengineering Handbook* (Indianapolis, Ind.: AT&T, 1991).

3. Masaaki Imai, *Kaizen* (New York: McGraw-Hill, 1986), xx.

4. *1995 Malcolm Baldrige National Quality Award Criteria* (Gaithersburg, Md.: National Institute of Standards and Technology, 1995).

5. Daniel Morris and Joel Brandon, *Re-Engineering Your Business* (New York: McGraw-Hill, 1993).

Chapter 5

*You never get a second chance
to make a first impression.*

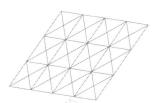

TQM in Services: How It Relates
to TQM in Manufacturing

Introduction

In service companies, quality has generally remained a philosophical notion. Insofar as it *has* been applied, its scope has been limited and defined merely in terms of effecting error-free transactions, as is the case in banking or insurance companies. Although quality control or inspection departments have always existed in manufacturing companies, no such departments exist in service organizations, even to this day. Although the manufacturing sector was the most important sector of the economy at the turn of the century, today, at the threshold of a new century, it is the service sector that dominates the economy. Two-thirds of jobs are in services, and costs are skyrocketing in sensitive areas such as education and health care. However, while they consider quality a manufacturing concern, most service organizations are still managed with a philosophy that is predominantly manufacturing oriented. Accordingly, to evaluate an organization's worth, emphasis is generally put on fixed assets that can easily be bought or sold on the market. The organization's real assets—the loyalty, creativity, and innovative capacities of its members—are not accounted for. Similarly, customer loyalty and faithfulness are not accounted for in any formal financial statement, except in the case of goodwill, which is roughly estimated when an organization is bought or sold. Accountants, known for their strict objectivity, have not found yet a truly objective way to account for such fundamental elements of the company's wealth.

I think it is Dr. Deming who once said that, save for a few rare exceptions, service organizations are not even aware that they offer poor-quality services. He went even further, pointing out that even if they were aware of it and wanted to do something about it, they would not know how to correct their errors and improve their quality. He may have been exaggerating somewhat, but given some of the improbably horrific service stories that make the rounds, one wonders. True, a lot of unquality still occurs in industry, but there is even more in services.

As Ronald Henkoff writes, in the new American economy, service—bold, fast, unexpected, innovative, and customized—is the ultimate strategic imperative, a business challenge that has profound implications for the way we manage companies, hire employees, develop careers, and craft policies. The changing nature of customer service demands a new breed of worker—one who is empathic, flexible, inventive, and able to work with minimal levels of supervision.[1]

In the manufacturing sector, product quality gives a competitive advantage. However, where two companies have products of equal quality, one can differentiate itself through the service it provides. Ideally, one should strive to both produce the best product and provide the best service simultaneously. Before launching the Lexus, Toyota observed that the weakness in the luxury car market was customer service. Now Toyota sells not only a luxury car but also a luxury service.

Henkoff suggests that a trend is now developing in the United States in which many manufacturers are moving to become service firms and thus drawing closer to their customers. For example, manufacturers, rather than simply designing, producing, and selling air conditioners and computers, now offer installation and servicing of complete air-conditioning and computer systems. A restaurant chain, the majority of whose personnel used to be employed in producing food, has outsourced food preparation to subcontractors, freeing up time and space for customer service.

Categorizing Services

Organizations, as well as departments and people within them, may produce goods and/or provide services for the benefit of either internal or external users. In this chapter, we shall discuss total quality in services. For clarity I have categorized services as follows:

- *Internal services:* These are services provided to individuals or departments within an organization, that is, services intended for internal users.
- *External services:* These are services intended for the company's customers.
- *Main services:* By main services we mean the central activity that is the raison d'être of a company, such as providing insurance coverage, health care, education, entertainment, accounting or computer services, travel packages (air travel, hotel accommodations), investment plans, and so on.

- *Ancillary services:* These are services that help provide the main services efficiently and effectively to the internal users or to the company's customers or that minimize any undue inconvenience to either of them.

These services, although similar in nature, do not all warrant being given the same importance or effort. Needless to say, the external and main services are generally the most important. However, when these are standard—as in the case of many banks offering the same interest rates on personal loans—effort must be put into upgrading ancillary services, because they become the key to the company's gaining a competitive advantage. Among the four types, internal and ancillary services, although still vital, are somewhat lower on the scale of importance.

All activities in a company, whatever their degree of importance, depend on what has been termed the *moment of truth.* This is when someone in the company—or someone working for an external partner, such as a distributor or a delivery organization—makes contact (face-to-face, telephone, fax, or otherwise) with the customer who needs the service. What transpires during such an encounter can make or break a long-term relationship with a customer. As they say, one never gets a second chance to make a first impression.

Quality: From Goods to Services

As indicated, organizations produce goods or provide services, both of which are supplemented by ancillary services (see Figure 5.1). Traditionally, quality has been associated exclusively with manufactured goods; in other words, with items that are tangible and whose characteristics can be checked, inspected, and tested by inspectors in well-equipped laboratories. However, nowadays many manufacturing companies realize the importance of ancillary services to keep their old

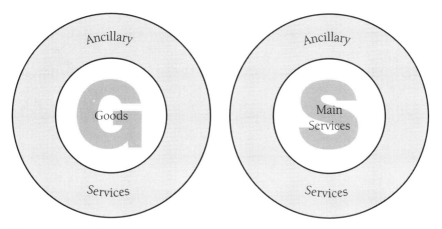

Figure 5.1. Services in manufacturing and service organizations.

customers or lure new ones. For example, Chrysler has developed a program—*Customer One*—aimed at its dealers and their 100,000 employees, as well as at its 1500 field representatives. This is a four-phase program (launch, reinforcement, anchoring, and perpetuation) with a mix of communication, education, motivation, and support tools linked to each phase. More than $1 million has been spent recruiting and training 180 of the best facilitators/trainers available to deliver it.

What Is Going On in the Service Sector?

Not long ago, I was to participate in an important conference in Western Canada, in Saskatoon. I headed for the airport to board what was scheduled to be a direct flight, with one stopover at another airport to change planes. I was already feeling anxious to get the trip over with. It was toward the end of the day, and I was looking forward to just getting there, finding a comfortable bed, and having some rest in order to be ready for the following day. Upon arriving at the airport, I was dismayed to be told—without reason, excuse, or apology—that the flight would be delayed for an hour.

When I finally arrived in the stopover airport I hurried to the departure counter, to board the plane for Saskatoon, where an attendant coolly informed me, "Sir, you've just missed your plane."

Furious, I reminded her, "You are the ones who made me miss my plane." She shrugged her shoulders and told me that she had nothing to do with it and that there was nothing she could do about it; I had to go to another departure counter elsewhere in the airport.

After I had waited for ages in a seemingly interminable line at that counter, a smartly uniformed young ticket attendant told me that there were no more flights for Saskatoon that evening! I could say good-bye to the trip to Saskatoon, the conference, my reputation, honor and the lot!

After some very laborious research she announced to me: "But I can send you off to Winnipeg, sir." Send me off, indeed! There I was, admired, respected, and appreciated by my children, boss, and friends, envied and admired by enemies and colleagues, being sent from point A to point B like a very ordinary, nameless package!

In another scenario outside a downtown cinema, a line of people, standing under freezing rain, was creeping along at the pace of a dying tortoise. The would-be viewers had turned up their collars and were suffering in silence when a uniformed cinema employee came out to say that the cashier would accept only the exact price of the ticket because she had run out of change. One gentleman politely told the employee that this was unfair because he had been waiting for more than half an hour. The imperious employee quickly shot back, "Well, if that doesn't suit you, you can always go to another cinema!"

An official at a multinational corporation, having decided to move to another house, informed the telephone company so that they could make the necessary arrangements to transfer his telephone line. He subsequently found that the new residence would not be ready for him on the planned date, so, to avoid having his line cut off prematurely, he immediately notified the telephone company about his change of plan. He was assured that due note had been taken of the change and that he had nothing to worry about. However, when the previously set moving day came around, his telephone service was discontinued anyway. It took many phone calls, going through all the digits on the telephone dial, before he could get a promise that the line would be reestablished "as soon as possible."

I had an appointment with my doctor for 8:00 one morning. The previous day, his secretary had telephoned to confirm the appointment, so I arrived about 10 minutes early. The waiting room was empty, so I picked up the magazine that was lying on the table to fill the time. It was incomplete and mutilated but, since it was the only magazine in the waiting room, I read it from cover to cover a few times. The doctor arrived at 9:18, and 10 minutes later I was ushered into his office. He didn't even raise his eyes from the contents of my file before he announced, "Everything is fine. You can leave now." No greeting, no apology for being late.

Recently there have been several articles written about the quality, or rather poor quality, of airline food. When airlines do manage to avoid losing an engine or a luggage cabin door while in full flight, or making a crash landing, they serve indigestible food to their passengers and, before you've had a chance to pop an antacid into your mouth, follow it up by misplacing your luggage.

I read somewhere that a study in the United States concluded that nurses had a 15 percent rate of errors (treatments not administered at the right time, at the right frequency, to the right patient, or in the right dosage). "If we were paid like the doctors, we wouldn't make mistakes!" they suggested. But that argument doesn't hold water. Two thousand autopsies were performed to measure the quality of the diagnoses made by doctors, and they showed that there was a 34 percent rate of error and that a third of these were fatal. One might therefore conclude, at least on the basis of statistics, that doctors kill 10 percent of their patients!

I went to train a group of managers in a downtown hotel and was very impressed by the luxurious hotel lobby: marble and gold everywhere. I immediately said to myself, "This is quality." I went to have breakfast in the dining room, where I was greeted with a severe gaze from the hostess. She asked if I was alone, showed me to a table, and gave me a menu. A few minutes later, a harried-looking waitress arrived, mechanically started pouring coffee in my cup while asking if I wanted coffee! I was somewhat taken aback and said that I preferred tea, if she didn't mind. I also ordered eggs and toast. After what seemed to me to be a rather long spell for such a short order, she returned with eggs but no toast. When I pointed out her error, she assured me that it wouldn't be long. I was hungry so started in on the eggs, but when she eventually arrived with the slices of toast, one was burnt and the other was virtually white.

By now thoroughly annoyed, I pointed to the mismatched slices of toast and blurted out, "I see you believe in the law of averages."

"The toaster's not working very well, sir," she explained, without seeing any need to apologize.

The little teapot she put in front of me had lost the knob on its lid and seemed to have been in use for rather a long time. When I remarked that I thought her teapot looked a little tired, she was quick to retort, "But it's the tea you're going to drink, sir, not the teapot." I hurriedly finished my breakfast and went off to my meeting place.

The room reserved for our meeting was a regular hotel room where the normal furniture had been replaced by tables. There were to be about 10 people occupying a room designed to comfortably accommodate, at the most, 2 people inclined towards shared intimacies. The rail in the closet promptly fell down when I hung my coat on it, taking down with it another couple of coats already hanging there, so I dropped my coat on a vacant chair. When all the participants had arrived, someone made a telling comment: "It is strange, but the situation here looks like the very ad from this hotel chain showing what their competition is like!" The ad in question, wonder of wonders, portrayed crammed meeting rooms much like our own—everyone rubbing elbows with their neighbors and people on top of each other, sticking out at odd angles. In all honesty, I must admit that this had been a last-minute reservation. However, it will be a long time before I darken the doorway of that hotel again.

On a more upbeat note, I had been searching for some time for a television set to use at home and finally decided on the model that I wanted to buy. I arrived at the store about four o'clock on a Saturday afternoon. I found the set that I wanted; discovered, to my delight, that the price was much better than the competitor's price; and agreed to buy it. I reached for my wallet and found that I had left it at home. I was quite upset because I really wanted to use the television set the next day. When the owner understood my predicament, he looked me up and down and, without hesitation, said, "Take it home today and you can come back and pay me on Monday." Without having me sign anything, without insisting on having my telephone number, my place of work, or my full family tree, he told an employee to carry it out to my car! Over the course of the years, I have bought all my appliances at his store, and, in the meantime, his business has expanded and become very successful. Today the business is 10 times bigger than it was on that memorable Saturday, and I'm still a loyal customer and keep recommending it to friends and family.

When the offices of a medium-sized company were moved to a new neighborhood, its president asked his secretary to make an appointment for him with the manager of the branch of the bank that faced his new office. He intended to have the bank look after all his financial interests. The secretary was told that the bank manager was busy on the phone and would call back. She made it quite clear that it was the president of the company who wanted to talk to the manager and was assured that the president would be called. There was still no news from the bank an hour later, so the secretary called again, and the bank manager himself told her that he had just had a meeting canceled and could meet the president right away.

The president arrived at the bank a few minutes later and introduced himself to the bank manager's secretary, who asked him to wait, as the manager was presently answering a phone call. The bank manager finally finished his telephone call, spoke with his secretary, then went away to talk to another employee behind the counter. A few minutes later, he returned to his office to make yet another telephone call. The secretary herself by this time was again on the telephone, so the customer-to-be president dropped his card on her desk and left. Half an hour later, the secretary in question telephoned the company and asked to speak to the president. She apologized and admitted that she had omitted to tell the bank manager that he had arrived. She asked if he could come back the following day. When the president asked why the bank manager had not taken the trouble to call back himself, she replied that the president would have to ask him that question.

Needless to say, the bank manager never did give any sign of life after that incident. His bank lost one customer for good and, if anyone subsequently happened to ask the president for his opinion of that branch or even that bank, one could presume that it lost a few others to boot.

Buying a new car is quite an adventure: selling the old model privately or letting the dealer handle the sale, timing it so that the sale of the old car is synchronized with the delivery of the new one, preparing a certified check in the name of the dealer—and any number of factors that one has to juggle, with gritted teeth, in order accomplish the mission. I remember the last time I arrived to take over my new vehicle. The salesman first of all made sure that I had the certified check with me. Next, he gave me a sheaf of papers and documents, then showed me which exit to take to get a fillup, as there was only enough gas in the tank to last for a few minutes. He added that I had several days' grace in which to register my car. He wished me good luck and wanted me to promise to come back and see him when I needed a new car.

After some time, that car began to show signs of wear so I decided to look for another one, though I dreaded going through all the rigmarole of changing vehicles. This time I dealt with a different dealership where the salesman assured me (not that I really believed him) that I would not run into any difficulties. When I had sold my old car, I called the salesman and found that the new car wasn't ready. This news threw me into a bit of a panic, but the salesman quickly solved the problem—he simply lent me his own car.

When the new car was ready to be delivered, the salesman called me. I had to tell him that I needed four more days before I would have the required amount available to make the payment. He seemed surprised that I would consider that to be a problem and asked me to bring along a postdated check. When I pointed out that I would not be able to certify a postdated check, he asked me why on earth I wanted to give him a certified check.

There were more pleasant surprises. When I went to get my car, I found that the salesman had taken care of everything and that my car was already registered. As I left, I asked him where the nearest gas station was so that I could fill up. His reply was a smile and an assurance that he had already looked after that; the tank was full. There's a man who knows how to do business and keep his customers.

I could go on and on, filling dozens of pages, even books, with instances in which I was frustrated by unquality service. Knowing how to keep customers, and knowing how to find new ones, is the very essence of total quality.

Why Is There So Much Unquality in Services?

According to Heskett, Sasser, Hart, and Christopher, "Services have replaced used car salespeople as the most frequent butt of jokes and complaints. In fact, abysmal quality of services in America has been made out by some to be a national scandal."[2]

Undoubtedly, it is not always very easy to define the quality of a service, let alone measure it. Moreover, when it is goods rather than services that a company produces, any item can be checked and, if necessary, corrected prior to sending it to the customers—or even when it is already in the hands of the customer.

But these are not the only reasons for unquality throughout service companies. As is the case for manufacturing organizations, service companies' managers still use introversive management, with emphasis on departmental objectives rather than on extraversive ones aimed at shareholder and customer satisfaction. The accountants still look after financial statements, personnel departments still devote themselves entirely to hiring and firing, while purchasing departments still try to satisfy internal users. The customer remains absent from the minds of the majority of personnel not in direct contact with the customer.

Another reason for unquality services is the public's tolerant attitude. The public, in effect, does not complain enough. People eat the terrible food served up by airlines; wait for hours in airports for planes that are often late; read and reread old magazines in the waiting rooms of doctors who are in no hurry to serve them—all without making any fuss, without complaining, rebelling, or grumbling.

I once had to visit a physiotherapist to undergo a number of treatments. My first time there, I was kept waiting for 20 minutes; the second time through, I had to wait for 15 minutes. On my third visit, I waited until the appointed time, and then marched up and informed the receptionist that I had an appointment at 4:30. It was 4:30 sharp. She looked at me, surprised, and said that I would have to wait for five minutes because the therapist was "finishing" with a patient.

When, after 15 minutes, the therapist did not appear, I asked the receptionist to cancel my appointment. She was taken aback and asked me why I would want to do that! I explained that I didn't like to be kept waiting every time I was there and that my time was as precious as the therapist's. She obviously didn't know how to deal with the situation since, as I was told, "nobody else complained" of that common practice of keeping patients waiting for 15 to 20 minutes.

I am convinced that if all customers walked out when they were not served on time, this clinic—and all other clinics—would darn well make sure they were.

Why, then, don't customers complain? Often because they have no other choice, no alternative. They can go to another bank, visit another clinic, but they are all the same; they can call on another doctor, but they run the risk of stumbling onto someone who is in less of a hurry than the previous one and whose waiting room boasts a selection of even older magazines, if indeed it can boast of any at all. When it comes to telephone, gas, electricity, or public services, what other choices do they have? It looks as though we are condemned to put up with these unquality services until at least one bank decides to offer better services, one airline company decides to provide better meals, or one doctor decides to bring his or her customer's interests to the fore. We should remember that *when people have a choice they choose quality; otherwise they endure unquality.*

Successful businesspeople realize that customers are kings and want them treated as such—that is, provided their employees are not staunch republicans. They know that it costs five times more to find new customers than to keep the old ones. The total quality concept boils down to having happy customers, happy people in the company, and happy shareholders. The notion that the customer is always right is not new; it is a notion that every elementary course in marketing has always underscored. Yet, in spite of knowing that their profits depend on satisfying their customers, service businesses seem to have difficulty in putting this fundamental principle into practice.

Characteristics of Quality in Services

Some oppose the word *service* to the term *product.* However, product is often used to cover services, as is the case when banks call loans and savings accounts financial products. Similarly, when a producer produces a play, his product is, in effect, a service that provides entertainment. To better differentiate between the two, when speaking of products in the limited sense of the term, we should use the word *goods.* In Canada, for example, there is a goods and services tax (GST).

Let us look at the definition of service. Webster suggests that a service is "useful labor that does not produce a tangible commodity," or "a facility supplying some public demand," like public transportation, or "one providing maintenance and repair."[3] Services are being characterized here by the fact that they are intangible, cannot be stored (in contrast with goods), and necessitate a direct contact with the customer and indeed the participation of the customer in their production. However, these characteristics do not apply to all services. Restaurant food, for example, is very tangible.

In manufacturing, the service dimension is, in fact, an integral part of the product, and all goods ordered, sold, and delivered are accompanied by ancillary services. *Pre- and after-sale services* include information and counseling required before the actual purchase of goods and maintenance and repair when the product is in use. Some authors argue that people never buy goods, but only services. We do not really buy a car, but, rather, transportation; we do not buy food but nutrition; never a house, but lodging. Why is buying a car considered acquiring goods while leasing one is considered obtaining a service, when in fact both are ways of acquiring a car, the difference being only on paper, and that generally for tax reasons.

In some manufacturing companies, no one has any contact whatsoever with a customer. Companies that sell only to other divisions of the same organization or to distributors, wholesalers, or even retailers have no direct relations with the end users of their products. They often, if not always, make the mistake of considering the former (distributors, wholesalers, retailers) as customers. As indicated before, these are external partners. By way of contrast, a great number of employees enter into contact with customers in most services, such as hospitals, schools, restaurants, stores, banks, and so on. Therefore, the attention given to customers is much more important in the service sector than in manufacturing companies.

Customer Loyalization

Although significantly different, the manufacturing and the service sectors bear a number of similarities—indeed, more than we would usually think. In short, one can say that a for-profit organization in either sector exists to produce a quality return for its shareholders' and owners' investment. To do so, as we have seen before, it has to produce products—goods and/or services—that satisfy customers through the organization's satisfied people. Companies in both sectors seek to build customer loyalty and faithfulness—to *loyalize* them, if you will. And, in actual fact, one cannot loyalize customers without loyal company people, especially where services are concerned.

The president of a small company confided to me that he used to buy from a certain distributor with whom he always dealt through a particular order-entry clerk. This clerk was extremely efficient and well-mannered; he never lost his temper, whatever the circumstance was, and always found ways and means to accommodate the president when a complex situation arose. When the clerk retired, this president started experiencing some difficulties with his replacement, who insisted on always working by the book. Shortly afterwards, he moved his business to the competitor—and he told me that many other customers had done the same.

It has been observed that, in some services using unskilled labor, little care goes into recruiting personnel. Fast-food outlets and stores hire minimum-wage employees and students. The turnover rate is extremely high. Training of these employees is limited to showing them how to use a cash register, pack goods, or prepare a hamburger. Successful companies train their employees not only to do their job, but to greet, welcome, and help customers. "The customer is king" is not an empty slogan.

In one instance in a department store, a cashier left the register to help a young woman who was struggling with a baby and a cart full of purchases and held her baby while she emptied her cart. The woman was clearly impressed, as were the customers watching the scene. At a parcel delivery organization, a delivery man whose truck broke down took the initiative to hire another truck to make his deliveries on time. This is how companies go about loyalizing their customers.

Another change in companies wanting to instill customer orientation in their employees concerns the commissions paid to salespeople. Traditionally, these have been related to the amounts of sales in dollars and cents. Now, a number of companies tie the amount of commission to the customers' satisfaction. They have explained to their employees that taking time to serve the customers well could reduce sales in the short term. However, in the long run, it increases the number of repeat sales and, therefore, total sales in general. In a similar vein, administrations in an increasing number of colleges offer a guarantee of satisfaction to organizations that hire their graduates, promising to retrain these graduates free of charge in subjects they are deemed to be weak in or lacking altogether.

QVALITY in Services

The QVALITY concept applies in services as well as in manufacturing. In services, customers require the following:

• A quality service (Q), that is, a main service that is suitable for their primary needs (such as health care, education, insurance coverage, savings, investment, loans and mortgages, retailing, groceries, transportation, travel, food and lodging, entertainment, repairs and maintenance, and so on) as well as all the ancillary services that go with that main service.

As they do with tangible products, customers avail themselves of a service for a functional use (playing golf at a country club, eating at a restaurant) or nonfunctional use (mixing with a certain class of people at a country club, conducting a business meeting at a restaurant). The quality of a service can be intrinsic (good turf in a golf course) or extrinsic (the good reputation of a country club).

• A certain volume (V) or quantity. Customers will need to borrow a certain *amount* of money, set up a computer system of a given *size* (payroll for 10,000 employees, order processing for 4000 orders a day), or get insurance coverage for a certain amount of money. Services could be required to serve a certain number of customers (10,000 students, 5000 patients, 100 patrons) simultaneously.

• Customer-friendly administrative procedures (A). Procedures that are required to obtain a service (enroll in a university, apply for a loan, request surgery, get insurance coverage), to pay for it, or to complain about it must be free of error and easy to understand and process.

• A convenient location (L). The site where the service is available must be suitable for customers' needs and easy to access (close to public transportation and highways); have ample parking space and inviting surroundings; be nicely decorated and offer comfort and a pleasant ambiance (soft music, studied lighting, interior decoration, magazines, videos, fax machines and telephones, coffee and other beverages).

• Friendly, efficient interrelations (I) with the company's personnel and representatives, whether face to face, on the telephone, or through correspondence (letters, faxes). Courtesy, politeness, promptitude. Another factor closely related to company–customer interrelations is the image of the company in terms of social, economic, and environmental issues (human rights, environmental protection, the company's contribution to the fight against unemployment).

• Timing and timeliness (T) when a service is provided. Waiting time reduced or eliminated, the required service provided in the least amount of time or when required. Most people in a restaurant at lunchtime like to eat rapidly to be able to return to work or to whatever matters they must attend to. In the evening, most people like to take their time wining and dining and treat it as a social activity; they do not appreciate being rushed. Some restaurants make a point of presenting the bill only when asked to do so by the customer.

• A good yield (Y) from the service. When considering this element, the customer poses an important question: How much will a service cost and what benefit will it generate? This is the economic dimension of acquiring a service, the cost–benefit equation of which the yield is the result.

When introducing total quality in a service organization, one should consider the following differences between manufacturing and service sectors.

• The manufacturing sector is relatively homogeneous in that the main production activities of most companies have the same general goal: to transform raw materials through a manufacturing process into finished, tangible goods either made to measure (to customer specifications) or mass produced (to manufacturer or trade specifications).

• Services vary significantly. In some sectors, the service includes as its main component a tangible physical product, such as the merchandise sold in the retail industry or the food prepared and sold by restaurateurs. In other sectors, where there is no physical product involved, the service is intangible. Such is the case when one purchases a train or an airplane ticket to travel from one point to another; when one deals with a lawyer, a consultant, or a marriage counselor; or when one undergoes a surgical operation or studies for a university degree. Unlike that of tangible products, the quality of intangible products is obviously difficult to measure in a precise, objective fashion.

• Some services require the physical presence of the customer (hairdressing, surgery, counseling, traveling, shows); others do not (car repairs, house maintenance, subscribing to a magazine, or applying for an insurance policy). In some instances, the customer is put in charge of the service rendered (self-service in supermarkets, department stores, or service stations; choosing a certain insurance combination plan).

• Although goods can be pretested before delivery to the customer, services (counseling, consulting) cannot. Furthermore, goods may be repaired or replaced when they are in the hands of the customer, whereas the unquality that occurs during services performed on or for the customer cannot be corrected. Cutting a customer's hair too short, operating on the wrong patient or operating on the basis of a wrong medical diagnosis—these errors are irreversible and, in the latter two cases, potentially deadly. The bit of gallows humor about physicians' mistakes being buried with the customer is really no laughing matter! Some patients have to endure unwarranted surgery, while others do not get the surgery they require because the surgeon fears the risk of making an error and consequently being sued. During the research done for a television documentary on medical laboratories, it was found that a great number of the laboratories had a high rate of errors. This becomes very critical, the program noted, when these errors lead to patients with cancer being diagnosed as healthy and healthy persons being diagnosed as having cancer!

• With the advent of new technologies, the way that services are rendered is changing drastically. In spite of their inconveniences, the new, automated telephone systems are spreading all across the business world and throughout government agencies, hospitals, and schools. Receptionists are disappearing and, in some of these sectors, contact with a human being is very difficult to come by, if not impossible! We hardly need to go to the bank anymore to cash a check or pay a telephone bill when all this can be done through direct deposits or through the electronic tellers that can be found on any street corner in any city throughout the world.

Once I went to a theater in Hamburg, Germany, to see the musical *Cats*. I didn't have enough cash and assumed the cashier would accept a credit card. The cashier indicated that the theater took cash only but pointed to a gas station/convenience store next door with an automatic teller machine. I scooted over to it, inserted my credit card, punched in the amount I required, got my cash, and got my tickets—the whole process taking less than five minutes in spite of the fact that I was thousands of miles away from home and from my bank.

The electronic information superhighway allows one to get all kinds of services simply by sitting in the living room, watching TV, and flipping the remote control. Press a few buttons and you can buy a washing machine, transfer funds from a savings to a checking account, reserve tickets for a show or a trip, make an appointment with a doctor or a lawyer, or pay the bills. When interactive entertainment television is fully developed, viewers will be able to watch a play or a movie on TV and change the ending at will to suit their taste, or even call the shots for the whole scenario as it unfolds. Happy ending? Sad ending? Did the butler do it? With interactive TV, it's your call.

As an indication of how diverse services can be, the following sectors are all considered to be service industries: health-related services (hospitals, laboratories, ambulance services, doctors' offices, dentists, and so on), maintenance services, public services (water, gas, electricity, telephone), commercial services (wholesalers, retailers), financial services (banking, insurance, bookkeeping services), professional services (lawyers, engineers, accountants, consultants), administrative services (data collection, personnel hiring), and scientific services (research and development). And as wide ranging as it is, this is but a partial list.

Quality in Financial Services

According to Robert Janson, the president of a management consulting firm, the fact that consumers are becoming increasingly conscious of the quality of the services they receive has given quality new value and power in the marketplace. This is particularly true in the financial services sector, where constant contact creates a close relationship between the person who is doing the selling and the one who is buying. Firms in this sector talk of creating *customer loyalty* in their efforts to counter the fact that consumers are increasingly aware that the services they get often do not really satisfy their expectations. Certain trends we see today are heralding this revolution.

• *There is a general perception that the quality of services is deteriorating.* The firms that neglect to integrate quality of service into their strategies will see their share of the market decline and their profits significantly reduced.

• *There is a growing demand for greater value.* With deregulation, investment companies are now offering savings services and current accounts for their customers, while banks are offering various financial services, such as insurance. In effect, the financial institutions are competing for clients by offering various new services in addition to those they have traditionally offered. They open on Saturdays, for example, and offer free services, such as counseling on retirement planning for older customers.

• *We now see a balance between technology and personal contacts.* Consumers have adapted quickly to the rapid, error-free service that new, computerized technology has made possible in many different areas of service. Nevertheless, they do feel the need for the personal touch, which can be lost as electronic technology takes over more and more functions that used to be performed by people.

• *There is a greater demand for personalized services.* Consumers expect their financial institution to personally guide them through the great diversity of services offered. In the past, financial institutions considered guidance services, but they were expensive and complicated. Now these institutions see in such services a strategic advantage. In effect, their customers are not only more satisfied and more dependent on their financial institution, but they, therefore, remain more loyal to it.

• *Customer's desire to do business with a single financial institution.* There is greater desire on the part of customers to take advantage of their leisure time, so they are looking for a kind of supermarket for financial services: savings, mortgages, personal loans, and auto and home insurance. The financial institutions, well aware of this trend, are beginning to design and offer these kinds of services.

Janson contends that a successful service company has the following characteristics.

1. A vision of customer service
2. A structure to support this vision
3. Customer-oriented attitudes
4. A system that empowers and gives responsibility to the front-line employees
5. Systems allowing customers to give feedback
6. Using technology as a vehicle to offer service
7. A plan for the gradual introduction of a client-oriented process

The Product Quality Cycle in Services

As indicated at the beginning of this chapter, we are often inclined to associate quality only with physical goods. In effect, how can you define or measure the quality of care in a hospital, a course at school, a management consultant's report, or a computerized system?

In spite of the obvious differences between the industrial and service sectors, the principles of total quality management apply just as much to one as to the other. Quality invariably means satisfying the customer's needs. Just like goods, services must suit the customer's intended use. This suitability can be functional, as when one goes to a restaurant to eat, or nonfunctional, as when one uses the restaurant for a business or social meeting and not specifically as a place to eat.

As with goods, the quality of a service can be intrinsic or extrinsic. The quality of a country club's golf course (that is, its layout and turf) is functional, whereas its reputation as a posh golf club and the prestige even nonplayers attach to it are nonfunctional. When someone deals with an institution (bank, insurance company) solely because he or she believes it is the best, that individual is being swayed by a quality that is purely extrinsic. Good mortgage rates, on the other hand, are an intrinsic factor that could persuade one to do business with a bank.

The product quality cycle notion is just as applicable to services as to physical goods. When a certain hospital wanted to introduce a quality system, hospital managers claimed that the quality cycle activities applied only to manufacturing. Figure 5.2, however, shows one such cycle as applied to a hospital. The needs to be satisfied in this case may be identified as the restoration or maintenance of the

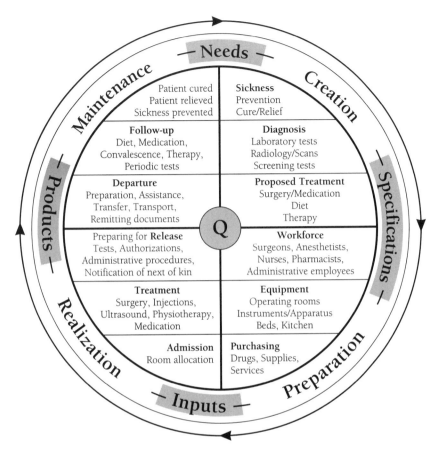

Figure 5.2. The quality cycle in a hospital.

Source: Adapted from J. N. Kelada, *Comprendre et réaliser la qualité totale,* 2nd ed. (Dollard-des-Ormeaux, Quebec, Canada: Quafec Publications, 1992). Reprinted with permission.

customer–patient's health and well-being, preventing sickness, curing diseases that can be cured, or offering what, for the hospital, translates into the imperatives of palliative care and relief for the incurable.

All treatments, just like physical goods, have to be produced. A treatment is designed after a diagnosis is performed and is based on the examination of X-rays; electrocardiograms; ultrasound, blood, and urine tests; and so forth. Next, the treatment so designed is *specified* in terms of type (surgery, therapy), dose (medication), and frequency. Then comes the preparation stage, when the availability of the workforce that will administer the treatment is checked (doctors, nurses, and support staff). Installations and equipment (operating rooms, therapy rooms) are verified to ensure that they are adequate for the task at hand. The availability and reliability of medications, supplies, and services are also checked, as is the reliability of the suppliers of these.

Then the treatment of patients can begin. First of all, they are admitted to the hospital and settled into a room. The treatment itself is administered and, after the appropriate period of recuperation, patients are ready to leave. When the treatment is over or the patients have left the hospital, they must be monitored. They may have to follow a certain diet and often must have regular examinations to prevent any risk of recurrence of the problem. The cycle ends when the patient is cured or (if the condition is incurable) relieved, or else when the patient has completed preventive treatment.

The preceding example illustrates that the product quality cycle can be used just as effectively in producing a service as it can for manufacturing goods. Similarly, the use of this cycle in the service sector demands that all of its activities be carried out correctly and that any errors be promptly analyzed and rectified to avoid their cropping up again in the future.

Quality Systems for Services

Recognizing the importance of quality in services, the International Organization for Standardization has issued, as part of the ISO 9000 series of standards, a standard that sets out guidelines for the elements of a quality system in services.[4] This standard—ISO 9004-2—encompasses everything in a quality system from the first marketing steps identifying customers' needs to the delivery of the service to the customer and the subsequent analysis of its quality. It applies to main services as well as to the ancillary services that accompany either a main service or a tangible product. It thus covers a number of situations, ranging from one in which a service accompanies a transaction involving a tangible product (as in the case of selling a car), to one in which the tangible product involved bears less importance in the transaction (as in the case of a restaurant), to one in which no tangible product is involved (as in the case of legal services). The needs of both internal and external users of services are also addressed by ISO 9004-2.

This standard is applicable in the case of a number of services, such as

- Restaurants, hotels, tourist services, entertainment, radio, and television
- Transportation and communications: airports and airlines; rail; road and sea carriers; telecommunications; mail services; computer networks
- Health care services: doctors, hospitals, ambulance services, medical laboratories, dentists, opticians
- Public services: water services; trash collection; suppliers of gas, electricity, and energy; firefighters; and police
- Trade: wholesale, retail, warehousing, distribution, marketing, packing

- Financial services: banks, insurance companies, credit unions, real estate agencies, accounting
- Professional services: architects, security, training and education, engineering, project management, quality management, consulting
- Administration: personnel departments, computer system departments, administrative departments
- Technical services: consulting, photography, test laboratories
- Scientific services: research and development, assistance for decision making, studies

ISO 9004-2 states that the requirements of the service to be provided must be clearly defined in terms of observable characteristics that can be assessed by the customer. It also states that the process used to provide the service should be defined in terms of characteristics that directly affect the execution of the service (such as the implementation of an internal procedure), even if they may not be observable by the customer. Figure 5.3 shows the main elements of a quality system for services, as presented by this standard. Customer interface stands at the center of the system, while the three factors that combine to affect it revolve

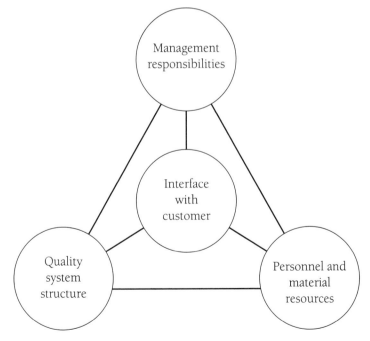

Figure 5.3. Key aspects of a quality system.

Source: ISO 9004-2:1991. Reprinted with permission of the Standards Council of Canada.

around it in constant interaction. These three factors are the management respon-sibilities; the quality system structure; and the personnel and material resources used to design, produce, and deliver the service.

Management's responsibility consists of establishing a quality policy and quality objectives and clearly assigning the responsibility for quality to all individuals or departments that directly affect the quality of the service provided to a customer. Management or a representative of management should ensure that an effective quality system is set up, applied, audited, and continuously analyzed for constant improvement. Management should vigilantly and regularly evaluate the results of the service provided, the results of internal audits of the quality system, and the impact of changes in marketing and social conditions on the quality of the service provided.

The standard requires that the personnel be adequately motivated, trained, and evaluated. Persons in direct contact with customers must have the training and the necessary skills to communicate effectively with the customer. Teamwork is recommended to improve communications among the personnel and to enable them to engage in participative problem solving. An appropriate information system is essential for good communications and for the production of the service required. The quality system should be well-documented.

The service quality loop (see Figure 5.4), another component of ISO 9004-2, comprises three main processes.

1. *The marketing process:* The marketing process identifies customers and their needs through market research, examining what the competition has to offer customers, and consulting with all departments within the organization to confirm their commitment and their capacity to meet the customers' requirements.

2. *The design process:* The design process ensures that the service is designed to suit the needs identified through the marketing process and to go beyond expectations. The service, the process required to produce it, and the process required to control its quality are specified.

3. *The service delivery process:* The service delivery process includes the following steps: providing information regarding the service offered; entering and processing orders; and invoicing and collecting payment. The service results are assessed by the supplier. They are also evaluated by the customer—and it is this assessment that is ultimately the most important one. The service-rendering process is analyzed, and based on this analysis and on the assessment by the supplier and by the customer, this process is then modified as necessary to improve the service.

Obviously, the more the service delivery process is formalized through a set of clear procedures, the easier it is to apply the structured, exacting principles of the type of quality system illustrated in Figure 5.4.

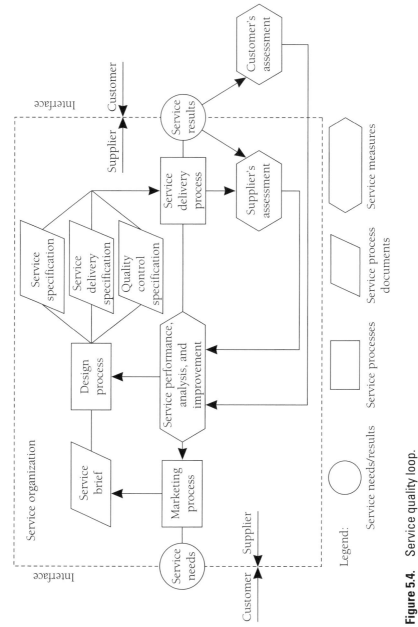

Figure 5.4. Service quality loop.

Source: ISO 9004-2:1991. Reprinted with permission of the Standards Council of Canada.

Total Quality in Public Services

The notion of quality may not be as popular in the service sector as in the industrial sector, but it is even less popular in the public sector. Governmental services have a captive clientele. Their customers cannot turn to other suppliers; they have no choice. Moreover, in contrast to the private sector, there is no motivation for the public sector to make a profit. However, many governmental services have gone the route of total quality in spite of their resistance to the idea. Indeed, faced with tighter and still tighter budgetary restrictions, public administrators are feeling pressed to do more with less. By embarking on the total quality path and focusing on a more humane and participative management style, they can increase productivity.

According to Hunter, O'Neil, and Wallen, quality improvement in the public services is based on three basic elements.[5]

1. A management philosophy that encourages all employees to emphasize continuous quality improvement.

2. A decision-making process based on factual data analysis rather than on intuition. All employees must follow and carry out detailed analysis of all the processes and know how to improve them.

3. A devotion to customers, bordering on fanaticism, in order to exceed their expectations.

Most managers have learned to control rather than direct. Organizations today use a management style that has its origins in the nineteenth-century military and virtually depends on the fear it generates. Orders and information go in one direction—from top to bottom—discouraging any initiatives on the part of the lower-level employees. In an attempt to increase productivity, human resources are reduced, but the remaining personnel are then expected to produce more. As a consequence, quality drops, time is wasted in rework and, as a result, productivity drops drastically.

A Case Study

Hunter, O'Neil, and Wallen cite a case in the public sector in Madison, Wisconsin. The city had been faced with all-too-familiar budget cuts and—regardless of a greater demand for services—was trying to fulfill an obligation to significantly reduce both its personnel and its operating costs: the city had to produce more with less. The city fathers decided to improve productivity by improving quality. They realized that managers are trained to *control* rather than *direct* their personnel, to manage by directives and procedures instead of by exercising enlightened leadership in an open and participative style of management. When a manager wants to raise production, he or she focuses on reducing costs and pushes people to work harder. The results are always disappointing. Cost reductions and increased workloads only succeed in lowering quality levels; the resulting rework then causes a vicious circle of increased costs and discouragement and disenchantment on the part of the employees.

An audit of the city of Madison's rolling stock showed very low productivity, mediocre work relations, and interdepartmental communications that left a great deal to be desired. All efforts to improve this situation had failed. The auditors recommended that certain quality improvement techniques be used in this sector. As it happened, the city's mayor had attended a seminar conducted by W. Edwards Deming and, therefore, realized that this approach could be used just as well in the public sector as in the private. Budgets were approved to introduce and test a quality improvement approach, beginning with the city's rolling stock department as a test case. Two groups of employees were established. The first group, after going through training on the quality improvement process, started by conducting an elaborate survey of their clients to prioritize the services offered by their department. Contrary to what they had expected, customers were looking more for safety than for reduction in cost. The survey's results showed the employees where to focus their efforts in order to provide greater satisfaction for their customers. In addition, this teamwork exercise had the effect of raising the morale of the employees who, hitherto, had merely followed orders without any discussion or questions.

The second group worked on work process and methods, trying to detect the causes for delays in the delivery of vehicles or for poor quality in the work done (see Figure 5.5). They concluded that the work done did not follow any order of priority and that the frequent lack of spare parts in the stores slowed down the repair work enormously. Instead of jumping to rapid conclusions and launching into a search for immediate solutions, the group took the time to gather and analyze a certain amount of pertinent data. In its report to the mayor, the group, in addition to giving a number of other pertinent recommendations, recommended that a system of preventive maintenance—which had been discontinued 20 years previously—be reinstated. Today, the number of vehicles with which the rolling stock department deals has gone from 546 to 725, even though the staff has been reduced from 35 to 29.

Wisconsin provides us with yet another example, this time concerning word processing in the state's department of revenue. In that department, it used to take from two to three weeks to return a one-page letter to its author—and even then it might contain several errors. The department had shelves full of backlogged requests. After several attempts to remedy the situation had failed, it was decided to try a quality improvement approach in the word processing service. A nine-member team, composed of managers, employees, and customers, met once a week for three months to find solutions to this thorny problem. This was the first time that workers and managers had ever met together on a formal basis.

Their first activity was to determine who the word processing department's customers were and who its suppliers were. By means of a survey, they deter-

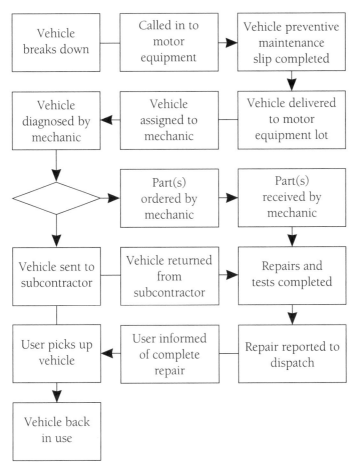

Figure 5.5. Vehicle-repair operations chart.

Reprinted with permission of ASQC.

mined customer needs and expectations. They also studied all of the stages of the work process, from receiving an order to prepare a text, right up to its delivery to the person who had requested it. This allowed them to determine that 27 percent of the customers' orders contained errors. Moreover, 49 percent of the requisitions were marked "Urgent" merely because customers believed that they would get more rapid service. Employees in the word processing department were given authority to refuse to accept illegible or poorly prepared texts, and customers were asked not to mark "Urgent" on any texts that were not required within three days. The employees were authorized to work overtime to reduce the backlog. Turnaround time was first of all reduced to two days and then to eight hours. The department was able to maintain this, and it is now the normal delivery time.

A Bank and a Maritime Transportation Company Launch Their Total Quality Processes

Three words sum up the nature of the relationships that financial institutions have to establish with clients: credibility, trust, and honesty. Any shortcomings in these areas seriously damage a financial institution and are likely to be remembered for a very long time. Given the present economic context and the increased competition between these institutions, banks realize the importance of stressing customer service.

R. Thomas, president of the First Chicago Bank, tells us that for his bank the customer is the highest priority. Every person who joins the bank is made aware of that right away and is reminded of it regularly.

At one point, the bank set out to be the quality provider of cash management services. They realized that they could not achieve that goal without initiating a serious quality program. To do that, they had to restructure the group in charge of these services into various strategic business units (SBU), each of which specialized in a specific family of products. Each SBU manager was given control over handling the expenditures and costs related to each of the products, establishing the price, developing the product and determining its characteristics, promoting the product, and ensuring the product's quality. Thus, each manager had the necessary tools to satisfy the customers' requirements.

The units went on after that to identify the customers' requirements in concrete terms, by asking questions and being constantly alert to what they were saying. Customers, they learned, were looking for *promptness, precision, accuracy, efficiency, good communications,* and *satisfactory service.* Armed with this information, those in charge took up the challenge of satisfying the requirements and destroying the myth that the quality of a service is difficult to measure. To measure the quality of services offered, they developed a detailed system that would, on a weekly basis, objectively assess 700 indicators that customers had found important. This system was publicized, not only within the bank to ensure its proper use, but also outside the bank to elicit participation among the customers. The units thus accomplished two objectives at the same time. The system improved continually, and the program caught the customers by surprise, evoking an enthusiastic response. As for concrete results, the rate of errors committed rapidly declined from one per 4000 transactions to one per 10,000. Processing telephone requests for funds transfers went from taking 20 minutes to only 13 minutes.

Although it received very favorable and positive reactions from their customers, the bank did not stop there. It pushed its quality improvement program much further. Researchers into bank services conducted a survey that found that the two most important problems for customers of these institutions were the *number of operational errors* and the *slowness in correcting problems*—which, of course, are purely and simply two aspects of poor quality. In general, following the introduction of a quality improvement program, the bank was able to save between $7 million and $10 million annually—and that is only the amount it was able to document; the actual savings can be estimated to be much higher. The costs have been significantly reduced and the prices of services have been maintained with no increase over the years, all of which has placed the bank in an enviable position.[6]

In 1986, and again in 1989, CGM (Compagnie Générale Maritime), an important French maritime transportation company, launched campaigns for total quality. President Claude Abraham had decided to implement the process very slowly because he was persuaded that this type of operation must not be rushed into without careful consideration.[7] According to Alain Buhl,[8] director for quality and communications at CGM, the company showed positive results for the first time on record in 1988 and again in 1989. And, in the words of its president, "Quality certainly had a lot to do with it." Year by year, CGM has widened its efforts to provide the training in quality concepts, practices, and tools that it began in 1986—and we know that training is one of the keys to success with this approach. Buhl adds that

> two essential elements led CGM to undertake the quality approach: a new marketing approach and a new management approach. A new marketing approach because, faced with lively competition and the emergence of large new shipping lines operating on a worldwide scale, we had to react to improve the quality of our service. That is to say, we had to go from a product-driven approach to a customer-driven approach in order to realign ourselves to meet the needs of our customers; we had to permanently adapt our processes to service customers who, themselves, were in a state of change. We needed a new management approach because, to make our realignment successful, we needed the support and commitment of all our personnel. In other words, we needed to initiate a participative approach to mobilize everybody's potential for initiative.

Buhl sums up the conditions for the success of a quality approach as follows.

> You have to believe in it, spell it out and do it. Quality has brought us ways to act, tools and methods that have made us more rigorous and disciplined, and a practice of internal and external partnership that is able to greatly enrich a service approach. Quality has reinforced our culture. However, there is still much to do: quality is not a destination, it's a journey.

Quality is therefore imperative for all enterprises. In service companies it is essential for success, progress, and longevity; in financial institutions, where billions of dollars are at stake, quality pays, and in a big way.

Quality Management in the Service Sector

As in industry, quality in a service organization is not the result of happenstance; it must be managed. It therefore has to be planned, organized, directed, controlled, and assured. Planning consists of identifying the customers and, with the help of their input, objectively defining the characteristics of quality required in both the main service and the ancillary service. And, of course, here I am talking about customer total quality—QVALITY. As for manufactured products, the objective is not merely to satisfy the customers' expectations with the services one offers; one has to go beyond their expectations and aim at eliciting their enthusiasm and delight. Consequently, a system of indicators has to be set up to measure each of the QVALITY characteristics. In the case of internal quality, a backtracking system must be designed that starts from the (external) customer and traces the *path to quality* back through each department, sector, or division of the organization, thus linking the internal partners' quality needs to the achievement of the customer-related quality objectives.

Mark B. Brown proposes a definition of the quality of a service which is composed of three dimensions: completion of the service, the behavior that accompanies it and the goods included with it. For example, in a restaurant, the *service completion* consists of preparing the food, taking the order, and cleaning the tables. The *behavior* includes greeting the customers, asking them what they want, and conveying the order to the kitchen. The *products* are the dishes and desserts that are prepared and the drinks that accompany them. In an accountant's office, completion comprises preparing tax returns, giving financial advice, and auditing financial statements. Behavior here includes collecting data, interpreting tax laws, and making recommendations concerning the improvement of certain procedures. The products are reports, forms duly filled in, and financial statements. Brown proposes a procedure comprising four stages in which one

1. Identifies the three dimensions of quality
2. Determines the factors to be measured
3. Determines the quality indicators for these factors
4. Establishes standards or requirements related to these indicators

For example, in a big store one would

1. Examine the behavioral dimension.
2. Ascertain from that which factors must be measured, one of these being how quickly customers are served.
3. Find out how much time elapses between the customers' entering the store and their being greeted (this being the quality indicator).
4. Establish that the standard should be, for example, about two minutes.[9]

However, even establishing standards for these three dimensions is not enough, for standards tend to only define the norm for what is minimally acceptable. Indeed, one has to rise above customer expectations (ACE) and beyond a banal satisfaction—and manage to do all this without stumbling into the costly pitfall of superfluous quality (which is giving customers something they do not need). This point is illustrated by the dry cleaner who restitches a button without being asked to do it or expecting payment for it; by the desk clerk at the automobile dealership knowing, and using, the names of his customers; and by the store that will alter the expensive clothes it has sold free of charge, should the client lose weight. This is how they build up their clientele and, above all, how they keep them.

To achieve total quality, businesses have to organize and structure themselves accordingly, externally and internally. The customer has to be considered, in much more than a figurative sense, as the sole boss of the company for, in effect, he or she is the one who foots the bills, including salaries and rent for the premises, and provides the company's profits. Businesses should draw their inspiration from the diamond-shaped organization, where all the people in the company work together as a team along with the upstream and downstream partners—as well as with any other people who come into contact with the customer.[10] Managers no longer have the responsibility of leading the troops into combat using strategies and tactics that they have developed in isolation. They become catalysts, discussion leaders, and counselors within the work team instead of remote figures perched on high administrative thrones atop the venerable, but antiquated, pyramid.

Directing the people in the company is fundamental to any approach intended to lead to the achievement of total quality. In practice, only people who are happy, well trained, and informed can achieve this goal. This is what successful companies have come to realize, and their results undeniably prove it. Activities designed to dramatize the necessity of total quality and to empower, sensitize, and continuously motivate a company's people will engender genuine and constant participation on the part of everybody in the company, regardless of position.[11]

Control of quality consists of putting the quality measurement system, set up during the planning stage, to work. Here, the notion of self-control—that is, of each individual being responsible for the work produced or the task performed—must come into play and replace the type of control enforced through policing. The latter leads to employees becoming disenchanted with anything to do with quality, and that, as we have seen in many instances, generates poor quality throughout the company.

Beyond quality control, there is also quality assurance, which is indispensable in view of the fact that its primary objective is the prevention of unquality, not control, which seeks after-the-fact detection and correction of errors and mistakes. It is much easier and much more economical to prevent unquality than to have to correct it and suffer the all-too-often disastrous consequences. It is also more motivating for the people.

Conclusion

As industry is driven by the pressure of massive imports of foreign goods and significant losses in the local markets, there are signs that quality in the industrial sector is improving. However, this is not the case in the service sector, where the situation gives cause for alarm. We could make interminable lists of instances of blatant poor quality in this sector. Even more alarming is the fact that this sector represents two-thirds of the economy and encompasses about 85 percent of all new jobs being created.

One reason that explains this state of affairs is the myth that one cannot objectively measure the quality of a service. Another reason is that we are so accustomed to unquality in services that we do not react to it. We suffer in silence as we endure long delays in airports, improperly serviced cars, doctors who keep us waiting for hours, and telephones that are always busy when we try to reach a public service. Nevertheless, the waves of deregulation, increasing competition, consumer-protection movements, and consumer education will force service organizations to turn to quality improvement approaches. Total quality management concepts and techniques are perfectly applicable to service sector organizations—as much as they are to those in the industrial sector—and will enable them to attain total quality and turn a greater profit.

Review Questions

1. What is different about total quality in the service sector?
2. What constitutes total quality in the following organizations?
   - The health-care system
   - Taxation department services
   - A hospital
   - A bank
   - An insurance company
   - A university
   - A chamber of commerce
3. Prepare a product quality cycle for the activities in a bank. How is it different from and how is it similar to an industrial company's product quality cycle?
4. In every organization, even in manufacturing, there is an important service component. Please discuss, giving examples.

Notes

1. Ronald Henkoff, "Service Is Everybody's Business," *Fortune,* 27 June 1994, 48–60.

2. James L. Heskett, W. Sasser Jr., Earl Hart, and W. L. Christopher, *Service Breakthroughs* (New York, Free Press, 1990), vii.

3. Robert Janson, "Achieving Service Excellence in the Financial Services Industry," *National Productivity Review* 8, no. 2 (Spring 1989): 129–144.

4. For a full discussion of the ISO 9000 series standards, see chapter 12.

5. W. C. Hunter, J. K. O'Neil, and C. Wallen, "Doing More With Less in the Public Sector," *Quality Progress* 20, no. 7 (July 1987): 19–26.

6. Richard L. Thomas, "Bank on Quality," *Quality Progress* 20, no. 2 (February 1987): 27–29.

7. Claude Abraham, "La qualité des services, une mode?" *Qualité Magazine* no. 13 (October–November 1989): 28–29.

8. Alain Buhl, "CGM: Former l'ensemble du personnel à la qualité," *Qualité Magazine* no. 18 (December 1990): 26–31.

9. Mark B. Brown, "Defining Quality in Service Businesses," *Quality* (January 1988): 56–58.

10. The diamond-shaped organization is explained in chapter 9, "Organizing for Total Quality."

11. These activities are discussed in chapter 7.

Chapter 6

It is better to aim for perfection and not reach it than aim for unquality and achieve it.

How to Implement Total Quality Management

As we all know, quality, long deemed a technical matter, was traditionally left in the hands of specialists. Then a concern for quality began to arise within company hierarchies. Hitherto limited to industrial operations, the notion of quality has penetrated not only service sectors but also government agencies. Moreover, many companies have shifted their concern from *quality* to *total quality*. On the other hand, a large number of organizations have failed in their attempt to achieve total quality, while others have been disappointed with the results they have so far obtained.

The reason may be that, before embarking on such a venture, these organizations do not take the trouble to convince every single person in the organization, from president to worker, that maintaining and constantly improving quality, in the *total* sense of the word, is of paramount importance. They put great effort into providing training on TQM techniques, yet make no effort whatsoever to arouse and maintain any enthusiasm among their members to practice the basic concepts of this approach systematically and continuously. Even if the training goes well, they fail to make sure that the interest and enthusiasm of their people is kept alive, day in, day out, year in, year out. Even a Rolls Royce will stop running if nobody puts gas in its tank! Recently, it has been observed that a number of these disillusioned organizations are reverting to business process reengineering which, they are told, is—rather than TQM—the way to go.

As indicated in chapter 1, failure to achieve total quality is not due to the ineffectiveness of this approach or its impotence to generate significant improvement. It is because top management is not committed to the total quality process, or, if that is not the case, then because management misunderstands its basic concepts, ignores its technology, or fails to reinforce the efforts spent to achieve and maintain total quality. This chapter is about how to successfully implement TQM.

Pitfalls to Avoid When Implementing TQM

As already indicated, TQM is not a time-limited project or program, with a starting point and a finishing point. It is a continuous process only ending if and when the business ceases to exist. Because this process is essentially based on a philosophy, on a way of thinking and acting, one cannot think of introducing it into an organization in the same way that one would install a new piece of machinery, a brand-new computer, or an inventory control system.

I suggest that companies that have failed to introduce and maintain total quality have tried to practice only some components of TQM. In effect, often without any prior groundwork or preparation, they have tried to introduce new techniques or methodologies which they took to be the essence of TQM, but which were really only visible manifestations of it.

If total quality is to succeed, 10 essential and indispensable conditions must be met, These are as follows.

1. Top management must have
   - A definite will to implement TQM.
   - The conviction that TQM is an absolute necessity for the company's progress, or even survival.
   - Personal commitment to and continuous involvement in the TQM process. This includes all members of the top management team, including the CEO.

2. The company must have a global, concrete, and measurable long-term vision of total quality. It should reach far beyond the quality of the company's goods and services and go to the extent of simultaneously satisfying the needs of the stockholders, customers, and the organization's people, that is, the total quality triad. The whole enterprise must adopt *extraversive* management.

3. There should be acceptance of the fact that the CEO has personal responsibility for total quality and cannot delegate this responsibility. He or she has to be implicated in, and visibly practice, total quality. The CEO's approval and support alone will not be enough to make this approach successful.

4. The CEO and the top management team must share the deep conviction that only teamwork involving genuine participation on the part of all the people in the company—lower management and workers, middle and upper management—can bring about total quality.

5. All the people in the company, as well as the stockholders and the customers, must be mobilized, sensitized, and even educated to the necessity and effectiveness of TQM.

6. People must receive appropriate training and be well versed in the notions and technology related to TQM (the means) and the effective use of this technology to achieve and maintain total quality (the objective).

7. All people must receive reinforcement in the form of

   • Formal recognition from the higher management as well as from all the managers, and informal recognition (personal recognition from managers and even peers)

   • Awards, or other forms of rewards

   • Periodic gatherings, bringing together the greatest possible number of managers and workers to celebrate the successes attained

8. There must be open and frank communication on the part of management, and generous dissemination of information that has traditionally been reserved for managers or those working in specific departments, such as marketing or finance.

9. Upstream and downstream partners must be sensitized to and educated about the necessity and effectiveness of long-term TQM, for their own good as well as for the company's.

10. Customers and stockholders must be educated about the necessity and usefulness of long-term TQM, in their own interests and the company's alike.

As indicated before, companies that have successfully introduced TQM did so by meeting *all* of these conditions. Top managers were strongly willing to change, and accurate and measurable definitions of both quality and total quality had been developed. Moreover, managers knew how to implement total quality, how to achieve it, and how to maintain it. In addition, all personnel understood and strongly believed that, for the benefit of everyone, a company must be profit oriented, customer driven, people centered, partner assisted, and environmentally conscious.

If any of these prerequisites are missing, you cannot call your approach TQM. Systems might be established for quality management, control, or assurance, but they cannot be considered TQM—there is a fundamental difference, and the results are not the same. Ideally, therefore, to introduce TQM, all people in the organization, from top manager to ground-level worker, must be completely convinced from the very outset that total quality is paramount. They have to realize that it ensures their jobs and their future and is the very source of their pride and satisfaction.

Once TQM is launched you can expect to see short- and medium-term results; but lack of spectacular or rapid changes in the very short term should nevertheless not be cause for discouragement. Some companies have successfully launched TQM and even received prestigious awards for it but have subsequently encountered serious problems. Undoubtedly, launching this process generally requires a change in the company's culture. This change demands special efforts: many procedures have to be formalized, and measuring and follow-up tools have to be implemented—all of which entails creating a certain amount of bureaucracy. This additional bureaucracy, if allowed to proliferate, becomes dangerous when the process has come to maturity and cruising speed is reached. Companies who are unaware that this is happening get bogged down, ossified in a bureaucracy which, although necessary when the process is started, affects their performance negatively when the maturity stage is reached, instead of improving it. When left untested, this bureaucracy can be likened to crutches, which, granted, help a wounded man to walk (or the process to be started) but then hinder him from walking properly once he is cured.

A. Sodano, a psychologist, and several colleagues have studied signs of change readiness and resistance.[1] They looked for the common traits of companies that adopt new business practices successfully. They have identified 17 factors that are essential to successful change.

1. Sponsorship for change
2. High-level leadership
3. A strong sense of urgency from senior management
4. Mobilization of all relevant parties—employees, the board, customers, and so on—for action
5. Performance measurements
6. A suitable organizational context
7. Flexible, functional executives to facilitate cross-functional efforts
8. Benchmarking
9. Customer focus
10. Rewards
11. Rare and well-received reorganizations
12. Communication
13. A horizontal organization with few hierarchy levels
14. Prior experience with change
15. High team spirit and morale
16. Innovation
17. An effective decision-making process

When TQM works, a company gets all its normally accruing benefits, such as better financial results and better returns for the shareholders, customer loyalty, market expansion, and a reputation for reliable products and services. However, a trend has been noticed in which some successful companies tend to slow down their total quality process. Let us take the Japanese example. Some time ago the French newspaper, *Le Monde,* ran an article entitled, "La qualité japonaise, la fin d'un mythe" ("Japanese quality: the end of a myth").[2] A French importer of Japanese cameras dared to admit, "On some models, 15 percent are defective when we unpack them." An official from an after-sales service company revealed that "12 percent of the video machines break down in their first year, regardless of make." On several occasions, the Japanese government has had to take its industrialists to task publicly.

The reasons for this decline in quality are numerous and provide some lessons worth learning. The main lesson, however, is that companies should not rest on their laurels and glide along, propelled by the momentum of past victories. First of all, the years of supremacy enjoyed by several Japanese industries has given them near monopoly on the world markets and has undoubtedly reduced whatever urgency they may have felt in facing any sizable competition. Secondly, their economic and technological success has resulted in constantly rising currency values and, sometimes, the obligation to invest abroad. The Japanese are thus importing more and more parts from other countries, parts that are not always of high quality. Thirdly, competition within Japan is such that industries are constantly innovating and, to counter competition, putting products on the market that have not been adequately tested. The Japanese are trying to remedy the problem, mainly by reorganizing companies, empowering personnel, and imposing stricter control on products manufactured abroad.

Implementing TQM: External Consultants

Most companies embarking on TQM call on external consultants, whose numbers are proliferating in direct proportion to the interest that company managers show in this subject. Care and caution must be exercised when choosing a consultant. Some of these consultants call themselves total quality "experts" or "specialists," but they are not, in fact, experts in the field.

Unfortunately, there is no magic formula to help those seeking assistance avoid these clever and expensive advisors—a necessary evil, as one of my clients calls them. Nor is there any organization, either able or willing, that can appraise the quality of these consultants. Only an *expert* expert could do that, and only then if there were some way to define what qualifies him or her as an expert above all others. All I can do is recommend that the choice of an external consultant be made carefully and objectively (if that is possible), because success or failure may depend on that choice. I have observed that it is better not to launch into the area of total quality than to do so and fail.

Generally, the company will have to choose its candidate–consultant after studying and comparing his or her achievements; assessing his or her reputation, knowledge and communication skills; and sizing up his or her ability to train the persons in the company to assume the responsibility of monitoring and participating in the introduction of TQM. All of these considerations are far more important than how well the consultant promotes and markets his or her services.

The Program for Implementing TQM

The methodology that we have developed and applied for implementing TQM consists of three phases and 10 steps, as follows.

    I.   Prerequisites for TQM implementation

       1. Sensitizing and familiarizing top management

       2. Creating a steering committee to manage total quality

       3. Appointing a coordinator or a coordinating committee

       4. Mobilizing internal and external partners

   II.   Preparing for the start-up

       5. Initiating a total quality diagnosis

       6. Establishing a training program

       7. Organizing for total quality

  III.   Starting the process

       8. Launching the process on a limited scale, then gradually extending it everywhere

       9. Continuously evaluating the process and its results; readjusting as necessary

     10. Setting up a continuous reinforcement process

Figure 6.1 shows a typical timetable for TQM implementation program. The time units represented by the numbers at the top of the chart are to be seen as variables without a fixed duration. In other words, the periods of time would differ in length for each case, depending upon a number of factors such as the size of the organization, the complexity and diversity of the products it offers, the geographical centralization or decentralization of the location of the main administrative and production units, and so on. For example, for a small business, these periods would represent a month, while for larger organizations they could represent two or even three months. Again, this timetable is applicable to most organizations but should be adapted to the specific conditions of any business about to introduce TQM. It is, in other words, a relatively good illustration of how such timetables are constructed.

Note that Xerox Corporation set for itself a five-stage program in order to implement total quality in five years at one stage per year.

    1. Inauguration

2. Awareness and comprehension
3. Transition and transformation
4. Identification of results to be obtained
5. Prematurity

Eight years after start, Xerox had reached only the third stage.

On the other hand, AT&T was able to obtain concrete and important results less than three years after starting its total quality process.

I: Prerequisites for TQM Implementation

The prerequisites for implementing TQM include the four first steps of the methodology indicated in Figure 6.1: sensitizing and familiarizing top management, creating a steering committee to manage total quality, appointing a coordinator or a coordinating committee, and mobilizing internal and external partners.

Step 1: Sensitizing and Familiarizing Top Management. The aim in this stage is to make higher managers, the CEO in particular, aware of the importance of the total quality approach and to familiarize them with its basic concepts and how

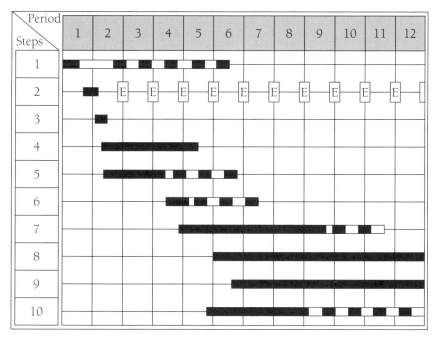

Figure 6.1. Example of a timetable for implementation of TQM. "E" indicates the evaluation periodically done by the steering committee. The intermittent line indicates intermittent activity.

CEO		Quality	Customer
Attitude	Action	Results	Reaction
Indifferent	Delegates	Poor quality	Dissatisfied
	Approves	Tolerable quality	Partially satisfied
Interested	Directs	Acceptable quality	Satisfied
	Is committed	Desired quality	Very satisfied
Obsessed	Participates	Unexpected quality	Surprised
	Is involved	Total quality	Delighted

Figure 6.2.   The CEO's attitude toward total quality and its relationship to quality results and the customer's reaction.

Source: Adapted from J. N. Kelada, *Comprendre et réaliser la qualité totale,* 2nd ed. (Dollard-des-Ormeaux, Quebec, Canada: Quafec Publications, 1992), 243. Reprinted with permission.

they are applied. A direct correlation has been noticed between the CEO's attitude toward total quality, his or her actions, and the resultant product quality as well as the degree of customer satisfaction (see Figure 6.2).

Granted that nobody is against quality, be it total or not, the CEO's attitude nevertheless can vary from indifference to obsession, with the results ranging from unquality to total quality, from dissatisfied customers to surprised and delighted ones. This demonstrates the paramount importance of this first stage. Some consultants attach no importance to it whatsoever, and others seem to be interested in this stage only.

Step 2: Creation of a TQM Steering Committee.   A TQM steering committee is generally made up of members from higher management, but it can also be restricted to the company's top management. This committee is created with the express purpose of guaranteeing that, in its regular meetings, total quality is the *only* topic on its agenda. This eliminates the risk that total quality will get lost in the thicket of topics usually discussed at regular management committee meetings, where day-to-day matters or pressing, short-term problems often take priority. In some companies, a member of the executive team leads the total quality discussion. His or her deep conviction constantly influences the other team members to keep pushing total quality to the forefront in spite of their everyday tasks and frequent crises.

Step 3: Appointing a Total Quality Coordinator.   The company appoints a coordinator to report directly to, and remain in continuous contact with, the company president. The president of a company for which I consult insisted that the coordinator's office be next to his, and the two had daily meetings to discuss the progress of the total quality process.

The total quality coordinator's task is to search, within the company and outside it, for people capable of setting up the various stages of the TQM implementation program. I have noticed that coordinators are often tempted to prepare some of the documents themselves and to propose activities to accelerate the program. However, I strongly recommend that the greatest possible number of internal staff be involved in ad-hoc quality improvement working committees and that they be the ones to write the documents and propose actions. This is a long, but infinitely more effective, process.

Rather than appointing a coordinator, large organizations frequently appoint a coordinating committee composed of representatives of all of its main sectors. Other companies assign the responsibility for the total quality process to a total quality manager, or even a total quality vice president, and provide an assisting staff. Although I am not totally against this practice, I can see a serious pitfall in it. There is great risk that the total quality manager, as well as his personnel, will be perceived, either rightly or wrongly, as wholly responsible for total quality. However, such a manager can function effectively if the CEO demonstrates personal involvement and makes it very clear to all the people that the total quality manager is his or her personal spokesperson. This entails continuous, direct contact between the CEO and the total quality manager. This does not generally happen, however. The president, always very busy, gives a great deal of latitude (in other words, abandons authority) to the total quality manager. The latter has no authority over his or her peers, however, who perceive the total quality manager as an intruder and usurper. In this situation, the only way the total quality manager can achieve his or her objective is by soliciting ideas, seeking out allies, and supporting, rather than proposing or, even worse, trying to impose, action plans.

When the coordinator has been appointed, prior to implementing TQM, work starts on a mobilization program and on a total quality diagnosis. Note that these two steps can be carried out concurrently.

Step 4: The Mobilization Campaign.   Before there is any thought of introducing TQM into an organization, the prerequisites in steps 1, 2, and 3 must be present. If any are missing, the result will be not TQM but merely quality programs limited in both time and scope. But when the first three prerequisites have been achieved, the next step is to instigate the will to change. All the people in the company must be brought to believe in the necessity of doing things differently, for their own sake as well as for the sake of the two other parties of the total quality triad, the shareholders and the customers. In order to achieve this, there must be a well-orchestrated *mobilization* program or campaign. In order to emphasize its importance, I would go so far as to call it a *dramatization* program, and it is the coordinator's or the coordinating committee's first activity with which to begin TQM implementation. I have chosen these terms in preference to *sensitization,* which does not confer enough weight to this all-important activity. Sensitization implies no more than an increased awareness. But mobilization and dramatization convey the urgency and imminence of action, the sense that *everyone* in the company must immediately be galvanized into action in order to initiate the process.

Managers engage in many activities during the mobilization campaign. These include holders meetings, in which employees begin to hear executives use terms like *we* and *us* instead of the traditional *you* (people) and *us* (management). Achievement of total quality has to be seen for what it really is: a joint effort on the part of all of the company's managers and workers. In addition, representatives of other companies are invited to recount their experiences, the pitfalls to avoid, the conditions for success and, of course, their successes. Once, I was invited to a mobilization meeting as a speaker and was surprised to find that, in addition to their own personnel, the company managers had invited suppliers, shareholders, and customers. In another case, the company's people and their spouses had been invited to hear my talk. What was interesting was that the spouses showed particular interest in the subject of total quality and actively participated in the discussions. They realized that this approach is applicable everywhere—in any particular bank, restaurant, office, or law practice where they might work. Mobilization consists of visualizing the absolute necessity of doing things well—and then going one step better—in all parts of the company. Mobilization can be positive or negative. It is positive when the positive aspects of total quality are brought out—pride in belonging to a winning team, being number one worldwide or nationally, winning prizes and honors in the business community, being presented with challenges, participating in company management, seeing one's own suggestions put into practice.

Negative mobilization shows the negative consequences resulting from a lack of total quality. Its call to action is like that of the captain who burned his ships, then told the crew, "The sea is behind you; the enemy in front of you," or the president of an auto manufacturing company who declared that if the quality of the product did not improve, he would close the factory. While consequences are not always that drastic, they can well be. The United States, which formerly produced and exported 50 percent of the steel used around the world, now *imports* about 30 percent of its steel. Meanwhile, paradoxically, many large U.S. steel producers are closing down their mills. Other, hitherto flourishing, American industries are now in constant and inexorable decline—clothing, machine tool, and consumer electronics, for example.[3]

Thus, everybody in the company should realize that

• No organization or company is completely shielded from its competitors.

- Although its survival may not be immediately threatened, a company could be tolerating performance that is only barely acceptable.
- A company may be just surviving, whereas it could be progressing.

It is up to top managers, aided by communications specialists, to launch the mobilization campaign, and to choose, carefully, the messages they wish to deliver. The messages can be based on well-known events that have had impact: the terrible nuclear accident in Chernobyl; the Challenger space shuttle explosion; the critical situation of North American steel companies; the invasion of our homes, offices, and highways by Japanese products, with the resulting loss of most of the domestic electronics market; the loss of a sizable part of the traditionally American-dominated automotive market. All of these are attributable to poor quality, which could have been avoided.

However, these incidents are of a general nature, and, to be really effective, the message must quickly focus on the specific reality of the industry and the organization that wishes to introduce TQM. And while that specific reality must be clearly depicted, often presenting a less-than-rosy picture, the rank-and-file cannot be left just to dwell gloomily on the negative. In fact, the mobilization effort must have appeal to the positive, rather than to the negative, aspects of TQM. One president wishing to inaugurate total quality gathered his troops together and, as a mobilizing tactic, told them that if the business did not launch total quality, the people most probably would lose their jobs. After that dramatic meeting, the best workers in the company started to look for other jobs. Many joined other companies where they felt less threatened. The mobilizing campaign, therefore, has to be balanced. Some negative (but real) elements may be used, but the emphasis should definitely be on the positive.

The prime objective in mobilization is to rouse, in each member of all levels of personnel, a deep, personal need to do something *himself* or *herself* as quickly as possible. Mobilization must prompt the realization that the organization's people are doing it for their own good and their own satisfaction, as well as for the good of others. They are also made aware that they are doing it to guarantee their jobs and security. Mobilization is the shock required to start the culture change fundamental to TQM. *Positive mobilization* stresses the success that results from the TQM process and the pride that can be derived from belonging to a company that manufactures products recognized, nationally or internationally, as being superior. Negative mobilization stresses the disastrous consequences of unquality on the economy, the society, the standard of living, and job security, as well as on the quality of life in general.

I strongly recommend that an external educational process (that is, sensitizing and training for upstream and downstream external partners, customers, and even shareholders) be conducted at the same time as the internal mobilization. Training helps individuals to change their way of thinking, attitudes, and behavior. Clearly, shareholders are more concerned about the short term (they scan the papers daily, checking the value of their shares), but they must also be educated in and converted to the total quality philosophy because they are the ones who generally appoint the company's executives, judge them, and, if dissatisfied with the company's performance, relieve them of their responsibilities. In Japan, a number of corporations, with the agreement of the stockholders, do not trade their stock in the market, to which the stockholders agree, to avoid speculation and to build long-term relationships within the company.

When all of the company's people have been convinced to take action and start the TQM process, the concepts of TQM have to be popularized and demystified if they are to become accessible to everyone. These concepts include everything involving total quality, in terms not only of the company's global performance but also of each individual department, system, activity, and operation. Introductory sessions should present the *why, who, what,* and *how* of TQM. Mobilization meetings can present the *why.* They should include, also the basic total quality concepts, indicating *what* TQM is all about. At this stage, procedures and techniques to show *how* TQM works may also be introduced so that the overall process can be visualized. Sessions are thus designed to combine both activities, mobilization and popularization, in the same agenda. Each session begins with mobilization—which stresses the importance of TQM to the company's progress and continued existence as well as to the people's welfare—and ends with popularizing the TQM concept.

Top managers are the first to go through these sessions. In subsequent sessions, all of the participants must become just as totally convinced as the CEO and the top management team of the necessity of undertaking this process. It is up to the CEO, however, to personally set an example of this conviction, not through dispatching directives or pitching slogans at an occasional company function, but by demonstrating a constancy of purpose, attitude, and action that can leave no doubt about the importance of the endeavor.

When they have finished the mobilization popularization session, participants realize that TQM means quality by all, everywhere, the first time, and all the time—quality in products, procedures, information, reports, marketing activities, personnel services, production, finance, and relationships with suppliers and distributors. They accept that they can benefit from total quality and that TQM is not limited to the consummation of customer and shareholder needs. In fact, in creating total quality, people satisfy and fulfill their own needs in terms of salary, job security, challenge in the workplace, personal achievement, recognition, and a sense of belonging to a winning team, as well as a satisfying personal life outside the workplace—all of which amounts to quality of life.

At the outset, TQM's introductory sessions—mobilization, dramatization, and popularization—are given selectively to certain levels of the hierarchy and some sectors of the organization. Subsequently, they are given to all the people in the organization and eventually extended to the company's external partners—its suppliers, subcontractors, distributors, and so on. Although essentially identical in content, the sessions are adapted to the level and nature of the participants' work.

It is important for staff in nonmanufacturing departments to realize that they have to provide quality service to one or several internal partners by using a work process that they control, but which is part of the global business process. The business process targets satisfaction of both shareholder and customer needs, a satisfaction that, in turn, is achieved through the satisfaction of the company's people. As we have stressed many times already, total quality is not restricted to the company's manufactured products or the services it offers, but extends to all of the activities connected in any way to the company. Big companies with sufficient means offer introductory TQM sessions to their suppliers, distributors, and all other external partners. In Japan, these sessions are obligatory. They also offer regular review sessions for staff, three to five years after they have taken their introductory sessions, or when they change positions or are promoted. Let us keep in mind that TQM is not a program; it is an ongoing process.

II: Preparing for the Start-Up

Following the mobilization performed in the preceding phase, a plan of action is developed to prepare for implementing TQM in an organization. The *action plan* identifies what actions are to be taken, the order in which they are to be undertaken, the people responsible for these actions, and what part the actions play in the entity that will become the TQM process. Furthermore, this plan includes the budgets required to implement the process. Responsibility for the plan of action lies with the president, or with a person or group of people who report directly to the president. I want to make it clear that I object to that responsibility being passed on to one of those numerous work committees who, when given a mandate, promptly forget it because there are more important things to worry about. It must lie with one person or with a group of people in constant and direct contact with the president. This plan comprises three steps: initiating a total quality diagnosis, establishing a training program, and organizing for total quality.

Step 5: Initiating a Total Quality Diagnosis.   During the time that mobilization and popularization are in progress, a diagnostic procedure is established for the present system. As will be explained in detail in chapter 8, there are two dimensions to this procedure: external (shareholders, customers, partners, environment), and internal (people and processes). It starts with carefully identifying the company's actual and potential customers and each department's internal upstream and downstream partners. Next, the various dimensions of total quality are defined, and the existing situation is evaluated in terms of the total quality requirements, as expressed by the customer and as compared with the standards in that particular industry (that is, benchmarking) and with the performance of the competition.

Next comes an evaluation of the morale and opinions of the people, both management and workers; and the business process and its components are mapped, examined, and analyzed to check that they are indeed capable of (a) achieving the required total quality and (b) preventing, detecting, and correcting any eventual occurrence of unquality or overquality. This diagnosis, complemented by a prognosis and forecasts, will either permit the improvement of the existing business process and the identification of specific problems requiring the attention of the continuous improvement teams, or call attention to the need for reengineering.

The company will need to devise its own diagnostic tools, borrowing from and modifying existing tools such as the Baldrige Award diagnosis, the ISO 9000 quality management and assurance standards, benchmarking, opinion polls and surveys, measures of customer and personnel satisfaction, process mapping and analysis techniques, and others.

The total quality approach does not recommend making a systematic examination of everything the company does. This diagnosis identifies activities and processes (including those concerning quality control and assurance) already underway in different sections of the company. It thus lays the groundwork for the subsequent addition of any missing elements and for the integration of all aspects of the business process into a coherent and efficient whole. In the past, most companies used a piecemeal approach and achieved a level of quality acceptable at the time. However, obviously, that level of quality is inadequate to face the fierce competition in today's world. The keynote then is *integration,* where all departments collaborate. Although TQM requires significant changes in the company's culture and in the attitude of its people and even its external partners, some already established technical aspects may be able to function very well and produce satisfactory, albeit partial, results. These, then, could be left in place and eventually integrated into a more global quality approach. However, process mapping and analysis may indicate the need to reengineer the business, the business process, or any work process within it.

Step 6: Establishing a Training Program.   After the TQM introductory sessions, a training program encompassing all company people must begin. It should enable each person to achieve, maintain, and improve the quality of whatever he or she has to do to contribute to the total objective. This program presents, in greater depth, the notions and concepts already introduced and provides training for all of the procedures and techniques used in the TQM process. It can last between three and five days. Whereas the introductory sessions are usually led by outside people, the training program is in the hands of internal staff previously trained to teach TQM implementation.

This program includes training managers to apply the new management style and techniques. Managers must cease playing supervisor and desist from giving out orders that others in their units have to carry out, with little or no discussion. They must now play a different role, coaching members of their teams in joint decision making about who does what, when, where, and how. They must learn that people do not work *for* them anymore, they work *with* them. This is a radical change for most managers. Indeed, chances are they were actually promoted to their positions because of their ability to manage the old, quasi-military way. This strategic about-face is complex because it is like changing the rules of a game in the middle of a match. If managers want to keep their positions and, eventually, move on to better ones, they have to learn and apply the new rules without delaying the game.

This program also includes training for everyone in the company, managers included. All of the people have to learn to work together in teams, use new practices, and apply new methodologies, tools, and techniques to improve and to innovate or reengineer as necessary, in order to achieve total quality.

Step 7: Organizing for Total Quality.   TQM advocates a highly participative style of management and teamwork throughout the company. If these are not to remain merely wishful thinking and pious expressions of hope, there must be a formal structure set up to bolster and sustain them. As indicated in Step 2, the TQM process is closely monitored by a TQM steering committee.

All people are organized into total quality teams. These teams recommend and implement continuous improvement and/or reengineering activities. They operate in a radically different way when a greater number of people are involved in decision making, problem solving, and improving or reengineering existing processes.

As indicated in Step 6, the manager's role within these teams changes from that of a supervisor to one in which he or she acts as a catalyst and resource for the team and a contact with other teams. The organizational structure thus tends to be flattened, with fewer levels of management between its top and its base and a large number of cross-functional teams in operation.

III: Starting the Process

The start-up phase consists of three stages: launching the TQM process on a limited scale, then gradually extending it everywhere; continuously monitoring and evaluating the process and its results, and readjusting as necessary; and setting up a continuous reinforcement process.

Step 8: The Launch.   This is the moment of truth; everything is ready for the launching. But let us remember that any company determined to introduce TQM has to take the first steps carefully, just as children hesitate as they learn to walk and learn to walk before they can run. It takes more than a few days, or a few months, to change an attitude or a habit; it might take a few years. TQM is not a simple solution; it is a way of doing things that has to be adopted over the long term, and therefore it is essential to proceed one step at a time. Seventy-five percent of the success achieved can be attributed to changes in attitude, 25 percent to procedures and techniques. Convince people that it is in their own interests to work toward satisfying the shareholder and the customer, and you have already taken a big step towards TQM.

Because introducing TQM is not a short-term project, there should not be an undue emphasis on short-term results, though results are indispensable to the credibility of the approach. In Japan, for example, many companies aim at applying for and obtaining the Deming Prize (one of the most sought-after honors among private and public organizations). In the United States, it is the Malcolm Baldrige National Quality Award. However, companies must set their sights on reaching this objective at the end of a period of, say, five years or more. The award then becomes one of their long-term TQM incentives and challenges.

The company has to ensure that the TQM implementation is done gradually. It should be given every possibility for success by initially introducing it into the sector or department judged capable of offering the greatest chance of success. Various factors can influence the choice of sector. The people may be more particularly inclined to, or interested in, the process; significant quality-driven activities may have already been successful there; or there may be some other reason to believe that positive and tangible results could be obtained over a reasonable space of time. I strongly advise trying an initial project in such a sector. Avoid calling it a pilot project, because that often implies a trial, undertaken in order to decide if one would proceed with it or not. This is not the case; the gradual start-up is intended as a learning or breaking-in stage where adjustments and fine-tuning can be carried out as the process is implemented. It should be closely monitored by an individual well-qualified in this area, but neutral, credible, and trusted by company personnel.

Step 9: Monitoring and Evaluating the Start-Up, and Readjusting If Necessary.
TQM's start-up stage must be carefully monitored. The process must follow the established action plan. It is useful to observe people's reactions to the initial activities related to implementing TQM because the whole process is based entirely on the willingness of everyone to participate. Any resistance to change must be analyzed, and the degree of people's participation must be noted. Often, the first activity in the TQM implementation process is for people in a given sector to identify the activities that make up their section of the *quality cycle*. This must be thoroughly done in a climate of dialogue and frank and open communication. An initial evaluation of this exercise provides a measurement of the group's degree of understanding and commitment. Nevertheless, one must avoid at all costs being swept up in the mechanics of the process and blinded by its technical aspects. What is important is that the mechanics be evaluated in terms of their effectiveness. For example, if you are more concerned about the tools you use than the ends they are intended to achieve, then you have to make some changes. One company tried to use SPC to improve quality in a certain work area. However, workers spent most of their time arguing about the statistical details—that is, about the mechanics of SPC—and disagreements created division within the group. This situation demonstrates that teamwork, which in my opinion is the fundamental prerequisite of SPC or of any other technique, was missing. When the teamwork aspect was reinforced and the people began to work as a team, quality improved. All this proves that, as someone has said, "Statistics do not improve quality—people do!"

The implementation process may have to be halted if it becomes evident that a group has not entirely assimilated the necessary knowledge and, therefore, requires more training. The group then receives further training, and the process is resumed.

The evaluation provides management with an important opportunity to reinforce motivation for the participants; it illustrates the president's and higher management's ongoing interest in following the implementation process and their intent to perpetuate that interest. It never fails to make a big impression on people in lower echelons. Continuous evaluation of the TQM implementation process must permit the identification of any deviation from the established objectives.

When evaluation of the start-up stage is complete and any necessary adjustments have been made, the process can then be gradually introduced into all of the company's departments. In addition to annual updating sessions for the company's people, there must be an introductory session and a training program for any newly hired employee or manager. Follow-up and continuous evaluation ensure the efficiency and continuity of the process.

Step 10: Setting Up a Continuous Reinforcement Process. Note that, up to now, we have mainly talked about *programs* for mobilization and training. At this point, however, we have to set up a reinforcement *process*. (Whereas programs have a definite beginning and end, I would define processes as being unlimited by a time frame and continual. A process may even be seen as circular because it stresses renewal by constantly going back to the beginning, back to the fundamentals.) When the knowledge acquired in the training program is put into practice, a continuous reinforcement process must come into play. This is what fuels TQM, making it function efficiently, effectively, and constantly. Reinforcement takes the form of several activities whose aim is to remind everyone of the necessity to always improve and innovate/reengineer. Positive reinforcement emphasizes pride in a job well done, the sense of belonging to a winning team, formal recognition of exceptional results, and rewards for having gone beyond one's normal responsibility to help a colleague or a customer. Negative reinforcement stresses the dangers that result from unquality: loss of orders, customers, and sales and the risk of frustration, bankruptcy, or job loss.

All people must adhere to the TQM philosophy. Otherwise, this philosophy cannot be introduced and practiced in a company. Everyone has to realize that TQM affects not only the company, but equally the people, and that, by improving the company's performance, TQM guarantees the people well-paid work, a motivating workplace where collaborative effort is the keynote, participation in a successful organization, a well-deserved pride, and great personal satisfaction.

The record of work relations in North America is not encouraging. There are organizations that still operate in a climate of distrust, hardly conducive to the type of collaboration required to practice true TQM. But seeking to lay blame on people or trade unions is not my purpose. I am more concerned with finding a common ground of understanding, because all parties stand to gain if they join forces against the threat of ever-increasing competition, both domestic and foreign.

But once you have mobilized all the forces before you, how do you reinforce total quality as your common objective during the TQM introduction process? A way that is often effective is to identify the "enemy to be conquered"—the major competitor against whom the company has to defend itself, the one it has to outdo. For Honda and Nissan it is possibly Toyota, for Pepsi-Cola it is Coca-Cola, for Komatsu it is Caterpillar—and vice versa. Frequent reports should indicate both the company's performance and the competitor's; all of the people in the organization must direct their attention toward these reports, which act as rallying points. These reports are not to be filed away in departmental economic and commercial research offices; they must be transmitted to all the people. Visiting one such company committed to the pursuit of total quality, I noticed at the entrance a huge poster of their competitor. For a moment, I thought I was at the wrong address. It was explained to me that the poster was there as a reminder for the people to be constantly alert. In addition, news about that competitor's performance was conveyed systematically to the personnel. When the competitor did well, it represented negative reinforcement; when it did badly, it was positive reinforcement. In both cases, the people were pushed to continue their efforts toward total quality.

Many a Japanese business continuously reinforces its workforce through organizing TQC or TQM conferences, usually held annually. Some of these are local, others are national if not international. The intent is to permit the company's various departments to publicly announce, before an assembly of the whole workforce, their achievements in terms of quality improvement in different sectors. The CEO, or a high-ranking company officer, presents total quality awards to the most deserving and shows his or her recognition of the results obtained. At the same time, the total quality teams present the assembly with the results they have achieved.

The company's executives and upper managers play a key role in constantly reinforcing the people's interest in and efforts toward total quality. They use every possible opportunity to show their commitment to total quality, which must be real, genuine, and sustained, not surfacing only when things go badly. Executives are encouraged to practice what they preach and apply the concept of *managing by wandering around.* This means frequently leaving their offices to meet and talk with people. People do not listen to speeches; they take far more notice of actions and behavior.

The companies that successfully implemented TQM have proven to have imaginative and innovative mobilization programs and reinforcement systems. What is more, these companies have demonstrated patience, perseverance, and confidence, all indispensable attributes for success in this approach.

Evaluating the Implementation Program

In order to evaluate the implementation program, I observe what a company does and then rate each of the 10 steps of the suggested program on a scale from 1 to

10. This adds up to a possible maximum of 100. This evaluation method has the advantage of being capable of rating each step as well as the whole process. No score under 60 percent should be allowed. This evaluation helps to identify both the strong and the weak points of the implementation, and permits the weak aspects to be corrected and the strong ones to be improved even further.

I use case studies to train people who have launched or are at the point of launching a TQM project so they can evaluate the implementation process. Appendix A contains such a case study. We start by listing the 10 steps and evaluating each on the 1 to 10 scale according to three criteria: Was the step done? Was it done on time? Was it done effectively?

Measuring Total Quality Results

There are usually some negative effects when the mechanisms to measure total quality are established. Generally speaking, individuals do not like being measured, because a measurement is perceived as a threat. The individual whose performance is low compared with the established standard feels at risk of being punished, demoted, temporarily laid off, or permanently dismissed. However, it would be wrong to say that individuals never like being measured. In fact, we often enjoy it. People who play bridge, tennis, bowling, or golf would no doubt abandon these games if no measures were involved; the Olympic Games would not exist; a Mozart would be held in no higher esteem than a Salieri—life would be very boring. Why, then, are we afraid of being measured when we are working in front of a machine or behind a desk? Clearly, outside the workplace, measurement permits us to take up a challenge, feel victory, and enjoy pride. That is the positive side of measurement and the one that the personnel reinforcement system has to concentrate on. I have always recommended that businesses drop punitive measurement systems and replace them with other measures that systematically reward the absence of error rather than hand out punishment for its presence.

Detractors of the Total Quality Approach

An article by Robert H. Schaffer and Harvey A. Thompson published in the *Harvard Business Review* states that the efforts made by some organizations to improve their performance have had about as much impact on the operating and financial results that shooting at a cloud has on the weather.[4] According to Schaffer and Thompson, the particular corporate attempts to find the miracle cure to all their problems, while accompanied by much pageantry and rattling, provide activities that look good and make the executives feel good but, in fact, contribute little or nothing to the company's performance. They claim that many of these activities appear under the banner of total quality or continuous improvement and that they propose a philosophy and management style based on interfunctional collaboration, greater delegation of authority to managers and middle managers, and increased worker involvement. Some activities are centered on a performance measurement, such as benchmarking, on evaluating the degree of customer satisfaction, or on statistical process control.

The authors point out that companies introduce such programs in the false belief that, if they undertake a large enough number of improvement activities, their performance cannot fail to improve. They maintain that at the heart of these programs is a faulty logic that fails to distinguish between means and objectives, processes and results. In their opinion, managers hide behind the fact that total quality is a long-term approach and thus justify continuing their so-called continuous improvement activities while providing themselves with an excuse for not demonstrating their effectiveness in the short or medium term.

Schaffer and Thompson support their opinions with concrete facts. They quote a survey conducted among 300 consumer electronics manufacturing companies which concluded that, of the 73 percent who confirmed having launched a total quality program, 63 percent had been unsuccessful in reducing quality defects by even one-tenth. The authors think that even that figure is optimistic and in no way reflects the magnitude of failure of these activity-centered programs, not only among electronics industries, which are well aware of the importance of quality, but in the world of business as a whole. All this leads the authors to propose that the solution lies in placing the emphasis on results rather than on means.

Such an article, squarely attacking the total quality approach, persuades many to conclude that, quite contrary to the statements of numerous theoreticians and practitioners, this approach is doomed to failure—like the great many others that have preceded it.

I have to admit that I agree with the conclusion and rate of failure this article cites. I also entirely concur with the authors that one should concentrate on the results and avoid emphasizing the means. But I differ with them when they state that these failures result when the total quality approach is used. As I have pointed out many times in this book and elsewhere, these companies are not practicing total quality; they are merely giving lip service to the term. The authors say that the total quality programs are focused on the means, and we cannot really blame them for saying that because many experts/consultants in total quality state that total quality is no more than process management. At a recent meeting with some of these experts, I was astounded to hear one of them unabashedly state that the primary objective of a private-sector company is to satisfy its customers, not to make a profit. According to him, profits are only a by-product! I was relieved when others joined me as I protested vehemently, but that did not prevent another participant from telling us, later on in the meeting, that "Total quality is nothing but process management!"

The trend towards introversive management—which was described in chapter 3—does, in fact, emphasize activities (accounting, inventory management, personnel management), or the results of those activities, rather than profit or short- and long-term profitability, that is, the company's true results. Of course, in the private sector, a company can satisfy all of its customers and still go bankrupt. But it cannot be truly profitable in the long term if its customers are often dissatisfied—unless, of course, the company has a monopoly and customers have no other alternative.

At CGM, where a TQM process has been launched, president Claude Abraham observes that "The main impediment holding the process back is a human one—and this is due to the fact that all managers do not necessarily have the same mind-set, nor do they have the same priorities or feel the same urgency to press forward. Consequently, the process evolved more quickly in some areas of the company than in others. However, the only directive [that mattered] was that we couldn't allow ourselves to fail." He adds, "I got personally involved right from the beginning—everyone knows that this is a necessary condition for success."[5]

As for the public sector, let us refer back to the case quoted in chapter 5 concerning the introduction of a quality approach in public services in the city of Madison, Wisconsin. Following its success, other quality improvement groups have been set up in Madison. They have not all been equally successful, and some have even failed completely. A study comparing the successes and the failures shows that teams have been most successful when projects

- Are clearly linked to customer needs
- Are important to the people in the company
- Are manageable, neither too large nor too small
- Concern processes responsive to changes
- Focus on statistically measurable processes, rather than on policies or attitudes

In addition, the most successful teams

- Include line workers who have hands-on experience with the processes under study
- Have supervisors and managers committed to quality improvement
- Include union representatives, when appropriate
- Become enthusiastic about their participation, and communicate this enthusiasm to individuals not on the team
- Are guided and coached by neutral, third-party facilitators who can keep teams focused on the data and underlying causes of problems.[6]

The manager of the unit must therefore be personally convinced of the necessity to improve quality. He or she has an important role to play which cannot be delegated. He or she must continually mobilize personnel by

- Demonstrating an attitude that makes his or her interest, personal conviction, and near-obsession for quality obvious at all times;

- Instigating formal activities to recognize all individual work done well
- Making symbolic awards to groups who achieve noteworthy results
- Arranging activities to allow groups to present their achievements to the whole staff (on a quarterly, semiannual, or yearly basis)
- Setting up activities to give constant visibility to the quality achieved
- Providing training and adequate support (internal and external) for the groups engaged in improving quality

Obviously, the executive or manager in question will need the assistance of external and internal resources capable of performing these activities. Reinforcement is to quality improvement what gasoline is to an automobile or water to a plant. The most expensive car, as well as the least expensive, needs a constant supply of fuel; the healthiest and strongest plant will die without regular watering. This is an often forgotten but essential point, and it is at the root of most failures to improve quality, even those that have initially been so promising.

TQM and Strategic Planning

TQM reaches into all activities within a company. Consequently it can be regarded as an internal network linking all departments and services. However, it also spreads outward, spanning the company's upstream and downstream partners, suppliers, affiliates, distributors, carriers, and installers. The external network can even go so far as to collaborate with the competitor in breaking into foreign markets. As I have said, apart from being a management philosophy, TQM is a business strategy which, like all other strategies, is the responsibility of higher management. This means that management has to take TQM into account in its strategic planning.

Strategic planning is the activity that allows management to choose its medium- and long-term goals, such as developing products, markets, and vertical and horizontal expansion and integration. It is the outcome of analyzing the company's strengths and weaknesses in relation to its immediate environment and its global, regional, national, or international environment.

The company's immediate environment primarily consists of its customers. The company must fully and completely satisfy them by

- Offering quality products and services
- Providing them in sufficient quantity
- Delivering products to the place and time specified, at the lowest cost
- Using a simple and uncomplicated administrative system
- Maintaining excellent relations with its actual and potential customers

That immediate environment also includes all the competitors who vie for or share the same market.

The global environment affects not only the company but also all of its domestic and international markets. The components comprising the global environment are the political (P), economic (E), and social (S) situations on national and international levels, as well as the prevailing technological changes (T) and ecological constraints (E)—represented by the acronym PESTE.[7]

Strategic planning specialists have found that companies whose products are superior in quality to their competitors', or who have a reputation for producing superior quality, have a distinct advantage over their competitors. This advantage is reflected in their profit margins, which can be as much as five times greater than that of companies whose quality is deemed to be inferior. This superiority is one of the defining characteristics of a high-performance company, having a direct and perceptible impact on the company's performance, success, progress, and continuity. Clearly, then, if the concept of total quality moves beyond the product to encompass all the company's activities, as is recommended in TQM, this advantage will be all the greater; and therein lies the main characteristic of an excellent company.

Successes and Failures in Implementing TQM

Stratton asked five professional quality specialists about the conditions of success and the causes of failure in the TQM process.[8] Largely speaking, there are four categories of factors that affect success: leadership, culture, the launching process, and training. There are other factors with some influence on the process, but they cannot be placed in any of those four categories.

1. A leader is needed to oversee the process. The leader champions the approach and is utterly convinced that the process and the direction taken are fundamentally sound. The leader is ready to risk his or her own career and position to persuade everyone of the paramount importance and necessity of creating total quality.

2. To achieve total quality, the experts state that the company's culture must be changed and a participative style of management set up everywhere in the company.

3. The launching process begins at the highest management level. Then, each division decides how it plans to join in the process. Isolated uses of the process (a smattering here, a smattering there) are not to be tolerated. The process, rather than being imposed, must be accepted before it can be implemented.

4. There must be training for everyone. The training is to be balanced, with equal measures of management and techniques. There is no selective training, where some employees are trained and others not. Managers and employees get the same training. The training sessions are not limited to sensitization sessions.

5. Other factors. The process is aimed at the long term. The goal is not simply to eliminate customer complaints. It must be to find out what customers want and then exceed their expectations.

Finally, let us look at some thumbnail scenarios to illustrate why some quality programs have failed in spite of their high implementation costs to the company.

1. *Cosmeticism.* The quality program, or a similar recommended alternative, is introduced on a superficial level, so that it remains an empty, outward form, like a Hollywood stage set. The company wants the cure, but it doesn't want to swallow the medicine.

2. *Firemanism.* When faced with a crisis or problem, the company rings the fire bell and tries to apply a quality approach rapidly. It pays no attention to the prerequisites; it looks no further than the short-term solution.

3. *Pontius Pilate-ism.* Quality has to be improved; managers all agree on that. They take immediate and concrete action: they hire a brilliant quality manager and give him or her free rein, or practically free rein. Management's conscience is clear; it washes its hands and turns to more important problems.

4. *Inadequatism.* Can you use a fire detector to put out a fire? Statistical process control cannot solve a lack of motivation, even if it is costly to implement.

5. *Individualism.* Each to his own! Designers devise their plans; workers carry them out; each has his or her own responsibility. What's there to talk about? The worker doesn't know how to draw up a plan, so how can she possibly discuss it with the designer? If the worker thinks that the plan is badly drawn and products are defective, it's assumed that she is looking for a scapegoat. If she knew how to design she wouldn't still be on the shop floor. Each individual barricades himself behind his own specialty, as though it were a fortress.

6. *Hidebound traditionalism.* We've always done it like that, as long as anyone can remember. Why should we suddenly change it now when it has always worked in the past?

7. *Sloganism.* Posters are plastered all over the walls. Someone must have gone to a Workers' Republic and decided that shouting slogans about quality in unison would somehow do the trick. "Zero defects!" "Do it right the first time!" (Why not "Do it right *every* time"?) "If you were a customer, would you buy this?" or even "Quality = Pride." Regardless of all the campaigns, the company continues to produce unquality products. Management can't fathom why—they thought the posters were so good!

8. *Copycatism (Keeping up with the Joneses).* Everybody is doing it, so we might as well, too. If the competitor has set up 10 quality improvement teams, we'd better have twice as many. What good will that do? "It'll improve the quality." "At least this is what we hear from people who have visited Japan."

9. *Gadgetism.* This thing about cross-functional teams is going to solve our problems. SPC does miracles—a consultant told us so. He must know what he's doing, at the price we're paying him.

10. *Compartmentalism.* They're implementing a quality improvement team in Workshop A and SPC in Workshop D. But what about Workshop E? We'll try quality assurance there. The rest of the plant is too big. We'll think about that later on.

Conclusion

By way of conclusion, let us look at an incident at Nissan, in Japan, that attracted my attention. Members of a quality circle had decided to work on a subject which, on first sight, seemed futile and in no way related to the company's performance or their production unit. The subject was the type of gift which should be given to foreign visitors. Several proposals had been made, and one was adopted.

As they explained to me, what the members of this team had indeed been working on was quality: the quality of relationships with present and future customers. They were convinced that the quality of these relationships was just as important as the products they made. It illustrates how a group of operators can be convinced of the importance of quality in every aspect of the company. This is certainly reflected in their daily work, where they assemble the thousands of parts of the products which, in turn, affect their company's performance.

When Western businesses were implementing quality circle programs, they expected members of the circle to work to reduce product defects or to improve productivity in their own work sectors. That was a perfectly legitimate expectation, but it aimed only at the short term and was very limited as far as the philosophy of quality circles is concerned. As could be expected, quality circles have disappeared in the West.

Techniques such as statistical process control are useful means of achieving total quality, but one should realize that they involve both human and technical elements. To achieve complete success, care must be taken to ensure that the technical aspects are not overly emphasized to the detriment of the human elements. These elements are the driving force that motivate and mobilize people toward the goal of total quality. Techniques don't improve quality, but people do!

TQM then, is primarily a question of attitude—the will and conviction to do well and to always improve on it. Moreover, while it is important not to overestimate the rational and technical aspects of TQM, it is equally important not to underestimate it. The use of different approaches or techniques reminds all the parties involved in the business, and its outside partners, how important it is for them to consistently maintain this attitude and avoid using the technical aspects simply for the sake of doing so.

Review Questions

1. List and explain the stages in the TQM implementation process.
2. What are the conditions for success and the causes of failure of the total quality process?
3. When TQM is implemented, which should be appointed— a coordinator or a manager? What advantages and disadvantages are there to each of these approaches?
4. Two companies get very different results in spite of using the same guru's philosophy. In some areas, one has great success while the other has a crashing failure. How can you account for that?
5. What role does the company CEO play in TQM implementation?

Notes

1. Thomas A. Stewart, "Rate Your Readiness to Change," *Fortune,* 7 February 1994, 106–110.

2. "La qualité japonaise, la fin d'un mythe," *Le Monde,* 19 April 1991, 31.

3. *Time,* 9 May 1988, 51.

4. Robert H. Schaffer and Harvey A. Thompson, "Successful Change Begins with Results," *Harvard Business Review* 70, no. 1 (January–February 1992): 80–89.

5. Claude Abraham, "La qualité des services, une mode?" *Qualité Magazine* no. 13 (October–November 1989): 28–29.

6. William G. Hunter, Janet K. O'Neil, and Carol Allen, "Doing More with Less," *Quality Progress* 20, no. 7 (July 1987): 19–26.

7. J. Nollet, J. N. Kelada, and M. Diorio, *La gestion des opérations et de la production,* 2nd ed. (Boucherville: Gaétan Morin, 1994).

8. Brad Stratton, "What Makes It Take? What Makes It Brake?" *Quality Progress* 23, no. 4 (April 1990): 14–18.

PART II
PRACTICING TQM

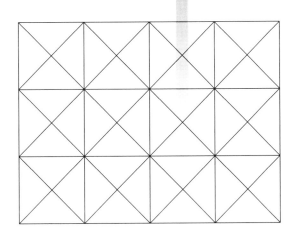

art II covers the TQM activities, starting with the human aspect of total quality and dealing next with planning, organization, control, and assessment.

The human aspect is a fundamental factor in the success of a TQM process. I present here several different concepts, such as motivation, mobilization, empowerment, and skill-based pay. I also indicate how they can be successfully applied.

I then move to planning for total quality; identifying the customers, actual and potential, and their needs; evaluating their degree of satisfaction or the causes of their dissatisfaction; and finding out ways to go above their expectations, beyond their satisfaction.

We have then to organize for total quality. Traditional organizational structures are no longer appropriate for implementing the total quality culture and its management practices. Horizontal organization and cross-functional teams are now suggested and explored.

Quality control is the best known aspect of quality management, at least in the manufacturing sector. It is in this sector that, since the turn of the century, formal quality control activities have taken place. Here, control is extended to total quality. Its main objective is the detection of un-quality so that it can be eventually corrected.

The objective of quality assurance is prevention. A quality assurance system allows a company to give its customers an *assurance* that the products it develops, designs, manufactures, and ships will meet their requirements. Although quality assurance systems are not new, many important customers around the world have decided to deal only with suppliers who have such a system. They require that their suppliers be registered according to the ISO 9000 series standards concerning such systems. I have therefore included a chapter on these standards and on their implementation.

In Part II we shall examine these five TQM activities, as illustrated in the following figure.

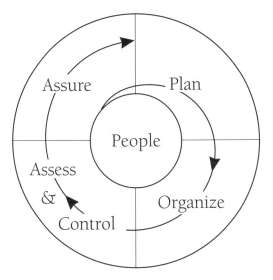

The five management activities.

Chapter 7

People are not the most important resource of a company; they are the company.

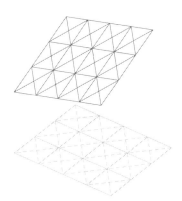

The Human Aspect of Total Quality

The People Aspect in TQM

TQM activities include planning, organization, assessment and control, and total quality assurance. At the center of these activities lies the human aspect (see Figure 7.1). No activity can be carried out effectively if the people involved are not willing to cooperate. In order to do so, they have to realize and be convinced that what they are asked to do is for their own benefit, rather than for another person or group of persons, be it the shareholders or the customers.

This chapter explores the human aspect to be taken into consideration if total quality is to be achieved and maintained successfully. As Chrysler's Bob Eaton puts it: "There's no magic. What will make all the difference in business will be how well you motivate and how well you empower."[1]

A Worldwide Concern

While competition is getting more and more ferocious, unemployment is running high all over the world. The challenge now is not to get people to work harder, but to get them to work "smarter" and more effectively, while reducing the prospect of massive job cutbacks.

Even countries like Germany and Japan, where workers long enjoyed high job security, are experiencing an employment crisis. The once ubiquitous "Made in Japan" label has been peeled off and replaced with a "Made by Japan" label as

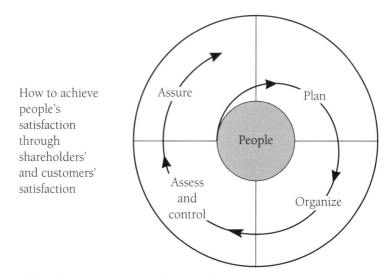

How to achieve
people's
satisfaction
through
shareholders'
and customers'
satisfaction

Figure 7.1.   The human aspect of total quality.

the Japanese move their manufacturing operations *en masse* to scattered locations around the world, ranging from neighboring areas such as China and other Asian countries to areas as distant as Europe and North or South America.

This situation resembles the one the United States was in a few years ago when American manufacturers exported a great number of jobs to low-wage areas in Asia (including Japan itself), South America, and elsewhere. German companies are also facing major layoffs (Mercedes-Benz at one point laid off 30,000 workers) and are opening manufacturing facilities in the United States, where labor is now relatively cheaper, thus reducing costs as well as getting closer to a huge potential market for their products. World competition, as well as the reunification of the two Germanys, is forcing the Germans to change.

So far, no country has found the magic solution. Shared work and a shorter working week are being tried out. Workers might work fewer hours and get lower pay, but they will face less risk of being laid off. After having lived in what was then termed the affluent society, we are now treated to a constant, needling refrain about the necessity of belt-tightening. We have come to the realization that we have been living beyond our means—and whoever's fault it is, if anyone's, somehow we have to pay for it.

Achieving total quality, however, does not necessarily mean downsizing or outsourcing, and thus eliminating jobs. In fact, it can lead to recapturing some of the lost markets and may even create more jobs than are lost when growth becomes a part of the total quality plan. And standing squarely at the center of the total quality approach is the human factor.

The Human Factor: The Fundamental Prerequisite for Success

It has been estimated that attempts to introduce TQM or to implement business reengineering in a company fail in 50 percent to 80 percent of the cases. A look at these failures indicates that one important factor that makes or breaks such an attempt is the human factor. This includes the company's culture; the leadership, attitude, and behavior of its top management; the management style practiced; the mobilization and reinforcement efforts, formal and informal, made by management; the compensation systems applied; and the education and training of the workforce. It also includes the relationship with unions as the representatives of employees.

As indicated in chapter 6, one consulting firm has identified 17 factors that measure the readiness of an organization to change and, therefore, to successfully implement an approach such as TQM. The majority of these have to do with human factors. Among them, just to mention a few, we have sponsorship from a senior level, leadership, motivation, direction, organizational context, rewards, communication, and morale.[2]

Management leaders still consider people in an organization to be an *asset,* a *resource,* and although an important one, still a resource to be *used* to produce goods and services. When top managers talk about themselves, they say "us" and refer to the rest of the people in the organization as "them." When they talk directly to the employees, they say "you" and "us." Two worlds, two solitudes. They forget that when a ship sinks, everybody goes under, the captain and the deckboy alike. In many instances, I have noticed that, in its mission statement, a company will use phrasing like "We consider our employees are our most valuable resource." When I ask who the "we" are, I get answers such as " 'We' is the company!" Do these managers mean that employees are *not* the company? Do they really think that such a statement would make the employees feel proud? Do employees like being somebody else's resource?

Moreover, when things go right in an organization, top managers take the credit and expect to be congratulated. In formal statements they explain how "*We* did it." When things go wrong for any reason, it is because of the mysterious "*them*"!

People Are Not the "Most Valuable Resource" of an Organization

In a company that I once worked for, I wanted a report that I periodically had to send out to be fitted with a different format and given a new logo representing the department I was heading. I went to see John F., the manager of the graphics and printing department, to discuss the matter. His response was categorical. He told me that the "company" would not allow any change in format, let alone the new logo. I suggested that the "company," as he put it, can neither allow nor disallow; only some people within the company can do so. I then inquired if he could tell me who those people were. John F. hesitated for a few seconds, then stated, "It's a committee. They make decisions like this about company publications. They're the ones who establish the procedures to be followed."

Taking the discussion a step further, I ventured to ask, "Is it confidential, or can you tell me who the members of the committee are?"

John F. appeared really embarrassed, then, faltering, he said, "Well . . . there is . . . myself, and . . . Mary G."

There was a silence, so I asked, "And?"

John admitted: "That's it!"

I immediately asked if the three of us could get together and discuss the matter.

John was now completely uncomfortable, and almost in a whisper, said, "Actually, Mary sits on the committee only in an advisory capacity."

"My God!" I almost shouted. "John, can we discuss the matter between ourselves then?"

The discussion ended there; I got my format and my logo with no further ado.

Companies, governments, organizations—these do not make decisions; people do. *People are not the most valuable resource of a company; they* are *the company.* A company cannot exist without owners or shareholders, it cannot exist without customers either: a truism. But a company *is* its people—management and nonmanagement, executives and workers, blue collars and white collars.

Note that I favor the term *people* instead of *employees* because this term includes both management and nonmanagement persons. Although most managers are employees, this word has been traditionally associated with nonmanagement. I also try to avoid the expression *human resources* where the emphasis is, generally, more on *resources* than on *human.* As for the word *workers,* it generally does not include managers, as if managers do not work!

Humans Versus Technology

Facing the tough Japanese competition in the 1970s, American car manufacturers reacted in different ways. While General Motors (GM) put the emphasis on high technology and massive robotization, Ford relied on its people. Ford executives asked the unions to collaborate with them to effect a change from an adversarial relationship to one in which management and union worked together to save the company and the workers' jobs. The union officials realized that they did not have much choice and relaxed their traditional, militant stand. The Ford management changed, too, and stopped viewing labor officials as enemies. Soon the two former enemies were working as partners.

In addition, Ford went on to offer awards such as the Q1 and TQE (Total Quality Excellence) awards which pushed quality consciousness among Ford's personnel and its supplier companies from a single line or product focus to a system/organizationwide focus. The result was that Ford's productivity significantly surpassed that of GM, allowing for Ford's comeback in the 1980s. Another difference between Ford and GM is the management attitude and involvement. Both companies had set up employee empowerment plans, but Ford's management was much more involved than was GM's.

As we can plainly see, Ford's success, as well as that of the Japanese, was based on putting the emphasis on the workforce. In contrast, GM's excessive robotization significantly increased its production capacity but reduced its manufacturing flexibility as compared to that of its competitors. GM lost the very flexibility essential for product diversity.

The Germans, who have always produced quality religiously, did so by relying on heavy and rigorous inspection and intense quality control. This was quality at any cost; any imperfect part or product was fixed as many times as necessary to produce perfect products. However, these products were expensive and took a long time to produce. Still, having a near-monopoly on such top-of-the-line products, the Germans had their own captive market—the elite looking for prestige and perfection. However, when the Japanese started chipping away at this niche, the Germans realized that they had to change their approach. Now, teamwork, self-inspection, and control have been introduced. The worker is trusted to produce quality and is given the responsibility to do so. Teams are allowed to plan their own production and develop their own work methods. From *quality at any cost,* Germans are now moving to the Japanese approach of *quality at least cost.*

The Total Quality Philosophy and Openness of Information

In a cardboard box manufacturing company, a salesman would contact a number of potential customers and finally meet with some of them. He would negotiate a tentative order, discuss it with the box designers, ask the estimating department for quotes, send the quote to the customer, and wait. Only when he had a firm order did he go to his superior, the sales manager, to break the good news. The sales manager then would notify the plant manager, turn to the box designer for a final design, and ask the production department to set a delivery schedule. The production department would fit any new order into its production schedule and order the required materials through the purchasing department. The operators on the production lines got the production schedule along with a kit of drawings and specifications. They then had to produce a box 32Z4566D77-T for the customer S-34667, order 5677-TR, quantity 800, for week 27.

If a worker from the production department, out of sheer curiosity, dared ask who customer S-34667 was, he was politely but firmly reminded to mind his own business. He did not need that information to do his job. Indeed, information was circulated only to people requiring it to perform a certain task or make a certain decision and to nobody else. Workers would be informed of, say, the acquisition of a new plant by their company or a deal with a new distributor by reading it in the newspapers or by watching the news on TV. This practice is called *rational information circulation.*

However, with the introduction of total quality and the application of the *market-in* concept, the plant manager, together with the sales manager, now informs all the people—production, accounting, engineering, personnel—about the contracts being sought, the potential customers, and the competitors likely to be vying for the contracts. Moreover, on visits to possible customers, the salesperson is now accompanied by a supervisor, a worker from the production line, or a clerk from the accounting department. Most potential and actual customers are invited to visit the plant and meet with the people who produce their boxes, prepare their invoices, or answer their telephone queries.

Meeting with the people in the cafeteria during lunch hour, the plant manager announces any contracts awarded to the plant or lost to a competitor. All people can then rejoice in or reflect on the outcome. They are regularly informed of any move by the head office, even if it will in no way affect them. Comments are encouraged and questions answered to the best of the plant manager's knowledge. Visits from people in key positions at the head office are also arranged on a regular basis. During such a visit, a plant worker once commented, "So that's what they look like, these people from the head office!"

At one company that had started implementing total quality, the president felt that progress was too slow and that people were not particularly enthusiastic. Granted, the company had to lay off some of its personnel, but that was due to the economic situation and in no way connected to the TQM initiative. A survey of the customers' needs and degree of satisfaction was also under way in an effort to increase sales. In the meantime, the company had to live with restraints. When asked if he had taken the time and effort to explain all this to his employees, the president was stunned. Why should he have done that?

In a total quality approach, good news as well as bad news should be shared and thoroughly explained. Information about efforts to solve a problem or to improve a situation should be passed on to employees, and suggestions toward these ends should be genuinely sought from everyone. Such an attitude on the part of management creates a climate conducive to cooperation and understanding. When we adopt this openness, we are, in effect, treating employees as adults. If we take the opposite approach, we end up treating them in the same patronizing fashion that we often reserve for our own children. Although we ask children always to consider the family a close-knit unit, as soon as a serious discussion starts, they are asked to leave the room! How can they then feel part of the family? One should not forget that when times are difficult we tend to ask for help and collaboration from the employees; but when things start rolling, we tend to revert to our old habits and stop involving them. This creates a mistrust among workers that, when times are difficult again, will escalate into skepticism and disillusionment.

TQM's Human Element

As I have indicated throughout this book, the human element is the fundamental constituent of every effort to achieve total quality. The efficiency of all of the systems, techniques, and work methods or control procedures depends on the good will, the motivation, and the ability of the people applying them. The complexity of managing people matches the complexity of human nature itself—a complexity documented in countless studies and analyses conducted in the "human" sciences of sociology, psychology, psychosociology, behavioral science, ethnology, and anthropology.

It was Frederick W. Taylor, much railed against for having reduced man to a machine, who made the point that employer and employee were similarly motivated. The owner seeking profit and the employee a wage, they have a common goal—making money. Taylor's mistake was to look only at the economic aspect and neglect all the other reasons why people work. Furthermore, even if there is respect for that common domain, there are still organizations in which the distrust that reigns between employer and employee destroys any possibility of collaboration between the two. This climate of distrust possibly dates back to when entrepreneurs had to share between themselves and their employees what was left after expenses had been paid. While the entrepreneur was thus a party to the act of sharing, he was also its arbiter. Trade unionism was born to protect the employee, powerless against the entrepreneur who was second only to God in his own enterprise. Given that the best defense is a good, aggressive offense, employer–union relationships could not possibly be friendly.

However, the situation has changed. Today, businesses are rarely managed by their owners and generally belong to a large number of shareholders. What is more, in the recent economic crises, we have seen that it is possible for management and trade unions to get along together. There have been instances, in businesses verging on bankruptcy, in which unions have accepted wage freezes or, better still, reduced wages, in order to save the business. In many businesses, top managers have made efforts to motivate and enhance the well-being of their personnel with the idea of improving the company's financial performance. Their efforts have concentrated on introducing into the business's current management process concepts, approaches, practices, and techniques developed by the practitioners of the various human sciences. However, I would do well to point out that some of the approaches advocated by these specialists have failed because business managers viewed them primarily as means of increasing productivity and improving financial performance. Moreover, the managers were not necessarily moved to action through any deep sense of conviction. They introduced these approaches and the practices that accompanied them either because other businesses were doing so or, sometimes, because they just wanted to try them out. For their part, the employees suspected top management of using devious means to make them work harder, produce more, and increase the profits.

People Needs and Quality

If we are to achieve total quality, we must also modify people's behavior with respect to total quality. To do this, we first have to understand the human mechanisms that engender the desired behavior. Every individual has beliefs that emanate from his or her own personal reasoning. From these beliefs emerge attitudes, which generate intentions. People first have to be mobilized by logically explaining and proving that total quality will benefit them and satisfy their own needs. When employees have been convinced, they will feel motivated; they will then develop a positive attitude and behavior toward total quality. This is where training becomes essential. After developing the will to change, the people must be imbued with the knowledge and skills that will provide them with the tools to achieve total quality. Now armed with will, knowledge, and skills, empowered people will undertake actions and achieve results in line with the total quality objectives, the outcome being a win–win situation for everyone involved.

Many an attempt to implement total quality has failed, not through a lack of effort at the outset, but because the process stagnated after the initial trigger of intense mobilization activities. Old habits die hard, and the high interest in total quality and the enthusiasm of the first days of its implementation disappear when management takes them for granted. As indicated before, lack of reinforcement is the culprit. Like the gasoline in a car, reinforcement is essential if the process is to keep going, relentlessly, inexorably, day after day, month after month, year after year (see Figure 7.2).

This whole process has to go on and on until total quality is no longer a set of concepts that one has to consciously adhere to, but rather an ingrained reflex no longer subject to doubts or questioning. Simply put, these concepts become *the* way of doing things. This is a change of culture—which takes time, patience, and perseverance.

Motivating People for Total Quality

No one would work to produce total quality merely to satisfy a customer or an owner. People will do it only to satisfy themselves. If, in their minds, achieving total quality is not directly and constantly related to their own satisfaction, they will not make the effort to achieve it. Motivation in itself is in no way a means to manipulate people toward a certain corporate goal. When used as such by a management eager to increase productivity and profits, it fails to produce any results and, indeed, even alienates the employees. Once employees feel used, a mistrust of management sets in that will be difficult to change in the future.

It has been argued that motivation is not an action, but a state. It is created by mobilization and reinforcement efforts. Motivation is achieved by genuinely establishing a clear relationship between total quality and the satisfaction of the spe-

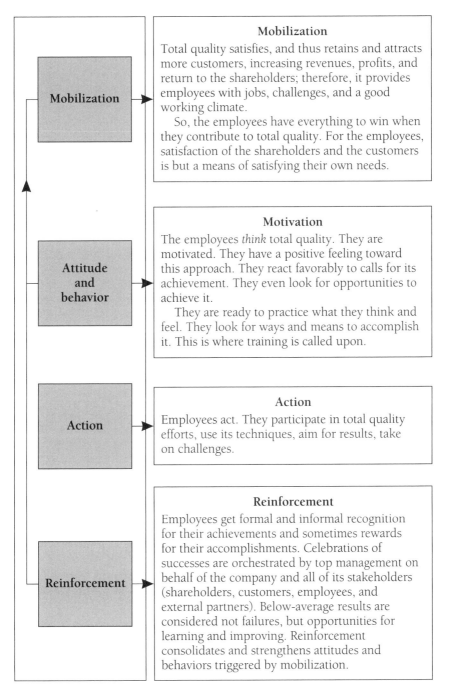

Mobilization

Total quality satisfies, and thus retains and attracts more customers, increasing revenues, profits, and return to the shareholders; therefore, it provides employees with jobs, challenges, and a good working climate.

So, the employees have everything to win when they contribute to total quality. For the employees, satisfaction of the shareholders and the customers is but a means of satisfying their own needs.

Motivation

The employees *think* total quality. They are motivated. They have a positive feeling toward this approach. They react favorably to calls for its achievement. They even look for opportunities to achieve it.

They are ready to practice what they think and feel. They look for ways and means to accomplish it. This is where training is called upon.

Action

Employees act. They participate in total quality efforts, use its techniques, aim for results, take on challenges.

Reinforcement

Employees get formal and informal recognition for their achievements and sometimes rewards for their accomplishments. Celebrations of successes are orchestrated by top management on behalf of the company and all of its stakeholders (shareholders, customers, employees, and external partners). Below-average results are considered not failures, but opportunities for learning and improving. Reinforcement consolidates and strengthens attitudes and behaviors triggered by mobilization.

Figure 7.2. Mobilization and reinforcement.

cific needs of the people. Rationally explaining this relationship to them creates in them the will to achieve total quality.

Using as a general guide the Maslow pyramid of human needs, we must correlate people's needs to the achievement of total quality. Basic human physical and psychological needs—satisfaction of hunger and thirst, a roof over one's head, clothing—are generally ones that require the expenditure of certain amounts of money; food, housing, and clothing are indeed things one must pay for. But what does total quality have to do with all that? There is, in fact, a direct relationship: to satisfy their needs, human beings require money; to get money, they generally need a job. In the present climate, where similar products compete on an international front, only total quality can generate sales. Obviously, sales generate profits which, in turn, maintain employment. Total quality, then, is synonymous with sales and profits; sales and profits are synonymous with jobs; hence, total quality is synonymous with jobs. The employees, therefore, have to realize that if they do not produce or contribute to total quality there is great risk that there will be no jobs for them.

People do not require only jobs, however; they require secure, long-term jobs. They must then sense that total quality can result in job security. The reasoning is the same as before. Long-term sales are the result of the well-established reputation that a company earns by consistently producing total quality. Now, long-term sales allow for long-term jobs and security. Therefore, consistently producing total quality results in job security.

Besides needing to be gainfully employed and to have a sense of security in their jobs, people also feel the need to socialize with fellow workers, to share a sense of belonging to a team—and, moreover, a winning team—whose members work together to achieve common objectives. This need can be fulfilled by group activities that require creativity and involve problem identification, problem solving, and problem prevention, and total quality improvements and innovations (reengineering). Work teams, while helping to achieve total quality, satisfy people's social needs.

People also need to have their efforts recognized. Management must establish both formal and informal ways of expressing the company's recognition for the total quality achieved. Some companies have numerous, imaginative ways of expressing their recognition: naming an employee of the week or month; setting up a publicized meeting with the president; or awarding a prize or gift.

Finally, some people feel a strong need for achievement and accomplishment, or what is termed self-actualization. There are always some particularly creative people who seek out opportunities to change, invent, innovate, and create. Top management has to find, within the total quality domain, opportunities to satisfy people's needs for self-actualization. They can start up easily accessible suggestion systems and encourage all people to use them. They can also launch innovation and reengineering teams that enable people to use their ideas and suggestions to change their own environment and work methods and allow them to take pride in what they accomplish.

While teamwork is to be encouraged, an individual's need for recognition and achievement must not be overlooked. It is possible for systems that encourage suggestions from both individuals and improvement teams to coexist. One very successful business, whose people were highly motivated to achieve total quality, introduced both a suggestion program and total quality teams. To avoid any conflict, everyone could present suggestions on his or her own behalf or through the team. However, the individual who presented an interesting idea would be immediately recognized and rewarded; the idea would then be passed on to the team for implementation. The team that successfully put such an idea into practice would also, in turn, be recognized and rewarded.

A recent study of worker attitudes and behavior was headed by psychologist G. C. Rapaille.[3] Its findings corroborate our contention that workers will produce total quality only to satisfy themselves. "To improve quality," the study says, "it's necessary to get workers to feel they have a personal stake"—to realize, in other words, that they personally stand to win or lose by the outcome of the total quality venture. The study goes on to indicate that American workers are not motivated by step-by-step improvements to increase quality, and it thus advises employers to "Ask for the big leap, rather than for tiny steps." On the other hand, as the study confirms, a big leap forward will not be accepted by people if it is imposed on them; if people are permitted to control and effect change themselves, however, it is likely to be met with a positive attitude.

As far as reinforcement is concerned, the study suggests not only rewarding workers for their achievements but presenting the right type of reward: "Instead of presenting tombstone-like plaques that imply the work is over, companies should reward employees with a new tool that will help them do their job better—a laptop computer, for example. . . . Although workers say they would prefer bonuses, rewarding them with a new tool results in better performance."

Prerequisites for Launching Motivational Programs

There are numerous approaches and techniques that are supposed to be able to motivate personnel to do the *right job* right the first time. However, our experience shows that some do not live up to expectations. Some programs, apparently specifically designed to be motivational, have been fruitless. Does this mean that the theories on motivation are not practicable? To answer that question, let us look at the steps often taken to motivate people. It all begins when someone notices that several errors have resulted in poor quality. The managers react by launching a motivational program, but the situation does not improve. They immediately jump to the conclusion that motivational theories are not as effective as their authors would have us believe.

In order to eliminate human errors, Juran suggests three requisites:

1. Knowing what the individual is supposed to do

2. Knowing what he or she is actually doing

3. Knowing how to correct any errors[4]

Let us point out that if an individual is to produce or contribute to the production of total quality, he or she must first have the knowledge, the skill, and the power or authority to do so and then be willing to do so. These are the four components of the human aspect of achieving total quality (see Figure 7.3).

The *knowledge* concerns the three conditions mentioned above, that is, one must know what to do, what one is doing and what one has done (feedback), then how to correct it if it has been done wrong. Acquiring the necessary knowledge to perform a job involves both education and information. Information concerns the work to be done (what, how, when, and where to do it). It also includes work instructions, procedures, and methods; design and technical specifications; work schedules; and so forth. Feedback information must follow upon this preliminary information. Without feedback, one cannot detect one's errors and is unable to correct them. Finally, information has to do with correction; one must know what to do in case one makes a error. With that knowledge one can correct one's own mistakes or, if company practice so dictates, take the necessary steps to have someone else correct them. Of course, all this information has to be willingly provided, and no motivational technique can possibly make up for the lack of it.

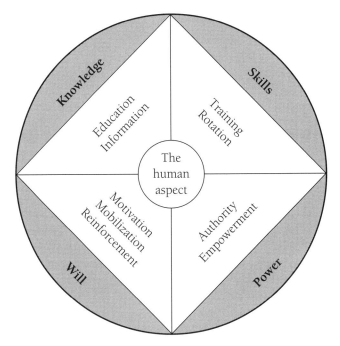

Figure 7.3. Components of the human aspect of achieving total quality.

Still, someone might have all the information required to do a really good job and to correct any possible mistakes, yet continue to make errors because he or she does not have the necessary *skill*. Skill is acquired through training and experience accumulated on the job and through job rotation. You might have a drawing with detailed instructions on an electric installation operation to be carried out, instructions that are easy to follow; you may also know the theory regarding this operation; but if you have not been trained as an electrician you cannot do an acceptable job. If a mistake is thus committed through lack of training, then training in this skill is required, and any motivational technique will be absolutely useless without it.

I should point out that, while skills can be acquired, they can also be inherent as aptitudes—aptitudes which, unfortunately, some people will lack no matter how much instruction or training they receive. Skills can be regarded as having both an innate aspect and an acquired one. The qualities and natural abilities that characterize an individual are innate, whereas the product of training and experience is acquired. To take tennis as an example, someone might know all the rules of the game, as well as the theory and strategy of how to play it (knowledge); might learn to play (through training); but still not have the sufficient experience (acquired skill) to perform well at a tournament. Even after long experience in playing this game, he or she will not necessarily succeed in becoming a competent player if the aptitude (innate skill) is lacking. If, in similar fashion, an employee lacks a necessary skill in the workplace and cannot acquire it despite intensive training, then he or she will have to be moved to another job. Even the greatest motivation cannot wish that skill into being.

Thirdly, one has to have the *power* (that is to say, control over things) or the authority to do or change things. For that, one has to be *empowered*—given the power to do, to improve, to correct, and to innovate. If the individual does not have that right, he or she will not do so. If employees do not have the right to exercise control over their own work, they will not try to spot their errors, let alone correct or prevent them.

The final condition for doing a correct job is the *will* to do it. Anyone who is not motivated to do a good job will not put out the necessary effort to do it. A question often asked by workers is, "What's in it for me?" Why should a worker go out of his or her way to do the job better or in less time? This is where individual motivation and group mobilization come into play. As indicated before, achieving or contributing to total quality must, in the individual's mind, be directly connected to the satisfaction of his or her personal needs.

Before launching a motivational campaign to reduce errors and mistakes, you must, first of all, be sure that the poor quality produced was caused by human error. Obviously, motivation cannot correct errors caused by equipment, machines, or, say, the chemical composition of a material. However, when you are certain that an error is, in fact, a human error, you have to find out where it occurred. Design errors are not corrected on the shop floor, nor can mistakes on the shop floor be redressed at the design stage—hence the importance of localiz-

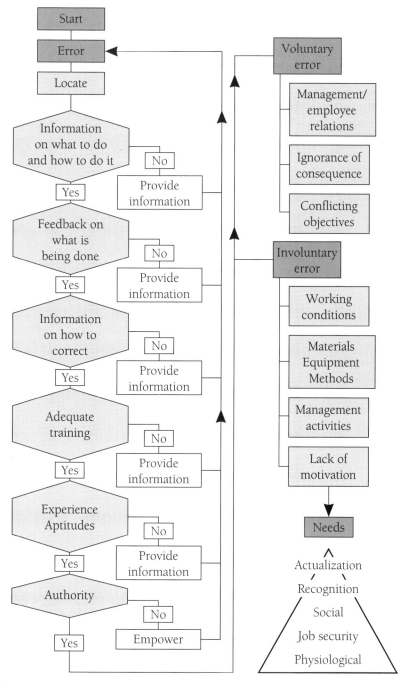

Figure 7.4. The motivational process.

Source: Adapted from J. M. Juran and Frank M. Gryna, ed., *Juran's Quality Control Handbook*, 4th ed. (New York: McGraw-Hill, 1988), 22.53–22.61.

ing the error and addressing the person who made it (see Figure 7.4). Therefore, before launching into motivational activities, you have to be sure that the errors in question can be rectified by motivating the person or group committing the errors.

On-the-Job Satisfaction and Quality

According to Kiechel's[5] findings, on-the-job satisfaction for employees is probably the single most researched topic in the realm of business management—there are more than 7000 studies on the subject, dating back to the early seventeenth century. We tend to believe that the happier the employees are, the more productive they will be, but it seems to be the other way around: The more productive employees are, the happier they are!

Surveys have been conducted among employees to determine the degree of their on-the-job satisfaction. The surveys asked questions like, "Do you like your work?" "Do you like your boss?" "Do you get along with your co-workers?" "Are you satisfied with your wages?" "Do you like your company as a whole?" The results revealed that, in certain cases, a positive correlation existed between employee satisfaction and productivity or quality; in other cases, however, this correlation was negative or even nonexistent.

It has been observed that employees who are constantly in demand demonstrate a level of job satisfaction that is higher than that of those who are less frequently solicited. This is explained by the fact that busy employees have their need for achievement satisfied. A business must therefore present its employees with challenges, both team challenges and the challenge of participation in the decision-making process.

Participative Management

Numerous executives have come to adopt a participative style of management in an endeavor to harness the creative potential of their entire workforce. Along the way, they have gone from an exploitive, authoritarian style of management to a benevolent, authoritarian one. Then they moved on to a consultative approach, before finally evolving into a participative system. In this final stage, objectives that used to be imposed or, at best, presented to the personnel (along with some commentary) are now either established only after discussion with members of the personnel or else directly defined by teamwork.

Participative management is based on a number of principles, namely that

- Participation generates motivation.
- Teamwork is an indispensable element in efficient management.
- The team, as a decision-making unit, is therefore given priority.

- Working in teams requires proper coordination.
- Participative management is based on collaboration between management and the entire workforce, at all levels of the hierarchy.
- Relationships between top management and personnel are based on trust rather than on authority.
- The free circulation of information is encouraged by top management.
- Self-control replaces management by domination.
- The individual is responsible for specific objectives that are in line with the company's objectives.

In this approach, the person at the top of the ladder acts in concert with those on the lower rungs to establish the targets and to assess achievements by comparing them with those that have been forecast. By incorporating the various levels of the hierarchy in this process, a narrow, introversive focus on the part of the departments is avoided. In this way, emphasis is placed on the ultimate objective rather than on the means to achieve it. Within that mandate, there is a freedom to act that fosters individual creativity. I would underline that this kind of management has the advantage of motivating the *empowered* individual, creating a pleasant work climate, and bringing about improved company performance. The major drawback is the possibility that people who do not see their own expectations fulfilled will be frustrated.

In effect, participative management is not really a technique that one can *apply,* but rather a philosophy based on company culture and on the executives' leadership styles. The necessity of providing adequate training to enable people to participate fully in managing the business must not be overlooked. Some versions of participative management have failed mainly because their adherents introduced certain techniques that, from the outset, took no account of the effect of the existing company culture, the style of executive management, or people training. For example, *management by objectives* would have proved impracticable for people untrained in how to determine an objective.

One of the best-known approaches based on participative management and on teamwork is that of *quality circles.* The contemporary context of the total quality approach, however, has seen quality circles give way to continuous improvement and reengineering teams.

Teamwork in Operation: From Quality Circles to Total Quality Teams

It may seem anachronistic today to still be talking about quality circles. They first saw light in Japan at the beginning of the 1960s, and Westerners discovered them in the 1970s, when they were very much in fashion. Every self-respecting company felt compelled to launch into quality circle programs. A virtual tidal wave of quality circles consultants and quality circles associations swept onto the scene in full force and then, within the space of a few years, receded just as fully from view. Today, we still find a few traces of these programs, as well as much disappointment. Because of their failure in our part of the world, there are some companies who do not want to hear any more about total quality, or even quality, let alone quality circles. However, the teamwork notion, which is an integral part of the quality circle program, is essential for the success of the total quality approach.

Total quality teams, which comprise *continuous improvement teams* and *reengineering teams,* have replaced quality circles. This is not simply a change of titles to humor the sensitive feelings of apprehensive companies who have gotten their fingers burnt in the fire. It is a threefold change: the disappearance or significant reduction of voluntary participation, the inclusion of these teams in a global and indivisible approach, and the emphasis put on cross-functional teams using new practices such as *concurrent engineering, quality function deployment,* and *policy deployment* (see chapter 15). Voluntary participation means the choice to participate or not, but no one has the right to choose not to participate in the common and ceaseless effort required in the production of total quality. Moreover, these teams must, perforce, be part of the more global TQM initiative, along with all of its human, logical, and technological components. They are an outgrowth of TQM and not a departure point. That fact must be understood; otherwise there is a great risk of further disappointment. Implementing total quality teams is not synonymous with introducing a TQM process; total quality teams are only a mechanism that allows the firm to bring the TQM process into play, but they are, nevertheless, one of TQM's important elements. Teamwork can fail for three reasons.

1. There is lack of genuine involvement on the part of top management.

2. The team approach is used as a technique to solve specific problems.

3. Teamwork is looked upon as a stop-gap technique to achieve short-term financial gains.

Celebration: A Tool for Reinforcement

During my visits to Japan, I noted that nearly all Japanese operators are members of quality circles. To get to this level of involvement, Japanese executives have to make quality circle activities very visible. They organize events that are highly publicized, not only in the particular department or section in which quality circles operate, but also companywide, regionally, or nationally. To illustrate the means that a Japanese company uses to maintain the interest of its personnel, let us take a look at the Komatsu Corporation (see Figures 7.5 and 7.6).

As we see, this tractor and heavy equipment manufacturer holds three annual meetings dedicated to allowing personnel from the company, its subsidiaries, and

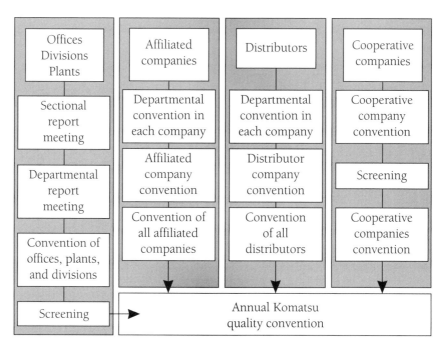

Figure 7.5. Komatsu's quality conventions.

Source: Komatsu Corporation. Reprinted with permission.

its distributors and suppliers to meet and show off the fruits of their endeavors. Komatsu's offices, divisions, and factories also hold quality circles meetings twice a year, and there is an annual general meeting for quality circles in which prizes are awarded to the circles with the best results. Three gold, three silver, and three special awards are presented. There are also six awards for the managerial quality circles at the annual meeting—three awards of excellence and three special awards. Three prizes are awarded for excellence in top management quality circles. Apart from these internal events, Komatsu participates in presenting regional and national awards ceremonies.

I would conclude by saying that total quality teams are one means used to allow company people—in particular front-line workers—to meet formally and regularly to participate in a concrete fashion in the effort to improve quality. The quality improvement and the reengineering teams take this a step further. They target all of the company's people, managerial and nonmanagerial, as participants and reject the notion of voluntary participation (how can one ask the members of a sports team to play only if they feel like it?). They enlarge the arena of team-work-analyzed problems and concerns to include all of the decisions made in the

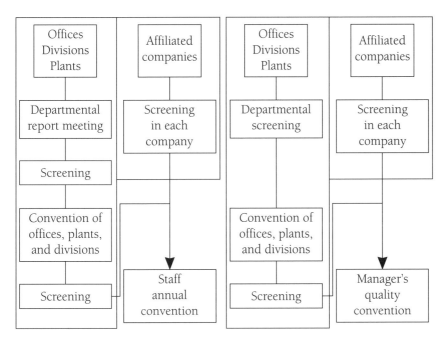

Figure 7.6. Managerial quality circles and Komatsu's top management.

Source: Komatsu Corporation. Reprinted with permission.

company, rather than limiting it—as is the case in quality circles—to problems related solely to the specific type of work that circle members do.

How Does a Team for Total Quality or for Reengineering Work?

Usually, total quality improvement teams, or reengineering teams, have between 4 and 12 members and meet regularly, on average once a week for about an hour. Their meeting room must be located in a quiet area, conducive to work. All of their work must be documented, and someone is chosen to take the minutes of each meeting. Members can take turns doing this task. The team members are free to call in a specialist to help in cases where they need more in-depth information, to identify causes, or to research acceptable solutions. The specialist's contributions should be recorded and given due recognition. Normally, total quality improvement teams are members of the same production or administrative unit, while reengineering teams are of a more cross-functional nature.

Other Types of Teamwork

While traditional quality circles or problem-solving teams can improve quality and reduce costs, their members have no authority to make decisions or effect important changes. According to Hoerr, some companies have expanded the concept of quality circles and set up groups or work teams with specific, designated responsibilities.[6] Teams such as these have been charged with designing and introducing new methods and technologies, organizing meetings with suppliers and customers, and coordinating different departments. In unionized companies, executives and the union collaborate in making operations-related decisions.

Hoerr observes that in North America, to be really effective, the teamwork must involve some participation in decision making and in actual management and not be limited to problem solving, as is the case with quality circles. Self-managing work teams, made up of between 5 and 15 employees, are assigned the entire responsibility for a product. Its members are able to carry out all of the tasks connected with the product and take turns performing these tasks. In addition, the team takes on the responsibility of planning and scheduling work, its members' vacations, and production-related purchases.

Organizations using this type of teamwork have seen a 30 percent increase in productivity and substantial improvement in product quality. It is a question of molding the organization into a horizontal shape, where there is no need for supervisors. Employees are, in effect, their own bosses. This type of teamwork, it seems, should be spreading. According to Hoerr, it is the organizational shape of the future for those who want to be, and remain, competitive.

Team Spirit

The notion of common objectives creates team spirit—an indispensable ingredient in the achievement of total quality—as everyone can share the pride of meeting challenges and achieving objectives together. At the very beginning of my professional life, I worked in the merchant navy. I observed that, on any given ship, there were groups that were practically autonomous. Navigation or deck officers made sure that the ship stayed on course, keeping themselves busy using maps, compasses, dividers, and sextants. Engineer officers spent their time making sure that the engines ran smoothly and were maintained correctly. Others looked after the galleys and administration. Everyone had his or her own problems, and no one dared step foot into another's territory. A lost map was the exclusive problem of the deck officers, a burnt meal was the responsibility of the cook, a squeaking engine was looked after by the engineers, and a passenger's lost passport was dealt with by the purser. People would commonly dismiss a great number of problems as not being *their* problems.

Members of the different groups were living among themselves, rarely socializing with each other. Actually, there was an unspoken antagonism among the groups, as the deck officers, with the captain of the ship at their head, thought of themselves as the masters of the vessel (the captain of the ship is, indeed, called the *master*). The engineer officers were frustrated because they were convinced that they were the most important people on board. Their job of running the complex engines of big liners was no small task, quite unlike that—or so they thought—of the immaculate, white-uniformed deck officers who spent their time gazing idly at the stars and playing with maps.

One day, while crossing the Atlantic Ocean, the ship sprang a serious leak in one of the cargo holds. For once in my sea life, I noticed that no one on board suggested that the leak was not *his* problem. Suddenly, the whole crew had a common problem, one of survival. Instantaneously, a spirit of collaboration was born. Rank or authority mattered no longer. The question now was one of having the appropriate skills to contribute to the solution. Uniforms, stripes, and titles were put aside, and officers and crew sat around a table to share ideas and suggestions without regard to rank or position. Strangely, with no previous discussion, everyone around the table—including the now uniformless, stripeless master of the ship—looked silently and respectfully at the chief engineer, not because of his title or his rank but because he was perceived as the most competent and skilled person available to solve the common problem.

The problem was solved, and the atmosphere on board ship was never the same again. A very strong sense of belonging to the same team had been instilled into all shipmates, officers and crew alike. They made an undeclared, unanimous decision to wear their uniforms only for official occasions. I have often recalled this incident as I have worked in companies and deplored the absence of an objective or common challenge that would unite its members. Yet it is this situation that I continue to see, and it brings home what that incident taught me: When different departments or groups in an organization systematically segregate and cloister themselves, energy is wasted. Many times I have dreamt of being able to pierce a hole in the company's hull to make everyone realize that they all have a common objective and that everyone is working for the same cause—to survive together.

To further emphasize this point, let me go back to the example that I presented in chapter 3, in which I visited a hospital where several of the managers themselves admitted that the words *patient* or *sick person* were never mentioned in their mission statement: the buyer bought, the computer specialist computed, the accountant accounted, the human resources manager hired and trained, the storekeeper looked after the inventory, and the chefs did the cooking. They were amazed when I asked them if they had ever had any patients in that hospital—the patients who should have been their common and only goal. Recently, a reengineering/total quality coordinator at a large railway company confided to me that the biggest discovery that the people in his century-old organization had made was that they had customers! He said that they had thought they were there because of trains, wagons, locomotives, tracks, cargo—and nothing else. It was a cultural shock, he admitted.

Working toward total quality is, in effect, a common cause that can unify everyone, regardless of prejudices, complexes about superiority or inferiority, or stripes and uniforms. People have to take off the blinkers that limit them to a view of only their own work. They must start to consider what contribution they can make toward accomplishing the common objectives—a quality life for all of the people in the organization achieved through profitability, total customer satisfaction, external partnerships, and concern for the environment and society in general.

In effect, the common objective in the total quality approach is a return to the concept upon which the artisan–customer relationship was based (see Figure 7.7). In days gone by, artisans dealt directly with their customers. They would choose their suppliers, their own work methods, their raw materials, and their co-workers. Today's artisans, now turned into employees or workers in the traditional and pyramidal type of organization, no longer focus on the customer. Lost in a sea of other employees and workers, crushed under the heavy hierarchy of big, intermediate, and little bosses, today's artisans maintain no contact with the suppliers of human resources, material resources, or financial resources. They have no connection with company backers, shareholders, or taxpayers. The only link that the company has with the customer is through the marketing and sales department. Even these departments are separated from the customer by a host of intermediaries: distributors, wholesalers, retailers, carriers, warehousers, and installers. Many companies do not know exactly who their customers are!

As we indicated above, the total quality approach proposes the concept of *market-in;* namely, bringing the notion of customer back into the company. Each employee must know that he or she is working for the customer, who is the company's real boss. The traditional approach, where the marketing department is the only department that knows and keeps in contact with customers, must give way and allow the cult of the customer to permeate through the entire business.

Let us again recall the manager of the cardboard box manufacturing plant mentioned earlier. He now tells all of the employees in his plant about any negotiations in progress with potential customers and indicates which manufacturers are competing for certain contracts. He also organizes meetings between his plant people and the customers. When he wins a contract, he lets all the people know about it, and they all share the joy of the victory. When a competitor gets a contract that the manager had been going after, he lets everyone know that, too, and they all share in the disappointment. When open communication, where everyone is informed of what is happening, replaces the notion of privileged information—that is to say, information that is distributed only to those who need it for their immediate work—a feeling of belonging to the company is created which is greatly appreciated among employees.

At John Deere, hourly workers now periodically visit farms to meet customers, see how they use equipment, and better assess their needs. Many workers travel across North America explaining John Deere's new products to dealers and farmers. Like an increasing number of companies, Deere figures that assembly line workers, with their intimate knowledge of the equipment, make a powerful

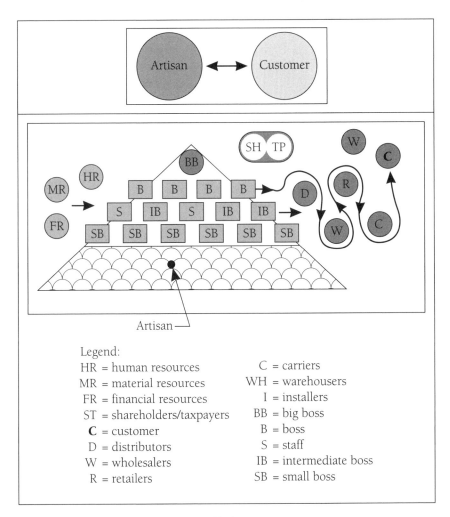

Legend:
HR = human resources
MR = material resources
FR = financial resources
ST = shareholders/taxpayers
C = customer
D = distributors
W = wholesalers
R = retailers

C = carriers
WH = warehousers
I = installers
BB = big boss
B = boss
S = staff
IB = intermediate boss
SB = small boss

Figure 7.7. Traditional relationship with the customer.

marketing team. In addition, Deere has begun an experimental program in which hourly workers' pay raises are tied to the completion of technical courses and the demonstration of their new skills on the job.[7]

Team Building[8]

Teamwork is essential to achieving total quality. However, merely organizing employees into teams is not enough. They have to learn how to work as a team, hence the very important role that team building plays in implementing TQM. It is an organizational development technique whose aim is to increase the efficiency of work teams within the organization. It is, in effect, a kind of apprenticeship for working as a team within participative management. The team-building exercise depends on everyone collaborating and participating to the utmost and is built on the assumption that all members of the team have mutual respect.

Before beginning to use team-building techniques, it would be wise to examine the qualities that make a team function well. The prevailing atmosphere in an efficient team is relaxed, everyone is at ease, and no one is unduly concerned. The discussions are lively and centered on the task at hand, and everyone participates. If the discussion ranges off the topic, someone quickly brings it back on track. Everybody understands and accepts what the task is, because open discussion to decide on the objective precedes the meeting and, thus, ensures that all team members feel fully involved. Members listen to each other. They don't jump from one topic to another, yet they are not afraid of making outlandish suggestions. The team copes with disagreements and does not seek to avoid conflicts. Disagreements are neither passed over in silence nor eliminated. The team seeks to resolve disagreement rather than suppress those who disagree.

Decisions are reached by a consensus which must be large enough to be considered acceptable as a team decision. Teams rarely use a formal vote. Criticism is frequent, frank, and spontaneous; it does not take the form of either open or veiled personal attack. Team members are free to examine their own feelings and ideas on problems or about team activity. The person who directs the discussion does not use his or her authority to squash the team, and the team does not allow him or her too much authority. Power struggles are rare. The problem at hand is knowing how the work is to be done rather than knowing who is in command.

Groups whose members have no experience in teamwork are often ineffective, and for them team building is an excellent apprenticeship tool. It is a formal means of making team members communicate about the way they interact as a team as well as about the tasks to be accomplished. People often find this apprenticeship stage difficult because, ordinarily, they would rarely be asked to express what they like or dislike about their interactions with their superiors or equals. Nevertheless, this type of apprenticeship is invaluable in situations fraught with latent tension or open conflict, because these are situations that lead to loss of human potential (in the guise of resignations, inhibition of creativity, lack of collaboration, and either interdepartmental or interpersonal rivalry) and are clearly obstacles to be circumvented on the path to total quality.

Mobilization and Reinforcement

To mobilize means to make something mobile, make it move, put it into motion. For some people, it also means to keep something in motion. I note, however, that there is a tendency to neglect the second part of the definition, that is, *to keep something in motion*. Some businesses put a lot of effort into the initial phases of launching, setting up, and implementing their total quality process but only realize too late that, with time, interest in the approach dies unless they continually fan its flame. In an effort to avoid this danger and reduce that ever-present risk, I have chosen to label the initial sensitization activity—whose intent is to trigger and stimulate everybody's interest in total quality—as *mobilization* and the activities intended to keep this interest continuously alive afterwards as *reinforcement*. The dictionary clearly tells us that to reinforce means to reward an action or response so that it becomes more likely to occur again. To use a common analogy with the automobile, one could say that the starter acts as mobilization, and the spark plugs are the reinforcement that provide impetus for the engine to turn continuously. I would do well to note, too, that when the spark plugs cease to receive electricity, the engine stops.

In a military context, mobilization can mean the call to serve under the national flag, be it by conscription or as a volunteer. Or again, it can mean to raise the troops' enthusiasm before launching an attack on the enemy. In the context of total quality, the objective of mobilization is to convince the troops—the entire workforce at all levels of the hierarchy—that this approach is useful, necessary, and indispensable to improving their quality of life (that is, their salaries, safety, sense of challenge, their feeling of belonging to a winning team, and their personal and family life). It must also demonstrate that this quality of life is attainable when one succeeds in exceeding the customers' expectations, which success translates into company profit that, in turn, translates into a quality return on investment for the shareholder. Finally, it also demonstrates that the shareholders, through their representatives—the company's executives—are able and anxious to offer the people the aforesaid quality of life. And the wheel continues to turn. . . .

Reinforcement occurs as activities are undertaken to keep this wheel in motion, namely to keep ensuring that the customers are more than satisfied and that the shareholders are happy with the dividends they collect. The people who have met the challenge of providing satisfaction must be recognized and rewarded. It should be noted that, just like total quality itself, reinforcement is not a program, but rather a continuous *process*. It must be kept in mind that people need constant leadership from the company's executives if they are to retain the lively enthusiasm that was triggered earlier. Executive leaders have to demonstrate through their behavior a firm and unfailing conviction that the total quality approach does indeed have all the advantages claimed for it. The common expression "walk your talk," meaning "practice what you preach," underscores the fact that behavior has a much greater influence on personnel than speeches.

In studying the use of recognition in the total quality approach, a committee at a public electrical utility in Canada found that companies working toward total quality give considerable weight to the practices involving recognition, and this includes spontaneous recognition on the job and making quality improvement teams visible. Recognition has always been part of sound management, but what is new about it is that companies who use the total quality approach recognize teams in addition to individuals. What is more, it appears that the celebratory aspect of recognition is essential, because the sharing and rejoicing after a team's success acts as a mobilizing agent within the company.

Team recognition should be highlighted, but not at the expense of recognition for the individual. The manager must know how to acknowledge work well done as well as diligence and behavior in keeping with the spirit of the total quality philosophy. I should also mention another possible source of resentment in the practice of team recognition. In instances in which teams have received recognition for a particularly important achievement, I have noticed that there is concomitant danger or risk involved if company managers have made that recognition without prior consultation with employees. The members of other teams may regard this recognition as unjust. This creates dissatisfaction and frustration, if not outright apathy, among these people. I always recommend that employees be allowed to evaluate the work that is to be recognized, although it is the manager who will make the recognition. When this is done, neither top management nor its representatives can be accused of unfairness or partiality.

Mobilizational Levers

In a seminar on total quality, Alain Rondeau, from the business school of the University of Montreal, presented four mobilization levers. He defines mobilization activities as "a set of management practices which are capable of influencing the intensity, persistence and direction of effort put out by the workers."[9] Reinforcement is obviously part and parcel of his definition. These *levers* take the form of information, appreciation, appropriation (the feeling of ownership over one's work), and identification with the company (see Figure 7.8).

1. *Information.* Before people can take their work and organization to heart, they must have a good understanding of what is expected of them, and they must also feel that the organization listens to their concerns and tries to respond to them. Management therefore has to set up an extensive and effective method of communicating information to the employees. This will underline the importance of openness of communication and show the respect that the company holds for its people. Activities that can be effective in this respect are meetings with the president, information sessions, audiovisual presentations, lectures, company newsletters, meetings between supervisors and employees, and surveys on the work climate.

2. *Appreciation.* The employees take their work and organization to heart if they feel that their contributions ultimately benefit them as much as the organization. This perception has to be fostered by directly associating the people's interests with the organization's results, and this must be done on all fronts. All people have to see that the company's results satisfy their interests on financial and symbolic levels as well as individual and collective levels. With regard to incentives—rewards and recognition—when the company's results are evaluated, care must be

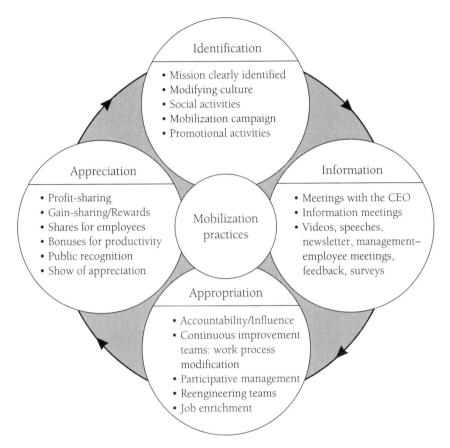

Figure 7.8. The four levers of mobilization.

exercised to consider only that part of the company's performance that is directly affected by the personnel and not that due to outside factors, such as an adverse world or national economic situation.

This lever brings out the importance of both the sharing of benefits and the appreciation of efforts made. Among the incentives practiced are profit- or gain-sharing, employee shareholding schemes, performance-based bonuses, public recognition, and mechanisms for expressing appreciation.

3. *Appropriation* (the feeling of ownership over one's work). Individuals also take their work and organization to heart if they feel effective and responsible for the results they obtain. The importance of meaningful work must be brought out by setting the employees in a system where work is divided rationally, so that they can see the logic, purpose, and utility of their work with respect to the end product or service delivered to the customers they are supposed to satisfy and delight.

The work assigned should implicate the customers just as much in the planning of objectives as in the control of results. People must be able to have a genuine impact on their work by being included in the decision-making process and by having both the autonomy and the right to take initiative. Furthermore, the notion of accountability can be properly brought to bear only after the employees are empowered, that is to say, given the authority to act.

Activities that promote a feeling of ownership of the work process include total quality teams, semi-autonomous groups, job enrichment, workplace layout, participative management, and quality improvement processes.

4. *Identification.* People take their work and organization to heart, as well, if they feel important to the company and if they share the values that it exhibits. This requires undertaking efforts to increase the pride that the workers have in their company and to induce them to be actively involved in its life. It also requires fostering the emergence of a system of values that target the results desired. This lever plays on the importance of the employees' feelings of belonging and their sharing of the company's values.

Activities that promote this feeling of attachment include the company mission statement, changes in the company culture, social activities, mobilization meetings, and promotional activities.

Comparing the Japanese with the American Approach

It has been long thought that there is a Japanese way of doing things based on cultural factors that cannot be duplicated outside of Japan. However, it has been observed that the Japanese-owned manufacturing facilities in the United States apply the same management approach toward American workers as they do toward their own and that this seems to result in high productivity and employee loyalty.

A study of practices in the United States and Japan found that Japanese-style management and employment methods, whether practiced by Japanese or U.S. plants, produce very similar gains in employee work attitudes.[10] These include cohesive work groups, participatory (but not delegated) decision making, and company-sponsored services.

The study found that Japanese supervisors seem to function as counselors and confidantes to their work groups, building communication and cohesion with a minimum of direct, authoritarian control. It also shows that, in both Japan and the United States, services offered to employees—social services, exercise facilities, and social activities—sometimes viewed by Westerners as being paternalistic, actually significantly improve employee motivation.

Although we must recognize the great difference between American and Japanese cultures, we cannot dismiss all Japanese management practices as being culture oriented and continue to think that anything that does not originate in the United States cannot be applied.

Skill-Based Pay: A New Strategic Option[11]

With the advent of the global marketplace, many firms have been forced to find ways of making themselves more competitive. Many organizations have been compelled to make drastic structural changes, the most telling of which are the reductions in hierarchical levels and personnel. Furthermore, the frequent changes in technological and operating processes have created a greater demand for more highly skilled people capable of learning new skills rapidly.

These conditions, as they emerged, have led companies to pay greater attention to the methods they use for deciding compensation and to question how well these methods suit their own organizations. This was how some of the traditional pay methods—notably the systems that base pay on the relative value of jobs and on the principle of seniority—came under scrutiny. The new method that has now emerged is *skill-based pay* (SBP).

With a teamwork approach, companies have increasingly begun to adopt this system. To put it very simply, traditionally, if a company needed 60 hours a week welding capacity and 20 hours a week electrical-work capacity, it would hire two welders and one electrician (because it could not hire half a worker). However, under a pay-by-skill scheme, the company would hire a welder (single skill) and an electrician–welder (double skill). The latter would be paid more since he or she has more skills. Now the welder would weld for 40 hours a week, while the electrician–welder would weld for 20 hours and do electrical work for 20 hours. The second worker has saved the company the need for a third person.

SBP systems are known under various names: knowledge pay, skill-based pay, and multi-skills pay systems. No matter what title is used, a skill-based pay method is usually defined as a pay system in which the individuals are paid for the number, type, or depth of the skills they have developed. In practice, in this type of program, the pay is determined by the variety of skills acquired or by the number of jobs that an employee is able to master. The more skills the employee acquires, the higher his or her wage will be. The underlying intent of this pay system is to encourage employees to acquire new skills, new knowledge, and increased versatility.

Essentially, there are three forms of skill development in an SBP system: vertical, horizontal, and specialized skills. When an organization adopts a *vertical skills* plan, it zeros in on the learning skills or the upstream or downstream knowledge that are connected to one or several functions. For an employee in a lower grade job, that can mean acquiring more technical skills or even acquiring management skills (in planning, organizing, and leading meetings, for example).

Horizontal skills plans are the most frequently used, and their aim is to offer employees the possibility of acquiring a multitude of very diverse skills that are relatively alike in terms of degree of difficulty. It may be a question of learning of all the activities associated with a work team or perhaps mastering all the activities leading to the production of goods or services.

The intent behind *specialized skills* plans is to enable employees to acquire skills or knowledge in a more narrow field of activities and develop a greater depth in each skill. This type of plan is not new and is fairly widely used in trades and highly technical jobs (for example, engineering).

Large companies as well known as Chrysler, General Foods, Johnson & Johnson, General Motors, Procter & Gamble, Northern Telecom, Honeywell, Polaroid, and General Mills, to name only a few, are said to have implemented this type of pay method.

The Differences Between Skill-Based Pay and Traditional Pay

As indicated in the preceding section, companies have two options: paying for jobs according to their value or paying individuals according to their skills. There are marked differences between these two approaches (see Table 7.1.)

Numerous reasons are given to justify implementing a skill-based pay system, but they fall into two major categories.

1. To produce greater flexibility in the workforce

2. To produce better quality products and services

Skill-based pay	Traditional pay
Linked to the person.	Linked to the job.
A list of skills.	A specific job.
Pay is a function of the capacity to master the skill.	Pay is a function of the position held at a given moment in time.
Pay increases depend on the individual demonstrating his mastery of the skills. Possible skill certification of employees.	Increases usually depend on seniority and sometimes on merit.
Usually wages do not increase when individual changes jobs.	Increases are usually automatic when individual changes jobs.
This plan encourages horizontal mobility.	This plan encourages vertical mobility or change of wage class.
The opportunities for advancement are greater.	Reaches a ceiling rapidly, in terms of both structure and content.
It is an in-house plan, suited to the organization.	The plan is more general and universal.

Table 7.1. Differences between skill-based pay and traditional pay based on job evaluation.

SBP increases functional flexibility. It enables the company to counteract the effects of absenteeism, overtime, personnel turnover, and training, because any available person can fill in any gaps that occur. Workforce flexibility is also a valuable instrument that contributes to the organization's capacity to adapt to changes in customers' needs by introducing changes in technology, production procedures, or even product lines.

It has also been observed that, with a skill-based pay system, mobility becomes much easier between the various jobs on the same team or in the same department. SBP undoubtedly represents one of the most appropriate means of blending *pay* and *total quality*. In fact, it seems that organizations devoted to total quality are significantly more inclined to resort to skill-based pay methods. Several writers also report that they have seen better quality in products produced under this new compensation strategy. SBP provides workers with better understanding of the operations, which, in turn, facilitates problem solving and better decision making. For example, people will have a greater ability to anticipate the problems that can arise during a product's or service's stages of production. Moreover, as a result of their varied training, members of a team working under a skill-based pay regime have a greater feeling of responsibility for quality.

These plans offer employees more opportunities for growth and professional and personal development and can also reinforce their feelings of personal advancement and self-worth. This concept can improve the quality of life and motivation in the workplace and increases employee satisfaction and attraction to the job. Employees involved in these programs are better satisfied because they perceive that there is greater equity in the level and administration of wages. There is also a greater sense of job security. (Actually, this security is often granted in return for employees' acceptance of this system of compensation.) Finally, there is less possibility in these programs of reaching a wage ceiling in a job. Job rotation, basic to SBP systems, gives employees variety and can minimize their feelings of having reached the upper limits of their jobs or careers.

The Training Program Leading to Total Quality

TQM is introduced into a company by means of a program that provides training in the TQM philosophy, process, and techniques, accompanied by sessions in awareness and familiarization. These sessions last between half a day and five days and may be offered as in-house or external courses, given by company personnel or external resources. All people, starting with the members of top management, must attend one of these sessions. Presentations for top management usually last for half a day or a day, whereas the other sessions are more comprehensive.

The management committee, coordinator, total quality facilitators, union representatives, and functional specialists are all made aware of the necessity for achieving total quality. They are taught the basic concepts of total quality along with the processes and the techniques used to identify, solve, and prevent problems, all of which they will need as participants of continuous quality improvement and reengineering teams. Coordinators and facilitators generally receive their training in externally organized courses and seminars.

Conclusion

When introducing and practicing total quality, the human element is the principal factor. The whole edifice is built on and buttressed by its human foundations. The rational and technical aspects will be useless unless all company people at all levels in all sectors are fully committed to the process of quality improvement.

Total quality teams are a valuable means of ensuring that all personnel participate in this process, but there are requisites that affect the results. Most importantly, people should no more be divided into categories like *management* and *employees* or considered a resource to be managed and exploited.

Managers, trade unions, and employees are just beginning to realize that the future belongs to those who will be able to change. Neither transition nor change is easy, but results do show that it is possible if people have the will, the knowledge, and the power to accomplish it.

Review Questions

1. There is evidence all over the world that successful companies have been able to achieve, maintain, and develop total quality by involving all of their personnel and managers in the total quality improvement and reengineering process. How does one go about doing this?

2. Most of the quality circle programs implemented in North America have not been successful. Their failure is often attributed to cultural factors. What do you think of that conclusion? Are there any other reasons for these failures?

3. How does the notion of market-in differ from the more traditional marketing? What are its advantages?

4. Several management theorists and practitioners claim that certain approaches can be used only in Japan. They go so far as to claim that the quality the Japanese produce is more a product of their culture than of their management style. What are your comments on this?

5. In the total quality triad, the company executive must satisfy the company's customers, shareholders, and people. How can he or she do all this?

Notes

1. Marshall Loeb, "Empowerment that Pays Off," *Fortune,* 20 March 1995, 145–146.

2. Thomas A. Stewart, "Rate Your Readiness to Change," *Fortune,* 7 February 1994, 106–110.

3. See "Developments to Watch," William D. Marbach, ed. "Quality: What Motivates American Workers," *Business Week,* 12 April 1993, 93.

4. J. M. Juran, *Quality Control Handbook* (New York: McGraw-Hill, 1974).

5. Walter Kiechel III, "How Important Is Morale, Really?" *Fortune,* 13 February 1989, 121–122.

6. John Hoerr, "The Payoff From Teamwork," *Business Week,* 10 July 1989, 56–62.

7. Kevin Kelly, "The New Soul of John Deere," *Business Week,* 31 January 1994), 64–66.

8. Jocelyn Bérard, "La consolidation d'équipe," *Qualité* 11, no. 4 (Winter 1990–1991): 11–13.

9. Alain Rondeau, "Four Mobilization Levers" (paper presented at Seminar on Total Quality, HEC Business School, University of Montreal, Montreal, Quebec, Canada, October 1992).

10. James R. Lincoln, "Employee Work Attitudes and Management Practice in the U.S. and Japan: Evidence from a Large Comparative Survey," *California Management Review* (Fall 1989): 89–106.

11. Michel Tremblay, "Rémuneration des compétences: une nouvelle option stratégique," *Info Ressources Humaines,* (Quebec 1993): 21–23.

Chapter 8

You cannot apply yesterday's tools today and expect to stay in business tomorrow.

Planning for Total Quality

In a nutshell, the intent of the planning activity is to establish objectives and determine the best means to achieve them. The total quality–oriented planning process must invariably take into account all of the shareholders', the customers', and the company's people's needs simultaneously, as well as any environmental issues, so that they can be fully satisfied or dealt with. Figure 8.1 illustrates this planning activity.

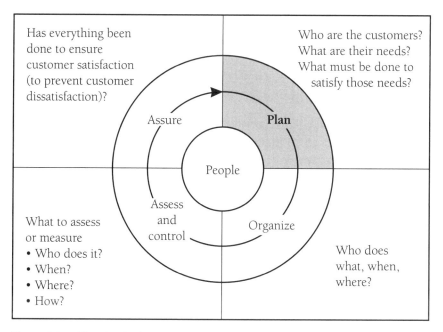

Figure 8.1. Planning in the management cycle.

Culture, Vision, Values, and Philosophy

In order to achieve total quality, a company has to change. This change goes far beyond altering a method or modifying a process. It is, at first, a change in culture that is required; all other major changes will then follow from that. *Culture* is the way things have always been done in a company. It is tradition and habits; it is an accepted, or even sought after, management and workforce behavior. It is a vision of the future and a set of mostly unwritten values. It is partly inherited, partly effected by people who exercise an influence on and in the company: the founders, the owners or major shareholders, top management, old-timers (managers or nonmanagers), and newcomers. The culture of a company is generally reflected and made tangible in its policies, which are essential to the planning process. These plans translate finally into action (see Figure 8.2).

Ideally, company executives—top management and middle management, as well as front-line management and supervisors—all share the same long-term global *vision* of their organization and of the environment in which they have to live and thrive. Consequently, every action they take will be inspired by and geared to this vision. As the owner of a small business told me recently, "My vision is a long-term dream that I have of my business, 5 or 10 years from now—a dream that I want to share and experience with all my people." When Coca-Cola started, it had a vision: *to quench the thirst of a nation.* And that goes much further

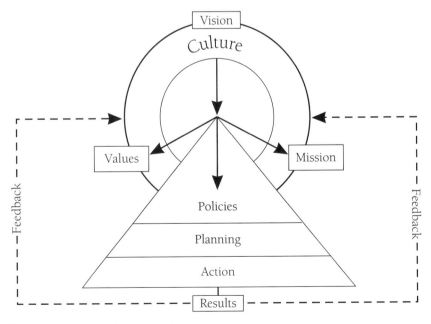

Figure 8.2. From culture to action.

than merely manufacturing herb-based soft drinks.[1] A Canadian paint manufacturer claims that his mission is to *beautify and protect the world,* thus underlining the two uses of paint, that is, to both please the eye and protect against the vagaries of weather or time.

A vision, however, is more than a cleverly worded slogan or a few nicely turned phrases. It involves imagining the market as it might be 5 or 10 years down the road and foreseeing where your competitors will be. But even beyond anticipating what might be, a vision amounts to inventing the future so that you can carve out the place you would want to occupy in it.

In companies as prestigious as GM and IBM, it was the top management's vision—in this case, a nearsighted one—that affected performance to such a large degree and caused the loss of a huge part of their market since the 1970s. Cocksure and blinkered by the success they had enjoyed for several decades, it seems that they saw the future unfolding as smoothly as in the past. In their vision, they would continue to reign supreme and unchallenged over their industry. GM, IBM, and many other huge corporations thought that they alone were able to determine customer needs, that they alone would design the products offered to fulfill them, and that they alone would dictate the standards that would be imposed on the rest of the industry worldwide. A vision based on false assumptions, indeed! In the case of GM, it worked as long as it did only because nowhere in the world was there any competition to be reckoned with until the 1970s.

Another example illustrating the importance of vision features the director of a printing company that I consulted with. The company specialized in the very complex process of printing lottery tickets. This director had to decide whether he viewed himself as a printing specialist or as a specialist in games of chance. If he chose to see himself as a printing specialist—and if games of chance started evolving, as seems to be the trend, toward a video format—he would sooner or later be faced with the problem of either having to close shop or finding other products to print. On the other hand, if he chose to view himself as a specialist in games of chance, he could end up producing something that had nothing to do with printing! His vision will therefore radically affect the type of business he is to be managing in the not-too-distant future.

It is thus plain to see that the philosophy of a company will affect the way it does everything, from its planning activities to its entire management process. Based on their vision, a number of German companies choose to produce quality at any cost, while many Japanese companies elect to produce quality at minimum cost, and still others—the majority of North American companies—produce quality at reasonable cost. Now, due to the fierce Japanese competition, Germans have started to think about quality at minimum cost as well.

Values emerge from top management's vision of the company's future. Top managers have to formalize and disseminate their vision as well as their values and ensure that they are shared by all and applied in all parts of the organization. What total quality–oriented organizations value are their customers, stockholders, and people; their upstream and downstream partners; and the protection and enhancement of the environment. Even if profits are the ultimate goal of any for-profit organization, total quality–driven companies will, by also emphasizing customer and people satisfaction, demonstrate their commitment to fairness to all three stakeholders.

Formal and official documents, policies, and directives should reflect these values, as should top managers in their attitudes, words, and actions. The company has to identify the kind of communication and plans that will best allow these values to be disseminated internally and externally.

In brief, culture consists of

1. A global, long-term *vision* of what the company wants to be: for example, "Number one thirst quencher of America" (Coca-Cola); "Number two but trying hard" (Avis); "The document company" (Xerox)

2. A set of *values* establishing the elements that must be adhered to when running the business: for example, a company that people love to do business with; a company that people love to work in; a company that you can always trust; a company that cares (about the customer, the environment, the society).

3. A *mission,* that, taking into hand the long-term goals expressed in a more general form by the company's vision, shapes them into explicit, concrete, and practical terms: for example, offering its customers (identified if possible—car owners, families, school-age children, teenagers, working mothers) good products (nutritious food, reliable cars, safe equipment) and its people a quality life; maintaining good relations with its outside partners; and ensuring its shareholders a quality return on their investment.

Culture—which comprises vision, values, and mission—is not a static concept or reality; it evolves with time and changes, often gradually but sometimes noticeably and abruptly. Cultural changes result from a constant feedback—whether formal or informal, conscious or unconscious—from the results of the culture, as illustrated in Figure 8.2. The process of translating the culture of the company into actions is illustrated in more elaborate detail in Figure 8.3.

Launching the Planning Process

As indicated in the preceding section, planning aims at materializing, in the long and short term, the vision, values, mission, and policies of the company. Planning begins with a diagnosis that leads to the establishment of the total quality objectives. Clearly, these objectives must be in line with the company's mission. Then a number of strategies that might best achieve such objectives are identified, considered, and narrowed down. The one that is most effective and suitable, given the company's available resources and constraints, is chosen. A plan of action is

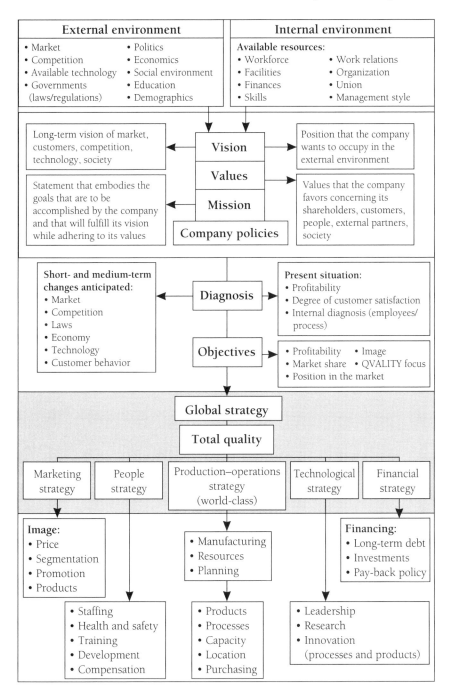

Figure 8.3. From vision to operational activities.

then developed to outline in detail all of the activities, the allocation of resources, the time schedules to be met, and the budget required to achieve the strategy adopted. When this plan is put into effect, a monitoring process is set up in order to ensure that the plan is adhered to and executed as outlined. A contingency plan is also prepared in case the plan originally chosen encounters any difficulties when put into action (see Figure 8.4).

As presented here, it would seem as though the planning process necessarily evolves in a logical and chronological order that starts with a total quality diagnosis and ends with the execution of the plan of action. In practice, this is not the case. In fact, the planning process is a never-ending, iterative process that often retraces its steps or goes back and forth between them. For example, when the total quality objectives are established, it may become evident that not all the information required on a certain aspect is available because the aspect was not studied in sufficient depth during the quality diagnosis. In that case, the diagnosis is reviewed in order to complete the information. Similarly, at the strategy-development stage, if it becomes apparent that some objectives are not easily attainable, these should be revised and, possibly, a whole new set of objectives established.

While this planning process is obviously used for the company as a whole, it is also used by each of its individual sectors and departments. Now let us look in detail at each of the activities that make up this process.

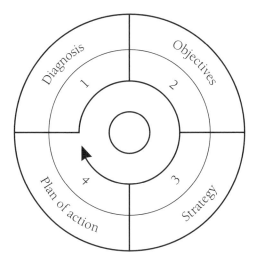

Figure 8.4. The planning process.

Source: Adapted from J. N. Kelada, *Comprendre et réaliser la qualité totale,* 2nd ed. (Dollard-des-Ormeaux, Quebec, Canada: Quafec publications, 1992), 72. Reprinted with permission.

Total Quality Diagnosis: Where Do We Stand?

Total quality diagnosis is one of the most important activities in any TQM improvement and/or reengineering project. It consists of researching all total quality–related facts, inside and outside the company, in order to assess where the company stands and where it is heading. It is comprised of the following six components.

1. Measuring the degree of satisfaction of the owner–shareholders of the company. This is not only limited to their financial needs and expectations, but also includes all nonfinancial elements, especially for small, family-owned companies. Examples of these nonfinancial elements include

- The pride of owning a successful or well-known company
- The satisfaction of being associated with a company that is recognized as a leader in its field
- The social influence the firm has in its community, state, or country.

2. Measuring the degree of satisfaction or dissatisfaction of the customers, whether they are actual or potential users of the firm's products, goods, or services. Potential customers are those who are not buying the product but could be, or who are buying it from the competition. What the company wants to know is why customers are not buying its products or using its services.

3. Measuring the degree of satisfaction or dissatisfaction of the people in the company, management and nonmanagement alike. This includes elements such as work content, challenges, working conditions, compensation (wages, salaries, fringe benefits), the perception and appreciation of the management style, rewards and recognition, work relations, the people's trust in top management, the relative importance of total quality for the people and for the company (as perceived by the people), and management–employee relationships.

4. Assessing the effectiveness of the company's systems, methods, procedures, facilities, equipment, tooling, and so on.

5. Evaluating the relationship with external partners, upstream and downstream. These include suppliers of goods and services (raw materials, components, supplies, banking and other financial services), suppliers of management and nonmanagement people (employment agencies, universities, colleges), carriers, security personnel, distributors, wholesalers, retailers, and so on. The evaluation includes their views on total quality and on the importance of good, trustful, and long-term relationships with the company.

6. Measuring the degree of caring for the environmental issues directly related to the business of the company (air, water, and noise pollution; green spaces; ozone layer preservation; preservation of species; and so on) and the results obtained from actions in this field.

It might seem obvious that one has to start by knowing one's customers, but we have often found that, although companies might think they know their customers, they really do not. Let us make it clear that, by *customers,* we include not only *actual* but also *potential* customers. Potential customers may be those who do not know the company's products and services, or those who may know them but deal with competitors; they also may be former customers who, for one reason or another which one must determine, have ceased to patronize the company. The potential customers can be classified as *possible* and *probable* clients. The objective will therefore be to convert possible customers into probable customers and probable customers into actual customers.

Besides knowing *who* one's customers are, one must erase any confusion about *what* a customer is. Companies have to recognize and separate the true customer conceptually from others who are not customers. It has to be stressed that a company should not consider distributors, wholesalers, retailers, or agents as customers, although they are the ones who initially decide to buy (or not to buy) the company's products. These have to be considered external partners, and the company has to secure their continuous cooperation and collaboration in wooing the end customers who are, generally, the actual users of the product. In some cases, it is the person or organization that decides for the user (to buy or not to buy) like parents who buy for their children (users), doctors who decide what medicine the patient will buy, or hospitals that decide what products or brands to buy that are used by patients (users of such products or brands).

In a certain building materials company that generally did not sell directly to the end customer, management always considered distributors as their customers. However, customers and potential customers were dissatisfied with the distributor's services or treatment, and this resulted in large losses of market share for the manufacturer. When the company started considering the distributor as a business partner, the distributor was made aware of the importance of this partner relationship for both parties. Joint customer surveys and promotion campaigns were then designed and implemented, with excellent results.

In a large pharmaceutical company, satisfying the customer posed a serious problem. Actually, the problem was to identify the customer: is it the patient, the doctor who prescribes the medication, the hospital, or the insurance company that pays for the drugs? It was finally agreed that the "customer" is whoever decides to purchase the product or influences that decision. This means that, in this example, the "customer" may consist of two or three persons (doctor, insurance company representative, patient).

After having classified them as being actual, probable, or possible, the next step is to find out what the needs of the customers are. This is accomplished by evaluating the seven QVALITY characteristics and researching ways to apply the ACE concept. Each of these characteristics is measured—as objectively as possible—in absolute or relative terms. This is done by means of total quality indicators that are deemed *absolute* when they are directly and objectively measurable (such as the number of errors in bank transactions, the waiting time for a service, the thickness of a piece of metal, or the number of times a telephone rings before it is answered) or *relative* when they cannot be measured objectively (as in the case of a company's people's courtesy). Though subjective, such evaluations can be measured by the customer on scales ranging, for example, from 0 to 10.

As we noted in chapter 5, the First Chicago Corporation studied customers' needs and expectations in terms of "timeliness, accuracy, efficiency, responsive service, and good communication. They developed an extensive performance measurement system that tracks on a weekly basis some 700 indicators that customers considered important."[2]

The aim of this research into customer satisfaction is to establish a *total quality diagnosis* which evaluates the company's performance by comparing that performance with the established objectives, past performance (of either the last month, the six previous months, or the last year), average performance in the industry, or the performance of a specific competitor.

What, then, are some of the total quality indicators to be analyzed during the diagnosis? Here is a partial list.

- The reception and treatment that present or potential customers enjoy or are subjected to by the company's personnel or that of an external partner.
- The proportion of products returned by the distributors.
- The proportion of products returned by the customers.
- The number of customer complaints, over a given period of time, related to the quality of the products, the observance of delivery schedules, the quantities delivered, and the administrative aspects (order processing, customer credit assessment, invoicing, and so on).
- The rate of internal failures (defective products detected prior to shipping, internal administrative errors, and other sorts of errors).
- The rate of external failures (defective products detected after shipping, external administrative errors) that affect the customer, such as errors in invoicing or order processing.
- The cost of unquality and overquality.
- The proportion of items returned to suppliers because of nonconformance to specifications.
- The proportion of time spent in rework and the extra time spent on repairing defective units.
- The proportion of defects due to product design, drawings, specifications, maintenance, improper handling, storage of raw materials, transportation, and manufacturing operations.
- Claims and lawsuits by customers.
- The sales of spare parts (these usually give an indication of the durability, rate of wear, and reliability of each part or each unit).
- The cost of refunds or repairs for products under guarantee.
- Product failure rate and frequency of repairs and maintenance.

- Media evaluation or criticism of the company's products (television, radio, and newspaper reviews specializing in product evaluations; consumer association critiques).

- The amount of scrap and waste (from raw materials, work in process, and finished products).

- The actual product performance as compared with desired or designed performance (does the finished product meet the needs for which it was made, does it have the desired durability and reliability, and does it meet all of the customer's requirements?).

- The interrelationships with actual and potential customers (communications by telephone, fax machine, correspondence, and face-to-face communication). Interrelationships include personnel's courtesy toward customers, promptitude in answering their queries, and the knowledge of the personnel in contact with the customers about any question they may ask. For instance, at Disney World, all personnel that the customers may encounter on the grounds (gardeners, maintenance personnel, security guards, entertainers, attendants, train drivers) are trained to answer a great number of questions that customers may ask. No employee is allowed to answer a customer with, "I don't know. I'm only here to sweep the floor (or clean the grounds, or sell tickets)."

In addition to obtaining such information about one's own company, attempts should be made to gather the same information about competitors. Some companies regularly buy their direct and indirect competitors' products so that they can make comparative assessments. Direct competitors are those who offer similar products; indirect competitors are those who offer substitute products (that is, plastic in place of steel, metal in place of wood, synthetic rather than natural). Evaluating a competitor's performance is often a good way for the company to evaluate its own success (or lack of it). This process, termed *benchmarking,* will be explained later on in this chapter.

If the diagnosis demonstrates that the company's current situation is unsatisfactory, the causes must be investigated. As we shall see in greater detail later, the search for causes involves a close and systematic examination of all of the factors that can influence total quality, both (1) during the four product quality cycle phases (from the definition of user needs up to disposal of the product after the user has used it to satisfy his needs) and (2) through the four phases of the A–I cycle.

Diagnosis should systematically examine all of the links of the product quality cycle and the A–I cycle and pose questions such as those in the following partial questionnaire.

- Have actual and potential customers been correctly identified? Were their requirements clearly understood? Was there adequate market research, and were surveys taken among the target clientele? Were the results of the research and the surveys carefully analyzed?

• Was the concept of the product properly developed? Were all possible concepts and avenues explored? Has a study been made of what the direct competitors (similar products and services) and the indirect competitors (substitute products) are doing?

• Did the product design take into consideration all of the customer's requirements? Were models and prototypes prepared to evaluate different possibilities? Was an effort made to get out of the old rut and use new materials? Were mock-up situations used to simulate and evaluate services before offering them to customers? Were designs, plans, and specifications checked? Were all of the relevant standards adhered to? Is there a reliable document-updating system that will serve the purchasing, production, and quality departments when there is a call for modification of product design?

• If the product has been designed and developed elsewhere, has a thorough *design review* been done to ensure that these activities and documents are free of error? Is there any proof that the documents have been checked by the organization, internal or external, that prepared them?

• Has a feasibility study been done to ensure that the available human and material resources are competent and capable of putting into effect the plans and specifications?

• Has a *producibility* study been carried out to ensure that the company is capable of not only carrying out the plans and specifications but also of producing the desired quantities of product within specified time limits?

• If the necessary workforce or equipment is not on hand, can it be acquired on time and at reasonable cost?

• Have purchasing department personnel researched and evaluated the suppliers to make sure that they are reliable and capable of delivering the materials, parts, and various services needed to produce the product or service at the required quality level?

• Is there an effective quality control system in place to verify items ordered and received, prior to introducing them into the production system? Are nonconforming items returned to the supplier or repaired and modified at the supplier's expense, and are statistics kept for subsequent analysis and decision making?

• During the manufacturing process, are updated procedures followed? (I have seen several instances in which, either by omission or by neglect, the latest version of a drawing had not been sent to the manufacturing division.)

• Is work in process inspected? Are nonconforming products well identified? Are errors and defects promptly corrected?

• Is verification carried out to ensure that each product is adequately packed prior to shipping?

• Are the means of transportation chosen to ship the finished products reliable, or do they present any danger that might affect the quality of the product?

• Are the finished products stored correctly, in conditions that do not affect their quality?

• Are the installation activities carried out by the company, the customer, or anyone else done in such a way as to protect the quality of the product when it has been installed? Do people follow the instructions? Are these clear and adequate?

• Have all the necessary operating instructions been provided to ensure the proper use of the product? Is the user clearly warned of any dangers or risks that may result if the product is misused?

• Can the product be maintained and repaired easily, rapidly, and at reasonable cost?

• Does the quality of the product satisfy the user? Is there any overquality that renders this product unprofitable or less profitable than if the level of quality had been simply sufficient and satisfactory?

• What are the costs of unquality and overquality? Can each be reduced and the quality improved?

• Do customers get efficient, speedy, and courteous responses to their requests for information?

• Does the accuracy of the information transmitted when orders are taken get checked?

• When carrying out an order, are requests for product modifications by the customer adequately met?

• Are there follow-up on activities related to the delivery of orders and after-sales service?

• Have all errors or irregularities been removed from the invoicing process?

It is not enough to answer yes or no to each of these questions. To complete the analysis, the specific question of who does what, how, when, and where must all be answered.

The diagnosis is an aid in identifying where and how much improvement is called for. The final step of the diagnosis links the areas of weak performance to their possible causes in the business process, and those where improvement is desirable to a means of improvement within that process. A subsequent analysis will determine whether a specific process within the mainstream or support processes has to be improved or completely reengineered. Moreover, in applying the total reengineering concept, not only should the business process be analyzed but also other dimensions such as the organizational structure, the management style, the mobilization of both management and the workforce, the existing job evaluation and compensation systems, the rewards and recognition system, and so on. Here again a subsequent analysis would indicate if improvement or reengineering are required.

In order to evaluate the quality management and assurance systems used by the company, a number of organizations use the ISO 9000 standards as a guide.

Moreover, companies seeking certification under these standards have to audit their systems—or have them audited—according to these standards. More and more companies also use these standards to evaluate their suppliers' capacity to provide them with quality products and services.

The examiners of the Malcolm Baldrige National Quality Award, the U.S. equivalent of the Japanese Deming Prize, use a number of criteria that can be integrated into a quality diagnosis. The seven areas examined are each accorded a relative value that changes every year. These areas are Leadership, Information and Analysis, Strategic Planning, Human Resource Development and Management, Process Management, Business Results, and Customer Focus and Satisfaction.[3] Details of the Malcolm Baldrige National Quality Award are given in chapter 13.

The diagnosis must be complemented by a study of any forthcoming changes—whether they be certain, probable, or suspected in the present situation. All foreseeable events and facts that could affect the company's operation in the short term have to be considered. These include

- The effect of anticipated legislation dealing with issues such as labeling, metric conversion, environmental protection, and so on
- The imminent arrival of a new competitor on the scene, or the disappearance of an old one
- The appearance of a new supplier, or the disappearance of an old one
- The signing of new important contracts with old or new clients
- The imminent launching of a competitive product similar to one already produced by the company or liable to become an attractive substitute
- New business acquisitions, such as the purchase of a competitor, a supplier, or a distributor
- Significant changes in the organization, such as new executives or managers; new policies, such as vertical integration or diversification; the introduction of new systems, new products, or new processes
- New technologies coming on the market
- Economic and social changes expected over the short and long term.

Total Quality Objectives: Where Do We Want to Go?

The total quality objectives are determined once the diagnosis has been completed and carefully considered. Traditionally, people corrected only what was wrong. Then the idea of improvement came along. Nowadays, even when nothing is glaringly wrong, the trend to improve is prevalent. That improvement can be either incremental, gradual, and continuous, or radical and aiming at a breakthrough.

Successful businesses establish their global objectives in close collaboration with the managers in charge of all of the various functions of the business. Then, in their turn, each of these managers, together with their staffs, establish objectives in line with the global objectives. There are many possible objectives; they often target certain percentage points of improvement, and they may aim at improving on the company's past performance, outperforming the competition in general, or outdoing one competitor in particular.

Benchmarking: Establishing Standards of Excellence

How can measurable indicators of total quality be established? Some companies are using a new approach—*benchmarking*. Benchmarking in its literal sense began long ago in the yard-goods trade—where merchants marked the benches on which they unrolled their cloth in given lengths of meters, yards, or smaller divisions thereof. They measured the amount of cloth their customers ordered against these marks. Today, benchmarking means comparing one's performance with that of the highest performer in the field, or comparing one's methods with the best way of producing a product, be it goods, services, tasks, activities, or operations.

Benchmarking is the process that establishes landmarks of performance and standards of excellence for a company's products and services and for the processes used to produce them. These benchmarks are reference points, based on the best performance in the world in a specific area, that the company, or one of its divisions, sectors, or departments, must endeavor to attain or even surpass. For example, Xerox, when researching its benchmarks, identified the invoicing system of the Japanese branch of American Express as the one which gave the best results in the world. Xerox studied the system, and it became the reference point for all invoicing-related activities at Xerox. They noted that American Express in Japan automatically suspends any invoice that the customer disputes and, in the meantime, asks the customer to pay all of his or her other bills.

Benchmarking can be defined as the search for the practices of the best performers in industry. Lawrence S. Pryor defines benchmarking as comprising

1. Measuring your performance against that of best-in-class companies
2. Determining how the best in class achieve those performance levels
3. Using the information as the basis for your own company's targets, strategies, and implementation[4]

In short, it is a question of comparing performances in a given function (accounting, invoicing, manufacturing, and so on) with what is done elsewhere in other companies. This exercise allows managers to compare themselves with others, particularly with those reputed to be the best, and to identify why their own performance is lacking.

Focusing

As we have seen, total quality for the customer lies in the satisfaction of the seven characteristics expressed in the QVALITY acronym. However, in practice it would be very difficult, almost impossible—and for that matter, undesirable—to try to achieve all of these objectives simultaneously. In any case, the customers themselves do not attach equal importance to all of the characteristics and consider only certain ones to be of predominant importance. Besides, the same customer will emphasize different characteristics according to the situation. To add to these difficulties, vastly different priorities may be held by any given set of customers. As the exasperated marketing director of a plastic products manufacturing company related, some customers demand low cost, others want a quality product, and still others require strict observance of delivery dates. One of his big customers changes his requirements with each order!

In this company, unquality was increasing at a dangerous rate, delivery dates were not being respected, and the cost of production was going out of control. An inquiry that I led indicated that, in the production department, workers and supervisors did not know which way to turn. For one order, they were required to pay particular attention to quality, for another, manufacturing completion dates were all important, and, for a third, they had to reduce production costs. They then found it particularly difficult when, for a given order, they were not told of any specific requirement. Should they watch the quality? Put the emphasis on quantity? Try to reduce costs? Attempt to respect completion and delivery dates?

In discussions with this company's management committee, I proposed that they use a *focusing* strategy. This means that the individual company must choose one, two, or three characteristics to emphasize (quality, delivery date; quality, delivery date, cost; quality, quantity; delivery date, cost) without, however, neglecting the others. For example, if the company decides to make quality its trademark, that requirement will be stressed. That does not mean that it would neglect the customer's other six total quality requirements, but it would mean that the quality of the product would never be sacrificed, even at a customer's request. The marketing director's immediate reaction was that such a strategy would instantly make them lose between 20 percent and 25 percent of their customers. When I delved further into the problem I found, however, that even if this were a realistic risk, the profits would still increase despite the loss of customers. In effect, the confusion that reigned within the company was engendering unquality and disrespect for the other requirements, all of which translated into very high costs.

When we examined this strategy together, we concluded that the arrival of new customers who would tolerate no compromise in terms of quality would largely compensate for the loss of some clients. After some thought, the marketing director then came to the conclusion that the company would be able to recover these lost customers if the customers were made aware of the company's new policy and were educated about it and convinced that the result would be a win–win situation. In point of fact, it meant that these customers would have to plan their requirements more precisely and plan far enough in advance so that quality would not have to be sacrificed in order to keep up with an overly demanding delivery schedule.

With a focusing policy in place, company personnel know what they are up against for each order and for all of their customers. This creates a work climate conducive to satisfying employees, managers, and customers and results in a noticeable improvement in company performance. The company becomes well-known in the market for the characteristics that it has chosen to emphasize as its distinctive mark, its *signature*. Naturally, the choice of characteristics to be favored depends on the strengths and weaknesses of the business, on the ability of its personnel, the complexity of its equipment, the type of product it produces, its competition, the market situation, and so on.

Backtracking

The total quality approach embodies simultaneously satisfying customer, shareholder, and people needs: the total quality triad. Moreover, in this approach, the manager adopts extraversive management and therefore looks outward first of all toward the shareholder (or the taxpayer) and the customer. Generally, in the private sector, the satisfaction of the shareholder, the owner, and the investors prevails (dividends stemming from profits and profitability), and, of course, if it were otherwise, they would take their investment elsewhere. Public government–owned organizations (health, education) should regard the customer as paramount, ahead of the taxpayer, even though they must operate within the budgetary constraints of the taxpayer's contributions.

The satisfaction of these various needs represents the point of destination for all organizations. And, obviously, all those who would undertake continuous improvement and reengineering activities do so because, having followed the charted course of their current business process, they have arrived at the wrong destination—that being the dissatisfaction of shareholders and/or customers. Thus, they must start at that point and work their way backwards to the beginning of the process, retracing the steps and identifying the wrong turns that led them to the unsatisfactory results. Using this system of *backtracking,* the elements of dissatisfaction can be traced to specific areas or causes within the organization. These should be tackled to eliminate such dissatisfaction, and the course recharted in order to achieve the required higher levels of satisfaction.

Because the effective linking of departments is also a crucial part of backtracking, a word of caution is necessary here regarding the concept of internal suppliers and internal customers.

Internal Customers or Internal Partners?

The customer dimension of total quality consists of exceeding the expectations of the company's customers. However, in a company, the vast majority of the people are not in direct contact with the customers. Therefore, it has been suggested that every department should be considered as an *internal customer* when receiving goods or services from the previous department and as an *internal supplier* when supplying goods and services to the subsequent department; the chain continues in this manner, with each department playing a dual role, until the last internal customer deals with the *external customer* (Figure 8.5). The logic of this approach is as follows: If department A serves its customer, namely department B, B serves C, C serves D, D serves E, and E finally serves the end customer, then any of those departments can be understood, by extension, to be at the ultimate service of the end customer.

This approach has the advantage of offering continuous contact with a customer who is no longer at a distant remove and who can easily and readily express his or her requirements to his or her internal supplier. However, I have noticed, on many occasions, that this has resulted in problems and ineffectiveness. In one instance, a recently promoted junior foreman, while talking to the company's human resources senior vice president, arrogantly pointed out that—as the company's total quality consultant indicated—being the vice president's internal customer, he expected to be treated as such and to have all his needs "more than satisfied." Furthermore, he insisted on the notion that the customer is always right!

In yet another company, I noticed that the internal customer concept was working against the notion of teamwork. This comes as no surprise because, generally, one works *for* a customer, while in a team one works *with* a partner. Moreover, the internal customer concept is inimical to cross-functional collaboration and seems to perpetuate the division of labor wherein each department is responsible for only one part of the whole process. Finally, to add to the general confusion, employees are told that managers are their customers while managers are told that employees are their customers. Indeed, everybody is a supplier and a customer—and often simultaneously. One incident illustrates this state of confusion. After a big electronic manufacturing firm promoted the internal customer concept, it was decided that every office would have a special chair with a sign reading "Customer" (internal, that is). This, I was told, created some problems. As the story goes, a personnel agent went to the purchasing manager's office to discuss the hiring of a new buyer as well as the purchase of some furniture that his department needed. As he entered the office, he hesitated for a few moments, not knowing on which chair he had to sit. He ended by standing up during his whole visit!

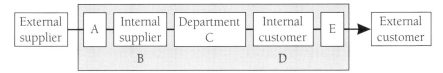

Figure 8.5.   Internal and external customers.

I do not use the expression *internal customer* anymore and use instead the expression *internal partner,* or even *teammate.* These expressions stress the importance of teamwork, of collaboration, of working *together* toward a common goal, of working *with* rather than *for,* or at worst, *against.* I prefer the expressions *internal user* and *internal provider* as they help clarify the role of an internal partner, without creating confusion with the notion of *customer* and *supplier.*

Each department, using a backtracking system, has to identify the means to contribute to the end customer's satisfaction. Starting from the customer's needs, expressed in terms of QVALITY, one determines the needs of the front-line people, that is, the staff in direct contact with the customer: the telephone receptionist, the delivery person who delivers the finished product, the salesperson who meets the customer, the accountant who prepares and sends the bill, the after-sales service staff called on to help the customer when he or she uses the product, the warehouse employee who prepares the merchandise for shipping, the order clerk who receives the order by mail, fax machine, or telephone. The second-line personnel, and those of all the other lines (the rear guard), must undertake activities and offer services or goods that fulfill the needs of each of these front-line people or departments. That having been said, however, I again underline that this fulfillment of front-line needs has to have a direct, logical connection to the satisfaction of the customer and the surpassing of his or her expectations.

Similarly, when the president and his or her immediate collaborators consider requests for resources from all of the departments, they take as their point of departure the needs of the customer. Using the focusing strategy that they have adopted, it is their job to find a way of distributing the company's available resources in a rational way. They must proceed in such a way as to ensure that each internal partner's or teammate's needs are always linked to the customer's needs.

Performance for any given department is measured by its direct contribution to and participation in the achievement of total quality. Obviously, this kind of exercise is neither simple nor easy; however, it is indispensable if one really wants to achieve total quality and enjoy its long-term results (see Figure 8.6).

Team sports, such as hockey or soccer, provide us with a useful analogy to illustrate this system. Goalkeepers would never be asked to score goals: Their job is to defend the goal, helped by the defense and the backs. Only the forwards or the players on the front line attack, and it is their mission to go to the opposite goal and score the points. Nevertheless, they will be able to accomplish their task only if the goalkeeper and the defense give them a strong hand by skillfully passing the ball or the puck to them. When they win, all of the members of the team share the honors of the success. When they suffer defeat, there is nothing to be gained in blaming one or another of the teammates; everybody shares the disappointment and the consequences of the defeat.

Each of the organization's quality performance indicators can be considered as an element to be improved. The question then becomes how to quantify this improvement. It is essential not to confuse an objective with the means required

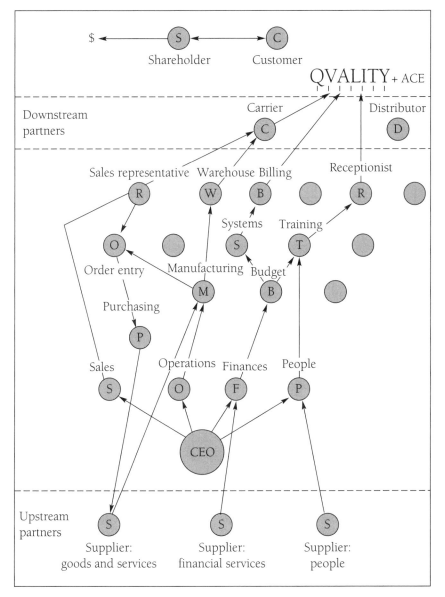

Figure 8.6. A customer-driven system.

Source: Adapted from J. N. Kelada, *Comprendre et réaliser la qualité totale*, 2nd ed. (Dollard-des-Ormeaux, Quebec, Canada: Quafec Publications, 1992), 87. Reprinted with permission.

to attain it. For example, we could take the reduction of the number of defective units or the improvement of product reliability as our objective. But, on the other hand, the improvement of the lighting system could not be considered a company objective because that kind of improvement is, in fact, a means to permit the realization of a given objective. Objectives should be revised when necessary, raising them or lowering them, each time any element justifies the change; they are not written in stone. The prime importance of establishing company objectives is to provide the company with a yardstick against which it can measure its performance. For this very reason, all company employees must be well aware of the objectives at all times.

Policy Deployment

Hoshin planning (also variously referred to as *management by policy, policy management,* or *policy deployment*) is an approach in which objectives are said to be *deployed* from the top downward throughout an organization. When I discussed this approach with certain Japanese managers, I concluded that this was a new management by objectives (MBO) approach, renamed in order to prevent its confusion with the traditional MBO and to identify it as a specifically Japanese approach.

To see how policy deployment works, let us take a brief look at the Komatsu Corporation of Japan. The Komatsu organization develops a document called the *President's Annual Policy.* This policy concerns the profits forecast for a given year and, as such, could be considered more as a statement of objectives than as a policy. Management begins its deliberations in April, on the basis of information gleaned from the business community connected with the company's markets. The first version of this policy is submitted to a group that then studies the strategies to be adopted. In September, a long-term plan is produced, and out of that comes a basic plan for the *President's Annual Policy* (see Figure 8.7). The basic policy for annual profits is then prepared in October and the policy is produced. It is distributed in December, along with notes of explanation, to all company department heads, their affiliated suppliers, foreign branches, distributors, and dealers. A company profit plan is prepared, and each department then develops its own activity plan to achieve this plan. This activity plan is then communicated to the quality circles so that they may direct their actions accordingly. I should note that in October and November of each year, the president initiates a *quality diagnosis* throughout the whole company. He may not personally conduct the diagnosis, but it is still known as the *president's diagnosis* to demonstrate how important the procedure is deemed to be. Usually the CEO, assisted by an external consultant, accomplishes this task.

In each plant, office, and division, the manager at the highest level also undertakes a quality diagnosis. The results of these diagnoses are communicated to managers at one of their monthly meetings and are used in preparing the next long-term plan.

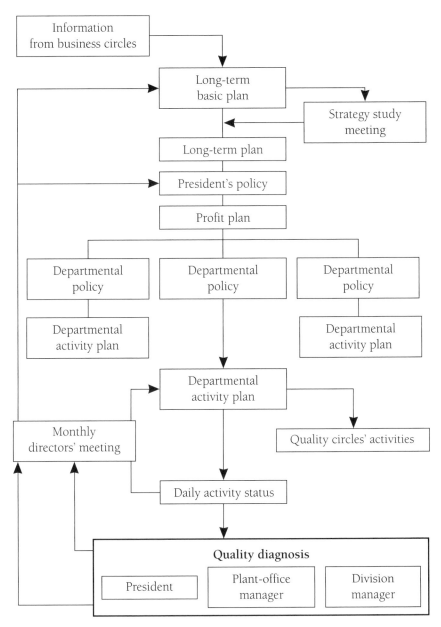

Figure 8.7. Komatsu's policy development system.

Source: Komatsu Corporation. Reprinted with permission.

The Strategy: What Do We Do to Achieve the Desired Objectives?

Establishing a strategy implies identifying the means necessary to achieve the objectives selected in each of the six areas that have been diagnosed. Detailed analysis of the business process will reveal the sources of the diagnosed shortcomings or problems and enable action to be taken to modify or reengineer them. It will also facilitate finding the ways and means to implement the opportunities for improvement found during the diagnosis.

Examples of such corrective measures could include

- Motivating the designers to eliminate, or at least reduce, errors in the design
- Introducing a new technology in design or drafting (computer-aided design—CAD, computer-aided manufacturing—CAM) that would reengineer the design process
- Introducing a rigorous supplier evaluation system, with a view to eliminating or reducing the number of nonconforming items delivered by certain suppliers
- Training operators to reduce manufacturing errors
- Increasing maintenance and service department resources to improve the after-sales service, or reengineering those processes
- Training telephone operators, delivery staff
- Improving the invoicing system to eliminate errors

For all these total quality–related activities to be effective, it is essential that they be coordinated throughout the company. In practice, several possible strategies are generally developed, and, after careful evaluation, a selection of the best one or best ones is made. I should stress that it is always a wise precaution to prepare an alternate strategy in case the one chosen proves to be difficult to put into practice.

Plan of Action: How Do We Implement the Strategy?

The plan of action puts the strategy to work and incorporates the following:

- The specific activities to be undertaken (for example, training, total quality management mobilization sessions, courses on statistical process control)
- The person or people responsible for each of the activities in the plan (committees, work groups, quality improvement teams, administrative units)

- The time limits connected with these activities
- The budgets required for each of these planned activities, projects, and programs
- The methods and procedures to be followed during the realization or implementation of the total quality activities

Control and evaluation procedures, designed to allow follow-up at all stages of the plan of action, must be clearly indicated. The plan of action is thus evaluated on a continuous basis, enabling any necessary corrective measures to be taken as soon as possible. People responsible for the evaluation are designated in advance. In addition, the plan of action specifies the documents that they will be required to produce and the recipients of these documents. The plan of action must include a contingency plan to be used in case difficulties in implementing the initial plan are of such a nature that corrective measures alone will not suffice.

Total Quality Management and Planning

Because total quality is ultimately the responsibility of management, the company is duty bound to develop a global total quality plan that incorporates the participation of representatives from all sectors of the company. Within the context of the global plan, activities concerning total quality are planned for each sector. It often happens, however, that each sector does its own planning, after which the individual plans of all sectors are consolidated into a global plan. This must be avoided.

Total quality must be subject to long-term strategic planning. Given that it emanates from an attitude and a philosophy, which are abstract notions, it is important for the organization to articulate its total quality policy in a formal fashion. That done, however, every major step the company takes must then follow the lines of this policy and draw its inspiration from it. I know of many companies that take pains to formulate their total quality policy in high-minded prose, then post and issue it everywhere in the company. But, unfortunately, the good intentions expounded in a policy often do not have much effect on company decisions. To ensure that total quality is produced, it is not enough for the company executives to simply declare that their organization is convinced that total quality underlies its survival, competitiveness, and progress. Their words, no matter how sincere, will count for nothing unless they find a way of deploying this policy, of putting it into practice.

As we have seen, in Japan the management team establishes formal total quality objectives for the whole company, as well as mechanisms throughout the enterprise for diagnosis, control, and distribution of results. The periodic distribution of results, usually on an annual basis, is done primarily for psychological rather than technical reasons. In fact, it is an opportunity to remind personnel in all sectors, at all levels of the hierarchy, of the importance that each person must attach to the quality of his or her work.

Conclusion

Planning is one of the most important management activities. If the previous stage could be regarded as a gestation period in which the vision is conceived and first sown, then it is the planning stage at which the vision is finally brought to term and total quality is created and nurtured. The whole process of generating activities to produce total quality is now set in motion. The companies that have reaped success are those that have been able to invest the necessary effort and time. Efficient planning requires that systematic procedures be adopted and that nothing be neglected; the smallest detail is important. Total quality is not a haphazard occurrence; it must be carefully and precisely planned. For this very reason, the necessary organization has to be put into place; staff must be managed and directed to carry it out; and every move continuously monitored to ensure proper results.

Before planning, company executives must go through a gestation stage to define their vision, values, and philosophy. Moreover, in a total quality approach, managers must use an extraversive approach, by first directing their attention outward to the shareholder and customer. In this way, the planning process focuses on the customer as a point of departure. Next, by applying the backtracking concept, all the company's activities are linked to the achievement of total quality. The notion of internal partners then comes into play, and great care is taken to ensure that their needs are met in a way that contributes directly or indirectly to the external customer's satisfaction.

Review Questions

1. A total quality diagnosis is the first step toward total quality. Describe how such a diagnostic process can be established in order to objectively assess the elements that are to be improved.

2. When the situation has been assessed and future events considered, objectives must be determined and a strategy and a plan of action developed, along with an alternative plan. Explain this process in concrete terms and provide examples as illustration.

3. Explain the *focusing* concept and its application.

Notes

1. Jim Clemmer and Art McNeil, *The V.I.P. Strategy* (Toronto: Key Porter Books, 1988), 70.

2. Richard L. Thomas, "Bank on Quality," *Quality Progress* 20, no. 2 (February 1987): 27–29.

3. *1995 Malcolm Baldrige National Quality Award Criteria* (Gaithersburg, Md.: National Institute of Standards and Technology, 1995). Note that the expression "total quality" is not used within the framework of this award.

4. Lawrence S. Pryor, "Benchmarking: A Self-Improvement Strategy," *Journal of Business Strategy* 10, no. 6 (November–December 1989): 28–32.

Chapter 9

The total quality approach:
neither project nor program, it's a process.

Organizing for Total Quality

We have seen the human aspect of total quality and the planning of activities required to achieve it. Having identified where we are, where we want to go, and what to do in order to get there, we now examine how we should organize for total quality, following the diagram in Figure 9.1. In other words, we examine who—individuals and groups of individuals—should do what and how people

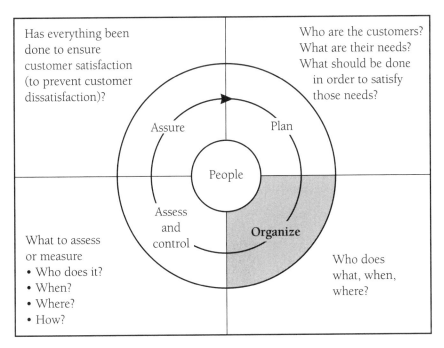

Has everything been done to ensure customer satisfaction (to prevent customer dissatisfaction)?

Who are the customers? What are their needs? What should be done in order to satisfy those needs?

Assure

Plan

People

Assess and control

Organize

What to assess or measure
• Who does it?
• When?
• Where?
• How?

Who does what, when, where?

Figure 9.1. TQM: Organizing for total quality

working with physical and financial resources and through processes should work together in order to achieve the total quality objectives.

Harold Koontz and Cyril O'Donnel assert that "in order to make it possible for people to work effectively toward accomplishing goals, an intentional structure of roles must be designed and maintained." Developing such a structure, according to the writers' succinct definition, "is the purpose of the managerial function of organizing."[1] This chapter deals both with the traditional organizational structures and with the recent trends in this field that have emerged as a means to achieve total quality.

Organizing for Quality

Before going into how to organize in order to achieve total quality, let us look at the more basic notion of organizing for quality. As clearly seen in chapter 2, when talking about quality we have traditionally limited ourselves to product quality. Although the total quality approach has greatly widened our scope in this regard, the quality of the products offered by a company is still a major factor in its competitiveness and performance. At the turn of the twentieth century, everyone was responsible for the quality he or she produced, and quality was not precisely defined, let alone measured. At the time, demand far surpassed supply, and customers were happy just to be able to acquire a product, any product. With the advent of big factories, quality responsibility was assigned to inspectors. From inspection, companies moved to quality control; complex destructive and nondestructive tests[2] were developed, labs set up, and statistical techniques applied. Even today, in many companies, most of these activities are grouped under a quality control (QC) department. Its main domain, manufacturing, has been extended to include incoming inspection of all materials used for production. Defective products returned by the customers are sent by the QC department to the manufacturing department for repair or rework. These are then retested by QC before being shipped to the customers.

It is evident, however, that the quality of the products of a company is affected by any number of departments or individuals outside the manufacturing department—these being the CEO, whose views on quality and policy in that area will permeate the entire organization; the marketing department, which has to identify the customer's needs or requirements and take care of guarantees, customer complaints, and after-sale service; the technical departments (research and development, engineering, and so on), which develop and design the product and the necessary manufacturing processes; the production department, which manufactures products in conformance to the previous departments' technical specifications; and the purchasing department, which acquires materials that must meet the required quality level. In addition, there is the personnel department, which provides training in quality for people in all the previous departments.

This broader view of quality was explained by A. V. Feigenbaum, in a book published more than 30 years ago. Feigenbaum stated that "as far as product quality is concerned, . . . Total *quality control* is an effective system for integrating the efforts of the various groups in an organization so as to enable production and service at the most economical levels which allow for full customer satisfaction. . . . Control must start with the design of the product and end only when the product has been placed in the hands of a customer who remains satisfied."[3] The reason for this breadth of scope is that the quality of any product is affected at many stages of the industrial cycle: marketing, engineering, purchasing, manufacturing engineering, manufacturing supervision, inspection and testing, shipping, installation, and service.

Generally, the quality control department is responsible for inspection, testing, and laboratory operations. Quality control is thus mainly aimed at the *detection* of poor quality. In contrast, *quality assurance*—as will be explained in detail in chapter 11—is mainly *preventive*. Therefore, many argue that the personnel in charge of the quality assurance activities must constitute an independent department that makes sure all other departments set up and use systems aiming at preventing poor quality. The quality assurance manager coordinates most quality-related activities in the different departments. Because of this role, this person must report directly to top management (see Figure 9.2).

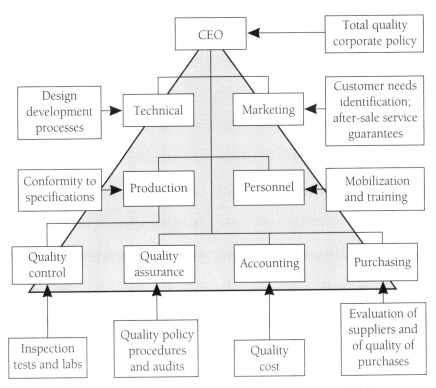

Figure 9.2. All departments are responsible for certain quality activities.

The Role of the Quality Control Department

A quality control department may be assigned a *line* role or a *staff* role. The line role is invested with the authority to give orders and make decisions, whereas the staff role provides support, counseling, and assistance. Each role has obvious advantages and disadvantages. Quality control personnel with a line role can stop a production operation or the shipment of an order if there is reason to believe that a product's quality is unacceptable. In a staff role, they would merely inform those in charge of production or shipping, and leave them to take any necessary corrective measures.

Ultimately, one cannot pronounce upon the effectiveness of one approach over the other because that effectiveness depends largely on the context of each situation, the complexity of the product, the current work relations, and the size of the company. Nevertheless, I notice that since the line role confers a police-like authority on the quality control people, they are regarded as always being on the lookout for a culprit, or at least a suspect. This perception makes people in other departments distrust line inspectors; they regard them as obstacles to be avoided, rather than as people who can help them perform better. Workers, therefore, spend more effort on avoiding being caught by an inspector than on improving product quality. Moreover, they are often astute enough to develop clever ways to achieve their own ends, such as keeping back certain products to show to a more lenient inspector or trying to get them passed at opportune moments, like Fridays near closing time, by marking them for urgent delivery. Along the way, an almost adversarial relationship develops, tearing away at the bonds of internal partnership.

The staff role has the apparent disadvantage of leaving decisions regarding product quality to someone who is also faced with producing specified quantities, on time and within budget, and who may therefore be tempted to sacrifice product quality in favor of the other requirements. You can allay this danger, however, by asking the staff quality control personnel, in cases they judge to be critical—and only in these cases—to notify company managers by simply sending them a copy of the report on a specific defective product or material. This exceptional procedure induces decision makers to refrain from making hasty decisions about nonconforming products. If they so decide, these nonconforming products can still be shipped to their destination, but the shipment is made with full knowledge of the facts and according to agreements prenegotiated with the customer. A quality department with a staff role usually enjoys the trust of personnel in all departments, providing that it is perceived as a source of assistance and support for any problems that might arise.

The Responsibility Grid

As indicated before, many departments and individuals share the responsibility for product quality and for the activities affecting it. But saying that quality is everybody's business does not mean it is nobody's responsibility. Unfortunately, though, that is often the conclusion that people draw when accountability is not explicitly charted out. For one thing, organization charts do not show how responsibilities are shared. That is why *responsibility grids* are so useful (see Figure 9.3). They serve to determine who is responsible for a decision, who participates in or is consulted for that decision, and who is informed when the decision has been made. Whereas a number of people or departments can participate, be consulted, or be informed during this process, there should be only one decision maker for each decision.

On the grid, D thus identifies the decision maker. He or she, alone, is responsible for the decision made for any given activity. P indicates participation in the decision-making process; *participation* is described for participants as an obligation to give their opinions and comments to the decision maker. The latter is obliged to take those comments into account but, if he or she chooses to reject them, the reasons for rejection must be justified to the participants and to a higher level of authority. When a person or a department is consulted on a certain decision, the consultee (C) also submits his or her opinion and comments to the decision maker. However, here, the decision maker may or may not take them into account in the decision. If he or she finds it appropriate to ignore them, there is no obligation to justify the rejection to anyone. Persons or departments identified with an I receive the information when a decision has been made but have no part in the decision-making process.

Responsibility Grid								
Activity \ Department	Top management	Research and development	Marketing	Production	Personnel	Purchasing	Finance	Quality assurance
Quality level	D	P	P	C	—	C	C	I
Motivation	C	—	—	D	P	—	C	I
Quality teams	D	—	—	P	P	—	C	C
Product reject	—	C	C	D	—	—	I	P
Choice of supplier	—	C	—	P	—	D	I	C

Legend
D = Decision maker   C = Person consulted about a decision
P = Participation in the   I = Person informed of the decision
    decision-making process

Figure 9.3. Section of a responsibility grid.

Preparing a responsibility grid is a very complex task. It is, however, a very useful exercise, because it clearly specifies each person's responsibilities in relation to certain activities. The preparation process is often an opportunity for co-workers who perform interdependent tasks to exchange views. As a result of this give and take, individuals come to an understanding regarding the distribution of these responsibilities, which would otherwise overlap and become a probable source of conflict. If, during preparation, participants do not agree on the role of any of the individuals, a temporary grid can be used on a trial basis for a certain period of time. Revisions and adjustments can be made as necessary, following trial and error. In any event, responsibility grids, just like organization charts or job descriptions, must be revised periodically in order to constantly improve the organization and keep it in good working order. They must thus accommodate any changes in the company and its environment, activities, or personnel.

From Quality to Total Quality Organization

As we know, total quality goes much further than product quality. Product quality may be vital but is not in itself enough to sustain a company's competitiveness. Therefore, we must organize for total quality. Being a new management approach, TQM requires a new type of organization, different from the traditional century-old model.

An organization that is business process–oriented is different from the traditional organization. The traditional company organizes its management activities and operations in a vertical hierarchy of departments, although its actual business process runs along horizontal lines and cuts through department boundaries (see

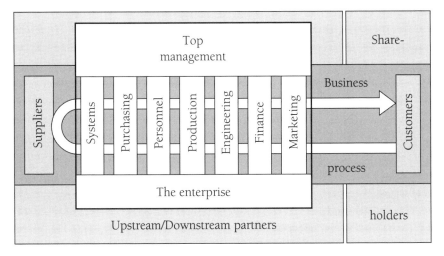

Figure 9.4. The business process and the traditional organizational structure.

Figure 9.4). This shows the necessity of rethinking the traditional structure and organizing the work around the business process and along its contours rather than around traditional functions such as marketing, finance, personnel, production, and so on. In the vertical structure, emphasis is on vertical functions, while in a seamless, streamlined, business-process approach, the emphasis is horizontal (that is, cross functional). Although functional departments would still continue to exist in a reengineered process, cross-functional teams would be the keynote of their modus operandi. This is organization by process rather than by function.

The Pyramidal Organization Chart

Most companies operate in a cascade-type, sequential process. They operate *in series*, which means that each department is assigned a part of the work to be done, then passes its products—goods or services—on to the next department down the line, which does the same thing with the subsequent department, and so on, until the work, having spilled down through all the levels of the cascade, is completed.

In general, as roughly illustrated in Figure 9.5, the order-entry department receives an order from the customer and sends it to the credit department, which checks the customer's credit standing. The credit department gives the go-ahead to the product design department, which produces a design and sends the product specifications to the manufacturing department. The latter orders the required materials through the purchasing department, which issues the necessary purchase orders to the suppliers. The materials ordered are received and stored, then delivered to the manufacturing department, which manufactures the product, ships it for delivery to the customer, and notifies the billing department. This department bills the customer and collects the amount due. All of this can be compared to a relay race, where each runner waits for the previous one to pass the baton before starting to run.

The risk faced with this approach is the probability of what communications experts call *distortion*. As the message gets passed along, there is likely to be distortion of the customer requirements at each step down the line. An error that goes undetected at any point along this process will be relayed to the next step. When the error is finally detected, retracing a number of steps could be required. By that time, added value (in terms of labor and/or material) would have been unnecessarily wasted on the product-in-process at each step along the way. Even worse, the error could be detected only when the product is delivered to the customers or even while being used by them. The defective product would then have to be replaced or repaired at high cost. Compensation may even have to be paid to the customers for damages caused by the defective product.

As opposed to this sequential approach, a *parallel* or *concurrent* approach would—at least in theory if not in practice—put all departments in direct contact with the customer (see Figure 9.6), thus obviating the risk of distorting the customer's message. This is achieved through emphasis on cross-functional team-

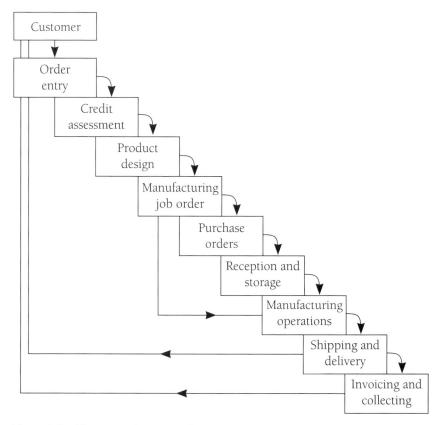

Figure 9.5. The cascade approach.

work. The voice of the customer is directly and simultaneously transmitted to all departments in the mainstream process.

The pyramidal organization charts now used almost everywhere are generally based on the cascade approach. Work is divided by specialty, the specialists being grouped in different departments (accounting, engineering, personnel, manufacturing, marketing). This is known as *departmentation*. Because work is rigidly divided among groups, each group needs a supervisor, a manager of some sort, whether the particular title be superintendent, vice president, line supervisor, general manager, section chief, or simply manager. Each group of managers, in turn, needs a super manager—and so on, all the way up to the CEO. This is how the organizational pyramid is built; and as the base grows wider, the number of levels of managers increases. These are then referred to as top management, middle management, lower management, and first-line management.

Although all of the people in a department report to one manager—the department manager—they may still find themselves in situations in which they re-

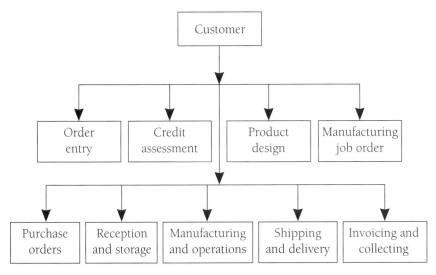

Figure 9.6. The parallel approach.

ceive orders from managers outside the department as well. This ambiguity in the chain of command has been criticized by some organizational structure experts, who argue that, for the sake of efficiency, each person should have only one boss. Henri Fayol—who is considered to be perhaps the real father of modern management theory—suggested the necessity of "a *unity of command*, which means that employees should receive orders from one superior only."[4] Where this vision of things prevails, communications tend to be vertical only; no horizontal contacts are provided for. However, to get around this constraint, integrative mechanisms have been invented, such as coordinators, ad hoc or permanent committees, cross-functional task forces, and the like. While these measures mitigate the rigidity of communications, they still work *within* (and at cross purposes to) a pyramidal structure, leaving its fundamentally vertical structure intact. To his credit, let us mention that Fayol himself indicated in his monograph, *Administration Industrielle et Générale,* which first appeared in 1916, that "the *chain of superiors* going from the highest to the lower ranks, while not to be departed from, needlessly, should be short circuited when its scrupulous following would be detrimental."[5] All the same, one can only conclude that, in Fayol's mind, this was to be the exception rather than the rule.

Again, because specialists do not specialize in everything, line managers—who are directly responsible for accomplishing the company's objectives—are assisted by staff personnel, who help the line accomplish those objectives. Staff personnel are grouped in departments, such as economic research, industrial engineering, internal management consulting, and the various types of analysis. In big corporations, *functional* departments at the head office—such as purchasing, accounting, personnel—have a *functional authority* (generally shown as a dotted line on the organization chart) over their counterpart line departments in the same function (that is why they are termed functional) in all other locations, regions, or divisions (see Figure 9.7). In short, a regional line department decides what to do and when to do it, while the functional department at the head office decides how the regional department will do it, by issuing policies and directives defining the methods. For example, a line department in a certain division might decide to hire four workers by a certain date. In doing so, however, they have to follow a policy and directive from the corporate functional department specifying, for instance, that they recruit from the inside before going to outside sources or that they refrain from (or encourage, if that be the case) hiring family members of employees.

Whether located at the head office or in regional offices, departments thus composed of specialists in one function are responsible for only a narrow segment of a product process. This focus on the internal mission creates isolated islands, as it were, of activity, none of which provide a good vantage point for a global outlook. Because no department is in charge of the product process as a whole, when there is any problem with a product to be delivered or a project in process, in the majority of cases no one can locate its cause, let alone solve it. Is it engineering or design? Is it purchasing, production, order entry, or credit assessment? For example, when a customer orders a product to be designed and manufactured, and the delivery dates are not met, marketing blames manufacturing, who blames purchasing for not delivering the material on time. In turn, purchasing blames engineering for late drawings, and engineering blames marketing for not forwarding to them the customer's order early enough. And while the customer is waiting, the buck is passed around from one department to the other! Responsibility for delays in such a case cannot be clearly identified.

To counter this, the *matrix organization* was invented, in which a product or project manager is placed in charge of the whole process surrounding a specific product or a particular project. However, even in this organizational system, the seat of authority remains ambiguous, causing loyalties to become divided. People—such as a designer A, an engineer D, and a buyer G (see Figure 9.8)—working on the same project or product (1) end up reporting to both the product-1 or project-1 manager and to a functional manager (design, engineering, or purchasing). Obviously this creates problems when these managers do not agree among themselves on priorities or on the way to do certain things. Besides, it has been observed that the specialists working on such a project tend to be more loyal to managers in their own area of expertise, especially when this manager—the functional manager—is also the one who decides who gets promoted and who gets a raise (or, in today's less optimistic shoptalk, who keeps his job and who gets the least cut in salary!).

All of these organizational concepts date back to the turn of the century, when they were proposed by people such as Henri Fayol. As a matter of fact, Fayol himself was inspired by the way the military had been organized for cen-

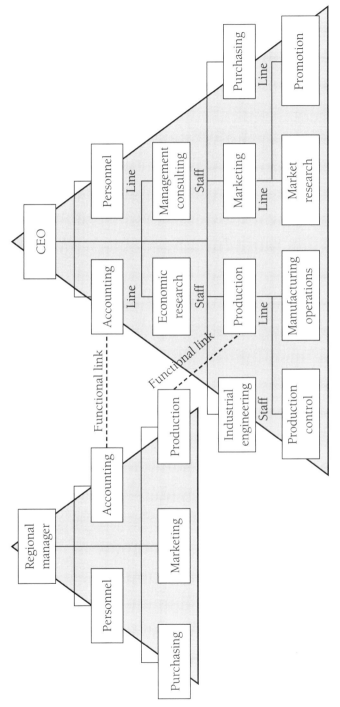

Figure 9.7. The traditional organization chart.

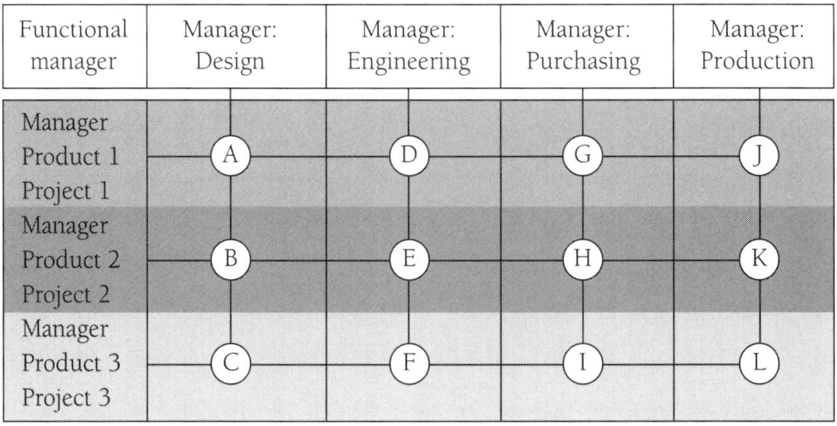

Functional manager	Manager: Design	Manager: Engineering	Manager: Purchasing	Manager: Production
Manager Product 1 Project 1	A	D	G	J
Manager Product 2 Project 2	B	E	H	K
Manager Product 3 Project 3	C	F	I	L

Figure 9.8. The matrix organization.

turies, and he adapted their style of organization to the business environment. Accordingly, the first of his 14 General Principles of Management is the division of work, "applied to all kinds of work, managerial as well as technical." However, his last principle hints at the eventual inadequacy of the vertical chain of command by dealing with an idea that is more timely than ever—that of *"esprit de corps,* emphasizing the need for teamwork and the importance of communication in obtaining it."[6]

New Organizational Trends

To recap, companies have been traditionally organized in functional, vertical structures, with specialists in each function being grouped in different departments and the strategic decision making left to the highest level in the hierarchy. This has led to introversive management, that is, each department developing its own mission and determining its own objectives, with little or no reference to the main company objectives. The matrix organization does not solve this problem because the functional organization still exists and decisions continue to be made by higher management.

Although a number of companies have reduced the number of management levels and have decentralized the decision-making process by empowering lower levels in the hierarchy to make some decisions, the functional boundaries remain intact, with each function protecting its turf and defending its territory. People are still loyal to their own function rather than to the customer and shareholder.

In order to change the way companies operate, different organizational models are being sought. The traditional, pyramid-shaped, hierarchical organization chart is being inverted or changed outright to take on other new shapes.

A number of companies, such as Xerox and Pepsico (which calls itself the right-side-up company), are replacing the pyramid-shaped organization chart with an inverted pyramid in which the customer, rather than the CEO, is at the top. Many attempts are made to modify the vertical structure. According to Rahul Jacob, "A consensus is beginning to evolve around a model corporation—the horizontal corporation." He adds,

> Rather than focusing single-mindedly on financial objectives or functional goals, the horizontal organization emphasizes customer satisfaction. Work is simplified and hierarchy flattened by combining related tasks—for example, an accountant-management process that subsumes the sales, billing, and service functions—and eliminating work that does not add value.[7]

Byrne indicates that

> Some AT&T units are now basing their annual budgets not on functions or departments, but on processes such as the maintenance of a worldwide telecommunications network. They're even dishing out bonuses to employees based on customer evaluations of the teams performing those processes.

He adds that

> Chrysler Corporation used a process approach to turn out its new Neon subcompact automobile quickly for a fraction of the typical development costs. Xerox Corporation is employing what it calls "microenterprise units" of employees that have beginning-to-end responsibility for the company's products.[8]

Companies are starting to organize around the different components of the business process, both using *functional* teams and bringing representatives of the different traditional functions together to work on *cross-functional* teams. There is thus a team corresponding to each work process, whether mainstream or support. At the same time, a coordinating team harmonizes and coordinates the efforts of all of these teams.

The same person could be working on two or more teams. For example, a design engineer would work on the customer needs identification process team as well as on the new products development team, together with marketing, production, and purchasing people. Similarly, an accountant would sit on the invoicing–collecting process team as well as on the general accounting process team in charge of preparing financial statements. With time, training, and experience, people shed the mantle of specialist and become generalists, capable of accomplishing multifunctional tasks (see Figure 9.9). That means that, after starting out with teams of various *unidisciplinary specialists,* the organization evolves toward teams of *multispecialists,* or *generalists.*

224

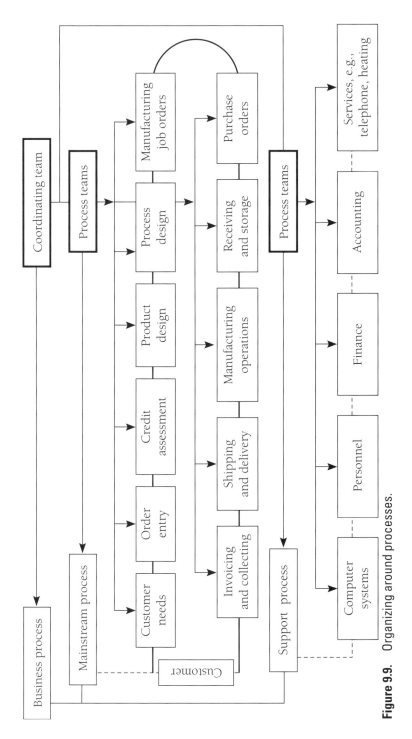

Figure 9.9. Organizing around processes.

The horizontal, process-oriented organization would tend to reduce the number of management levels and eliminate boundaries between functions. No one would specialize exclusively in order entry or credit assessment processes. Rather, people would work in a number of different process teams. All of these teams would be self-managing. Even if a company were to have a basic, functional structure, people would be continuously moving from one team to the other. As I have indicated, this worker mobility requires training and a different approach to compensation. Rather than being tied to a position or a specific job, compensation would be based on the skills of a person, that is, on his or her capacity to perform a number of jobs and work effectively in teams. The emphasis thus shifts from what an individual does to what he or she can do and from individual performance to team performance. (This pay-by-skill approach is discussed in detail in chapter 7).

In the extraversive management approach, the performance objectives of processes should be linked to profitability or shareholder needs through customer satisfaction. No organization around processes should be undertaken until these links have been clearly and unequivocally established. However, one should realize that this is no simple task. Furthermore, requiring people who have always identified themselves as specialists in one particular function to forget about their function will always meet with their resistance.

Byrne explains that

> GE's $3 billion lighting business scrambled a more traditional structure for its global technology organization in favor of one in which a senior team of 9 to 12 people oversees nearly 100 processes or programs worldwide, from new-product design to improving the yield on production machinery. In virtually all the cases, a multidisciplinary team works together to achieve the goals of the process. The senior leadership group—composed of managers with "multiple competencies" rather than narrow specialists—exists to allocate resources and ensure coordination of the processes and programs.[9]

In no way does all this mean that companies have abandoned the more-than-century-old, traditional, pyramidal organization chart or that they will abandon it in the foreseeable future. There will always be a CEO, managers, and employees, and the pyramidal representation is still the simplest and most logical way to represent it, because the CEO will always be the person at the top, and because the employees at the base will always outnumber the managers in the middle.

The new shapes of organization are only graphic representations of the way the pyramidal organization must operate. For instance, the latter in itself cannot effectively represent the way cross-functional teams are organized. Indeed, the pyramidal shape, hamstrung by its hierarchical scheme, would be hard put to depict the same person working in two or three different teams, some of them permanent and others temporary. Some authors argue that a concentric shape better represents the type of organization that should be adopted because, when the pyramid is flattened, the person at the top becomes the person in the center. When Xerox Corporation or Pepsico show their company as an inverted pyramid with the customer at the top, the main effect is to convey the idea that the company is customer oriented or even customer driven. Their top management is still at the top. To further illustrate, let us take the example of the diamond- and the daisy-shaped organizations.

Diamond-Shaped and Daisy-Shaped Organizations

The diamond-shaped organization also reflects the TQM imperative that an organization be customer driven. If the customer is placed at the top of the chart (see Figure 9.10), there is no doubt as to who is the source of the company's profits

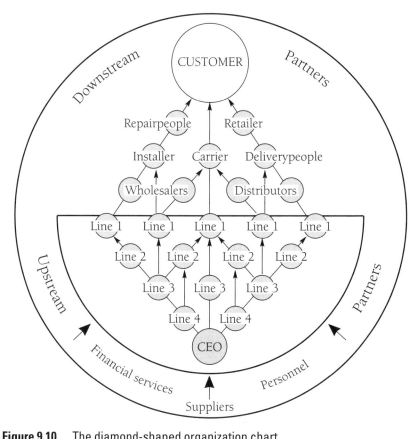

Figure 9.10. The diamond-shaped organization chart.

and who ultimately pays for the stockholders' dividends, the salaries, the rent, and all of the company's other expenses. If the customer were to disappear, the whole company would disappear as well!

The diamond shape is actually composed of two pyramids joined at their bases by a center line. On one side of the center line—the *contact* line at which the company has its interface with the outside world—are all of the company personnel, starting with the front liners, that is, the people in direct contact with the customer's environment. These are followed by second liners, third liners, and so on, ending with the company's top management and its CEO at the bottom. Here, too, are the external upstream partners (including suppliers and subcontractors) who assist the company's personnel in realizing total quality. All of the company's downstream partners—who transport, store, distribute (wholesale or retail), deliver, install, and repair the finished product—are on the other side of the center line. All organizational elements on both sides of the contact line collaborate to produce total quality, thus exceeding customer expectations as expressed in terms of QVALITY.

Another type of organization is daisy shaped. Its organization chart represents a flat organization (see Figure 9.11). The CEO works with a team composed of

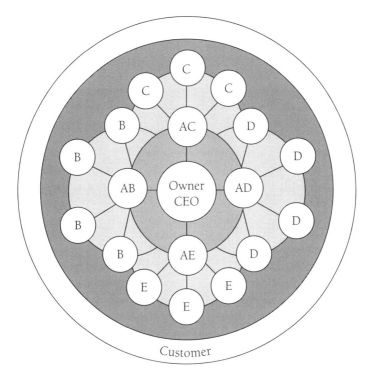

Figure 9.11.   The daisy-shaped organization chart.

managers of other teams. All of these team managers, however, are no longer managers in the narrow sense of the word. Rather, they act as team leaders, catalysts, and coaches for team members who work *with* them, not *for* them. Contrary to the departments of the traditional, vertical, *mechanistic* system, in which the employees interact exclusively with their own manager in a superior–subordinate relationship, these administrative units promote free communications among all of the members, as well as with external partners. Thus, this is an *organic* organization. Within the company, the people in direct contact with the customer environment are recognized as holding a special place. These are the front-line troops, so to speak—the telephone receptionist who answers the customers' calls, the accountant who sends them their bills, the shipper who ships their orders, and so on.

In the center of this type of organization, we have the owner or, in the case of owner–shareholders, the CEO, who generally represents them. Constelled around the CEO within that central circle are the A team, the executives who work with the CEO. Each of these executives is also part of a second team and constitute the center of another circle. For example, executive AC is also part of team C. This pattern continues radiating outward, with any member of the C team being also a member of, say, either teams F, G, or H. These members would then be referred to as CF, CG, and CH. Members common to two teams act as what Likert once called a "linking pin."[10]

Consensus Management and Team Organization

Nowadays, many decisions are made not by individuals, but by groups practicing *management by consensus*. Consensus management presupposes participative teamwork. The concentric organization shown in Figure 9.12 works on principles similar to those of the daisy shape. One member of a team at Level 1 is also a member of a team at Level 2. In turn, a member of that Level 2 team is also member of a different team at Level 3. The same overlapping pattern continues all the way to Level 5, the last level.

Again, as in the daisy-shaped organization, a member common to two teams acts as a linking pin between them. Contrast this with the situation in traditional organizations composed of a hierarchy of a big boss (BB), bosses (B), small bosses (SB), and very small bosses (VSB), where middle managers act as intermediaries between top management and the employees at the base of the pyramid. It is their job to communicate management's (often unpopular) decisions to the workers. Also, as the management's representatives, they must face the employees' comments and frequently negative reactions to these decisions. They are in the uncomfortable position of being squeezed between the top and bottom of the pyramid. However, in team organization, they are equal partners of members of both groups, and, as such, participate actively and share their opinions with the members of the respective groups (see Figure 9.13).

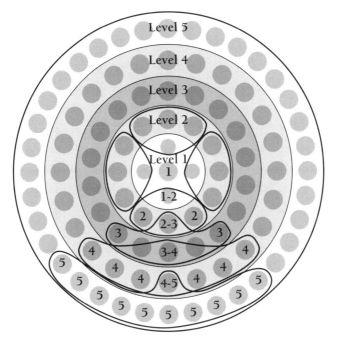

Figure 9.12.   Team organization and consensus management.

Source: J. N. Kelada, *Comprendre et réaliser la qualité totale*, 2nd ed. (Dollard-des-Ormeaux, Quebec, Canada: Quafec Publications, 1992), 117. Reprinted with permission.

One of the companies that has crossed over from a pyramidal organization to a *concentric* organization is Semco. According to Ricardo Semler, the owner and president of this company,

The organizational pyramid is the cause of much corporate evil, because the tip is too far from the base. Pyramids emphasize power, promote insecurity, distort communications, and make it very difficult for the people who plan and the people who execute to move in the same direction. So Semco designed an organizational circle. It consists of three concentric circles. The central circle contains the people who integrate the company's movements. A second, larger circle contains the heads of eight divisions. Finally, a third, huge circle holds all the other employees. Some of these are permanent and temporary team or task leaders we call coordinators. They are the linchpins of the system, a group that includes everyone formerly called foreman, supervisor, manager, head, or chief.[11]

With consensus management, if executives at Level 1 want to make a decision, each one of them meets with his or her teammates from Level 2. Each of the

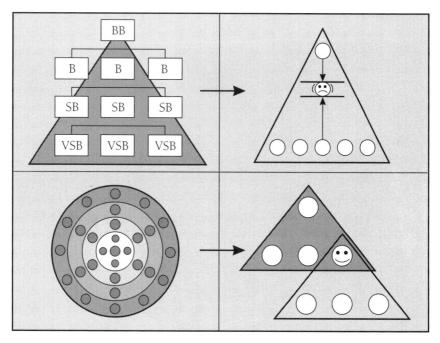

Figure 9.13.   Traditional organization and team organization.

Source: J. N. Kelada, *Comprendre et réaliser la qualité totale,* 2nd ed. (Dollard-des-Ormeaux, Quebec, Canada: Quafec Publications, 1992), 117. Reprinted with permission.

latter then meets with his or her own teammates from Level 3, and so on. The decision is made only when there is consensus (not necessarily unanimity) among all of the participants. I must differentiate between unanimity and consensus about a decision in a group. Unanimity, someone once said, means that everyone would die for a decision, whereas consensus means that everyone feels they can live with it. Obviously, this approach cannot be used for all decisions. But, in general, all of the people who are affected by a decision or who will have any impact on its implementation participate in the decision-making process. It is believed that this way of making decisions is lengthy and cumbersome—and, indeed, it does take longer. Once the consensus is built up, however, the implementation of the decision takes much less time than it would under the traditional system, and it is much more effective and wholehearted.

In an article called "The Payoff from Teamwork," John Hoerr wonders: "The gains in quality [from team organization] are substantial—so why isn't it spreading faster?" According to Hoerr, despite

> productivity gains that exceed 30 percent in some cases, resistance to teamwork organization remains widespread. Many managers won't

allow participation because it entails sharing power with employees. Low level supervisors, whose interests often are ignored in the employee involvement (EI), tend to fight it. Some militant unionists see "teamwork" as a new form of the age-old "speedup." However, while angry union officers still rail against participation, more and more workers and labor leaders are willing to risk EI in hopes of making their employers more competitive—and the jobs more secure.[12]

One corporation that is gradually enlisting the support of all of the parties above is GE. Combining teamwork with *flexible automation* and other computerized systems, GE has raised productivity in a number of its plants by leaps and bounds. For example, by 1989 one GE plant had increased productivity by a remarkable 250 percent compared with GE plants that produced the same products in 1985.

One of the best-known approaches based on teamwork and the principles of participative management is the Japanese-inspired quality circles. Unfortunately, this approach did not have the success it deserved when it was used in the West. The main reason for failure was the error companies using it made: They did not integrate quality circles into a global management approach. So top managers washed their hands of it, delegated the quality circle program to middle managers, and hoped to see all their problems resolved. When that failed to happen, they did away with the circles and promptly forgot them.

Getting Organized for Total Quality

In order to save total quality initiatives from the fate that struck down the quality circles, I recommend that a global organization be implemented to support teamwork. To set up such a global organization, one must begin by defining the role of the firm's CEO. The onus is on the CEO to be the firebrand of the initiative, to participate actively in the process, and to constantly maintain a visible presence in all sectors of the enterprise. Similarly, the conduct of the other managers must demonstrate a profound conviction in the total quality approach as a way of life that permeates the entire company and extends to its relations with the external partners as well. The top managers actively participate in the dramatization program and are involved in continuously mobilizing the personnel (see Figure 9.14).

The president chooses a member of the top management team to champion the cause of total quality. The *champion* devotes a significant amount of time to the task of piloting the total quality process. This sends a very clear message to everyone in the company. It shows the degree of importance that the president attaches to the initiative and to its success. This designated person comes to personify total quality. He or she presides over the total quality steering committee and stays in constant contact with the president on the one hand and the coordinator on the other.

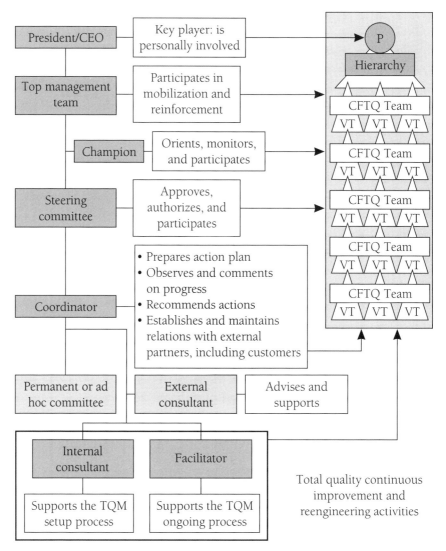

Legend: CFTQ Team = Cross-functional total quality team
         VT = Vertical team

Figure 9.14.   TQM organization.

Source: J. N. Kelada, *Comprendre et réaliser la qualité totale,* 2nd ed. (Dollard-des-Ormeaux, Quebec, Canada: Quafec Publications, 1992), 120. Reprinted with permission.

The steering committee is formed of influential members of the top management team. It closely follows the evolution of the total quality teams as they set up and begin operation. It comments on, approves, and authorizes proposals put forward by the total quality coordinator. The latter works alone or with a coordinating committee. This committee can be permanent or ad hoc, depending on the size of the company and on the complexity and geographical breadth of its activities.

The coordinator prepares an action plan and establishes the company's links with its external contacts—the upstream and downstream partners, the various associations involved in promoting total quality, the governmental organizations offering technical and financial support, the organizations offering training services, and so forth. He or she keeps up to date with all that is happening in the field of total quality, attends lectures on the subject, and visits companies that, like his or her own, are taking total quality initiatives. He or she is the main link between the company and its one or more total quality consultants. The coordinator also makes sure that management and the rest of the company are in accord on all issues regarding total quality and, occasionally, even acts as a consultant to the company.

Depending on the size of the company, the coordinator may receive back-up from one or more internal consultants and one or more facilitators. The internal consultant is responsible for support during the TQM set-up stage, while the facilitator supports the functioning of the TQM process. Support for the set-up includes preparation, training, and the planning of various activities, while support for the actual TQM process comprises operational aspects, such as the arrangement of meeting sites, the facilitation of internal and external data collection, the writing of progress reports on jobs undertaken by total quality teams, preparation for certain events (such as annual meetings), and the public presentation of results.

Unlike quality circles, where participation was strictly voluntary, these teams are not formed on a volunteer basis: All employees, white- or blue-collar, managers or workers, must be part of at least one team. There are four types of total quality teams: vertical (or natural) teams; horizontal (or cross-functional) teams; ad hoc teams; and common interest teams. The *vertical,* or natural, teams (VT) are made up of members from the same traditional organizational unit: The former boss and his or her subordinates have now become team leader, or coach, and teammates. The members of horizontal, or *cross-functional total quality* teams (CFTQ) represent different functions—purchasing, production, marketing, personnel, and accounting—and deal with topics of concern common to a number of departments. The *ad hoc* teams are formed to resolve specific problems or to undertake given projects. Each ad hoc team member is chosen for his or her expertise in and experience with the problem or project in question. As the name indicates, the team dissolves when its mandate is fulfilled. *Common interest* teams bring together people working in the same domain but not in the same unit—for example, all people using word processing. By meeting, they can pool their expe-

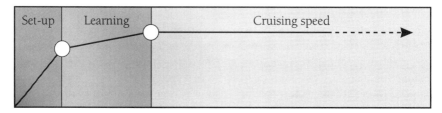

Figure 9.15. The three phases of implementing TQM.

riences, solve common problems, improve their work methods, and reengineer their work processes.

This system of organization may seem complicated. And, indeed, at the outset it is. But people get used to it, and, eventually, teamwork becomes the natural way of working. At that point, everyone wonders why it was ever done any differently before.

I should note that the organizational set-ups must reflect and keep pace with the teamwork, which evolves from a carefully calculated system of interaction into a natural reflex. One should not use the same organizational set-up for all three phases of TQM implementation (that is, the set-up, learning, and cruising speed phases shown in Figure 9.15). When TQM is well under way (the cruising speed phase) and becomes *the* way of doing things, formal teams are gradually disbanded. People will have acquired the habit of working in teams and will no longer need formal teams meeting at a specific time in a specific room with a specific agenda, as was the case in the launching phase and the learning phase. Actually, a number of TQM attempts have failed because the original organizational set-up was perpetuated, turning itself into a complex, unnecessary bureaucracy that eventually paralyzed the whole company. This is analogous to a sailboat that continuously uses its starter engine, even out in open waters, when the engine is meant only to maneuver the boat out of its moorings or to bring it to shore should the winds completely die.

The Union's Role

What is the union's stance toward total quality initiatives, and what part does it play in them? Let us point out that, in North America, relations between unions and management are generally tinged with a certain amount of distrust. We must not forget that trade unions came into being to protect weak and defenseless workers against powerful entrepreneurs who were exploiting them unscrupulously. Work conditions were almost inhuman; men, women, and even children were exploited, with no regard for their health or well-being. Fortunately, this is no longer the case. We have labor legislation, fixed minimum wages, and unions that are well organized and capable of negotiating satisfactory conditions for their members. Nevertheless, whatever else one might say about the progress made in labor–management relations, one can hardly say that they are now brimming over with affection and blind trust. The situation has to be analyzed, not to cast blame on one party or the other, but to find a way to collaborate and thereby find a satisfactory solution for all those concerned.

As I have already shown, the total quality approach is based on the stockholder–customer–people triad. The term *people* also includes the union that represents them. Thus, wherever they exist, unions are one of the pivotal points around which the total quality process turns. If they are seen as lying somewhere outside the machinery of the process, or if they decline to participate in the process, they will serve only to put a wedge in the machinery and stop the wheel of motion dead in its tracks. An article written by a union executive, a work relations director, and a total quality consultant noted that when new approaches, such as statistical process control or quality circles, are introduced, executives do not feel the need to involve the union. They ignore the union yet hope to be able to count on the unconditional support of the employees. The authors call this a naive attitude and cite numerous examples showing how unions have reacted negatively and opposed these changes.[13] We should not assume, however, that union representatives would have been in any hurry to collaborate with management, even if they had been invited to do so. Let us not forget the climate of distrust that still lingers over relations between many company managers and union representatives. In the end, however, each party must be unfailingly committed to cooperation. It is the only way to set the wheel of progress in motion and to enable companies to withstand the ever-mounting competition and stringent market conditions created by the globalization of economies.

Businesses face widespread changes all around them—political, economic, technological, social, and environmental. On the economic front, a number of North American industries have disappeared, thousands of jobs have been irrevocably lost, and international competitors in Europe and Asia are redoubling their efforts to retain the markets they have gained and to conquer others. TV sets, microwave ovens, and stereo sound systems—so many quintessentially American products—are for the most part no longer manufactured by American interests. Given all these hard facts, employers and unions cannot allow themselves the luxury of an adversarial relationship. They have to learn to live in a new type of relationship that will produce a medium- and long-term win–win situation for all parties involved—and this holds doubly true where total quality initiatives are concerned.

And yet it would be nothing short of utopian to suggest that long-time adversaries could be transformed into close associates without considerable effort on both sides. Cooperation, partnership, a win–win situation—these are all well and good; but how do we set about achieving them? Some union executives see in the total quality approach a new and positive way of approaching labor relations; others feel that the proposed changes amount to selling their souls to the company executives. The article mentioned earlier suggests that both company and union executives should receive training in the basic concepts of total quality, such as communications, teamwork, and problem solving. While I concur, I would add that receiving a grounding in the concepts alone is simply not enough; company and union executives must undergo sensitization to become aware of the *why* as well as the *what* of the approach. To this end, they must be sensitized to the necessity of the total quality approach as a means of survival, to the stakes that are hanging in the balance, and to the results each can expect from the changes. At the present time, this kind of sensitization is blatantly lacking in most existing initiatives and programs.

When I lead sensitization and training sessions for company managers and employees, I notice that union representatives are seldom invited. Even when they are present, they are conspicuously outnumbered by executives, managers, and employees. Union executives should perhaps take the initiative and offer similar sessions to their own executives and officers.

Company executives and union executives must respectively convince their managers and their members that collaboration is an absolute necessity. Recently, a union official told me that he, for one, was ready to shoulder responsibility for total quality initiatives—if he could see in it an *honest* effort to improve company performance and working conditions, job security, and general well-being for the employees. Admittedly, however, some companies that have launched total quality initiatives see them only as a new way of increasing worker productivity, just as they did when pursuing management by objectives, quality of work life, or quality circles. In the eyes of union officials, already wary of double-talk, this could hardly be perceived as a sign of good faith. For collaboration to take place—and the time is certainly ripe for it—all parties must feel they stand to gain by it. The notion of quality of life must be brought to the forefront of discussion as an essential condition of bringing labor into the fold.

Changing labor–management relations is a major challenge, just as great for the company as for the union. However, the success of the total quality initiative, and of our companies and our society in general, depends on it.

Conclusion

The company must reorganize itself to achieve total quality. One trend that has emerged in response to this need is the recasting of the traditional, pyramidal organization into new forms. The diamond-shaped organization is a case in point. In it, we find, on the one hand, the upstream environment—the company with all its departments, partners, suppliers, and contractors—and, on the other hand, the downstream environment—the company's salespeople, partners, distributors, installers, and service representatives. It is a flat rather than a vertical organization. In this revamped picture, the customer is the boss and is recognized as the very lifeblood of the company. The manager no longer makes subordinates work, but works with them as a colleague and partner; no longer a dictator, the manager becomes a leader, a coach, and a counselor for those with whom he or she works. Total quality management means teamwork, and any firm using it must transform its organization into a network of interrelated teams.[14]

Companies that entrust responsibility for total quality to a quality department make a serious mistake. Quality is everyone's business. The activities necessary to achieve it can, and must, be coordinated; and therein lies the total quality department's mission.

Review Questions

1. Some claim that a quality control department must have line authority to be able to function properly—to be able to stop inadequate production, reject a defective unit or lot, halt shipping of substandard finished products, or return any incoming unquality material to the supplier. Others are convinced that a quality department with line authority acts as a policing body that instills fear and mistrust. In this atmosphere, everyone does his or her utmost not to get caught instead of concentrating effort on improving quality. A quality department with a staff role encourages self-control and assists other departments to improve their quality. Give your comments.

2. If we profess that quality is everyone's business, what we are saying, in effect, is that no one in particular is actually responsible for quality. Therefore, it is better to have a central department whose personnel includes the best specialists in quality control and make them responsible for quality throughout the company. What are your comments?

3. During recent attempts to introduce teamwork management and consensus management into the United States, company executives, union representatives, and employees themselves announced that they were against this type of organization. Explain their attitude. How could they be persuaded to adopt such strategies?

4. In an organization, the business process and all of its components work horizontally through the different functions. Traditionally, structures of an organization are vertical, arranged by function. Today, many companies are being organized by process, which seems to be more logical. Please discuss why and how these companies organize themselves by process.

Notes

1. Harold Koontz and Cyril O'Donnel, *Principles of Management: An Analysis of Managerial Functions* (New York: McGraw-Hill, 1972).

2. An example of a destructive test is crashing a car to measure passenger safety. Nondestructive tests are, for example, road tests to measure car performance.

3. A. V. Feigenbaum, *Total Quality Control* (New York: McGraw-Hill, 1961). This is a revised version of the book originally published under the title *Quality Control*.

4. Koontz and O'Donnel, 23 and 25.

5. Ibid.

6. Ibid.

7. Rahul Jacob, "The Struggle to Create an Organization for the 21st Century," *Fortune*, 3 April 1995, 90–99.

8. John A. Byrne, "The Horizontal Corporation: It's About Managing Across, Not Up and Down," *Business Week*, 20 December 1993, 76–81.

9. Ibid.

10. R. Likert, *New Patterns of Management* (New York: McGraw Hill, 1961).

11. Ricardo Semler, "Managing Without Managers," *Harvard Business Review* 67, no. 5 (September–October 1989): 76–84.

12. John Hoerr, "The Payoff from Teamwork," *Business Week,* 10 July 1989, 56–62.

13. John Persico Jr., Betty L. Bednarczyk, and David P. Negus, "Three Routes to the Same Destination: TQM," *Quality Progress* 23, nos. 1 and 2 (January 1990 and February 1990).

14. The network notion is proposed by John Naisbitt and Patricia Aburdene in their book, *Re-Inventing the Corporation* (New York: Warner Books, 1985).

Chapter 10

*Only what can be measured
can be managed.*
—paraphrased from Lord Kelvin

Total Quality Assessment and Control

We have seen in the previous chapters, total quality being planned, an organization set up, and management providing direction for personnel, who then execute the plans, gets results that, if all goes well, meet the planned objectives. In order to achieve total quality, the system of people, equipment, materials, and procedures now in place has to be assessed and the obtained results evaluated and controlled in order to detect any absence of total quality (the terms *quality* and *unquality* relate exclusively to the product itself) and correct it, or else improve on whatever was successfully achieved (see Figure 10.1). This is the assessment and control stage, which is the subject of this chapter.

Defining *Control*

Control comes from the French word *contrôle*, whose original form, *contre rôle,* or counter account, refers to the historical accounting practice of keeping a double of each account for verification or auditing purposes. Though retaining its original meaning of *checking, testing,* or *verifying*, the definition of control has been extended: "to exercise restraining or directing influence over: regulate or have power over; rule."

Traditionally, control has been the best-known management activity in the field of quality. It was on the factory shop floors that the first formal quality control activities saw the light of day. Prior to the Industrial Revolution, the artisan was responsible for the quality of his or her own work. With the advent of factories, arti-

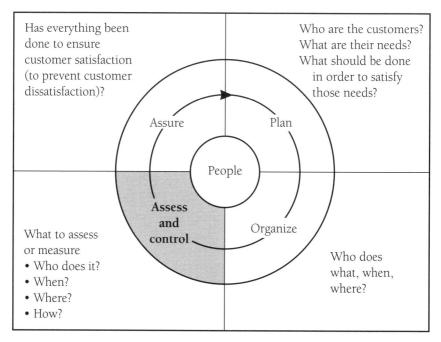

Figure 10.1. TQM: Total quality assessment and control.

sans were grouped together and became mere operators, the responsibility for quality devolving to the line supervisor. Eventually, when the line supervisor's job became more complicated and onerous, inspectors assumed responsibility for controlling quality: formal "quality control" was born. Historically, quality control consisted of measuring the conformity of a product, part, or material to a given technical specification, whether at the receiving stage, during the work in process, or prior to shipping. This was done by inspection and testing and, in fact, quality control is still limited to this in many companies.

More than 30 years ago, Feigenbaum introduced the concept of total quality control to lift the idea of control from its limited context of shop-floor inspection. It now not only applies to manufacturing operations but has been expanded to include all activities affecting product quality, from the product design phase all the way to the product's delivery to the customer.[1] He suggested that control be extended to all product-related activities in the following stages of the industrial cycle: marketing, engineering, purchasing, manufacturing engineering, manufacturing supervision and shop operations, mechanical inspection and functional testing, shipping, installation and service. However, Feigenbaum indicates that he uses "quality control" and "total quality control" interchangeably.[2]

Management specialists Koontz and O'Donnel state that "controlling implies measurement of accomplishment of events against the standard of plans and the correction of deviations to assure attainment of objectives according to plans."[3] This is the original meaning of control and the one that I will use. In this chapter, I speak of control in the sense of measuring, inspecting, verifying, and detecting any variation between what one gets as an outcome and what one is supposed to get, or in other words, between the result and the objective. Therefore, to detect, and thus correct, all incidence of mistakes, errors, or defects is to be seen as the main thrust of control activities.

Total Quality As the Object of Assessment and Control

As indicated above, controlling consists of measuring the result of some continuing or completed set of activities, be it a physical output, such as a product, work in process, or document, or a service, such as repair work on a car or machine. This should be done by objective means whenever possible, but should that prove to be impossible, subjective means may also be called upon. This measure (that is, the obtained result) is compared to some desired result in order to assess any discrepancy.

In the total quality approach, control should start by focusing outside the company (extraversive management) and evaluating both the shareholders' and the customers' satisfaction. It should then proceed by evaluating the satisfaction of the partners and the employees—management and nonmanagement alike—as well as their inputs (that is, their contribution toward shareholders' and customers' satisfaction). Finally, it must include assessing the degree to which the environmental objectives have been achieved. Therefore, it goes far beyond the mere control of quality of goods and services produced, although this, traditional quality control, is still included.

Besides measuring or evaluating the *results*, the *means* used to achieve the results must be assessed in order to identify the opportunities for performance improvement and the causes of any lack of total quality—weaknesses, errors, defects, or, in general, dissatisfaction on the part of the three parties of the total quality triad or the external partners, or any undesirable impact on the environment. With all these bases now being covered, the object of assessment and control has shifted from quality to total quality.

What to Assess and Control

For the shareholders, one must measure the financial results of the company—which, in specific terms, translate into return on investment (ROI), dividends per share, the market value per share, profits per share, and the like. These figures are compared to objectives that will have been predetermined, to the performance of comparable companies in the same industry or region, or to economic indicators at large regarding the whole economy, national or international.

The costs related to achieving total quality (that is, the costs of running the business) directly affect the profits earned and, as a consequence, the dividends available for the shareholders after the retained earnings necessary to cover required capital expenditures have been deducted. Hence the importance of evaluating those costs as closely as possible.

Besides scrutinizing the financial aspect, one must evaluate the degree of satisfaction of the shareholders regarding a number of factors: the company's image; its management's vision; its marketing and financial policies in terms of taking or avoiding risks; the technological standing of the company in relation to its competitors in the marketplace; the question of whether it tends to be a leader or follower of trends in the setting of its general policy; its degree of environmental consciousness; and the balance achieved between short-term and long-term concerns.

Regarding the customers, both actual and potential, one should measure their degree of satisfaction, dissatisfaction, or indifference. Obviously, potential customers who buy from the competition are not completely satisfied with the company's products and services, either because of a lack of familiarity with them or because they believe that the company's products and services are unable to satisfy their needs. I am referring here to QVALITY and ACE. A separate value or degree of importance should be attached to each of these factors, because, as I indicated in chapter 2, customers do not give the same weight to all of them. Some will seek quality regardless of cost, others quality at a minimum cost, while others still will emphasize on-time deliveries. Thus, among the seven QVALITY factors, customers will generally tend to highlight only a certain number of them—whether they be QAL, VLITY, or any other possible combination; and each factor within that combination will be seen by the customer as having a different degree of importance. Comparing these company survey results with those of the competition is important. Here again, because the costs related to achieving total quality could directly affect the price charged to the customers for the company's goods and services, a special effort to evaluate these costs (in terms of their yield) is evidently important.

As far as the people in the organization are concerned, both their satisfaction and their contribution—what they get from the company and what they give to it—have to be evaluated. Their satisfaction includes their feelings about the company; the management; the content of their work; the wages, salaries and fringe benefits received; the working climate; the impact of their work on their personal and family lives; the challenges with which they are presented; the recognition and the rewards they get; the opportunities for advancement and promotion they have; and the fulfillment of their personal needs.

What people *give* to a company must be thoroughly evaluated in terms of the results of operations. These consist of their contribution to shareholder and customer satisfaction as well as, on the negative side, anything that could cause shareholder or customer dissatisfaction—errors, mistakes, and defects produced and the time and materials required to correct them. The results also include all nonproductive time that has to be paid for, including time wasted as a consequence of lateness, absenteeism, or waiting for materials, drawings, plans, schedules, or work orders. All of these are reflected, as we shall see, in the costs related to total quality. Therefore, they affect the satisfaction of the customers (a low rate of failures and low prices or a high rate of failures and higher prices), of the shareholders (more profit, less profit), and of the employees themselves because they enhance or reduce possible benefits, rewards, bonuses, or even basic wages and salaries. In addition, good or bad operational results also affect the people's morale and, therefore, their quality of life.

Moreover, the relations with the external partners—upstream and downstream—must be assessed, as well as these partners' contributions to total quality. The upstream partners affect the customers indirectly, while those downstream have a direct effect on them. We might recall the incident in chapter 2 where the regrettable behavior of a delivery person—who did not even work for the company—nonetheless had disastrous consequences. The driver, who worked for the company's downstream carrier, managed to lose the company its most important client by attacking its president in the parking lot of the customer's receiving area. Now that's what you call a direct effect! At the opposite end of the spectrum, decent and courteous behavior by such partners toward customers has a very positive impact on sales and revenues. Relations with the external partners are of utmost importance for, beyond all formal and legal aspects of the relationship, their collaboration could prove to put a crowning touch on a successful total quality venture.

Finally, the way the company affects the *environment* has to be assessed, since this could, and generally does, affect the shareholders, the customers, the employees, and society at large.

All results have to include trends observed over a given period of time, extending as far back as possible to indicate any improvement or deterioration in the company's performance.

How to Assess and Control for Total Quality

As far as the measuring of the financial results is concerned, I shall not go into any detail on this extremely important point; a number of books and publications deal with this aspect very thoroughly. However, one thing I should call attention to which is not being practiced—at least not effectively—is the assessment of the degree of shareholder satisfaction through surveys or interviews where shareholders can, should they so desire, express their views on the company, the way it is run and managed, its policies, record, and so on. This would generally exclude shareholders who are mere speculators, interested only in short-term buying and selling, who "play" the stock market rather than look at long-term investments.

As indicated before, when considering customer satisfaction, one must include all of the actual customers as well as the so-called *noncustomers,* those potential customers who buy from the competition or do not buy at all. (Note, however, that I place those that some consider customers—such as distributors, wholesalers, or retailers—in the category of external partners.) Methods of measuring or evaluating the degree of customer satisfaction or dissatisfaction include looking at the frequency and nature of returns, complaints, or lawsuits; conducting surveys (especially for noncustomers), focus groups, and visits to customers; listening to comments from sales representatives, distributors, wholesalers, retailers, and critics; obtaining evaluations by consumer groups or journalists; soliciting opinions (via opinion polls and comment cards in restaurants, airplanes, theaters, and so on); and setting up toll-free telephone lines. Some companies conduct informal surveys by requesting all of their employees to actively look for comments on the company, its products and services, its management and personnel, and its competitors, and to subsequently report such comments to a designated individual in the company for analysis and evaluation.

In addition to satisfaction or dissatisfaction, knowledge and perception of the company or its products and services by the customers or potential customers should also be assessed. Misconceptions, if any, are to be identified.

The people's degree of satisfaction is usually measured through surveys, interviews, suggestions, and meetings. The analysis and assessment of this factor will be helped by periodically repeating these activities in order to establish trends and fluctuations.

Operations results are measured all along the mainstream process that comprises the product quality cycle and the A–I cycle, as well as in the support processes (see Figure 10.2).

Assessment and Control Along the Product Quality Cycle and the A–I Cycle

We must keep in mind that, for the customer, quality implies that his or her expectations are exceeded in terms of QVALITY. This is achieved through a set of activities grouped under what we have named the product quality cycle and the administration–interrelations (A–I) cycle.

At each stage of these cycles, total quality management techniques can be used to find ways and means to achieve improvements in performance or to seek out the causes of problems and find solutions to eliminate them. Obviously, some techniques are appropriate only for tangible and objectively measurable aspects of total quality, whereas one often also has to consider the intangible—though very real—subjective aspects of total quality, such as a customer's perception of a product or his or her (not always rational) loyalty to certain products, companies, or brands. TQM techniques can also have a marked psychological benefit above and

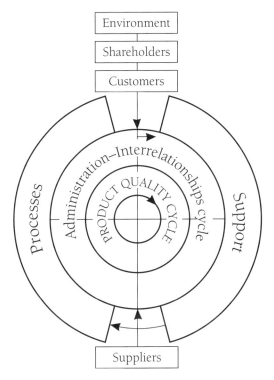

Figure 10.2. The mainstream process, including the A–I and the product quality cycles.

beyond their use for the intended technical purposes of improvement and correction. I have noticed that when TQM techniques are used on a regular basis, it is possible to create a constant quest for improvement over past performance, a feeling that, regardless of how successful the previous performance was, it can still be outstripped. Let us not forget that Japan's first steps on the road to quality after World War II were to launch a massive training program in quality techniques for all personnel in industry. They called in the statistician, W. Edwards Deming, to help them in the task. Even today, the Deming Prize for Quality is one of the most highly coveted honors among Japan's industrial and service companies.

In summary, the assessment and control activities—like total quality itself—are not, as common belief and practice would have it, limited to manufacturing, construction, and production. They should extend to all four phases of the product quality cycle: quality creation, preparation, realization, and maintenance. As Figure 10.3 illustrates, they constitute an iterative process, which should begin by identifying the need to be satisfied (point N); continue through the design phase, which ends with the issuing of the product specifications (S); move on to the acquisition of materials and other inputs (I); then proceed to the actual manufactur-

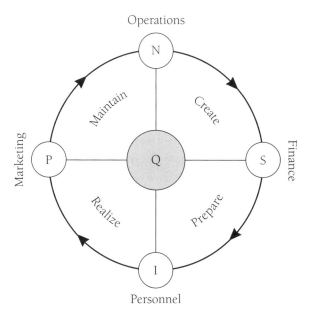

Operations

Personnel

Figure 10.3. Total control of quality throughout the company.

Source: J. N. Kelada, *Comprendre et réaliser la qualité totale,* 2nd ed. (Dollard-des-Ormeaux, Quebec, Canada: Quafec Publications, 1992), 171. Reprinted with permission.

ing of the product (goods or services) (P); and finally be brought full circle with the delivery, utilization, and servicing of the product—the maintenance (M) phase. Assessment and control activities should also be extended to all four phases of the A–I cycle and to all of the administrative procedures that customers must undergo.

A Total Quality Assessment and Control System

Total quality assessment and control thus extend throughout all of the company's functions: marketing, engineering, production, finance, and personnel (see Figure 10.3). Bear in mind that I are not talking exclusively of product quality; now we have a wider focus for quality of performance—the quality of performance in all of the functions throughout the company. This is precisely why I insist on calling it *total* quality. Assessment and control of total quality should begin at the quality creation phase, when the customer is first identified. This may be stating the obvious, but, surprisingly enough, many companies really do not know exactly who their customers are! Assessment and control at this phase consists of verifying that each person really knows, on the one hand, who his or her customers are and, on the other hand, who the internal upstream and downstream partners are. The next step in this phase comes when the potential customer's needs and requirements are identified. Following this, specifications are established relating to the product and the services accompanying it, to the customer–company interrelationships, and to the administrative procedures required to order, deliver, repair, modify, update, and pay for the product.

Thus, the ultimate objective of control at this phase is to verify that the specifications drawn up have the capacity to satisfy the need for which the product is being designed while simultaneously accommodating the various constraints imposed by the company's immediate environment (laws, culture, and competition) and the customer's additional stipulations and requirements (volume, time, location, and cost). To strip all this down to its essentials, the quality creation phase must end by having product specifications (S) matching the customer's needs (N) (S = N).

Some of the principal means of assessment and control used at this phase are

- Opinion polls and studies to verify that the eventual customer's needs have been properly identified
- Meetings between company representatives and the customer—in cases in which the latter is an industrial or commercial concern—to verify that the customer's requirements have been clearly and precisely stated
- Producibility studies to verify that the production facilities, whether already in place or to be installed, not only have adequate capacity to meet the specifications, but also are able to meet the additional demands imposed by volume, time, and cost requirements
- Tests on different models and prototypes, and computer simulations to verify the projected performance of the product
- Verification of calculations and designs, blueprints, and technical specifications to detect any possible error
- Project reviews to detect all anomalies in the preliminary or detailed engineering
- Checks to verify the availability of materials and components needed for the production of the required level of quality

Each person responsible for each of these activities in the assessment and control system is identified. The various means of control and the different tests can be undertaken internally or done externally (in specialized laboratories or on the customer's premises). The design and specifications can be controlled by their author (self-inspection) or by a colleague, a superior, or someone specially assigned to do so. The frequency of these controls, together with the instruments and apparatus to be used and the methods and procedures involved, must be specified.

In the preparation phase, assessment and control consist mainly of verifying the quality—here I am talking about *qualification*—of the workforce, the equipment, and the suppliers that will have to provide the company with materials, parts, supplies, services, and the various components required to manufacture the product or produce the service. The activities involved in the qualification of the workforce include evaluating its capacity to achieve the required levels of quality; making sure its members are certified, when hiring in the trades and professions; providing recruits with training and information; undertaking retraining and development; and supplying motivation as needed. The personnel department collaborates in these activities with the managers of the various departments. To succeed in achieving product quality, it is indispensable that equipment, production materials, handling and measuring procedures, and storage installations and methods be qualified. In manufacturing, this qualification exercise should include the assessment of *process capability* in order to evaluate the production facility's capacity to accommodate the specified dimensions and their tolerances (the amount of variation that will be tolerated: for example, 5 inches, plus or minus 5/1000 of an inch).

Assessment and control must extend to all administrative procedures that affect the customers—that is, procedures that they undergo before placing an order, when they place the order, while they wait for the order to be produced, when they receive service, when they are invoiced after product delivery, and, finally, when they have used the product and find that they have a complaint. It must also include all of the aspects related to the interrelationships and communications with the customers, be they written, verbal, face to face, by phone, fax, computer, or other means.

Controlling Product Quality in Manufacturing

Setting up a quality control system in a manufacturing environment includes the following six steps (see Figure 10.4). In a service environment, similar, although not identical, steps can be followed.

What to Control
Generally speaking, not everything should or can always be controlled. However, essential characteristics to be evaluated or measured should be identified, such as physical or chemical characteristics, dimensions, weight, performance (speed, power, reliability), appearance (finish, color), taste, and durability.

Who Controls
It is important to know who is responsible for controlling. In some cases it is the operators themselves who perform self-inspection. This is the current tendency because it is efficient and has a motivating effect on the person who is doing the job. The latter may, at times, be helped by personnel from the quality control department or by representatives of the client company that has placed the order; however, the operator always remains responsible for controlling what he or she

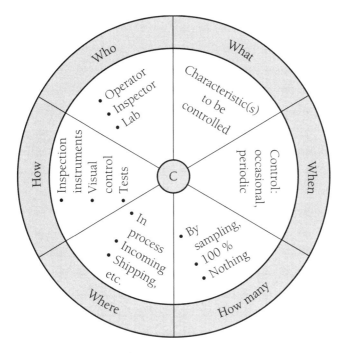

Figure 10.4. The quality control system.

Source: J. N. Kelada, *Comprendre et réaliser la qualité totale*, 2nd ed. (Dollard-des-Ormeaux, Quebec, Canada: Quafec Publications, 1992), 174. Reprinted with permission.

does. It may also happen that an inspector does the control. This can be an internal inspector or, again, someone representing the customer or a governmental agency.

How to Control

Items can be controlled by simple visual inspection or by dimensional inspection in which one or more dimensions are measured using instruments or other apparatus. Another way to control is to conduct destructive or nondestructive tests. A destructive test, as its name implies, completely destroys the article being tested, as in the case of a match, which is tested by being lit. Because these tests can be very costly, for certain products nondestructive tests are used. For example, in a foundry, X-ray techniques are used to detect cracks, air pockets, or other abnormalities.

One can further control by attributes or by variables. Controlling by *attributes* is a question of choosing an attribute and simply stating its presence or absence. For example, one can check to see if a label has been placed on a bottle or a box. One can also find out whether a product is good or defective, as in the case of an electric light bulb, which either lights up or does not. As one can see, there is no measurement involved in this type of control, and the outcome is always to accept or reject the item being controlled.

One can also control by using *variables*. In the case of control by variables, however, a measurement of one or more of the characteristics being controlled is undertaken. This is a more complicated type of control because it requires the use of instruments of measurement. In the case of the electric light bulb, for example, one can measure the intensity of the light, the length of its life, and its rate of energy consumption. Although control by variables is much more complex, it can also be more useful than control by attributes, for it provides a greater amount of information about the reasons that the part was rejected and it can clearly indicate the magnitude of the error as well as the statistical tendency for good or defective product occurring in all of the parts produced. Therefore, control by variables permits some often useful and even indispensable analysis to be carried out.

Where Control Is Applied

The precise points at which control should take place are to be indicated throughout the manufacturing process. For example, one can control the following:

- When raw materials, parts, and components are received
- When passing from one stage of a procedure to another
- Before a complicated or costly operation
- Before assembling parts that would make access to other components difficult
- Before a series of operations that would be difficult to interrupt
- Before finishing operations (painting or enameling)
- Before packing, warehousing, storing, or shipping out products
- Before transporting a product that has been ordered

In addition, one should control

- Operations that result from customer complaints
- Operations that have undergone recent changes in design and specifications
- Operations whose methods, procedures, and processes have been modified
- Operations that would incur high costs for correction
- Simple operations that are, nevertheless, critically important for the product's performance
- Operations specified by the customer
- Operations that can affect the safety of the user of the product

How Often Control Is Done

One has to establish if the control is to be done on a regular or a sporadic basis; if it is to be done systematically or only after complaints or incidents of error; if it is to follow a preestablished plan or occur upon customer demand; and if it is to be applied in a continuous fashion or at predetermined intervals.

How Much to Control

One must determine if one has to exert exhaustive, 100 percent control (that is, controlling all units produced), perform control by sampling, or apply no control at all. Indeed, you should never control just for the sake of controlling. Sometimes—when there is no justifiable purpose—it can be more advantageous not to control than to control. In other words, if a reliable supplier meticulously controls everything he or she sends out, it is futile to undertake the same kind of control when you receive the goods. In some instances, unit control is not as efficient as it is thought to be. This is certainly the case in the repeated inspection of a great number of similar items; after several hours of inspection the control efficiency can be reduced by as much as 80 percent. This is the reason that people avoid calling this type of control 100 percent control, which might lead one to believe that it is 100 percent efficient. Aside from the risk of inefficiency, 100 percent control has other disadvantages, particularly (and obviously) when it means using destructive tests. Other technical aspects can play in favor of control by sampling, such as in the case of a lack of personnel or specialized instruments. Finally, the cost of control can be very high, and, at some point, it becomes more economical to control by sampling.

At Motorola, executives set themselves a very ambitious program, with a common objective entitled "6 Sigma." Without going into statistical details, we may explain this as simply representing a rate of one defect or error per 3.4 million units produced of either goods or services.[4] This objective applies to administrative as well as manufacturing departments. A metric called the defect per unit (DPU) is used throughout the company to calculate the *sigma level*. The DPU is equal to the total number of defects detected in a product batch or a service (letter, report, or statement, in the case of administrative operations) divided by the number of units produced. To calculate the sigma level, the DPU is divided by the average opportunities for error in one unit, then multiplied by 1,000,000. A typewritten or computer text with, say, 2000 characters per page would represent 2000 opportunities for error per unit (or page). A drawing with 22 dimensions would represent 22 opportunities for dimensioning errors.

For example, let us assume that a product or a service contains 80 opportunities for error—the maximum number of possible errors for that unit. In 2500 units processed, a total of 45 defects is discovered. To calculate the defects per unit,

$$\text{DPU} = \frac{\text{total number of defects}}{\text{total number of units}} = \frac{45}{2500} = 0.18$$

To calculate the defects per million opportunities for error,

$$\frac{\text{DPU} \times 1{,}000{,}000}{\text{average number of opportunities for error in one unit}} = \frac{0.18 \times 1{,}000{,}000}{80}$$

$$= \frac{180{,}000}{80} = 2250$$

Number of Defects per Million Opportunities for Error	Associated Sigma Level
66,810	3.00
38,950	3.25
22,750	3.50
11,870	3.75
6,210	4.00
2,890	4.25
1,350	4.50
560	4.75
233	5.00
86	5.25
32	5.50
10.5	5.75
3.4	6.00

Table 10.1.   Sigma levels of defects per million.

This figure is then correlated to the sigma level in Table 10.1, giving between 4.25 and 4.50 sigma.

The Quality Index

Quality control consists of measuring the conformity of a result to an objective that is desired or required. Generally, the result of this activity is expressed as a number or a proportion of *defective units,* or as a number or proportion of *defects.* If, as in the first case, we simply label a number or proportion of units as defective, we are making no distinction between one defective unit and the next, for the actual number of defects in each unit is left unspecified. Consequently, when the result is expressed in defective units, we will not know if a given unit contains a single defect or a great number of defects, nor will we know the nature of those defects.

If, on the other hand, the result is expressed in a number or proportion of defects per unit or certain number of units (it being often expressed as defects per hundred units), we can then more effectively compare one defective unit or batch of units with the next—but this still leaves us in the dark about the relative importance of each defect. A television set can have an exterior casing that has a defect (color or finish) just as it can have a defect in the way it works (poor sound or scrambled picture). Although both of these fall under the broad category of defects, they are two very different types of defects that are not comparable. Consequently, if we simply add up all the defects in a set of products, that total will not give a proper indication of the quality of that set of products. Additional measure-

Type of Defect		Description	Demerits
Critical	(A)	Prevents the product from being used. Produces a safety or health hazard.	20
Serious	(B)	Significantly reduces product's use and safety. Injurious to health.	15
Major	(C)	Affects usage but not injurious to health and safety.	10
Minor	(D)	Affects neither product usage nor health and safety. Defect in appearance, finish, and so on.	2

Table 10.2. Defect weighting measures.

ment or weighting is required to differentiate between the various types of defects and their gravity. Instead of defects, then, we will consider *demerits*. A demerit is the weighted value of a specific type of defect. Defects can be ranked as critical, serious, major, or minor. As a defect mounts in severity, so does its value. For example, defects can be weighed as shown in Table 10.2.

Other types of defects (E, F, G, and so on) can also be found and demerit points accordingly determined for each. By converting the defects into demerits and then adding them up, we can accumulate some interesting statistics. This method is one way in which the quality performance of two suppliers or two production departments can be compared or followed over a period of time. It can also be useful in establishing a quality index. Generally speaking, an index is a relative value. To determine a quality index, we can calculate the number of demerit points over a given period in relation to a preestablished value. Following the variation of this index over a period of time will indicate if the quality improves or deteriorates. In detail, the procedure is as follows: The quality index (QI) is arrived at by dividing the number of demerits for a given week by the maximum number of demerits that are to be tolerated. The index is then calculated regularly, thus indicating the variation (improvement or deterioration) in the level of product quality. Let us take the example of a given week in which the defects shown in Table 10.3 have been detected.

12	A defects	=	12×20	=	240 demerits
20	B defects	=	20×15	=	300 demerits
31	C defects	=	31×10	=	310 demerits
51	D defects	=	51×2	=	102 demerits
		Total		=	952 demerits

Table 10.3. Calculating the quality index.

If the production rate is constant, you can then calculate the index by dividing the total number of demerits by a number representing the *ceiling* for demerits, say, 400. Thus, QI = 952/400 = 2.38. If the QI for the following week is, say, 3.21, it means that the quality has deteriorated. The target objective expressed in this case is an index equal to or below 1. By calculating the quality index for each week, you can follow the evolution of the quality level over long periods of time and take the proper corrective methods when necessary.

If the rate of production varies, you can divide the total number of demerits by the number of units produced and express the result in demerits per unit. In this fashion you will get the average number of demerits per unit produced rather than the total number of defects detected. Thus, if we take the same example as used in Table 10.3 (952 demerits detected) and further assume a production of 100 units, we will obtain the following calculations.

For a production of 100 units:

$$\text{Proportion of demerits} = \frac{952}{100}$$

$$= 9.52 \text{ demerits per unit}$$

$$\text{Ceiling for demerits} = 4 \text{ demerits per unit}$$

$$\text{QI for the week} = \frac{9.52}{4} = 2.38$$

For a production of 80 units:

$$\text{Proportion of demerits} = \frac{9.52}{80}$$

$$= 11.9 \text{ demerits per unit}$$

$$\text{QI for the week} = \frac{11.9}{4} = 2.98$$

The QI is a supple tool that can be set up and used in a number of different ways. Sometimes the QI is the relationship between the proportion of demerits for a given week and the average daily proportion of demerits for the previous year. The QI can also be calculated on a weekly, monthly, or annual basis to track its development, and this may be done equally for the products that the company produces and for the ones it buys, as well as for those of each of its suppliers taken separately.

A company may compare its QI with that of a given competitor or with the average for the industry. It may even take the QI for one of its plants and compare it with the average for the rest of its plants.

As a further refinement, the number of defects can be integrated into the calculation. (Note that in the QI calculations above, we have looked at the number of demerits but not the number of defects.) In practice, a car, for example, might have 1 defect worth 20 demerits or 20 defects worth 1 demerit each. Although, in both instances, the figures add up to 20, the message to be drawn from each of them would differ. While one 2-demerit defect may well be attributable to human error, 20 defects—no matter how small—surely amount to negligence. One formula that may be used to integrate defects is the following:

If a QI of 200 represents the ideal QI (that is, 0 defects, 0 demerits), then

$$QI = 200 - \frac{(defects + demerits)}{2}$$

The Introduction of SQC and SPC into Companies

I should point out that the techniques for *statistical quality control* (SQC) and for *statistical process control* (SPC) have been in existence since the end of the 1920s; they are thus not a 1990s innovation. Though they were developed in the United States, they have been used there only on a relatively limited basis. It was the spectacular invasion of Japanese products, after the oil crises of the 1970s, that awoke the West to the importance of these techniques. A number of companies who recently introduced statistical quality control and, especially, statistical process control have been most disappointed by the results. We must not forget that *statistics do not improve quality, people do,* and they use numerous means to do so, statistics being but one of them.

As with any other techniques, there are conditions requisite to obtaining the best results when SQC and SPC are introduced. Company top management must realize that SPC is only a part of SQC; SQC is only one aspect of control; control is only one activity within quality management; and, finally, quality management itself must be part and parcel of the enterprise's overall philosophy, which is, in sum, total quality management. In this way, quality management is not limited to the technical aspects of the products or processes but, rather, starts from the definition of the need and extends right up to the satisfaction of this need, with all of the functions in the enterprise contributing to it either directly or indirectly.

This in no way means that the company has to be completely revolutionized every time some particular SQC technique is introduced. It does, however, mean that such techniques have to be introduced within the context of a global vision that is shared equally by all, from top management right down to the shop-floor workers at the base of the hierarchical pyramid.

The very costly failures sustained by many companies who have launched SPC and SQC programs are due, in the majority of cases, to the fact that these programs have been left exclusively in the hands of middle managers. Top management thinks that its only role is to approve budgets for the program. The workers suspect that top management uses the programs as a means to make them work harder and to save on salaries for inspectors. Everybody's attention is caught up in the means rather than being focused on the end, the company's common goals of survival and progress. The time when soldiers fought simply because the generals told them to has gone; nowadays they want to know why and against whom they have to fight. Therefore, in my opinion, before introducing SQC programs, there must be a systematic effort to make everyone fully aware of their usefulness and, indeed, necessity if company progress is to be furthered and jobs protected. This sensitization program must include top management, starting with the president and upper management, and permeate down to the shop-floor workers. It is the only guarantee of success in the short and medium term and of tangible and significant results in quality improvement.

Statistical Process Control

To define SPC, we should remember that control is a quantitative or qualitative evaluation of a characteristic or group of characteristics of a product (goods or services) in relation to an established value which is desired or required. *Statistics* is a science that collects, analyzes, represents, and interprets quantitative data. A *process* is a system composed of operators, machines, work methods, materials, and their immediate environment. It is used to transform *input* into useful *output*.

More and more, manufacturing companies—small, medium, or large—are introducing SPC. They do so either by choice, with a view to improving the quality of their products, or by necessity, to comply with their client companies' requirements. Indeed, many companies who outsource most of their production activities to suppliers stipulate that the suppliers use SPC as a condition of doing business with them.

The following is a list of seven of the characteristics and advantages of SPC.

1. It facilitates improvement in the quality of the products and consequently increases the company's competitiveness.

2. It focuses on defect prevention rather than on detection. This contrasts with control by sampling, which, as an after-the-fact control, serves only to confirm a situation that already exists.

3. It eliminates, or at least reduces, emotional discussions about the process, because work is done on the basis of fact rather than opinion.

4. It allows an objective evaluation of the capacity of a process to produce results that fall within a specified range of tolerances.

5. It gives the customer the assurance—some would say proof—that the quality of the product he or she is ordering will satisfy all of his or her requirements.

6. It is a tool that permits the operator to visually monitor quality as it is being manufactured; hence he or she can make any necessary corrections when required.

7. It permits an evaluation of the impact of a change in the process on the quality of the finished product.

Big companies that require their suppliers to use an SPC system also offer them courses in SPC, if they so desire, so that they will be able to meet the required specifications. In this way, the client company makes sure that it receives quality products and, in addition, is no longer obliged to set up a rigorous incoming control system on its own premises, as has been the case until quite recently. This saves precious time and money that would have been spent on returning to the supplier all of the items judged to be of inferior quality.

There is another point to bear in mind: With the knowledge that no process—however sophisticated it might be—can reproduce a given dimension with absolute precision, the potential purchaser of a part or product indicates a range of *tolerance* that he or she would accept. In other words, he or she indicates what degree of deviation from the required specification, or *nominal value,* is admissible. Unfortunately, this has given birth to a sloppy habit in industry. Manufacturers no longer target the desired specification, but remain content with falling somewhere within the permitted range of tolerance. Tolerances are confused with the quality level sought, as represented by the value specified. However, as the word itself denotes, tolerances refer to inferior quality which, at best, is only to be tolerated, not set up as a target to aim for. To produce products that are as near as possible to the dimension required or desired, one has to use certain techniques, among the most efficient of which is SPC. SPC has the additional advantage of being a motivating force for the operators who are trained to use it. They are given responsibility for the quality of their own product and the tool with which to achieve it. Everybody wins. The company can offer better quality at a better price and thereby increases its profits; the operator is proud of what he or she produces; and, above all else, the customer's needs are fulfilled.

The Basic Concept of SPC

The basic concept of SPC is that every process, however precise it may be, produces variations. Some variations are inherent in the process and are due to random, *nonassignable* causes. To illustrate the point, ask someone to write the letter *a* several times on a sheet of paper, with the same pencil, under the same lighting and the same ambient conditions. You will see that the individual letters written under the same conditions are different, although the difference may be only very slight. Inherent variations of a process may be caused by vibrations from a machine, minor irregularities in raw materials, imperceptible changes in temperature, or other ambient conditions. Whereas inherent variations are *random* and due to chance, other variations are due to *assignable* causes which have to be researched and eliminated where necessary. When a process produces variations due to assignable causes, it is said to be *out of control.* These variations can be caused by wear in a tool, machinery that is out of order, operator negligence, poor raw materials, or a power failure.

SPC's basic tool is the *control chart.* Control charts are used to monitor a process in order to reduce the variations and limit them to those produced by nonassignable causes, thereby keeping this process *under control.* SPC is also useful in measuring the capability of a process to meet the specified tolerances for product characteristics.

Every process has a number of variable characteristics, such as the speed of the machines, ambient temperature, weight or composition of the raw materials, and so on. Variations in these characteristics can influence the output of the process and can be due to assignable or nonassignable causes within the process. You can follow the variations in any process with the aid of a control chart.

Just as a car must be smaller than a garage door to be able to fit the garage, so the span of variations produced by a process must be smaller than the specified tolerance range for a process to be capable of complying with it. This ability to fit in is called the *process capability*. If the span is wider than the tolerance range, the process obviously does not have the process capability needed to meet the specifications. In this case, one must change the range of tolerances, change the process, or simply tolerate the production of a certain proportion of defective units. SPC gives an objective measurement of the capability of a process. Though control charts are the principal tool of SPC, other techniques can be used, such as Pareto analysis and the scatter diagram, which form part of the PISP process. PISP is an acronym for problem identification, solving, and prevention. (For more information on this process, see chapter 13.)

Acceptance Sampling

The concept of acceptance sampling is the same one as applied in surveys used to evaluate the opinion of a population based on a relatively small sample. Opinion polls during an election period, customer surveys on specific products and services—these are immediately recognizable examples of this concept at work. The objective of acceptance sampling is to help those responsible to decide if a given lot should be accepted or rejected in cases in which 100 percent control is impractical or undesirable. There are a number of reasons for which one might resort to acceptance sampling, ranging from economic or technical reasons to matters of efficiency. Acceptance sampling can be succinctly described as follows: When a batch of items is received for control, a *sample* is drawn from it, and the number of defective parts in the sample is noted. If this number does not exceed a certain *acceptance number,* the lot is accepted; otherwise it is rejected. If rejected, it is either completely sorted through so that the defective units can be picked out or returned to its internal or external source.

Before statistical acceptance sampling was introduced, an intuitive sampling approach was used that arbitrarily determined sample sizes, arbitrarily ruled to accept or reject a lot, and gave no idea of the risk of error entailed in using a specific sampling plan. Acceptance sampling is used to choose a sample size and an acceptance number and to calculate the risk, or probability, of rejecting a good lot or accepting a bad lot. Acceptance sampling saves time and money, and although it presents risks, these can nevertheless be precisely evaluated.

Measuring the Costs Related to the Absence of Total Quality

Operating costs can directly affect both the shareholders, since they affect profits and resulting dividends, and the customers, because costs may be passed on to them in the form of higher prices. They can also affect employees, because the more they rise, the less is left over for employees' salaries, fringe benefits, and bonuses. Therefore, control measures must be brought to bear on the costs related to total quality (that is, the cost spent to achieve total quality and the cost resulting from any un- (total) quality or over- (total) quality produced). Control being based on measuring, those overseeing the controlling—quality specialists or *qualiticians*—have traditionally discussed quality in purely technical terms: number of errors, rate of defects, number of nonconforming items, variations, deviations, and so on. But for that matter this heady jargon and these figures are hardly likely to make top management, or any other management, break out into cheers. They are actually somewhat more likely to elicit an indifferent yawn.

There is an anecdote about a quality control manager who was at his wit's end to get someone, anyone, in higher management to listen to him and to look at his reports, his charts and graphs, his figures about defects, defectives, and nonconformities. His attempts always failed. Everyone was busy with more important strategic matters. One day, however, this manager had a revolutionary idea. He asked to meet with the president, this time using as his lure some serious information on how to triple the company's profits. Although more than skeptical, the president could not afford not to listen, if only briefly, to what the quality manager had to say. The meeting was set and the manager showed up with a thick file in his hand. Without any introduction, social or otherwise, he threw his file on the president's desk and stated that, for the previous fiscal year, unquality had cost the company 24 percent of its total revenues! In a company that was running at a 7 percent profit, that meant it was losing more than three times its profits on unquality. Saving even 14 percent of the 24 percent would triple the profits. Simple mathematics.

The president immediately hung up his phone, asked his secretary to hold all calls and not to interrupt him under any circumstance, and then pulled down the blinds on his windows to shut out any distractions. He offered the QC manager a cup of strong coffee, regretting that in this smokeless era he could not offer him an expensive cigar, and sat down and asked for facts and figures, with which he was presented. Shortly after this incident, the QC manager was promoted to a senior position. For once, he had used a language anyone could understand, regardless of his or her position on the organization chart. In fact, Juran has even suggested that QC specialists should be bilingual: fluent in the technical language surrounding the quality of what has been produced, yet still able to talk to top managers in their own language.

In another instance, when asked about the cost of poor product quality, the CEO at a small manufacturing company said that his feeling was that it was about 3 percent of his sales. He added that this seemed reasonable and so he did not deem it necessary to do anything about it. He commented, "This is the cost of doing business." When the cost was later evaluated and found to be closer to 22 percent of sales, he was at first very skeptical, but then realized that this figure was actually closer to the truth than his original 3 percent. The 3 percent figure was based exclusively on defective products that had been returned by customers and had to be either repaired or replaced with new ones. Other companies include in that cost only the expenses of the quality control or quality assurance department, nothing else.

Most quality experts estimate the cost of poor product quality to run around 25 percent of the sales revenues in an average manufacturing company.[5] In service companies, the cost of poor quality is a high percentage of the operating costs. For example, a Chicago bank noticed that a money transfer, when done correctly, cost about $10. However, if there was an error in the transaction, it cost the bank about $400 to correct it—4000 percent of the regular cost! Based on these estimates, the United States loses $1 trillion a year on poor quality.

As indicated in chapter 1, a study by the Strategic Planning Institute showed the direct impact of quality on the return on investment and on the profits on

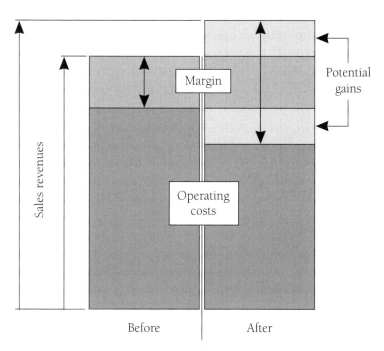

Figure 10.5. Gains resulting from continuous improvement and reengineering.

sales for different-sized companies in different sectors. For a company with a small market share, profits on sales vary from 3 percent for companies with low relative quality to 8 percent for ones with high relative quality; if the market share increases, profits could go as high as 12 percent, a 400 percent increase. According to the French Standards Association (AFNOR), poor quality costs an estimated $4000 per worker per year. The association indicates that the evaluation of the cost of quality is a fundamental aspect of the management of an organization because it leads to the implementation of actions targeting continuous improvement and reengineering, which result in increasing its revenues and decreasing its operating costs (see Figure 10.5).

It has been observed that executives in most organizations, big or small, do not know how much the absence of quality costs. They often do not seem to have even a clue. Generally, they tend to largely underestimate such costs. In fact, a great number are even convinced that improving quality and increasing customer and employee satisfaction is an expensive proposition that they cannot afford, especially in recessionary times. This ignorance goes a long way toward explaining why most of them do not get personally and genuinely involved in any quality or total quality effort. They may support it, encourage their subordinates to consider and emphasize it, even agree to participate in some events to show they care. But, in the end, because they fail to grasp its bottom-line value, they lack the commitment to truly practice what they preach.

Evaluating the Costs Related to Total Quality

As indicated before, the costs related to total quality include both the costs incurred in order to achieve it and the costs resulting from the failure to achieve it. To put it in terms of the total quality triad, they include the costs of the specific activities necessary to satisfy shareholders, customers, and employees, and the costs of the consequences resulting from the dissatisfaction of any of these people.

Measuring total quality costs is an important element in the controlling activities of TQM. It is often a factor that will trigger the introduction of TQM in an organization. Besides, no diagnosis is complete if it does not include information on this cost. However, many attempts to measure such costs in precise terms have proven to be arduous. Moreover, the evaluation of this cost does not, in and of itself, improve a company's performance as far as total quality is concerned. One has to know how to interpret the results of that evaluation, then use them to develop a plan of action to reduce this cost and improve performance. Interpretation cannot be done intuitively or haphazardly. Continuous improvement and reengineering techniques have to be mastered and effectively applied at both strategic and operational levels in order to effectively prepare this plan of action.

What makes the computation of total quality costs difficult is the fact that most existing accounting systems are simply not designed to do it. Traditionally, accounting systems are mainly used to calculate the profits and losses and the taxes to be paid or, better, saved. There are exceptions, of course. More sophisticated accounting systems have been and are still being developed to serve more integrally as management decision-making tools. Activity-based costing (ABC) is such a system, as explained in chapter 13. Another difficulty stems from the fact that a sizable proportion of the cost of the absence of total quality cannot be objectively and precisely measured. For example, one should evaluate the impact of an unsatisfied shareholder, customer, or employee on the revenues of a company. Indeed, a dissatisfied customer may cancel an order for some products or may stop dealing with a company and go elsewhere for all subsequent purchases. The dissatisfaction may stem from any of the seven QVALITY factors and not necessarily from unquality products only. In one instance, a number of customers stopped buying products from a certain company because it became known that the company's production process polluted a nearby lake (this is the image factor in QVALITY). Moreover, a dissatisfied customer may cause a chain reaction when he or she expresses dissatisfaction to a number of other customers, with the possible result that a company loses an entire market.

The same applies to shareholders. There is a case in which some institutions sold off the bonds they held in a public utility because it was suspected that the utility planned to engage in construction projects detrimental to the environment. To cite another example, an aeronautical company decided to develop a housing project on a huge piece of land that it had previously used as an airfield. Its shareholders questioned the wisdom of this decision to venture into real estate, which they, at the time, considered to be a highly unstable, unpredictable, and quickly declining field. They decided to sell their shares and invest elsewhere. The results of these actions have to be measured and attributed to the absence of total quality (that is, the dissatisfaction of the shareholders) rather than to a general trend in the stock market, to the recession, or to other prevailing economic conditions.

The fact that costs related to total quality or its absence are somewhat difficult to calculate in no way means that one should not make serious efforts to evaluate them. On the contrary, it means that even greater efforts must be made to calculate such costs, for even subjective data and rough evaluations may prove indispensable to improving the company's performance and ensuring its survival and progress.

A Historical Review

Efforts to calculate the cost of product quality and unquality began a number of years ago. In his book *Total Quality Control,* Feigenbaum suggested that the two major segments of a company's quality costs are the failure and appraisal costs, the third and smallest segment being the prevention costs.[6] As we shall see, these categories can be extended to include all aspects of the total quality approach. Let us see now what these costs represent.

- *Failure costs* can be broken down into internal and external subgroups.

— The *internal failure costs* are those incurred due to unquality in the product detected before the product leaves the company or while it is still under its control.

— Conversely, *external failure costs* are those incurred due to unquality in the product detected when the product has already left the company and is no longer under its control.

• *Appraisal costs* include all monies spent on the detection of errors or defects by measuring the conformity of different items to the required level or specifications of quality. Items include incoming materials and supplies, work in process, and finished products.

• *Prevention costs* include the sum of all amounts spent or invested to prevent or at least significantly reduce defects, that is, to finance activities aimed at eliminating the causes of possible defects and errors before they occur.

As we can see, these costs pertain only to preventing and correcting poor product quality and, even then, they represent only the direct, tangible, and visible portion of the real and total costs. Obviously, they do not include, among other things, costs incurred by producing overquality, that is, developing product characteristics that do not benefit the customer or user in any way.

The total quality costs include direct as well as indirect costs, be they tangible and measurable or intangible and estimated. In this global spectrum, some costs can be calculated with a very high degree of precision or level of certainty, while others can be only roughly estimated with a very low degree of certainty (see Figure 10.6). They include, on the one hand, expenditures and investments required to introduce, promote, monitor, control, and achieve total quality and, on the other hand, the costs resulting from the absence of total quality. When measuring the total quality costs, it is recommended that one start with the costs that are easily quantifiable, tangible, and visible, then move on gradually to include costs which can be estimated with only some degree of certainty, and end with the costs that can be no more than very roughly estimated with a very low degree of certainty.

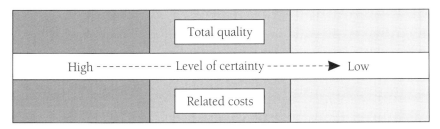

Figure 10.6. The spectrum of costs related to total quality.

Source: J. N. Kelada, *Comprendre et réaliser la qualité totale,* 2nd ed. (Dollard-des-Ormeaux, Quebec, Canada: Quafec Publications, 1992), 326. Reprinted with permission.

Let us further extend this model and examine total quality costs in the light of these categories.

Direct and Indirect Costs Related to Total Quality

TQ costs include the customer-related costs of external failures and the costs of internal failures, as well as those of appraisal and prevention. I present here some examples of such costs, not with the intention of compiling a complete or exhaustive list, but to illustrate the nature of these costs.

Customer-Related External Failure Costs

Customer-related external failure costs include all costs resulting from a failure to meet, on the one hand, the Q requirements (product quality per se) and, on the other hand, any of the VALITY requirements (Q + VALITY = QVALITY).

Costs Related to Not Satisfying the Q Requirements

- Compensation, complete refunds, or free replacement to customers who are forced to return substandard products or who receive substandard services. A restaurant, for example, might give out free meals to unsatisfied customers.

- Replacements for items returned by client companies, distributors, retailers, or wholesalers.

- The cost of processing complaints.

- Warranties covering parts, labor, and so on.

- Transportation costs for defective products.

- Costs resulting from legal procedures and settlements when customers sue companies for breach of contracts regarding products and services or for damages ensuing from faulty products (product liability). In one recent example of service liability, a judge ordered a dentist to pay $163,570 in damages to a couple he treated. He had ignored their complaints of persistent pain while performing crown and bridge repairs on them.[7]

- Voluntary or compulsory recalls of defective products. Recently, a publisher had to recall a cookbook for an error in a recipe that might have endangered the health of anyone trying it.

- Insurance against malpractice and product liability.

- Rate increases in insurance due to history of malpractice and defective products.

- Loss of an order, a customer, or a whole market due to poor product quality.

Costs Related to Not Satisfying the VALITY Requirements

- Compensation to customers who receive quality products or services but who do not receive them on time (T), in the required quantity (volume, V), or at the agreed-upon location (L). Some restaurants, for example, offer free meals if the customers are not served within a certain period of time (as short as 15 minutes in some cases). In the case of delayed deliveries to commercial clients, penalties are often written into the contract itself.

- The cost of administrative errors (A) in order taking, credit assessment, invoicing, and complaint processing. These include interest foregone or paid on amounts that could not be collected because of such errors. The correction of these errors (if it is not too late to do so) will, of course, also incur costs.

- Loss of sales or contract biddings due to noncompetitive pricing (lower yield, Y, for customers).

- Loss of a sale or cancellation of an order due to improper behavior toward a customer by an employee, company representative, or external partner (I).

- Loss of a sale or cancellation of an order because of an image problem (I) due to the behavior of the company towards the environment. Loss of sales due to image being affected by a massive recall of defective products.

- Loss of potential customers due to an image problem (I) caused by dissatisfied actual customers who tell other customers or potential customers.

- Loss of revenues due to incorrect assessments of a customer's credit. Through incorrect credit assessment, one can end up selling to customers who cannot pay or, conversely, not selling to customers who can.

- Higher interest rates on loans and difficulties in borrowing due to the deteriorating image of the company (bad quality, recalls, effect on environment, and so on).

- Loss of an order, a customer, or a whole market due to customer dissatisfaction with any of the VALITY characteristics.

Internal Failure Costs

As mentioned earlier, internal failure costs result from errors or defects detected prior to the defective item leaving the company or while it is still under its control (for example, in a warehouse or truck) and thus include such items as work in process, finished products, documents (reports, financial statements, purchase orders, work orders), and services (machine repairs, maintenance of equipment). The following costs, among others, fall under this category.

- Cost of rework due to errors or defects which, if not corrected, could affect the satisfaction of either the shareholders, the customers, or the employees. This includes repairs and corrections. Obviously, the later the error is detected in a process (mainstream, support, or work process), the higher the cost. For example, an error in a drawing entails correcting or modifying the drawing or producing a new one. Now, if the drawing was used to actually produce something, the item produced would have to be modified to match the new or modified drawing.

- Discounts given to customers on items that are deemed of a lesser quality than required. This occurs, for instance, when defective clothes or garments are produced. The defective product may be salvaged, but can only then be sold at a loss, with the recuperated costs amounting to less than the production costs.

- Cost of scrap produced, when defective, nonconforming items cannot be repaired or salvaged.

- Nonproductive work, such as waiting for parts, information, or instructions.

- Cost of scrapping or modifying substandard purchased materials which, for any number of possible reasons, cannot be refunded by suppliers.

- Costs incurred because of work accidents, absenteeism, and repair work and loss of production entailed by equipment breakdown.

Costs Common to External and Internal Failures

- Repairs and modifications of defective products or unsatisfactory services. These include costs of parts, direct labor (production personnel), and indirect labor (storekeepers, supervisors, and so on).

- Correction and modification of faulty drawings.

- Subcontracting production as a result of an increase in rework and repairs that significantly reduce the production capacity of the company.

- Administrative costs resulting from dealing with any of the failures mentioned here—long-distance telephone calls, faxes, letters, mail.

- Meetings to discuss causes of these failures and find solutions.

- Reinspecting modified and repaired products prior to their delivery to the customers.

- Drop in both productivity and employee morale when employees have to do the same job over and over again until the customers are finally either satisfied or give up altogether. Cost of high turnover.

- Cost of all of the activities that have to be carried out to compensate for faulty parts or scrapped material: modifying plans or rescheduling work; adding supervisors to cope with the increased general workload; increasing the inventory levels to make up for a high percentage of parts and material that are not fit for use; the proliferation of administrative work when additional parts and materials have to be purchased, received, and stored.

- Higher inventories of materials of work in process and of finished products in order to prevent production or shipping stoppages due to the high occurrence of unquality in these items.

- Indirect labor and paperwork involved in activities related to rework, shipping and receiving, and scrapping of defective materials.

- The reduction in the life of equipment and facilities caused by their additional use for modification and repair of defective products.

- New competitors entering the market with better products or acceptable or better substitutes.

There is the danger that recurring failures will creep up, settle in at an insidiously comfortable level, and, at some point, no longer be noticed by anyone. If they occur regularly enough, they either become invisible or come to be regarded, with complacency, as the cost of doing business. What is in fact a chronic malaise becomes normal, and "the trouble with normal," as one thoughtful songsmith put it, "is it always gets worse."

Actually, whatever percentage of work (that is, finished product) is taken up by failures, that percentage increase is mirrored across the board and tacked on to everything that is done, bought, or stored. Thus, if failures represent 3 percent of regular work, this would lead to everything else being increased by 3 percent: inventory levels, time for supervision, production and storage space, delivery dates, cycle time for administrative procedures, and so on. The time element obviously translates into costs. These costs are then buried in what would be considered normal operating costs.

Prevention and Appraisal Costs

These include costs such as the ones related to the following:

- Sensitization of the workforce to the importance of total quality and of the role of teamwork in achieving and maintaining it. Opinion surveys to measure the degree of satisfaction of the people in the company.

- Sensitization and education of the customers regarding the importance of the TQ approach, the benefits it can bring to all concerned, and the spirit of mutual assistance ("help us to help you") necessary to achieve it. These activities include organizing visits to and from customers (market-in) to establish better relations and enhance customer orientation in the company. They also include press campaigns and communication programs as well as advertisements. Opinion surveys to measure the customers' degree of satisfaction.

- Sensitization and education of shareholders. Total quality is a long-term joint effort, not a short-term scheme for grabbing a quick return on investment. Invitations to shareholders to participate in the life of the company and in its special events.

- Sensitization of and collaboration with upstream and downstream partners to achieve total quality for the benefit of all parties (company and partners).

- Benchmarking activities to assess the company's products in comparison with those of the competitors and the company's processes with those of competitors and noncompetitors. (These processes include production, accounting, warehousing, communication, and so on.)

- Additional personnel and activities necessary for follow-up of the different activities related to total quality: coordinators, facilitators, steering committee meetings, and administrative work.

- Reinforcement activities to keep the interest in total quality running at a high and continuous level. (These include recognition and rewards, pamphlets, literature, and participation in external activities, such as conferences, information exchanges, and national awards.)

- Setting up and operating quality assessment and control systems and procedures.

- The quality assurance system: manual, procedures, audits, and certification as put forth in the ISO standards. (See chapter 11 for a detailed discussion of quality assurance.)

- Inspectors' salaries and fringe benefits; inspection and testing laboratories and facilities; calibration of instruments; and so on.

- Salaries and fringe benefits of all personnel working on activities related to total quality in different departments.

- Products destroyed for testing purposes.

- Total quality information and reporting systems.

- Total quality motivation programs for personnel.

- Training in quality management, control and assurance, problem solving, reengineering, and so on.

- Quality promotion material (booklets, videos, and so on) aimed at enhancing quality awareness and maintaining interest among personnel, suppliers, and subcontractors.

- Continuous quality improvement, innovation (reengineering), and problem-prevention activities.

- Cost of competitors' products bought for analysis and evaluation.

- Frequent preventive maintenance operations to improve quality or reduce the risks of unquality.

- Improving plant and office layout and work instructions to reduce poor quality.

- Evaluation of suppliers and help extended to them to set up quality systems.
- Standardization activities.
- Development of new and better-performing products.
- Development of new and better-performing processes.

The Total Quality Cost Curve

In order to achieve and maintain total quality, a company must spend a certain amount of money on prevention, on assessment and control, and on corrective actions directed toward any absence of total quality. The graph in Figure 10.7 illustrates the effect of these costs on the revenues and profits of the company.

If we plot the internal and external failure costs (dotted line A) and prevention and appraisal costs (dotted line B), we are able to obtain the total quality cost line $(A + B)$.[8] When, as at the beginning of the chart, there is no prevention or appraisal, total costs related to total quality are at their highest and the company loses money because it cannot compete with companies offering total quality at less cost. With the increase in prevention and appraisal activities, total costs decrease substantially, and the company starts making some profits. At a certain

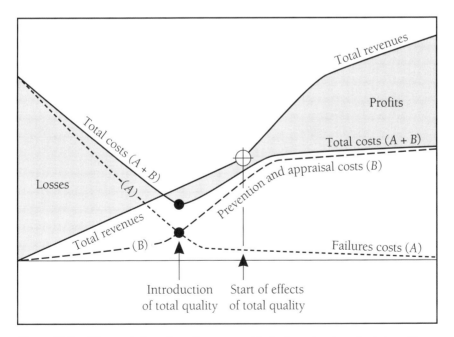

Figure 10.7. The evolution of quality costs with the introduction of total quality.

point, the total quality effort is introduced, and, accordingly, prevention and appraisal costs begin to mount at an even quicker rate. The effect of the TQ effort on revenue starts after a certain delay, when it begins to positively affect the satisfaction of the three members of the total quality triad. After a period of time, as the process is stabilized and moves into cruising speed, total revenues increase at a slower rate and total costs related to total quality taper off, as do both failure costs and prevention and appraisal costs.

In the short term, increasing prevention and appraisal costs increase total quality for the customers and employees; however, as we can see in the chart, it negatively affects the shareholders' satisfaction because it reduces the profitability of the company. With time, and with the maturing of the process, however, profitability will be improved by these costs, as continually mounting profits combine with a reduction in unnecessary waste to widen the profit margin. Eventually, we will have achieved satisfaction for all three players of the total quality triad.

An additional aspect to be considered is the economics of total quality–related costs. As underlined by Professor Hitoshi Kume, of the University of Tokyo, these costs are very high for new products, whose prices, sales revenues, and profit margins are also generally high. When a product has been manufactured for some time, and competition increases, total quality costs decrease but so do the price, the sales revenues, and the profit margin. However, with products hitting the market for the first time, profit margins are higher in spite of high quality costs, and such products are more profitable than other, established ones of higher quality levels. One can consider the example of videocassette recorders which, while they were of low quality when introduced to the marketplace, were nevertheless five times more expensive than they are now and still profitable.[9]

The calculation of total quality costs may serve two purposes: (1) to convince top managers of the critical importance of quality in their organization and the necessity of their personal implication in some total quality achievement and improvement process, and (2) to measure the improvement in total quality in dollars and cents. However, setting up an accurate total quality–cost accounting system alongside other existing information and accounting systems generally proves very costly. In many instances, inexpensive rough estimates have usually proven sufficient to serve both these purposes.

Conclusion

Total quality assessment and control activities aim at measuring the results of a company or a division within it and at evaluating the means used to achieve such results. The objective of these activities is to detect any absence of total quality in order to correct it and to identify opportunities for improvement of performance, either through continuous improvement or innovation (that is, reengineering).

The performance of a company has to be measured in terms of the achievement of the triple objective of the total quality triad—satisfying its three players through the collaborative effort of the company and its upstream and downstream partners. Moreover, that evaluation must take into account the impact of the company's activities on its environment. The performance of a division or a department within a company should not be evaluated by the criteria of its internal departmental objectives, but by its contribution to the company's global objectives.

Review Questions

1. How is the customers' satisfaction to be evaluated? Do satisfied customers mean that management has achieved the company's basic objectives?

2. Some management theoreticians and practitioners claim that profitability should not be seen as the only objective of an assessment and control system. Please comment.

3. Total quality should be measured in terms of dollars and cents. It is the only language everyone understands. Please comment. What would Juran and Crosby think of this statement?

4. According to Philip B. Crosby, quality is free. Please comment on this statement.

Notes

1. A. V. Feigenbaum, *Total Quality Control* (New York: McGraw-Hill 1961).

2. Ibid.

3. Harold Koontz and Cyril O'Donnel, *Principles of Management: An Analysis of Managerial Functions* (New York: McGraw-Hill, 1972), 579.

4. Actually, this represents 4.5 sigmas, since Motorola allows a deviation from the center (or nominal value) of plus or minus 1.5 sigmas (thus, $6 - 1.5 = 4.5$).

5. "Gallup Survey: Top Executives Talk About Quality," *Quality Progress* 19, no. 12 (December 1986): 49; and "1987 ASQC/Gallup Survey," *Quality Progress* 20, no. 12 (December 1987): 16.

6. A. V. Feigenbaum, *Total Quality Control* (New York: McGraw-Hill 1961), 83–84.

7. Geoff Baker, "Dentist ordered to pay couple $163,570 in damages," *The* [Montreal] *Gazette,* 10 March 1994, A5.

8. The total quality cost line is calculated as follows: At any point along the horizontal axis, the vertical distance measured from the base line to line A plus the vertical distance measured from the base line to line B will give us the corresponding point in line A + B. When this calculation is effected all along the horizontal axis, the points that have been derived are then connected to form the new line A + B.

9. Hitoshi Kume, "Business Management and Quality Cost: The Japanese Review," *Quality Progress* 18, no. 5 (May 1985): 13–18.

Chapter 11

An ounce of prevention is worth a pound of cure.

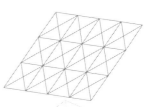

Total Quality Assurance and Standardization

Section 1: Total Quality Assurance

The cycle is now complete. The people have been given direction and guidance, total quality has been planned and organized, the plans have been executed, and the obtained results evaluated. The absence of total quality has been detected and corrective action undertaken. Even if all objectives have been achieved, there are still opportunities to improve on the results obtained. Assessment and control activities will help improve performances by detecting and correcting the absence of total quality as well as pointing out opportunities for improvement and innovation. However, more important than detection will be the emphasis given prevention—for prevention is by far the best cure. And while assessment and control may help detect, it is assurance that helps prevent (see Figure 11.1).

Quality Assurance: Concept and Definition

Assurance differs from planning, organization, and control—the other management activities—in that it is continuous and runs parallel to them. In effect, it is an overall auditing and monitoring system to ensure that the other management activities are performed effectively to achieve the common goal of total quality.

Companies traditionally put great importance on quality control, using it as a filter to separate the bad units from the good ones. Controlling the incoming goods and services, materials, parts, components, information, and documents, if done efficiently and effectively, allows one to stop any substandard items from entering

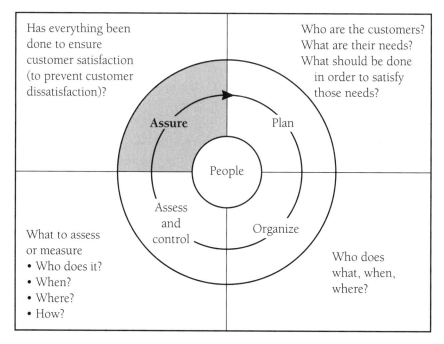

Has everything been done to ensure customer satisfaction (to prevent customer dissatisfaction)?

Who are the customers? What are their needs? What should be done in order to satisfy those needs?

Assure

Plan

People

Assess and control

Organize

What to assess or measure
• Who does it?
• When?
• Where?
• How?

Who does what, when, where?

Figure 11.1. Position of assurance in management activities.

the production system or any errors from entering the information or administrative system. Similarly, controlling work in process prevents errors or substandard products from proceeding any further in the administrative or production process. Finally, controlling finished products—goods or services—stops unquality units from being shipped to the customers or buyers, or errors being forwarded to external partners. Although this is all very well and good, it is performed *after the fact,* that is, after the incoming materials, documents, and information have been received, or the work in process, finished products, documents, reports, and so on have been produced. Therefore, time and money will have been wasted on the faulty material, documents, or products that are detected, returned, and then corrected or rejected.

The idea of *product quality assurance,* or *quality assurance* (QA) is not new. It was conceived during World War II when it was found that controlling materials, equipment, or ammunitions at the front made no sense. The time and resources to control them were lacking, and, even if they had been available, it would not have been practical to return the faulty items to the manufacturers thousands of miles away and wait for replacements. Rather than detecting unquality, it was decided that the emphasis would be placed on preventing it.

The concept of quality assurance consists therefore of setting up a system that can give the customers the *assurance* that no poor quality will occur in design, production, or delivery of the product. To sketch out the specifics broadly, this means making sure that everyone knows what to do (information, instructions), what has just been done (control, feedback), and how to correct any error immediately, wherever it happens, before proceeding to the next step in the global business process that carries the product from its specification stage to its final delivery and use.

External quality assurance may comprise either the QA system that a customer requires a company (its supplier) to set up or the system that the company itself wants to set up for its own benefit. Having begun by being applied externally, the concept of quality assurance was subsequently extended to company management when companies sensed the need to seek assurance that their own products were designed and produced to an optimal level of quality. This is *internal* quality assurance, which, thus, denotes a QA system set up by a company by its own volition and for its own use. Note that the company's own requirements for an internal quality assurance system can sometimes happen to coincide with the system required by a customer or a number of customers. If not, a company will generally set up one QA system that satisfies both the external and internal needs.

Let us take a look at what happens when a company with no external QA system purchases manufactured goods or raw materials. The receiving department uses control procedures (inspections, tests, verifications) to filter out any incoming materials, parts, or products that do not conform to the buying companies' specifications. This method, although it should eliminate the possibility of any defective items entering a company, has several disadvantages. First of all, it translates into additional costs and significant delays for the buyers. By performing the inspection of incoming materials, they are paying for an activity to detect a poor quality that should not exist in the first place, because they are supposed to be receiving and paying for items that meet their specifications.

The buyers often incur further significant loss of time and money (transportation, reinspection procedures, and so on) in returning nonconforming items to the suppliers. The burden of proof that these items truly meet the specifications should be on the suppliers, not on the buyers. Furthermore, in cases where manufacturing processes are lengthy (months, perhaps years), it would be absurd to wait for delivery only to find that the item is defective and has to be returned to the supplier. For example, it can take two years to have a hydraulic turbine delivered. To be forced—after a two-year wait—to reject such a product would be extremely costly and could have terrible consequences, economic and otherwise.

Large organizations that rely heavily on subcontracting, like the department of defense (arms, weapons, ammunitions), automobile manufacturers (parts, components), and electric utility companies (turbines, boilers, reactors) now all resort to quality assurance.[1] Even prior to ordering, they need to have *proof* that the product will be designed, produced, and delivered to meet their exact requirements. External quality assurance—a QA system set up at the supplier's premises—consequently eliminates, or at least substantially reduces, the need to implement an incoming quality control system in the buyer's receiving department.

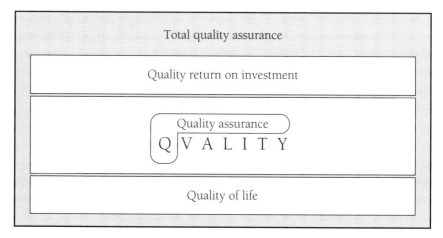

Figure 11.2. Quality assurance and total quality assurance.

Source: J. N. Kelada, *Comprendre et réaliser la qualité totale*, 2nd ed. (Dollard-des-Ormeaux, Quebec, Canada: Quafec Publications, 1992), 1791. Reprinted with permission.

Total quality assurance (TQA) goes further than product quality assurance. It constantly targets the three components of the total quality triad, namely: a quality return on their investment for the stockholders; QVALITY and the surpassing of customer satisfaction and expectations; and quality of life for the employee (see Figure 11.2). Just as total quality includes and surpasses product quality, so total quality assurance also includes and surpasses product quality assurance. It touches on all of the activities within a company and extends to its external partners, upstream and downstream. QA aims at ensuring that the customers get the *right* product, *on time,* and *at the least cost;* TQA aims at ensuring that the customers get QVALITY and ACE, that the shareholders get a quality return and employees a good quality of life, and that the environment is protected and enhanced.

The Philosophy Behind Quality Assurance

Even if a quality assurance program is clearly established—whether it be by a client setting out external quality assurance requirements or by management setting up a quality assurance system internally—the parties concerned are not absolved of the responsibility of verifying that products are properly designed, their specifications properly executed, and products manufactured on schedule. Because no system can act as a 100 percent guarantee of quality (can a good legal system ensure that no crimes are committed?), one cannot afford to rely just on the system. While it is true that quality assurance tends to confer responsibility for product quality on the supplier (whether internal or external), this in no way eliminates the customers' responsibility regarding the quality of the product they order; it only changes its nature and limits the customers to occasional supervision.

Quality assurance is based on an attitude on the part of the customers and suppliers toward each other that is quite different from one on which quality control has been traditionally based. The latter reflects an adversarial relationship and is a product of the element of distrust often felt by the company toward the suppliers and the company's own workers. When this attitude prevails, we often see customers playing the policeman's role, trying to catch suppliers or workers, whom they always suspect of wanting to sneak a substandard level of quality past them. In the receiving department, inspectors act like customs officers, trying to expose any attempt suppliers make to smuggle in poor quality. But within the framework of total quality assurance, that attitude has to change; the supplier must be perceived (and act) as a responsible partner, able and eager to exercise self-inspection. Making sure that the supplier actually does this is the essence of quality assurance. In this kind of working climate, total quality assurance has a double aim: to allow the buyer to achieve total quality and to help the supplier help the buyer achieve it, in a relationship of partnership.

Unfortunately, I see inappropriate uses of the concept. Some purchasers *impose* self-inspection on suppliers and use quality assurance as a means to keep an eye on potentially dishonest suppliers. This violates the essential spirit of quality assurance, which is to have suppliers voluntarily adopt self-inspection, not to drag them into it kicking and screaming. When there is distrust between a customer and a supplier, the supplier assumes a defensive attitude and concentrates all of its efforts on mounting the proof that the customer's quality requirements are being met, rather than focusing on actually satisfying those requirements. The supplier will often devote more energy to preparing a comprehensive quality manual and developing procedures than to rigorously applying those procedures. It becomes a matter of making expansive, dramatic gestures that yield poor results. Of course, customers with a large purchasing power can impose conditions on their suppliers, but this is counter-productive; the underlying concept of quality assurance is to allow the supplier to willingly exercise greater self-control and the buyer to use less control. As the old adage goes, "A man convinced against his will is of the same opinion still."

Mutual trust between the two parties is far more constructive and will not cost them any more. The onus lies with the buyer to make the suppliers understand that the demand for the implementation of a quality system at the supplier's end is not a bureaucratic procedure intended to increase the supplier's paperwork and costs while reducing its own; it is a system allowing both parties to function better, at a minimum cost, over the long term. It is a win–win proposition that can benefit both.

Such an earnest attempt to communicate with suppliers may be found in a document entitled *Supplier Quality Manual*, produced by General Electric's major appliance Business Group.[2] Through a series of messages, signed by representatives of the company, this document underscores two factors.

1. The company's concern to achieve the highest levels of quality in the field of household appliance manufacturing
2. The supplier's predominant role in this common objective

In this document, the buyer tries to get the suppliers to associate their own aspirations and objectives with the buyer's. First of all, the manual points out to the suppliers that they have everything to gain by improving the quality of the products they sell to their customers. Next, it goes on to give a detailed description of the new philosophy of quality, which has evolved from an effort to *detect* unquality when items are received to an effort to *prevent* the occurrence of unquality in the supplier's plant. The manual then presents possible approaches and techniques for putting this philosophy into practice.

One approach it advocates is to express the proportion of defective units produced or delivered in parts per million (ppm) instead of in a percentage, as is widely done currently. The advantage of this is primarily psychological. A 5 percent proportion of defective units may seem acceptable or even tolerable; expressed in ppm, however, 5 percent translates into 50,000. A figure like this is bound to attract and retain a manager's attention and galvanize him or her into the necessary corrective action.

The Quality Assurance System

The objective in using a quality assurance system is to provide proof that an optimal level of quality is being obtained at all stages of the product quality cycle. It is an overall system of *monitoring* activities and mechanisms that aims, in the first place, to prevent all unquality and, in the second place, to give early warning of any unquality produced in this cycle, from the design of the product to its delivery and use by the customer.

When customers started asking their suppliers to implement such systems, the suppliers would call in consultants who prepared a quality manual documenting all the required instructions and procedures in great detail. Often, these consultants had manuals prepared in advance that could be slightly altered or customized to give the impression they were designed specifically for a given company. These manuals could be presented by the company to the potential customers as proof that it indeed had a quality assurance system. In some cases it was observed that these manuals would never even reach the people who were supposed to be using them in engineering, purchasing, or manufacturing! If truth be told, they never left the offices of sales and marketing. In practice, then, situations can vary enormously. Some companies do not have any quality system, others may have one but it is ineffective, and still others have an effective system but nobody uses it. That is why the customers have to make sure that the supplier *has* a formal quality system and that it is *adequate* and effective (this can be done by looking at the supplier's quality manual), and then verify that it is in fact being *used* (by paying a visit to the supplier).

The validity of the quality system is checked by means of *audits*.

- Systems audits: work procedures, inspection and test procedures, organization charts

- Process audits: verifying that manufacturing processes as well as design and purchasing processes are used correctly and as specified

- Product audits: raw materials and various purchased parts, finished products, work in process

- Suppliers' audits: in some cases customers control not only their own suppliers but also their suppliers' suppliers, so that they can be sure that the raw materials used are of the required quality

The Role of the Quality Assurance Department

The traditional quality assurance department is supposed to have both an advisory and a supportive role. It should monitor operations, report any deviations to the appropriate managers, and suggest possible corrective measures. This department does not, however, carry out such measures itself. Its task is to ensure that they are carried out by the right people. It helps the various other departments to implement systems and mechanisms that will enable them to attain the required level of quality, but it is not the role of the quality assurance department to act as a substitute for anyone in charge of an operation. Usually the department has three types of responsibilities.

1. It assists in *formalizing* activities connected with quality-related planning, organization, directing, and control. These activities must be formalized, by documenting them; otherwise it is not possible to show proof of quality. The quality assurance department can help management and the other departments to develop a formal policy regarding quality, as well as the directives for putting it into practice and the indicators for evaluating it. It can act as advisor during standardization activities or when the quality manual is being prepared or updated. Documenting all of these activities is an essential exercise that always proves to be profitable. It makes the analysis of eventual problems much easier and facilitates inquiry into their probable causes. It allows for *traceability*.

2. The quality assurance department audits systems that are in place and evaluates their effectiveness, their adequacy for the intended use, and their updating methods. Activities that are audited involve design, writing of specifications, workforce and equipment qualification, research into and evaluation of suppliers, complaint systems, procedures for handling returned goods, recall systems for defective products (auditing, here, takes the form of a simulation to

evaluate effectiveness and response time), and metrological systems (processes for the selection of measuring instruments, maintenance procedures, standardization, and calibration).

3. Finally, the quality assurance department compiles statistics and produces reports on deviations from specifications; disparities between results and objectives; and anomalies found in procedure plans, processes, materials received, work in process, and finished products. The reports should note the number of these that occur, the trends that arise from them, and the manner in which these problems are handled.

The formal quality assurance system includes the following elements.

1. An organization that clearly defines the responsibilities of each department or of certain employees with respect to the quality management activities that will affect the product from design stage to scrap heap. These responsibilities are set out in organization charts and in job descriptions.

2. Formal, quality-related activities at the product design and development stages.

3. Quality-related activities concerning purchasing, described in procedures for the purchasing department personnel.

4. Documented methods related to receiving, storing, and handling that ensure that the level of quality received is maintained.

5. Work instructions that are clear, accessible, and practicable for all personnel concerned.

6. Precise and adequate measuring instruments, not only for the quality control department (if there is one), but also for receiving and manufacturing.

7. A system for *calibrating* all the measuring and testing instruments.

8. A detailed plan for inspection and testing that defines the various controls throughout the manufacturing process (what, where, when, by whom, and so on).

9. Identification and labeling of the items to be controlled or already controlled, conforming or not conforming to the desired specifications.

10. Physical isolation of nonconforming items, so that there is no risk that they will get mixed up with conforming products (for example, setting up a quarantine area).

11. The ability to determine at what stage the control process currently is. At any time the company must be able to find out what has been controlled and what remains to be controlled.

12. A quality manual, regularly updated, and always available to the personnel involved.

13. Audits to verify the systems, procedures, and products.

To transform quality assurance into total quality assurance, this series of items and activities must be complemented by other activities ensuring that the product will be delivered in sufficient quantity, on time, to the desired location, and at the lowest cost to the customer. At the same time, they must be accompanied by efficient and cordial *relations* with the customer and by an administrative system designed to allow customers to receive information, place orders, obtain credit, request modifications to orders in progress, pay their bills, and so on, in the easiest, least aggravating manner possible. *Profitability* must be the underlying objective of the entire process (which is not necessarily the case in quality assurance). To accomplish all this, one must see to it that

- Actual and potential customers are well identified.
- Their needs in terms of QVALITY are well identified.
- The competition's products and services are known and analyzed.
- Sound financial management principles are applied.
- Error-free, customer-friendly administrative procedures have been established.
- The personnel recruited and hired are capable of achieving total quality and are eager to do so.
- External upstream and downstream partners are capable of helping the customer achieve total quality and are eager to do so.
- Particular attention is paid to the company's personnel (that is, mobilizing them and making sure that the attitudes of the managers reinforce the concern for total quality).
- The various mobilization techniques presented in chapter 7 are used.
- All of the above is done with a constant eye to targeting profitability (or, in the public sector, respect for financial restraints and reduction of the tax burden for the taxpayers).

Business Process Mapping

In order to help put the concept of total quality assurance into practice, one generally proceeds by schematizing, or mapping out, the business process. Business process mapping thus defines the company's external environment and examines the following:

- Stockholders and their needs (return, image, and so on)
- Actual customers and potential customers (possible and probable) and their needs (QVALITY + ACE)
- Competitors and what they offer their customers
- Governments (constraints, financial and technical assistance, and so on)

Business process mapping also defines the internal environment and examines the business process, along with its mainstream and support processes. An analysis of unsatisfactory results would identify problems and weaknesses which could then be traced back to the probable causes within the business process just mapped.

I will discuss how business process mapping is set up in chapter 13. Each system, process, procedure, activity, or task within the firm must be linked to achieving total quality—that is to say, quality for both customer and stockholder—while, at the same time, taking into account all of the other external environmental components (government, ecology, and so on) and ensuring quality of life for the employees. Throughout this process, one must ensure that mechanisms exist or actions are taken to prevent any negative effects on the customer (QVALITY) or the stockholder (profitability).

The Quality Manual

In a quality assurance system, the quality manual takes on great importance. This document formally sets out the entire quality system in relation to the company's products and processes. In practice, a company may choose to have a manual for each product. This can happen if a customer stipulates it in the contract or if products are appreciably different and do not require the same degree of attention in terms of quality.

Some organizations that undertake large projects prepare a quality manual for each project. Sometimes companies have separate quality manuals for each one of their products. Depending on its particular situation, a company can choose to have a single manual that includes all work instructions and control procedures or a general manual and a procedure manual. If the contract with the customer stipulates a manual, it must be approved and signed by one of the supplier's executive officers.

Quality and Purchasing

On the average, in manufacturing firms, the cost of purchasing goods and services represents 60 percent of the total sales revenues, although in some cases it can reach 92 percent![3] In service businesses, the proportion is not as high, but it is still relatively significant. All of this indicates the suppliers' potentially enormous influence on the quality of the finished products as well as on the profitability of a company. Think of the impact caused by a delivery of an insufficient quantity of services, materials, parts, or components. Now take it a step further: Imagine this sort of miscue on the part of suppliers occurring repeatedly throughout the quality cycle, and you will get an idea of the potential snowball effect. If we take another look at the quality cycle (see Figure 11.3), we can then examine just how many opportunities there are for this to happen.

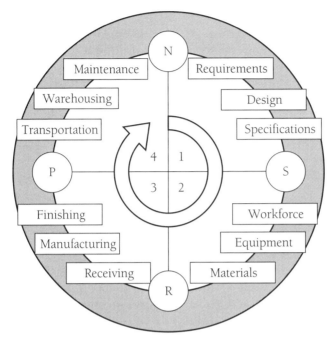

Figure 11.3. Purchasing and the quality cycle.

Source: J. N. Kelada, *Comprendre et réaliser la qualité totale,* 2nd ed. (Dollard-des-Ormeaux, Quebec, Canada: Quafec Publications, 1992), 206. Reprinted with permission.

In fact, a business may have dealings with external suppliers at each stage of all the four phases of the cycle. As far as its dealings with downstream partners are concerned, the firm can subcontract market research and surveys and product design and development in order to prepare product description and specifications. The company can also rent labor, buy or rent equipment, and buy materials. It can also subcontract manufacturing. As far as upstream partners are concerned, it can entrust the shipping, storage, and maintenance of products to external organizations. Obviously, quality must be assured at each of these stages.

The Customer–Supplier Relationship and Quality

As companies have introduced more recent management philosophies, the customer–supplier relationship has taken a whole new direction: The former adversaries now collaborate in close partnership. W. Edwards Deming has advised that companies stop searching for the lowest price when looking for a supplier. He has also proposed that companies significantly reduce the number of suppliers and genuinely collaborate with them at all stages of product development, design, and subcontracting. I saw this advice put into practice when I accompanied him on a visit to General Motors in Detroit, where a meeting had been arranged to bring together two suppliers to whom GM wanted to entrust important, complementary work contracts.

The suppliers had been invited to participate at the development stage, which is not the usual practice when calling for tenders. No tenders were called, and the suppliers had already been promised contracts and had been chosen for their ability to fulfill those contracts. They were agreeably surprised with this new procedure, for it meant that the automobile giant considered them as partners and was asking for their collaboration. One of the suppliers, obviously delighted with the change, said that he would never have imagined that the day would come when he would collaborate with the other supplier, a long-time competitor and opponent on the field of battle.

The positive effect of reducing the number of suppliers can be seen in what happened at Xerox after its then president, David Kearns, had introduced major changes. In the early 1980s, the company was placing orders for various parts and components with 5000 suppliers scattered all over the world. When Kearns asked his purchasing personnel to reduce the number of suppliers, he encountered strong objections. In their opinion, it would be better to increase the number of suppliers to safeguard against the hazards of unforeseen events, such as strikes and plant closings, and to promote competition among the suppliers in order to obtain better prices. Adamant, Kearns held his ground, and the number of suppliers was reduced to fewer than 400. The result was amazing. Quality improved significantly and costs were reduced. Over four years quality improved from 92 percent to 99.2 percent. Today this has become a general practice adopted by a great number of companies.

The Purchasing Department's Responsibility for Quality

Many players are involved in the purchasing process: the potential user of the product who submits a purchase requisition; the personnel involved in market research or surveys, research and development, purchasing, and finance; and the suppliers and subcontractors. So we must then ask who is responsible for the quality of the goods and services to be purchased. But this is a difficult question to answer because the division of responsibility is not always very clear. Purchasing's role, in accordance with its objectives, is to supply the enterprise with the goods and services needed, at the requisite volume and level of quality, at the proper location and time, and at minimum cost. The potential user also has similar responsibilities, but the degree of emphasis he or she puts on each of these objectives may not be the same as that of the purchasing department.

In order to clarify these responsibilities, it has been suggested that there are two aspects to be considered as far as quality is concerned: *technical quality* and *economic quality.* The potential users have the exclusive responsibility for technical quality (that is, the specifications), for only they can determine what specifications are required for the product. The purchasing department has exclusive responsibility for the economic quality, or quality at least cost; thus, when the specifications have been established, this department must provide them at the least cost.[4]

Although the purchasing department has no responsibility for establishing the specifications for a product, it can, and often must, influence them. Because of its close contact with the potential users, the department is well acquainted with the technical specifications called for by all of the various sectors of the company. This knowledge, linked with its concern for profitability, may lead the purchasing department to look at the possibility of standardizing orders. For instance, if one user needs a $1/4$-inch thick sheet of steel and another uses steel sheets $5/16$ of an inch thick, the purchasing department might well step in and suggest that the users make the necessary technical modifications so that each can use the same thickness—providing, of course, that no other technical barriers exist to prevent the standardization. In this way the purchasing department can consolidate orders, reduce inventories, and possibly negotiate to obtain better deals. Often, this department is more aware than the user of the availability of certain items that are on the market and of the introduction of new items. All of this available information enables users to modify their specifications so as to bring them into line with what is available on the market and/or what will incur the least cost.

From the Definition of Needs to Their Satisfaction

The purchasing process starts when a need first arises and ends when that need is satisfied. All along the process, great attention must be paid to the various aspects of quality. This process comprises four stages: (1) needs definition and description; (2) the search for and the evaluation and choice of a supplier; (3) a control system acting preventively to ensure that the product will be delivered at the required level of quality and acting after the fact to ensure that the product indeed has been delivered at the right level of quality; (4) a group of procedures that govern the eventual handling of products that are rejected on delivery (see Figure 11.4).

Definition of Needs

Every acquisition a company makes is driven by an internal user's need that has to be satisfied. This need is defined, as indicated in chapter 2, by the acquisition's fitness for use, durability, reliability, maintainability, and a certain number of other characteristics. For example, a user might need to make a certain number of photocopies a day, at a reasonable speed, and on a machine (or through a process) that can produce copies of certain sizes and in certain colors. The user might further require that this machine last for a reasonable period of time, be easy to in-

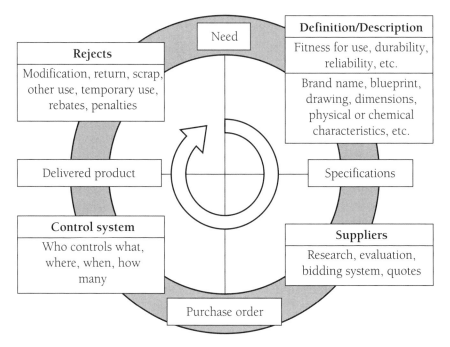

Figure 11.4. Purchasing and the quality cycle.

Source: J. N. Kelada, *Comprendre et réaliser la qualité totale,* 2nd ed. (Dollard-des-Ormeaux, Quebec, Canada: Quafec Publications, 1992), 206. Reprinted with permission.

stall and operate, be able to function with a minimal number of repairs to avoid downtime and service interruptions, not take up too much space, and harmonize with the office decor.

Obviously, only the potential users fully understand what their specific needs are. Yet I have noticed that users never specify their own *needs* to the purchasing department—cutting, transporting, weighing, measuring, heating, lighting. In general, they merely specify the *product* that, in their opinion, will meet their needs. Here, as well, the purchasing department has a role to play.

To show how useful it is for the purchasing department to be involved in the process of defining needs, consider the example of the user who wanted to order a type of truck with a very complex design. When the purchasing agent understood that the user needed to transport transformers weighing 50 tons around the company premises, he researched several truck suppliers to find the equipment best suited for this kind of job. One supplier suggested using air cushions, and this proved to be the most efficient and economical solution.

An order must contain a clear, detailed description of the product to eliminate any risk of error. All efforts must be made to avoid any possible ambiguity. Moreover, an order is a formal agreement, a legal contract between buyer and supplier which is binding on both parties. Once the need is defined, a description is written to ensure that the product can satisfy the potential user's need as he or she defines it. A buyer can use many different ways to describe the product required from the supplier.

Product Description

Among the numerous possible ways of describing product quality in a call for tender and, subsequently, in a final order, Lee and Dobler suggest the following:

> Market grades, brand or trade names, commercial standards, chemical or physical specifications, performance specifications, specifications for materials and for the manufacturing process, blueprints or engineering drawings, samples, or a combination of any of the above.[5]

Each of these has advantages and drawbacks. For example, ordering a product by brand name is the method that generally presents the least ambiguity; however, it could prove to be the most expensive. The purchasing personnel should carefully weigh the pros and cons before deciding which method to apply for each purchase requisition.

Aspects of Quality Assurance and Control

There are several facets to quality in the purchasing department. These are the quality

- *Required* by the potential user
- *Defined* or expressed by the potential user
- *Conceived* by the research and development or engineering staff
- *Specified* by the design staff
- *Ordered* by the purchasing department
- *Provided* by the supplier
- *Delivered* to the buyer
- *Received* by the buyer
- *Stored* by the buyer or user
- *Used* by the end user and then scrapped
- Sometimes *discarded* without having been used at all

To prevent the occurrence of unquality and avoid its disturbing consequences, quality must be assured at each of these stages. The delivered products must conform to the predetermined description. The buyer must be able to evaluate this conformance as objectively as possible. It is preferable that the evaluation be preventive, since after-the-fact control can often cause significant delays for which one cannot hold the supplier responsible. Prevention is best begun at the supplier evaluation stage. The aim, in effect, is to ensure that the supplier has the capability to produce and deliver products that meet the standards of quality specified. Supplier evaluation, then, is of supreme importance.

Supplier Evaluation

Supplier qualification is an important element in quality assurance. In order to evaluate a supplier correctly and effectively, a company has to know what to evaluate, who will do the evaluation, and when and how it should be done. One way to do it is to limit the examination to the products that the supplier has produced in the past, provided that these products are similar to the those that the company wants to order. Another way is to conduct studies among the supplier's customers to evaluate their satisfaction with the quality of the products bought from the supplier. It is advisable to evaluate the supplier's financial situation as well as its technical capacity to produce products with the required level of quality. There would be no sense in giving a contract to a supplier who might have difficulty finishing it because it was either operating under financial constraints (and thus lacked cash flow, borrowing capacity, or credit with its own suppliers) or teetering on the edge of bankruptcy.

The major factors that can influence the quality of the supplier's products are the workforce, the equipment, and the quality management systems. To produce a quality product, the workforce must be well-trained, well-informed, and motivated. Although elaborate studies to evaluate the supplier's workforce are not feasible, certain indicators should lead a buyer to treat a supplier with suspicion. You may be sure that any company with strained personnel relations, numerous strikes, or a high staff turnover will not have a highly motivated workforce.

As for equipment, experts in that area have only to visit the supplier's premises to evaluate the capacity to produce the requisite products. Obviously, this type of evaluation cannot be entrusted to nontechnical personnel in the purchasing department. If a visit is not possible, capability studies of the supplier's equipment are in order. This is part of what is called SPC.

However, even qualified and motivated personnel working with adequate equipment is not a guarantee that the requisite quality will be produced. In addition to all that, the supplier must have an adequate system, capable of preventing poor quality or correcting poor quality should it occur. It must, therefore, have quality planning, organization, direction, control, and assurance activities in place to produce the product as specified. It can be ascertained that the supplier has an adequate and properly applied quality system in place by visiting the premises or by specifying one of the accepted quality assurance standards, such as ISO 9000, when the call for tender is issued.

If it proves impractical to evaluate the supplier on its own premises, there are various other options. Ask for a sample, order a trial batch, send in a partial order, or even send in a conditional order. The advantages and drawbacks of each type of order, however, must be assessed. A sample may not be representative of the normal product; a trial batch, although usually expensive, gives the company wider scope to evaluate the supplier's ability to produce to specifications; a partial order is less costly than a trial batch order because, although some suppliers may demand a higher price for a trial batch, a partial order is usually priced as a global order. If, however, the supplier does not agree to a partial order at the same price and the same conditions of the full order, one can opt to make a conditional order—that is to say, a full order, but placed on the condition that if the quality delivered does not completely satisfy the buyer, the buyer can unilaterally cancel the order at any time or return the goods to the supplier, without any liability.

Before submitting an order, the buyer must clearly identify the form of control required or the one that will be carried out. This is just as important as setting out precise and detailed quality descriptions in the call for tender and orders. The buyer must state

- The characteristics that will be evaluated by the control activities.
- How frequently evaluations are to be performed.
- Who is responsible for the controlling (that is, who decides that a product is not of an acceptable quality—the customer's inspector, that of the supplier, or a third party).
- Where the control activities will take place. There are numerous possible locations: the supplier's premises as soon as raw materials are received, during manufacture, or before shipping; or the customer's receiving area or manufacturing departments during product assembly. If a product is guaranteed for several years, control activities may take place even after the product has found its way to the user.
- The quantity to be controlled. Where control is done by sampling, the supplier must know what method the customer is using so that it can assess the risks under this type of control.

Finally, there must be prior agreement on what actions will be taken if the products delivered are refused. Provisions may be made for the goods to be

- Returned to the supplier at its own expense, following prior notification
- Scrapped according to given procedures
- Temporarily accepted until they can be replaced
- Accepted at a discounted price
- Accepted but modified at the supplier's expense

The whole process of quality in the purchasing system is illustrated in Figure 11.5.

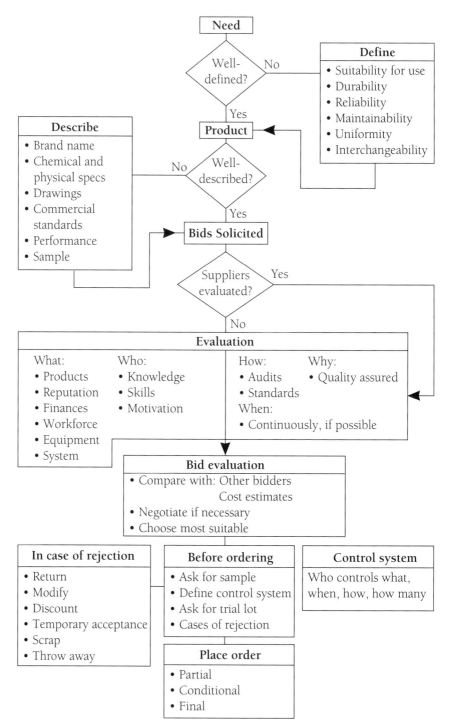

Figure 11.5. Quality in the purchasing process.

Section 2: Standardization

Standardization helps reduce inventories and costs, allows interchangeability, promotes safety and quality in general, and facilitates the relations between buyers and suppliers. Moreover, in the field of quality assurance, it helps both buyers and suppliers by providing preestablished guidelines for the quality systems that the suppliers have to set up in order to assure the buyers that they will get the required level of quality. This section deals with standardization, how it is defined, what its advantages are, and the way standards are developed and used.[6]

Standardization, an important facet of total quality management, provides companies with the potential to markedly improve quality and enhance productivity. In our everyday lives, we are surrounded by an intricate thatchwork of standards and norms. The roofs over our heads and the walls around us are held up by beams of standard width and thickness. We are clothed from head to foot in garments of standard sizes. History's first measuring instruments were undoubtedly hands or feet, but, because not all hands and feet are the same size, a suitable common measure, such as the tribal leader's hand, had to be used. Undoubtedly, the leader was not always there when measurement was called for, so the members of the tribe may have scratched the size of his or her hand on a flat stone and placed it in a central position for everyone's use. Later, these marks were transposed onto a stick to measure objects farther away from the stone.

For a long time, the purpose of standardization was simply to make the replacement of worn-out parts easier, but its uses today go far beyond that and have spread to many new domains, to front-line technologies or to developing branches of activity where there is often much at stake in the economic sense—for example, in the information superhighway, new energies, or agribusiness. The underlying intent of standardization is to standardize products or parts according to their characteristics (weight, size, dimensions, chemical composition) to facilitate production, use, and marketing. Thus, a nut made by one manufacturer will fit a bolt made by another. Automobile manufacturers and tire manufacturers use common standards, just as the clothing industry uses standard sizes for their off-the-rack merchandise.

The main purpose of standardization is to increase the usefulness or safety of a product. The standard thickness of the insulation in walls is calculated to reduce energy loss. Car manufacturing standards were developed to reduce gas consumption and pollution and to increase public safety. Standardization can also affect manufacturing procedures. In the food and pharmaceutical industries, hygiene standards (to eliminate the possibility of product contamination) imposed on manufacturers become regulations and act as a safeguard for public health protection. Standardization plays an ever-increasing role in areas that are vital to society, such as health, energy, transportation, and environmental protection.

Common standards for measuring and expressing time, linear dimensions, weight, and energy have been hallmarks of cultural achievement throughout recorded history. In the present century, common standards for ensuring quality, compatibility, safety, and reliability are the logical consequence of continuing industrial and social development. Standardization is both the process of coming to an agreement on common solutions to recurring technical problems and the result of having put those agreements into practice. The process and the practice are inseparable and dynamic, as are the technological societies they serve.

Trading partners throughout the world have grown to appreciate the importance of internationally agreed-upon standards for transport vehicles and cargo containers; for storage and handling requirements of perishable products; and for compatible universal facilities and administrative procedures to ease the movement of goods, people, and services internationally. Equally important to the smooth functioning of trade are internationally sanctioned standards for specifying and testing traded products—standards such as those for grading rubber, for testing the safety of gas cylinders, or for achieving interchangeability and compatibility of components for machine tools and earth-moving machinery.

Standardization has become an important tool for reducing the risk of injury in the home, at work, and during travel and leisure activities. International standards relating to workplace safety include provisions to protect operators of industrial machinery, procedures for the safe handling of hazardous materials, specifications for the design and performance of protective clothing, and requirements for colors and symbols for safety signs and warnings. Minimizing the risk of human injury in automobiles and aircraft has meant requiring the use of several hundred standards covering safety glass, seat belts, lighting and braking systems, signaling devices, and exhaust systems. The development of international agreements on safety standards and regulations has been especially important for international trade in automotive products.

In the home, standards provide for the safe installation and operation of household equipment, for the reliable performance of fire protection and alarm systems, for the appropriate use of glass and other building materials, and for the general safety of children's toys. Internationally agreed-upon standards can also significantly reduce the risk of injury in sports and recreational activity, as in the case of the safety requirements specified for gymnastic and skiing equipment.

The procedures used for coming to agreement on standards, whether within a company, at the national level, or internationally, are essentially similar. Differences mainly reflect the extent of application intended for the standards under consideration. The guiding principle in each case is that standards should be prepared and agreed upon by those who will use them and those who will be affected by their use.

Background

The inch is a standard of measurement. Money is a standard of exchange. Words are standards of communication. Traffic lights are safety standards. Octane numbers of gasoline are quality standards. "No more than 1 percent shrinkage" is a performance standard.[7]

As this indicates, standardization has a major impact on our lives, yet most people know little about the process or about the standards themselves. They know that camera film marked ISO 100 is likely to give good results in a camera with the film speed set at 100, but few understand that the ISO 100 marking on the package means that the film conforms to a standard established by ISO—the International Organization for Standardization. Few people question whether three-holed notebook paper will align with the three rings in most notebooks, yet such a matter-of-fact assumption would not be possible without standards. While driving, we are on the lookout for hexagonal, not round or square-shaped, stop signs, just as we know that inverted triangles invariably indicate where traffic should yield. These are just a few of the thousands of standards that have an impact on our lives.

The National Standards Policy Advisory Committee defined a standard as

A prescribed set of rules, conditions, or requirements concerning definitions of terms; classification of components; specification of materials, performance, or operations; delineation of procedures; or measurement of quantity and quality in describing materials, products, systems, services, or practices.[8]

Though often unrecognized, standards can help to ensure health and safety and to increase the quality of life. Standards are vital tools of industry and commerce. They often provide the basis for buyer–seller transactions; hence, they have tremendous impact on companies and nations, and even on the economic fabric of the world market. In the United States alone, approximately 30,000 current voluntary standards have been developed by more than 400 organizations. In addition, numerous foreign national, regional, and international organizations produce standards of interest and importance to United States manufacturers and exporters.

International standardization is a natural consequence of the development of international trade and technical collaboration. The recent, remarkable achievements in international standardization have been made possible through the collaborative efforts of national standards organizations and with the cooperation and support of producers, consumers, and governments from all over the world. There are, of course, many important international standardization problems left to be solved, and others are sure to follow new technological developments and expanded international trade. International standardization is an investment based on confidence in the rational application of technology for the benefit of all of the world's people.

Notwithstanding the ever-growing number of internationally accepted and applied standards, there still remain several hundred thousand standards and technical regulations in use throughout the world containing special requirements for a particular country or region. Finding information about all of these standards, technical regulations, or related testing and certification activities can be an onerous task.

There are numerous international organizations that produce standards. The International Organization for Standardization probably produces the largest number of international standards, having issued approximately 6000. ISO's work is carried out through technical bodies using the resources of experts from all over the world who participate each year in the development of ISO standards. The international General Agreement on Tariffs and Trade (GATT) (now the responsibility of the World Trade Organization) has as one of its major components the Agreement on Technical Barriers to Trade, usually referred to as the Standards Code. The framers of the Standards Code recognized that standards and standards-related activities, if misused, can seriously hinder the free flow of goods in international commerce. The Code established some requirements for the procedures by which standards are developed, adopted, and used, and for the systems that determine conformity with such standards. The Trade Agreements Act of 1979 implemented the Standards Code in the United States.

Historical Notes on Standardization

The history of standardization is both fascinating and demonstrative of the scope and variety of such activities. Standards are known to have existed as early as 7000 B.C. The first known attempts at standardization in the Western world occurred in 1120. King Henry I of England decreed that the *ell,* the ancient yard, should be the exact length of his forearm and that it should be used as the standard unit of length in his kingdom.[9] History also notes that, in 1689, the Boston city fathers recognized the need for standardization when they passed a law making it a civic crime to manufacture bricks in any size other than $9 \times 4 \times 4$. The city had just been destroyed by fire, and the city fathers decided that standards would ensure that rebuilding would be completed in the most economical and fastest way possible.[10]

Eli Whitney is sometimes referred to as the Father of Standardization in the area of interchangeability, having originated and implemented the concept of mass production in the United States in 1780. He was awarded a contract to produce 10,000 muskets by then vice president Thomas Jefferson. Although standardized parts had been successfully used in other parts of the world, Whitney brought the concept to this country when he divided the manufacturing process into individual steps and put different groups to work on each step of the process. All parts of the same type were copied from a model musket and were made to be interchangeable. Subsequently, when he appeared before Congress with a collection of assorted parts and proceeded to assemble 10 working muskets by selecting the required parts at random, Congress was convinced of the benefits of mass production made possible by standardization.[11]

The great blaze in downtown Baltimore in February 1904 provided tragic and undeniable evidence of the importance of standards. While the fire in Baltimore raged, fire engines from as far away as New York rushed to the scene only to discover that their hoses would not fit Baltimore fire hydrants. The inferno burned for more than 30 hours, destroying 1526 buildings and covering more than 70 city blocks.[12] In contrast, 23 years later, help from 20 neighboring towns saved Fall River, Massachusetts, from destruction because hydrants and hose couplings had been standardized in these communities.[13] Probably the most significant standard ever developed in the United States, however, was the railroad's standard track gauge. This standard, now used in Great Britain, the United States, Canada, and much of continental Europe, enables railroad-rolling stock to cross the country.[14]

It was World War II, however, that brought the urgency of extending standardization from the domestic level to the international level. Allied supplies and facilities were severely strained because of the incompatibility of tools, replacement parts, and equipment. The war highlighted the need for standards aimed at reducing inventories and increasing compatibility.

Types of Standards

Standards may be classified in numerous ways. ISO Draft Guide 2 differentiates eight types based on the purpose that each serves.[15] A basic standard has a broad effect in a particular field. An example might be the standard for metal, which affects an array of products from cars to screws. Among the types of standards, I might mention terminology standards, testing standards, product standards, process standards, service standards, and interface standards. Standards may also be classified by the intended user group. These classifications range from company standards, meant for use by a single industrial organization, to international standards, which may be voluntary or mandatory in nature. A harmonized standard can be either an attempt by a country to make its standard compatible with an international, regional, or other standard, or an agreement by two or more nations on the content and application of a standard, the latter of which tends to be mandatory.

There are still other classifications, such as industry standards and military or government standards. Standards that describe how a product is supposed to function are called *performance standards*. In contrast, *design standards* define characteristics, or how the product is to be built. For example, a performance standard for water pipes might set requirements for the pressure per square inch that a pipe must withstand, along with a test method to determine if a specimen meets the requirement. On the other hand, the specification that a pipe be made of a given gauge of copper would characterize a design standard. The distinction, however, between these two types of standards is not always clear cut. It is possible to include two different requirements within the same standard, one of which is stated in terms of performance and the other in terms of design. Design standards may be appropriate, as in testing methods where the need for comparability may outweigh other considerations. In general, however, performance standards, though usually more difficult to write and enforce, tend to be less restrictive than design standards, and more likely to encourage innovation.

Still another classification scheme distinguishes between *voluntary standards,* which by themselves impose no obligations regarding use, and *mandatory standards.* A mandatory standard is generally published as part of a code, rule, or regulation by a regulatory government body and imposes an obligation on specified parties to conform to it. However, the distinction between these two categories may be lost when voluntary consensus standards are referenced in government regulations, effectively making them mandatory standards. Voluntary consensus standards may also become quasi-mandatory due to conditions in the marketplace. For example, the health care industry is sensitive to the need to have available the safest products to ensure patient safety and to protect manufacturers, vendors, and health care providers against lawsuits. Informed buyers of health care products will frequently insist that products meet all appropriate voluntary consensus standards. If they wish to compete effectively, manufacturers of such products are obliged to conform to such standards. It is clear, then, that standards cover a broad range of types and serve a wide variety of purposes.

Private Standards Organizations in the United States

Many private standards organizations operate in the United States. In all, more than 400 organizations develop voluntary standards of many different types for a broad range of services, products, and tests. Among these, let us mention the following:

• The American Society for Testing of Materials (ASTM), which produces the largest number of nongovernmental, voluntary standards in the United States.

• The American National Standards Institute (ANSI), which serves as the coordinator of voluntary standards activities in the United States and as the agency that approves standards as American national standards. ANSI is also the coordinator and manager of United States participation in the work of two nongovernmental, international standards organizations, ISO and the International Electrotechnical Commission (IEC).

• The American Society of Mechanical Engineering (ASME), which first issued the ASME Boiler Code in 1914. Today, that code is mandatory not only in the United States but in many other countries throughout the world. It may be the most widely used voluntary standard in the world.

• The Society of Automotive Engineers (SAE), which led to the pioneering efforts of the American automotive industry to achieve substantial intercompany technical standardization.

• Underwriters' Laboratories (UL) is a major standards writer; it also operates nonprofit testing laboratories whose mission is to investigate products and materials with respect to hazards that might affect life or property.

• The National Fire Protection Association (NFPA), which has produced the National Electrical Code used in building construction and many other standards affecting safety from fires and other hazards.

• The safety of aircraft is the object of the standards produced by the Aerospace Industries Association of America (AIAA).

• The Association of American Railroads' (AAR) standards affect the railroad industry.

• The quality and size of paper is standardized through the work of the Technical Association of the Pulp and Paper Industry (TAPPI).

• The Electronic Industries Association (EIA) is a standards developer in the areas of electrical and electronic products and components.

• The Institute of Electrical and Electronics Engineers (IEEE) maintains more than 500 standards, with 800 more under development. IEEE is responsible for the National Electrical Safety Code, widely used by governments and regulatory agencies for electrical supply and communications installations.

• The National Sanitation Foundation (NSF) develops standards for health and sanitation products.

• The Factory Mutual Research Corporation (FM) is a *product listing* type of organization, as is UL.

• Building code organizations, such as the Building Officials and Code Administrators International (BOCA), the International Conference of Building Officials (ICBO), and the Southern Building Code Congress International (SBCCI), are involved in standards development.

The broad range of organizations participating in standards development reflects the impact standards have on a vast spectrum of interests and disciplines.

Standardization in Canada

In Canada, standardization goes back to 1919, when the Canadian Engineering Association began to use it. Subsequently this organization became known as the Canadian Standards Association (CSA). In 1970, the Canadian government created the Standards Council of Canada (SCC), which coordinates the National Standards System (NSS). Members of the NSS write standards, test products, or register the quality systems of organizations. The SCC also coordinates the contribution and representation of Canada in ISO and IEC.

The SCC's main aims are to foster and promote voluntary standardization for the benefit of industry, consumers, and the economy. It coordinates the contribution of Canadians to the two most prominent international standards-writing forums—ISO and the IEC. The SCC operates accreditation programs which ensure that members of the System meet all of the necessary criteria for the services they wish to provide. It also operates an information and sales service to help organizations compete in the global marketplace.[16]

SCC has five registered bodies, authorized to set standards in various domains.

- The Canadian Standards Association (CSA)
- The Canadian General Standards Board (CGSB)
- The Canadian Gas Association (CGA)
- Underwriters' Laboratories of Canada (ULC)
- The Quebec Standards Bureau (QSB)

These bodies have the power to submit to the Council standards which they feel respond to a national need and merit recognition as Canadian national standards.

The SCC has also accredited other certification and testing organizations. About 10 years ago, it created the Canadian Point for standards information service (part of ISONET), which continually receives requests from business, industry, government, and educational institutions on standards, codes, specifications, and certification systems in force in Canada and abroad. The SCC answers questions by referring to its collections and databases of more than 800,000 documents. It can provide valuable information for companies planning to enter local and foreign markets and is, in fact, the Canadian representative on Technical Help to Exporters (THE), which is a service of the British Standards Institute. For several years, that organization has been gathering essential information on the technical requirements and standards that products must meet in many foreign markets. As the ISO and IEC representative in Canada, the SCC also provides Canadians with a focal point to purchase international, national, and foreign standards, without the communications troubles, foreign exchange, or customs issues.

The CSA is the best-known standards organization in Canada. It levies no membership fee, is nonprofit, and has no regulatory power. Some of its standards are used in several provinces as provincial regulations. Approval by the CSA is mandatory in various areas, such as electrical safety, elevators, and hoists.

Standards Development Procedures

A standard is a reference document that establishes—depending upon the circumstances—definitions, dimensions, methods for testing and analyzing, performance, regulations for use, safety rules, and acceptance sampling plans. In essence, it is a collection of requirements that a product or technique must meet. The product or technique must be capable of providing the services that the deliberating body expects of it. When a standard is being developed, the standardization body forms a committee of representatives from all of the sectors with a vested interest in the standard. When setting the standard for a product, the committee invites representatives from manufacturers, buyers, universities, governmental organizations, and experts in the particular field to give their input. The committee members agree to work in a volunteer capacity and meet until they reach consensus. If the committee is unable to reach consensus, they can call in a subcommittee of experts to further enlighten them on the topic under debate and help them reach their final decision.

The standardization process can be set into motion at the request of users or producers, or by the standards body itself when it perceives that there is a need in a given area. Before forming a committee, the standardization body does bibliographical research on the standard that is to be developed. Existing standards, either local or from abroad, are studied, and technical and commercial practices in the areas potentially affected by the standard are analyzed. This means that the standardizing body has to meet with the technical production and quality control staff of the various manufacturers and with the people who will use the given product. They also need to get a good grasp of the manufacturing procedures and the raw materials that are used. Finally, they consult the laws and regulations applicable to producing, marketing, or using the product under study. In reality, they can impose restraints that the standardization committee must take into consideration.

A preliminary study is then undertaken to establish the following:

- *The purpose and area of application.* This is the most important element of the project because it sets the framework in which the product to be standardized is to be used and, at the same time, delimits the boundaries for its use.

- *The documents.* This part of the study determines what documents are available to provide other related information. We should note that in Canada national standards often make reference to foreign standards such as the American Society for Testing of Materials (ASTM) or the American Society of Mechanical Engineers (ASME). Not only that, but some of these standards themselves refer to yet other standards. The difficulty here is that the standardization body has no control whatsoever over the foreign standard in terms of its contents, the changes made to it, or its withdrawal.

- *The vocabulary.* This section presents, when necessary, a list of defined terms related to the document's contents, to avoid any interpretation inconsistent with the spirit or letter of the standard.

- *The classification.* This part sets up a classification or codification system for products that conform to the standard's specifications.

- *The technical aspects.* This describes the characteristics chosen as relevant when studying the area of application: the measuring or controlling methods chosen, the limitations of the results, acceptable tolerances, description of tests, and operating modes.

There must be consensus among all committee members before any standardization project is approved. Projects must then go through the public inquiry process. Interested parties receive a copy of the project and the standardization committee analyzes their comments. A standard can concern raw materials, manufacturing processes, characteristics of a finished product, and inspections and tests to be used for controlling the quality of the product. When the standard touches upon the question of apparatus that the producer, buyer, or specialized laboratories need for testing activities, one standard can refer to another. Details concerning the product's packaging or labeling can also be included in the standard.

Two of the most widely used procedures for ensuring consensus in the development of standards are the committee and the canvass methods.

The Committee Method

Committee standards are subject to wide review and consideration by all interested parties. The requirements of this process vary among organizations. In some organizations, consensus may be defined as an agreement of at least 51% of the participants. Other organizations may also include requirements for due process, appeals procedures, the mandatory consideration of negative votes or comments, and for committee balance. Balance is achieved when all parties having an interest in the outcome of a standard have an opportunity to participate and where no single interest can dominate the outcome. Standards organizations differ widely in the emphasis placed on each of these requirements. Organizations that emphasize all four factors, in addition to achieving substantial agreement among participants, produce standards that are more likely to be adopted and used.

The Canvass Method

The canvass method is frequently used by an organization that has prepared a standard under its own internal procedures. To gain greater stature for and acceptance of the drafted standard, the developer may then submit it to balloting by a set of organizations representing a variety of interests, such as manufacturers, consumers, government, and others. Any objections or comments from organizations on the canvass list must be addressed and satisfactorily resolved. Changes in a proposed standard, as well as any unresolved objections and the developing organization's rationale for its response, must be resubmitted to the canvass list. It is crucial that all interested groups be included on the list. Two problems sometimes arise: the response level may be low, and consumers and others on the canvass list may have difficulty commenting on a standard because they did not participate in the initial drafting and may not understand the reasons for or implications of particular provisions.

Benefits and Problems of Standardization

On the whole, the benefits of standardization far outweigh the difficulties and potential for abuse. Standards promote understanding between buyer and seller and make possible mutually beneficial commercial transactions. Product attributes cannot always be evaluated by individual purchasers by inspection or even on the basis of prior experience. However, a product's conformance to accepted standards readily provides an efficient method of conveying complex information on the product's suitability. Architects use standards when drafting plans for buildings. Purchasing agents can also use standards as an easy way of communicating their needs to potential suppliers. In a host of situations, standards are or may be used to replace large quantities of complex information.

Standards underlie mass production methods and processes. They also promote more effective and organized social interaction, as is the case in the example of the standardized colors for traffic lights and in many other widely accepted conventions. Standards are essential in efforts to improve product safety and to clean up the environment. Standardized and interchangeable parts can reduce inventory requirements and facilitate product repairs. They can also promote fair competition by facilitating the comparison of standardized commodities. In general, standards permit society to make more effective use of its resources and allow more effective communication among all parties regarding particular activities, transactions, or processes. Indeed, standards are crucial to every form of scientific and industrial process, and, without them, the quality of life would be significantly reduced.

No system, particularly none as complex and diverse as the U.S. voluntary standards system, is without problems. In 1982, in the highly significant case of the American Society of Mechanical Engineers (ASME) v. Hydrolevel, the United States Supreme Court rendered its decision in favor of Hydrolevel, a manufacturer of low-water fuel cutoff devices. It found ASME liable for conspiring to restrain trade because it was determined that two subcommittee officers, serving as volunteers but acting in the name of ASME, had issued a misinterpretation of a standard and produced an adverse effect on the competitiveness of the plaintiff. Similarly, the Federal Trade Commission held hearings on standards and certification and uncovered "substantiated complaints of individual standards and certification actions that have, in fact, unreasonably restrained trade or deceived or otherwise injured consumers."[17]

In part, problems result from the sometimes substantial costs of participation in standards development, making it difficult, if not impossible, for small firms and nonindustry representatives to be active in the process. The standards themselves may cause problems highly technical in nature. It is frequently difficult, if not impossible, to get qualified consumer representatives to participate actively. This seriously complicates the attempts to achieve a balanced representation of all interests concerned.

Other problems may occur when a standard undergoes review and revision. Unless the original writers of the standard participate in its revision, the reviewers may not be able to understand how the document was prepared, what was eliminated from consideration, and the reasons or assumptions underlying decisions and the resultant provisions. Problems can also occur in the application of specific provisions if the intent behind them is unclear. Rationale statements, which sometimes accompany a standard, are specifically designed to define the purpose and scope of the standard, to explain the criteria used in developing its requirements, and to put all other relevant information at the disposal of the developers. However, the use of rationale statements is not yet extensive.[18]

Product Certification

In order to satisfy the requirements of regulations or contracts, a product must be declared to be in conformance with the standard in question. This conformity can be indicated by the manufacturer or certified by the buyer or the regulatory body. A group responsible for standardization can certify that a product conforms to a given standard. Then, the manufacturer provides written agreement to the standardization group that it will respect the certification protocol. This protocol demands control of supplies, a quality management system, and a quality control system.

The manufacturer must notify the standardization group of any changes made to the product, which must undergo a series of tests stipulated in the standard. The manufacturer must also agree to receive visits during the course of the year, at prearranged intervals, from representatives of a testing laboratory appointed to do specific controls set out in the certification protocol. The laboratory prepares a report on its visits and the tests it carries out. Then, if all is satisfactory, the certification committee recommends that the product be certified. If need be, a certified product can be submitted to a decertification process. This involves more frequent visits from the testing laboratory, advice notices, formal demands, and finally decertification.

Apart from certifying one particular model of product, a standardization body can certify a line of products. Random samples are tested, allowing a complete line of products to be certified. A category of products can also be certified. This certification is for cases in which production is affected by continual technical change. In such instances, the producer evaluates the products and prepares the necessary documentation for their certification. A representative of the standardization group visits the producer's factory to ensure that the design, manufacturing, and testing activities are all adequate.

Product certification schemes range from the simple to the complex. There are more than 100 private organizations and more than 60 federal programs in the United States that certify products ranging from electrical cords to kitchen cabinets. In addition, many certification programs are operated at the state and local level.

Consumers see evidence of the extensive reach of certification when they note the UL or CSA certification mark on many products, ranging from coffee pots to fire extinguishers, or the U.S. Department of Agriculture (USDA) mark on meats, poultry, and other agricultural products. These are only a few of the many certification programs conducted in North America. The intention of product certification is to confirm that a particular product conforms to one or more specified standards, thus providing the user with explicit or implicit information about the characteristics and/or performance of the product. Certification is a method for increasing a buyer's confidence in a product and for furnishing product information.

In the United States, if a manufacturer or supplier attests to the fact that his or her product meets one or more standards, the process is called *self-certification.* This process is also known as a manufacturer's declaration in other parts of the world. The manufacturer's capability, integrity, and reputation determine the degree of confidence that can be placed in self-certification.

Third-party certification is the term applied to the process by which an organization independent of either the manufacturer or supplier assesses the product's conformance to one or more standards. A manufacturer's overall quality control program may also be examined as part of the certification process. There are hundreds of third-party certification programs in the United States operated by federal, state, and local governments and by many private organizations. Third-party certification programs differ greatly from one another, and the degree of confidence to be placed in the resultant certification depends on the program's type and comprehensiveness.

The methods used in third-party certification programs can be classified as follows.

• *Type testing/initial inspection.* This ensures that the manufacturer's design specifications can produce a product that conforms to a particular standard. Products from a production run are not inspected or tested, and there is no information on whether products from a production run also consistently meet the specification.

• *Audit testing.* In this procedure, test samples are selected at random from the marketplace. Extensive testing is usually required to provide adequate assurance that products meet the desired standard.

• *Surveillance of the manufacturing process.* Assessment of a manufacturer's production and control processes can, at relatively low cost, provide assurance that the manufacturer's quality control procedures are adequate.

• *Field investigations.* Alleged failures of products under use conditions are investigated to determine the cause of failure and to suggest appropriate corrective action.

• *Batch testing.* A sample of products is selected from a production batch and tested for conformance to the standard. If the sampling procedure and the sample size are adequate, batch testing makes it likely that all products in that batch conform to the standard. It does not, however, ensure that a specific untested product in the batch will meet the standard, nor does it furnish information on the quality of products produced in earlier or subsequent batches. Batch testing is used in many certification programs for building products, such as those for energy conservation.

- *100-percent testing.* Each individual product is tested to determine if it meets the designated standard. If the testing procedures are adequate, the procedure provides the highest possible level of assurance that the product conforms to a particular standard. It is also usually the most expensive method and can be applied only where the test has no adverse effect on the product.[19]

Many programs apply two or more of these methods in their certification process. The choice of methods depends on the needs of both the buyer and the seller and on the nature of the product. The methods chosen can greatly affect both the cost of the program and the level of confidence that can be ascribed to it. ANSI and ISO have each developed criteria to evaluate certification programs. ANSI has also developed a program to accredit certification schemes that meet its criteria, but only two programs have been accredited to date.

Laboratory Accreditation

Laboratory accreditation is a process for evaluating testing facilities and designating those laboratories judged competent to perform specific tests using standard test methods, where available. The National Voluntary Laboratory Accreditation Program (NVLAP) in NIST, U.S. Department of Commerce, and the American Association for Laboratory Accreditation (AALA) are the two largest accreditation agencies in the United States.[20]

It should be emphasized that laboratory accreditation assesses the capability of a laboratory to conduct testing, generally using standard test methods. The accreditation process should not be confused with certification nor with the validation of a certification, which is "an action by a third party to assure that the producer (or certifier) is adhering to the requirements of a given certification program."[21] Laboratory accreditation neither reviews nor assesses products, nor does it check the tests conducted on specific products or product batches. In addition, laboratories may be accredited to conduct tests (such as the EPA's accreditation program for laboratories testing drinking water) in fields where no certification program exists.

Laboratory accreditation, however, can affect the quality of certification programs by requiring evidence that a certifying laboratory has competent personnel, adequate equipment, and sufficient knowledge of the testing procedures for which accreditation is sought. Also, laboratory accreditation is assuming increased importance in trade. As countries seek acceptance of their test data by trading partners, they must assure them that the data comes from competent laboratories. Laboratory accreditation can help to provide that assurance.

Impact of Standardization and Related Activities

Standardization, product certification, and laboratory accreditation are closely linked. In many developing countries, all three activities are conducted by the same organization. Certification programs are communication tools designed to reduce the cost of exchanging information between buyer and seller. The quality of the information conveyed depends on both the competence of the testing laboratory selected and the adequacy and appropriateness of the standards against which the product is to be evaluated. Certification can result in widespread consumer deception if performance characteristics or test methods contained in the standard are insufficient to assure adequate product performance or if the testing laboratory is incompetent or has biases that affect the reporting of test results.

As attested by the number of standards in existence and the variety of fields covered by private-sector standards development and certification organizations, the United States has one of the most developed and complex standardization and certification systems in the world. Furthermore, the number of federal, state, and local government standardization and certification activities and the large volume of standards, regulations, and procurement specifications that these agencies have developed result in standardization and related activities having an enormous impact on almost every aspect of life in the United States. Not only are considerable resources invested in this country in such activities every year, but buyers depend on standards and certification to ensure that products purchased are safe and perform satisfactorily. Recognition of the impact of standards and certification on trade, as evidenced by the Standards Code, is also increasing. Society depends on standardization and related activities for its existence.

Standardization Benefits

Standardization permits industrial firms to rationalize production and increase the competitiveness of their products. Savings in raw materials and energy, as well as consumer safety, are all direct results of its use. Construction, electrical, or mechanical equipment industries need to have materials available in standard sizes. The codes set out in the standardization documents provide them with the assurance that the proper regulations have been respected. Standardization has allowed the industrial sector to prolong product runs and to eliminate useless variety and make corresponding reductions in cost. Standardization is a boon to firms interested in exporting products to new markets because it provides them with advance knowledge of the new market's requirements in terms of the quality of the products that it will import.[22]

Standardization also affects procedures. There are many benefits for industries that adhere to it. Their production costs decrease because they need to invest less in developing products; they rapidly update their quality management, control, and, assurance; they are better informed about the materials they use; and they can simplify their processes. Moreover, standardization has rendered marketing activities much easier for companies who offer products that conform to the recognized values in the reference documents. These documents act as a composite guarantee of product quality and reliability, parts compatibility, rapidity of maintenance, and reduced maintenance costs.

Because standardization is based on dialogue and consensus, it can be used as a tool of global economic policy. This policy emerges from the collective responsibility of the economic participants themselves and is the very essence of standardization. Standardization can play a significant, supportive role in technological innovation. It constantly integrates new technologies and makes them available to users, providing easy access to technical expertise and proving instrumental in putting that expertise to work.

Standardization also has a very important social role. It acts as a vehicle for environmental and consumer protection and enhances the safety of machines and the workplace. Consumers who buy standard products are assured of a minimum level of quality and safety and—because standardization facilitates the interchange of parts—are afforded the possibility of easily replacing worn-out parts and components.

Standardization and Quality Assurance

As I indicated before, the concept of quality assurance was born out of the need for a customer to be assured, even before ordering from a supplier, that the product ordered will be designed, made, delivered, transported, stored, and installed as a quality product; in other words, that product will respect all of the requirements of the person who places the order. In short, the customer seeks proof through quality assurance that the supplier has put into place effective and adequate means to guarantee that the customer's requirements, as stated in the order, will be met. All this amounts to what can be called in this context a *quality assurance system.* When the customer receives the product, it can then dispense with quality control. The customer must, nevertheless, check that the supplier's quality system is effective and efficient.

In the past, purchasers required that their suppliers use a quality assurance system that reflected their own perception of what such a system should amount to. This state of affairs created major difficulties for the supplier who had several customers and several products; a different system was necessary for each customer and for each product, with some products needing a less rigorous system than others. A number of standardization groups have spent time studying this problem in both the United States and Canada, as well as elsewhere in the world. Among these are the following.

- The American military standards MIL-Q-9858A and MIL-I-45208, and the Canadian Ministry of National Defense standards DND 1015, 1016, and 1017. The latter have been replaced by the AQAP 1, 4, and 9 standards adopted by the NATO countries.
- The CSA standards CAN3-Z299.1, 2, 3, and 4–85.
- The British standards BS 5750–1, 2, and 3.
- The ISO 9000 series standards, which are discussed at length in the next chapter.

Prior to adopting the ISO 9000 series, General Motors published a standard for its internal and external suppliers that goes far beyond quality assurance. It is known as *Targets for Excellence* and it contains six sections: continuous improvement, company management, quality, costs, delivery dates, and technology.[23] Clearly, this standard goes beyond the purely technical aspect of quality. It presents a model for continuous improvement and for company management in general (administrative structure, management efficiency, communications, business planning, human resource management, supply management, and evaluation of suppliers). As for quality, the standard presents a fairly complete guide to a quality assurance system. Where costs are concerned, it touches on all of the aspects of establishing standard costs and production costs and deals with cost reduction, price structures, and cost estimates. The standard also indicates General Motors' expectations of and requirements for its suppliers in terms of technology and production capacity. General Motors sends its own examiners to assess the suppliers according to this standard, which, covering as much ground as it does, is quite a program.

Conclusion

Quality assurance is more than a system. It is primarily a philosophy based on responsibility and, consequently, on self-inspection. In effect, the company's workers and suppliers are made responsible. By allowing them to exercise self-inspection, control effectiveness is increased, its cost is reduced, and both the internal workforce and the external supplier are motivated.

Self-inspection is not synonymous with laissez-faire. To be effective, self-inspection must be supported by quality assurance. The quality assurance system, and the personnel who apply it, give those practicing self-inspection the necessary tools and support to allow them to carry out their jobs properly.

My observations of the present changes in the management of modern companies lead me to believe that the new management philosophies are increasingly based on confidence, decentralization, and delegation. For the purchasing department, this represents a new mission in which quality takes on a central role. Whereas, before, purchasing would simply purchase and leave the matter of quality to the quality control department, they are now invested with the responsibility of quality assurance.

Total quality assurance is based on the same concept as quality assurance. Indeed, it means putting in place a system capable of *preventing* the absence of total quality, that is to say anything with a negative impact on the company's profitability, customer satisfaction (as expressed in QVALITY), or employee satisfaction.

Standardization is a process undertaken by companies and countries to bring format and uniformity to the technical descriptions of products and manufacturing processes and systems, such as quality assurance systems. In contrast to the mandatory nature of regulations, the use of standards is voluntary. Standardization is also one of the tools for achieving total quality. It establishes the form of products, processes, and procedures and facilitates continuous quality improvement.

The process of standardization involves dialogue between the producers, manufacturers, and users of a product. The exchange between these various parties at the development stage of a standard translates into technological and economic development. As this dialogue has taken on a global dimension in order to deal with the common changes overtaking the countries of the world, the importance of international standardization has been magnified.

Review Questions

1. Why do buyers seem to lay more stress on their suppliers' quality assurance than on quality control in their own organization?

2. Quality assurance is based on a philosophical approach more than on a technique. Discuss.

3. Evaluation of suppliers is supremely important in the purchasing management process. Is this really true? Explain a supplier evaluation process. Who is responsible for it? When and how must this type of evaluation be carried out?

4. What is a quality assurance system? Explain it in detail, using examples to illustrate.

5. Standardization encourages technical development in local enterprises. International standardization bolsters trade relations between countries. Discuss.

6. What is the main objective of a quality assurance standard? What are its main components?

7. How does the standardization process start off? What steps does it go through and how does it end?

Notes

1. In general usage, the term *quality assurance* refers to external quality assurance, unless specifically qualified by the adjective *internal*. I shall follow suit and also use it to mean external quality assurance.

2. Major Appliance Business Group, General Electric Corporation, *Supplier Quality Manual* (Louisville, Ky.: General Electric Corporation, 1983).

3. M. R. Leenders, H. E. Fearon, and W. B. England, *Purchasing and Materials Management,* 9th ed. (Burr Ridge, Ill.: Richard D. Irwin, 1989), 6.

4. Lamar Lee Jr. and Donald W. Dobler, *Purchasing and Materials Management: Text and Cases* (New York: McGraw-Hill, 1977), 32.

5. Lee and Dobler, 37.

6. Material for this section and for chapter 12 has been kindly provided by the National Bureau of Standards of the U.S. Department of Commerce, Pierre F. Caillibot, the International Organization for Standardization (ISO), the Standards Council of Canada, and the Canadian General Standards Board.

7. USA Standards Institute, "What Is . . . a Standard? the USA Standards Institute? a USA Standard?" (New York: USA Standards Institute, [date]), 1.

8. *National Policy on Standards for the United States and a Recommended Implementation Plan* (Washington, D.C.: National Standards Policy Advisory Committee, December, 1978) 6.

9. American Standards Association, "Through History with Standards," *Speaking of Standards,* Rowen Glie, ed. (Boston: Cahner Books, 1972), 38.

10. Ibid., 42.

11. Ibid., 44.

12. Rexmond C. Cochrane, *Measures for Progress: A History of the National Bureau of Standards* (Washington D.C.: National Bureau of Standards, 1974), 82–86.

13. Glie, 60.

14. Ibid., 50

15. Draft revision of ISO Guide 2, *General terms and their definitions concerning standardization, certification and testing laboratory accreditation* (Geneva, Switzerland: International Organization for Standardization, July 1985).

16. More information on the services of the SCC can be obtained from Communication Branch, Standards Council of Canada, 1200–45 O'Connor Street, Ottawa, Ontario, Canada, K1P 6N7. Telephone (613) 238-3222.

17. David A. Swankin, *Rationale Statements for Voluntary Standards Issues, Techniques, and Consequences* (Gaithersburg, Md.: National Bureau of Standards, November, 1981).

18. Ibid.

19. Douglas B. Thomas, "NVLAP Glossary of Terms for Laboratory Accreditation," *Product Certification and Standardization* (Washington D.C.: U.S. National Bureau of Standards, 1980).

20. Charles W. Hyer, *Principal Aspects of U.S. Laboratory Accreditation Programs* (Gaithersburg, Md.: National Bureau of Standards, October, 1984).

21. Ibid., 21.

22. AFNOR, *La normalisation en bref . . . ,* (Paris: AFNOR, 1982).

23. "Standard for Supplier Performance Evaluation and Reporting (SPEAR)," *Targets for Excellence* General Motors Purchasing Activities, (Detroit, Mich.: General Motors Corporation, 1990).

Chapter 12

ISO *is Greek for* equal.

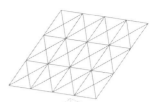

Total Quality and the ISO 9000 Standards

Introduction

Quality improvement has now become a key domestic and international business strategy, and worldwide interest in quality systems as one method of ensuring the consistent conformity of products or services to a defined set of standards or expectations has mushroomed. Nowhere is this more apparent than in the ever-increasing international adoption and use of the ISO 9000 series standards. Growing demand by both buyers and regulators within and outside the European Union (EU) for conformity to ISO 9000 requirements has made these standards and their use a matter of considerable importance and concern to North American companies.

This section deals with the ISO 9000 standards and quality system registration. Special attention is given to ISO 9000-related events within the European Union that might affect North American trade.

Information About ISO[1]

ISO is Greek for *equal*. Contrary to a popular belief, it does not stand for the name *International Organization for Standardization,* the body that has chosen ISO as its international symbol. ISO is the symbol of this specialized, international agency for standardization—a worldwide, nongovernmental organization that is a federation of national standards bodies, presently comprising more than 90 members, one in each country, representing more than 95 percent of the world's industrial production. The object of ISO is to promote the development of worldwide stan-

311

dards and related activities, including conformity assessment;[2] to improve international communication and collaboration; and to promote the smooth and equitable growth of international trade, with a view to facilitating international exchange of goods and services and to developing cooperation in the spheres of intellectual, scientific, technological, and economic activity. ISO work results in international technical agreements that are published as international standards. The scope of ISO covers standardization in all fields except electrical and electronic engineering, which are the responsibility of the International Electrotechnical Commission (IEC).

The IEC came into being in 1906. ISO and IEC have established a formal agreement stating the relationship between the two organizations. In accordance with this agreement, ISO and IEC form the specialized system for worldwide standardization. It is agreed that questions related to international standardization in the electrical and electronic engineering fields are the concern of IEC. Other subject areas are the responsibility of ISO. In matters of international standardization not related to any particular technology, ISO, in consultation with IEC, undertakes to safeguard any electrotechnical interests that may be involved. To ensure the necessary technical coordination, ISO and IEC have established a joint ISO/IEC technical programming committee.

The members of the IEC are the *national committees,* one for each country, which are required to be as representative as possible of all electrotechnical interests in the country concerned: manufacturers, users, governmental authorities, and teaching and professional bodies. They are composed of representatives of all of these interests. National committees obtain a large measure of support from industry and are, for the most part, recognized by their governments. In order to carry out work related to technical standardization, numerous liaisons have been established between ISO and IEC committees, and a joint ISO/IEC technical committee has been established in the field of information technology.

ISO came into existence when, following a meeting in London in 1946, delegates from 25 countries decided to create a new, international organization, the object of which would be to facilitate the international coordination and unification of industrial standards. The new organization began to function officially in 1947. In its preparation of international standards, ISO brings together the interests of producers, users (including consumers), governments, and the scientific community. ISO work is carried out through a number of technical bodies. More than 30,000 experts from all parts of the world participate each year in ISO technical work, which, to date, has resulted in the publication of over 8600 ISO standards. International standardization is a natural consequence of the development of international trade and technical collaboration. The recent remarkable achievements in international standardization have been made possible through the collaborative efforts of national standards organizations and with the cooperation and support of producers, consumers, and governments from all over the world. There are, of course, many important international standardization problems left to be solved, and others are sure to arise following new technological developments and expanded international trade. International standardization is an investment based on confidence in the rational application of technology for the benefit of all people.

A *member body* of ISO is the national body most representative of standardization in its country. It follows that only one such body for each country is accepted for membership. Member bodies are entitled to participate and exercise full voting rights in any technical committee of ISO, are eligible for Council membership, and have seats in the General Assembly. There are more than 70 such bodies. Most of the ISO member bodies (over 70 percent) are governmental institutions or organizations incorporated by public law. The remainder have close links with the public administration in their own countries.

A *correspondent member* is normally an organization in a developing country that does not yet have its own national standards body. Correspondent members do not take an active part in the technical work but are entitled to be kept fully informed about any work of interest to them. They may attend the General Assembly as observers. Nearly all the current correspondent members are governmental institutions. The number of correspondent members exceeds 20. ISO has recently established a third category, *subscriber membership,* for countries with very small economies. These subscriber members, while not eligible to attend the General Assembly in any capacity, pay reduced membership fees that allow them to keep abreast of developments in international standardization.

Lowering the Barriers of International Trade

A primary objective of ISO is to replace the often-divergent standards of its member countries with international standards. Interest in ISO work has developed over the years to the extent that, today, ISO is the world's largest international organization for technical and industrial collaboration. As ISO has grown, so has the importance of other cooperative, multinational efforts to achieve international agreement on standards and technical regulations. For example, as part of the General Agreement on Tariffs and Trade (GATT)—now the responsibility of the World Trade Organization—more than 30 governments became signatories to a special Standards Code.

International standards developed by ISO cover a wide variety of needs ranging from the placement of motor vehicle control symbols to the designation of film speed for photography. Yet the basic idea of removing unnecessary impediments to international communication, collaboration, and trade is a common thread in all ISO work.

In the development process for ISO standards, the need for a particular international standard is first considered by an expert committee made up of representatives of all interested parties. When agreement is reached at the technical level, the draft form of the standard is proposed for approval by all ISO members. When voting results and comments show that the proposed standard is the best possible solution for international application at a particular time, the standard is accepted for publication by the ISO Council.

Experts participate in ISO technical committee meetings each year, and they, in turn, are supported by comparable national committees representing all interests that will be affected by the standard in question. Many other international organizations—such as the specialized agencies of the United Nations and international and professional trade associations—participate actively in ISO technical committees as liaison members. The work of each ISO technical committee and subcommittee is managed by a committee secretariat provided by one of the ISO members. These secretariats, currently from 34 countries, work closely with the ISO Central Secretariat in Geneva to ensure that the total program of ISO work is well-coordinated and proceeds in a timely manner. The ISO standards development system is, by design, highly decentralized and has shown itself to be remarkably effective. Each working day of the year, on the average, nine ISO technical meetings are in progress somewhere in the world. The timetables are coordinated by the Central Secretariat, and a calendar of meetings is published monthly.

Notwithstanding the ever-growing number of standards agreed upon and applied, there still remain several hundred thousand localized standards and technical regulations in use throughout the world. These contain special requirements for a particular country or region. Finding information about all of these standards, technical regulations, or related testing and certification activities can be an onerous task.

The ISO Information Network (ISONET) is a worldwide network of national standards information centers that have cooperatively developed a system to provide rapid access to information about standards, standards-type documents, and testing and certification activities currently used in different parts of the world. Individuals needing information about any standard or governmental technical regulation in another country need only contact the ISONET member in their own country to receive information and assistance from any of the more than 50 other ISONET members. Within the ISONET system, each member is responsible for documents issued within its own territory. Information about international standards, whether produced by ISO or another international organization, is provided by the ISO Information Center at the Central Secretariat in Geneva. The many aspects of the work of ISO are presented in various publications, which can be obtained through any ISO member body or directly from the ISO Central Secretariat.

The list of all published ISO standards is recorded in the *ISO Catalogue,* issued annually and updated by cumulative supplements. The structure and administration of all ISO standards committees are described in detail in the *ISO Memento.* Information updates on the achievements in international standardization of the organization as a whole are provided in the annual *Activities Report.* News about international standardization is given in the illustrated, monthly *ISO Bulletin.* In order to make international standards more accessible to a wider audience, ISO standards are compiled into *handbooks* covering each technical field. The most comprehensive reference source, and one that helps to identify all existing international standards for a given subject, is the *ISO KWIC Index of International Standards,* prepared in key-word-in-context format. In addition, ISO publishes a variety of manuals and textbooks that provide selected information on standardization and related activities.

As indicated before, the technical work of ISO is carried out through *technical committees* (TC). The decision to establish a technical committee is taken by the ISO Council, and the committee's scope is approved by the ISO Technical Board on behalf of the Council. Within this scope, the committee determines its own program of work. Work in the field of information technology is carried out through a joint ISO/IEC technical committee.

Each technical committee may, in turn, establish *subcommittees* (SC) and *working groups* (WG) to cover different aspects of its work. Each TC or SC has a secretariat, assigned to an ISO member body—in the case of the former, by the Technical Board on behalf of the Council, and in the case of the latter, by the parent committee. For each working group, a conveyor is appointed by the parent committee. By the end of 1992, there were 179 technical committees, 620 subcommittees, 1885 working groups, and 25 ad hoc study groups. A proposal to begin work in a new field of technical activity normally comes from within ISO itself, but it may also originate from some other international organization. Because the resources are limited, priorities must be considered. Therefore, all new proposals are submitted for consideration by the ISO member bodies. If accepted, either the new work will be referred to the appropriate, existing TC; or a new one will be established.

To ensure coordination of work in all matters of common interest, liaisons are established between related technical committees. Each member body interested in a subject for which a TC has been authorized has the right to be represented on that committee. Member bodies that decide to take an active part in the work of a TC or SC are designated as *P members* (participating members) of that committee or subcommittee. They have an obligation to vote and, whenever possible, to attend meetings. One of the P members is designated to act as the secretariat of the committee or subcommittee.

Member bodies that wish only to be kept informed of the work of a TC or SC are registered as *O members* (observers).

How an International Standard Is Developed

An international standard is the result of an agreement between the member bodies of ISO. An international standard may be used as such, or may be implemented through incorporation in national standards of different countries. A first step toward an international standard is the committee draft (CD)—a document circulated for study within the technical committee or subcommittee. This document must pass through a number of stages before it can be accepted as an international standard. This procedure is designed to ensure that the final result is acceptable to as many countries as possible.

When agreement is finally reached within the committee, the CD is sent to the Central Secretariat for registration as a draft international standard (DIS). The DIS is then circulated to all member bodies for voting. If 75 percent of the votes cast are in favor of the DIS, it is accepted for publication as an international standard. Normally, the fundamental technical issues are resolved at committee level; however, the member body voting procedure provides assurance that no important objections have been overlooked. The greater part of the work is done by correspondence, and meetings are convened only when thoroughly justified. Each year some 10,000 working documents are circulated.

Most standards require periodic revision. Several factors combine to render a standard out of date: technological evolution, new methods and materials, or new quality and safety requirements. To take account of these factors, ISO has established the general rule that all ISO standards should be reviewed at intervals of not more than five years. On occasion, it is necessary to revise a standard sooner.[3]

Questions Asked About the ISO 9000 Series Standards

As far as the ISO 9000 quality management and assurance standards are concerned, the most commonly asked questions regard the definition of quality and of quality systems; the content, application, and revision of the ISO 9000 standards; quality system approval/registration; European Union requirements for quality system approval/registration; and related topics. The increasing number of inquiries about these topics is indicative of the expanding interest in quality in many sectors of the economy.

Quality improvement has now become both the corporate and the international business strategy of the 1990s. Large companies are making a public pledge of their dedication to quality: Cadillac and Milliken and Company each advertise their having won the Malcolm Baldrige National Quality Award, Ford Motor Company proclaims in a prominently featured slogan that "Quality is Job 1" and many other companies are following suit. Under the Automotive Industry Action Group (AIAG) banner, Ford, GM, and Chrysler have joined efforts to develop and deploy a common quality standard based on ISO 9000. The result is the QS-9000 standard, which was put into place in 1994. At the international level, interest has mushroomed in quality systems as a means of ensuring the consistent conformity of products or services to a given set of standards or expectations.

There has, however, been little agreement among either corporate management or professionals in the field regarding the meaning of quality. The ISO standard 8402 defines quality as "the totality of features and characteristics of a product or service that bear on its ability to satisfy stated or implied needs."[4]

However, there are problems with this definition. "To satisfy stated or implied needs" is good as far as it goes, but exactly *whose* needs are we talking about? Who are the customers of a product or service? There are situations where the question of whose needs are being addressed may lead to some ambiguous, even contradictory, answers.

A case in point is the testing services field, where the service being offered is the testing of a product for a manufacturer. Totally erroneous test results may serve this client's need quite handsomely if the faulty test report can be used as a rationalization to allow the client to sell its product; in this instance, an accurate test report would only hamper the sale. Nevertheless, those erroneous results, felicitous as they may be for the manufacturer, are unlikely to satisfy the needs of the potential buyer of the product or the standards of the agency responsible for regulating the product. In this situation, the needs of the manufacturer and the needs of the user are clearly at odds.

Another situation in which one may have difficulty in pinpointing whose needs should be targeted occurs when a product or service is passed on by one company unit to another for use by the latter, and then subsequently delivered to the customer for its use as well. (An example of such a product would be a car manufacturing division that produces batteries and sells them to another division, which installs them in the car.) Although this could seemingly create a conflict between the needs of the internal customer and the external customer, in reality, this dilemma has no horns: As I have said before, there is no internal customer and this concept serves only to muddle the ultimate goal of all parties in the company—that of serving the external (and, indeed, the only) customer.

In an attempt to address this problem of customer identification, ISO has added seven footnotes to its definition, including some making the further qualifications that "needs can change with time" and that "in a contractual environment, needs are specified, whereas in other environments, implied needs should be identified and defined." This still leaves us with the problem of determining all of the parameters of the definition, for needs can be variously defined in terms of safety, useability, availability, versatility, compatibility with other products, reliability, maintainability, overall cost (including purchase price, maintenance costs, and product life), environmental impact, or other desired characteristics.

Even if all needs can be identified and adequately defined (often no easy task), what about the issue of what is known as an acceptable quality level (AQL)—the traditional idea of a maximum percentage of nonconforming products or service units that may be considered satisfactory as a process average? Stated in other words, how many mistakes can you make and still produce a quality product or service? A manufacturer's production system may be considered by its customers to produce a quality product if the AQL is 0.1 percent, that is, only one in 1000 products contains defects. Yet a 1 in 1000 error rate for nurses whose job it is to hold babies (only 1 baby dropped out of a 1000!) or for containers that hold highly toxic or hazardous materials (only 1 deadly leak for every 1000 containers produced!) is obviously not acceptable. There is a belief among many quality experts and their disciples that the only acceptable quality level for any manufactured product or service is 100 percent (zero defects), and that any failure to do it right the first time is not tolerable. This is not a universally held opinion.

Product quality depends on many variables, such as the caliber of the components or materials used; the type of equipment used in design, production, handling, installation, testing, and shipping; the equipment calibration and maintenance procedures employed; the training and experience of production and supervisory personnel; the level of workmanship; and, sometimes, the environmental conditions (temperature, humidity, level of dust particles) in the area in which the product is produced. The process, organizational structure, procedures, and resources that manufacturers and suppliers use to control these variables to produce a product of consistent quality which meets defined specifications is called a *quality system.*[5] The standards that are being adopted globally for quality systems are the ISO 9000 series standards.

Development of the ISO 9000 Series Standards

A few years ago, the then 12 members of what was called the European Community (EC) decided to unify their market by January 1, 1993. On that date, all barriers to free movement of goods, services, capital, and persons among these countries were to disappear. In view of this radical change in the world scene, the EC, seeking to assure buyers of the quality of goods and services purchased, suggested the replacement of national standards regarding quality management and assurance systems by a common one to be applied throughout the Community. Foreign suppliers to the member countries would also be required to comply with such standards. ISO was then requested to start working on such standards. In North America, the North American Free Trade Agreement (NAFTA) did not suggest the development of continental standards. In fact, however, Canada, the United States, and Mexico have all adopted the ISO 9000 standards as quality management system standards.[6]

In 1979, ISO formed Technical Committee (TC) 176 on Quality Management and Quality Assurance to address two related issues: the worldwide trend toward increasingly stringent customer demands with regard to quality, and the growing confusion in international trade resulting from differing national and subnational quality system requirements. TC 176 held its first meeting in 1980 at the Ottawa-based headquarters of the Standards Council of Canada, which represents Canada within the ISO. Twenty-one countries participated. Toward the end of 1991, the committee had 40 member countries with 23 observers. TC 176 meets, on the average, once a year. More than 220 delegates attended the November 1991 meeting in Madrid.

TC 176 has three permanent subcommittees. These subcommittees generally form a working group for each new standardization project. Before the projected

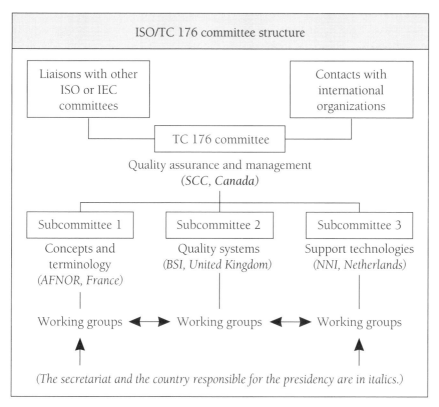

Figure 12.1. ISO/TC 176 committee structure.

standards are finalized and published, they are discussed and deliberated at two international consultation sessions.

Origin of Quality Assurance Standards

Quality assurance standards first came to be developed for use in a military context. In 1959, the U.S. Department of Defense (DOD) established a quality assurance standard that it called the *Quality Management Program* (designed as MIL-Q-9858). The purpose of this standard was to unify the requirements concerning quality systems for all of the suppliers of the department. In 1968, the North Atlantic Treaty Organization (NATO) essentially adopted the provisions of the MIL-Q-9858A Quality Program Requirements in the form of the Allied Quality Assurance Publication (AQAP). In 1970, the United Kingdom's Ministry of Defense adopted the provisions of AQAP as its Management Program Defense Standard.

The year 1979 saw the introduction of the first quality management system standard for commercial use when the British Standards Institution (BSI) developed the standard known as BS 5750. Meanwhile, the Canadian Standards Association (CSA) launched its CSA Z299 series, which later became the national standard CAN Z299. The British and Canadian standards became known and used worldwide. Nevertheless, some countries developed their own standards separately, and the resulting proliferation of standards started to cause some problems for suppliers exporting to different countries.

In 1987, based on these predecessors and on the work of TC 176, ISO created the ISO 9000 series standards—a series of five international standards on quality management and assurance: ISO 9000, 9001, 9002, 9003, and 9004. These standards were formed by garnering considerable input from a number of countries, especially the United States, Canada, and the United Kingdom. In particular, the ISO 9000 standards were largely based on the British Standards Institution's BS 5750 series.[7]

The ISO 9000 series, together with the terminology and definitions contained in ISO 8402, provides guidance on the selection of an appropriate quality management program or system for a supplier's operations. The publication of this series has paved the way for meshing the concepts, terms, and guidelines related to quality assurance and management on an international scale and, thus, has sustained the growing impact of quality as a factor in international trade.

Since the ISO 9000 standards were set in 1987, they have been promulgated widely in a number of different countries and organizations. That same year, they were adopted in the United States under the guise of ANSI/ASQC Q90 standard series; and, in the United Kingdom, BS 5750 was revised to render it identical to the ISO 9000 standards. Canada has also adopted the ISO 9000 series (under the name of Q9000), with supplements added to make it equivalent to the CAN Z299 series. NATO has revised its quality system standards to incorporate the ISO 9000 standards. ASQC has assumed responsibility for managing the adoption of the ISO 9000 and 10000 standards as American national standards. In Europe, they have been adopted by the European Committee for Standardization (CEN) and the European Committee for Electrotechnical Standardization (CENELEC) as the European Norm (EN) 29000 series. In 1991, the ISO 9000 series was adopted in Japan as the Japanese Industrial Standard (JIS) Z 9900 series.[8] According to a survey by ISO, some 50 countries have national standards that are identical or equivalent to the ISO 9000 series standards. At this time, additional countries are considering their adoption, as the ISO 9000 standards continue to rapidly supplant previous national standards.

The ISO 9000 standards were intended to be advisory in nature and were developed primarily for use in two-party contractual situations or for internal auditing. However, the standards are currently being applied under a much broader range of conditions and circumstances. In some cases, compliance with one of the ISO 9000 standards (or their equivalent) has been or is soon to be mandated by domestic, foreign national, or regional government bodies. Conformance to ISO

9000 standards is also being required in purchasing specifications with increasing frequency.

According to ISO procedures, all of its standards must be reviewed and then revised or reaffirmed at least once every five years. The initial ISO 9000 standards published in 1987 (ISO 9000, 9001, 9002, 9003, and 9004, without subparts) were scheduled for review in 1992/1993, as was ISO 8402, *Quality—Vocabulary*, which contains relevant terminology and definitions. Minor modifications to the original ISO 9000 series were made in 1994, with major revisions—referred to as the phase 2 revisions—scheduled for 1997/1998.

For the 1994 modifications, the Registrar Accreditation Board (RAB) established that all registered suppliers would have to demonstrate that they met the requirements of the revised standards within one year after the date that the revisions were published. According to RAB, this requirement would apply to both existing supplier registrations and all registrations occurring after the publication date. Registrars are free to establish additional guidelines for administering their own activities, such as setting earlier interim deadlines for suppliers, to ensure that the one-year time limit for conversion to the revised standards is met.[9]

ISO 9000–9004 and their ANSI/ASQC counterparts are equivalent. However, the latter has been modified to incorporate customary American language usage and spelling (such as *program* instead of *programme*). Some supplementary guidance on sampling and other statistical methods and on product liability and user safety has also been included in the appendices to ANSI/ASQC Q94. ASQC renumbered the ANSI/ASQC Q90 series as the ANSI/ISO/ASQC Q9000 series to clearly indicate its equivalency to the ISO 9000 series.

ISO has continued to supplement the ISO 9000 series. Some of these standards have been included as parts under ISO 9000 and ISO 9004, while others have been included in the ISO 10000 series.

Information Contained in the ISO 9000 Standards

The ISO 9000 series is generic in scope. Each standard addresses a different aspect of quality assurance, and each user will consult a different standard, depending on his or her needs.

ISO 9001, 9002, and 9003 describe three distinct quality system models of varying stringency for use in different applications. Common elements addressed by ISO 9001, 9002, and 9003 include the need for

- An effective quality system
- Ensuring that measurements are valid and that measuring and testing equipment is calibrated regularly
- The use of appropriate statistical techniques
- Having a product identification and traceability system
- Maintaining an adequate record-keeping system

Standard	Title	Use
ISO 9000-1	*Quality management and quality assurance standards—Part 1: Guidelines for selection and use*	Explains fundamental quality concepts. It defines key terms and provides guidance on selecting, using, and tailoring ISO 9001, 9002, and 9003.
ISO 9001	*Quality systems—Model for quality assurance in design, development, production, installation, and servicing*	Covers all element listed in ISO 9002 and 9003. In addition, it addresses design, development, and servicing capabilities. This is the most comprehensive standard in the series.
ISO 9002	*Quality systems—Model for quality assurance in production and installation*	Addresses the prevention, detection, and correction of problems during production and installation. It is more extensive and more sophisticated than ISO 9003.
ISO 9003	*Quality systems—Model for quality assurance in final inspection and test*	Addresses requirements for the detection and control of problems during final inspection and testing. This is the least comprehensive standard.
ISO 9004-1	*Quality management and quality system elements—Part 1: Guidelines*	Provides guidance for a supplier to use in developing and implementing a quality system and in determining the extent to which each quality system element is applicable. ISO 9004-1 examines each of the quality system elements (cross-referenced in the other ISO standards) in greater detail and can be used for internal and external auditing purposes.

Table 12.1. Title and use of the five main ISO 9000 series standards.

- Having an adequate product handling, storage, packaging, and delivery system;
- Having an adequate inspection and testing system, as well as a process for dealing with nonconforming items
- Ensuring that personnel have adequate training and experience

Table 12.1 shows the number, title, and uses of the five main ISO 9000 series standards. Table 12.2 shows and compares the elements contained in ISO 9001, 9002, and 9003.

Requirement, 1994 edition	ISO 9001	ISO 9002	ISO 9003
1. Management responsibility	●	●	●
2. Quality system	●	●	● *
3. Contract review	●	●	●
4. Design control	●		
5. Document control	●	●	●
6. Purchasing	●	●	
7. Purchaser supplied product	●	●	●
8. Product identification and traceability	●	●	● *
9. Process control	●	●	
10. Inspection and testing	●	●	● *
11. Inspection, measuring, and test equipment	●	●	●
12. Inspection and test status	●	●	●
13. Control of nonconforming product	●	●	● *
14. Corrective and preventive action	●	●	● *
15. Handling, storage, packaging, and delivery	●	●	●
16. Quality records	●	●	● *
17. Internal quality audits	●	●	● *
18. Training	●	●	● *
19. Servicing	●	●	
20. Statistical techniques	●	●	● *

Table 12.2. Comparison of elements—ISO 9001, 9002, and 9003.

* Requirements are limited by the scope of each specific standard.

Several other standards and guidelines have been added to the basic standards (see Figure 12.2). They fall into four distinct categories.

1. Guidelines for quality management
   - ISO 10011-1, *Guidelines for auditing quality systems—Auditing* (1990).
   - ISO 10011-2, *Guidelines for auditing quality systems—Qualification criteria for auditors* (1991)
   - ISO 10011-3, *Guidelines for auditing quality systems—Managing audit programmes* (1991)
   - ISO 9004-2, *Quality management and quality system elements— Guidelines for services* (1991)

2. General requirements for quality assurance
   - ISO 10012-1, *Quality assurance requirements for measuring equipment—Management of measuring equipment* (1992)

3. Guidelines associated with quality-related technology
   - ISO 9000-3, *Guidelines for the application of ISO 9001 to the development, supply and maintenance of software* (1991)

4. Terms and definitions[10]

Other ISO standards that deal with various aspects of quality management are also being prepared. For example, there is a quality standard for companies engaged in continuous production, another on quality in services, and a third on quality improvement. The following standards are under development in TC 176's subcommittees.

- Quality systems terminology
- Guidelines for processed materials
- Generic guidelines for the application of ISO 9001, ISO 9002, and ISO 9003
- Guidelines for quality improvement
- Guidelines for quality plans
- Guide to quality assurance for project management
- Guidelines for configuration management
- Guidelines for developing quality manuals
- Guide to the economic effects of quality
- Continuing education and training guidelines

In the work accomplished to date, the subcommittee for the quality improvement standard recognizes that improvement is only possible after a company completes a number of projects using a structured method based on gathering and analyzing information in a coherent and disciplined fashion. One of the projects, involving research, diagnosis, and problem solving or improvement activi-

Guidelines for quality management	General requirements for quality assurance	Quality technology
ISO 9004-1 Quality management guide	**ISO 9001 ISO 9002 ISO 9003** Quality assurance models	ISO 10011-1, 2, 3 Quality audit
ISO 9004-2 Services		ISO 10012-1 System for metrological qualification of measuring equipment
	Supplements	
ISO 9004-3 Processed materials	ISO 9000-1 Basic document for selection and use	ISO 10012-2 Quality assurance for measuring equipment
ISO 9004-4 Quality improvement	ISO 9000-2 Guide for implementing ISO 9001/2/3 standards	ISO 10013 Quality manual
ISO 9004-5 Project management	ISO 9000-3 Quality assurance of software	ISO 10014 Economics of quality management
ISO 9004-6 Quality plans	*Terms and definitions*	ISO 10015 Continuing education and training
ISO 9004-7 Configuration management	ISO 8402	ISO 10016 Inspection and tests records

Figure 12.2. The ISO 9000 series and related standards.

Source: Pierre F. Caillibot, "La normalisation internationale, pour gérer et assurer la qualité," *Qualité totale* 13, no. 2 (Summer 1992): 10. Updated in 1995. Reprinted with permission.

ties, identifies the possible gains that would result from quality improvement in any part of the company.

This process starts out by instigating measures to achieve new levels of performance. Quality improvement projects can be very complex and lengthy and require the involvement of upper management. They can also be relatively simple and be carried out by groups of employees or workers during the course of their regular work. The project for this particular standard also proposes a number of useful techniques for quality improvement projects.

Some national and regional standards bodies are developing supplemental guides for the application of the ISO 9000 series to specific industries. CEN and CENELEC, for example, are developing more specific requirements for the application of the ISO 9001 to the medical device industry.[11] The U.S. Food and Drug Administration (FDA) is planning to revise its Good Manufacturing Practice (GMP) regulations for medical devices to follow ISO 9001 with appropriate additional requirements.

"Vision 2000—A Strategy for International Standards' Implementation in the Quality Arena During the 1990s" is a long-range plan through the year 2000 developed by an ad hoc task force of ISO TC 176. The plan includes providing additional guidance on how to apply the ISO 9000 series standards to four generic product categories (hardware, software, processed materials, and services), as well as providing guidance on related issues, such as quality system auditing. As noted above, these documents are in various stages of development. Major revisions in the original ISO 9000 series are expected in 1997. The long-range goal, according to Vision 2000, is to have a single total quality management standard by the year 2000.

ISO has established a forum to serve the needs of ISO 9000 users by

- Providing information (including a newsletter, the *ISO 9000 News*)
- Facilitating international discussions on new developments and issues affecting the application of the ISO 9000 standards
- Promoting the exchange of experience in training and other such areas
- Promoting and operating relevant schemes
- Harmonizing practices in the application and interpretation of the ISO 9000 standards

A Word of Caution

The ISO 9000 standards may not be perfect; however, they are now with us and many companies will have to play the game. According to J. T. Burr,[12] the series has some shortcomings, the greatest being as follows.

1. These standards are generic. They represent the minimum requirements that a quality system needs to be effective and to ensure that the product will meet customer requirements.

2. These standards are written for all suppliers regardless of their industry base, their company size, or what portion of the company is being registered. Still, the ISO 9000 series is one set of standards that does have almost universal acceptance. It is recognized by some 150 countries.

3. The ISO 9001, 9002, and 9003 standards define what must be in a quality system but do not tell a company how to document the quality system. What is a quality manual? What is a quality plan? What makes up an adequate quality policy? Who should be responsible, and what is authority?

4. According to J. M. Juran, the series does not mention or make provision for continuous improvement. This is a serious drawback.

5. The series requires no evidence of a satisfactory track record of performance, for example, in product quality or delivery. Because the applicable standard will usually be identified as a part of a purchasing contract, it is expected that the contract itself will provide controls on performance. A company not satisfied with the track record of a supplier will look for another supplier that will meet its needs all the time.

As Yves Van Nuland puts it, "ISO 9000 are quality standards that assure customers that an organization is working in accordance with specific requirements."[13] You will note that the customer thus receives an assurance regarding the organization, not product quality per se. In other words, what customers are being told is that the tools and the procedures are there—and that these have the *potential* to produce quality. But when, then, can customers be sure that they are receiving only conforming products? Only when their suppliers work in accordance with the principles of total quality. Many companies, however, are unsuccessful in introducing total quality because they make the mistake of emphasizing only one of its elements. The technical element is the most obvious, and, thus, most companies generally start with that point (and, I would add, end at that point). Technical elements include such tools as ISO 9000, just-in-time, statistical process control, problem-solving techniques, and measuring techniques. According to Van Nuland, there are three essential elements in the successful introduction of total quality: technical input, committed management, and the right attitude. He concludes that the practice of ISO 9000 will be successful only if total quality management is already present in a company or if it is introduced at the same time as ISO 9000.

Ian S. Kalinosky comments that continued success at improving competitiveness and providing a product or a service that meets customer requirements is like a journey. Quality policy provides the map and the rules for the journey, quality management is the driver, and the quality system is the vehicle. He adds that, rather than making compliance to an external quality system standard the focus of a company's effort, the focus should be on the designing of a total quality system and on integrating elements that enhance competitiveness.[14]

A number of quality specialists prefer ISO 9004-1 to 9001, 9002, and 9003. J. J. Klock from AT&T suggests that ISO 9004-1 is more comprehensive and covers more aspects of a companywide quality system.[15] For example, ISO 9004-1 does not require that a specific quality organization (department, committee, coordinator, and so on) be responsible for quality. Some manufacturers, especially Japanese manufacturers, have achieved high levels of quality by integrating quality into their operations, taking what had hitherto been a loosely conceived, unstated intention, formalizing it as an explicit goal, and making the individual operators responsible for its achievement.

In all fairness, one should keep in mind that, since the above comments were made, the ISO 9000 series have undergone a major revision and significant modifications. For example, while the old version (1987) did not require a quality manual, this is now a requirement. (One may consult ISO 10013, *Guidelines for developing quality manuals,* published in April 1995). Also, the 9002 standard now includes a requirement concerning services to customers, which was previously limited to the ISO 9001 standard. Moreover, while the previous standards required *corrective* actions to be undertaken when required, the revised standards have added a requirement for *preventive* actions as well.

In brief, no company should consider the implementation of an ISO 9000 standard as an objective. The objective should always be the design, production, and delivery of quality products and services. The ISO 9000 standards are a means—a valuable and efficient means, but still a means—toward that end.

ISO 9000 and the Malcolm Baldrige National Quality Award

The Malcolm Baldrige National Quality Award examination process is designed to recognize and reward those firms with outstanding records of quality performance. The purpose of the program is therefore very different from the purpose behind the development of the ISO 9000 criteria. While the use of the ISO 9000 standards may be a good starting point for establishing a quality system, the criteria used in evaluating candidates for the Baldrige Award are much more detailed and extend beyond those areas covered by the ISO 9000 series. The Baldrige Award criteria are results oriented and cover all operations, processes, and work units of a company. The evaluation procedures emphasize the means and mechanisms involved in the integration of all aspects of a firm's quality system and in the firm's continuous improvements in quality.

Quality System Evaluation and Registration

Manufacturers may choose to evaluate their own quality systems. Such *self-audits* are usually major components of the quality system itself. They can increase the confidence of management in its production system and demonstrate to personnel that the firm is committed to quality management. *Second-party* evaluations are also common. In these cases, it is usually the buyer who requires and conducts quality system evaluations of the suppliers. These evaluations are mandatory only for companies wishing to become suppliers to that buyer. *Third-party* quality system evaluations and registrations may be voluntary or mandatory and are conducted by persons or organizations independent of both the supplier and the buyer. According to a recent ISO survey, more than 30 countries reported the existence of one or more third-party registration schemes in their countries.

There is a good deal of confusion surrounding the terms *certification, registration,* and *accreditation,* and this should be cleared up from the outset. Although certification and registration are frequently used interchangeably when spoken of informally, they are, strictly speaking, two different things. Certification traditionally applies only to products. It is the procedure by which a third party gives written assurance that a product conforms to specified requirements. Registration, on the other hand, applies to the assessment and approval of quality systems, not products. In everyday usage, however, people will use the word certification indiscriminately to refer to either of the two activities, thus skirting the danger of blurring these concepts entirely.[16] If certification must be used to mean quality system registration, then care must be taken to qualify it as *quality system certification.*

Meanwhile, the last of these terms, accreditation, is completely distinct in meaning from the other two. While the first two terms have to do with certifying a product and registering a system, the third accredits people or organizations in order that they are able to certify and register others. Accreditation is therefore the procedure by which an authoritative body gives formal recognition that a laboratory, certification body, or quality system registrar is competent to conduct specified conformity assessment tasks.

Quality system registration or approval involves the assessment and periodic audit of the adequacy of a supplier's quality system by a third party, known as a *quality system registrar.* When a supplier's system conforms to the registrar's interpretation of an ISO 9000 standard, the registrar issues the supplier a *certificate of registration.* Interpretations of an ISO 9000 standard may not be consistent from one registrar to another. Note again that the supplier's *quality system* is registered, not an individual product. Consequently, quality system registration does not imply product conformity to any given set of requirements. Registration programs can be conducted in conjunction with or independently from a certification program. Registrars may or may not concurrently operate a product certification program. *Conformity assessment,* a more comprehensive term, is the systematic evaluation of a product, process, or service to determine the extent to which it complies with specified requirements. Conformity assessment activities include quality system registration; product or service testing and/or certification; and laboratory, certification body, or quality system registrar accreditation.

The European Accreditation of Certification (EAC) is an association of the European national accreditation bodies. The overall objective of the EAC is to create a single European system for recognizing certification/quality system registration bodies that will provide the marketplace with adequate assurance that certification/registration is equivalent in all European countries. A Memorandum of Understanding was signed by Belgium, Denmark, Ireland, the Netherlands, the United Kingdom, Germany, Greece, Italy, Portugal, Iceland, Norway, Sweden, and Switzerland on May 22, 1991. Specific objectives of the EAC, as defined in the memorandum, are to

- Maintain and strengthen market confidence in certificates issued by accredited bodies
- Establish mutual confidence between participating bodies and promote collaboration and agreements as a means toward a European system of assessment and accreditation
- Provide the means for a continuous flow of knowledge relevant to assessment and accreditation between participating bodies and other relevant bodies
- Work toward a multilateral agreement on the equivalence of the operations of the participating bodies and a declaration of their commitment to fostering general acceptance of the equivalence of the certificates issued by the certification bodies they accredit
- Promote the harmonization of the operations of participating bodies

Until recently, U.S. companies relied on quality system registration firms in Europe and Canada to register their quality systems, but this is no longer the case. Today, the number of U.S.-based organizations offering consulting services, assessment, and/or quality system registration is growing rapidly. In the United States, in 1989, the Registrar Accreditation Board (RAB) was established as an affiliate of ASQC to develop a program to evaluate the quality of services offered by registrars. RAB issued its first approval in March 1991, and several more firms have been approved since then. RAB and ANSI agreed to form a joint U.S. program in December 1991. In February 1992, RAB announced the establishment of an ISO 9000 auditor certification program. Programs similar to that of the RAB have been under way in Canada, in a number of European countries, and elsewhere in the world for some time.

The demand for ISO 9000 registration in Europe and elsewhere seems to be coming primarily from the marketplace as a contractual obligation assumed voluntarily rather than as a regulatory requirement. As conformity to the ISO 9000 standards becomes recognized and required by foreign and domestic buyers and used by manufacturers as a competitive marketing tool, the demand for ISO 9000 compliance is expected to increase in nonregulated areas. It is therefore critical for manufacturers to determine what their buyers' requirements are regarding ISO 9000 compliance. The degree of interest and pressure that specific manufacturers are experiencing from their buyers to seek registration currently varies significantly by industry. In many of the high-technology or high-safety and health high-risk product areas where product reliability is crucial (such as electronic components, aerospace, autos, test equipment, and health care products), the market pressure on manufacturers to seek registration is likely to increase.

The U.S. Aerospace Industries Association, in its April 1992 Study, *Impact of International Standardization and Certification on the U.S. Aerospace Industry,* noted that in its industry "some European and other foreign customers are now including a requirement that potential bidders be ISO 9000-compliant." This growing demand from buyers for registration is being noted in many other industries as well. Procurement authorities and buyers are increasingly including ISO 9000 registration requirements in their purchase contracts. Suppliers desiring to sell to such entities will have to be audited and registered as being in compliance with an ISO 9000 standard under terms acceptable to those buyers.

According to Morrow,

> One of the most common complaints about the ISO 9000 series registration is that registrars often have differing opinions on how to interpret specific clauses of the standard. . . . Some companies solve the problem by hiring consultants familiar with a particular registrar's audit practices. Other companies use the same registrar for the preassessment and the final audit . . . effective methods but not ideal. The Independent Association of Accredited Registrars . . . has established a committee to offer common interpretations of the series standards . . . at least registrars and their customers will have a benchmark that represents consensus opinion. . . . Worldwide estimates for ISO 9000 registrations range from 30,000 to 35,000. Despite the frantic pace of registrations, the standard cannot live up to its full potential without agreement and consensus on such basic issues as consistent interpretation.[17]

According to the same author, the very methods that companies use to get around this problem of inconsistent interpretation on the part of registrars creates its own set of problems. The fact that some registrars, as mentioned above, perform both the preassessment and assessment audits for the same client and that others provide their client with both registrar and consulting services approaches a conflict of interest which puts the registration movement in danger of losing credibility.[18] The quality community must address these issues to make the best use of the ISO 9000 series standards.

There is no reference to ISO 9000, or to quality management systems, in EU legislation related to private sector procurement of services such as accounting, engineering, or legal services. The proposed EU directive on procedures for the awarding of public service contracts does note that some government-owned, -operated, or -controlled contracting entities in the public works and supplies sectors do impose quality management system requirements in their qualified supplier programs. However, ISO 9000 registration is not mandatory under this directive. The EU Commission has noted that

> Quality control certification . . . exists at the national level in particular service sectors such as the field of engineering. It has been observed that

contracting authorities tend to require such certificates whenever a quality assurance body exists in their country. This may have the effect of discriminating against foreign suppliers. . . . The directive should therefore recognize the existence of quality assurance schemes, and reconcile the way in which they are used with the need to grant a fair chance to suppliers from other countries.

Prerequisites for Product Certification

Having a registered quality system will not be a blanket requirement for all products. However, for suppliers of construction products, certain classes of medical devices and personal protective equipment, telecommunications terminal equipment, gas appliances, commercial scales, and possibly other products (such as pressure equipment, recreational craft, cable ways, and lifting equipment for people), registration of a supplier's quality system will be a key component of the EU's legal requirements for product certification. It should be noted that manufacturer compliance with ISO 9002 or ISO 9003 is usually combined with some type of product testing for full product certification under EU requirements. The full quality assurance (ISO 9001) option includes an assessment of the product's design to ensure that it conforms to the applicable *essential requirements.*

Manufacturers of some products will be permitted to self-declare that their product conforms to the requirements and to place the EU mark on the product. However, they must maintain a file on the manufacture of those products, including information on their quality system. It is possible that the ISO 9000 (EN 29000) series standards could be used within the EU to evaluate the adequacy of such quality systems.

In the nonregulated product area, producers desiring to do business in the EU and elsewhere may be required by procurement authorities or buyers to be audited and registered as being in compliance with an ISO 9000 standard. This is especially likely in industries such as aerospace, autos, electronic components, measuring and testing equipment, or in industries where safety and liability are concerns. Such requirements will result from marketplace demands, as opposed to regulatory requirements. Other foreign government procurement authorities have already or are likely to follow suit.

Product Safety and ISO 9000

The EU Directive on General Product Safety 92/59 (commonly known as the Product Safety Directive) was approved by the then EC Council on June 29, 1992. This directive covers all products placed on the EU market—whether regulated by the EU or not. The directive applies to the safety of products from the time that they are first placed on the EU market and extends throughout the product's foreseeable life. The objective of the directive is to impose a general requirement on producers to introduce only safe products into the EU market. A *safe product* is defined as follows:

> A product that does not present, in particular in respect of its design, composition, execution, functioning, wrapping, conditions of assembly, maintenance or disposal, instructions for handling and use, or any other of its properties, an unacceptable risk for the safety and health of persons, either directly or indirectly, in particular through its effect upon other products or its combinations therewith.

Products intended for consumers should not present any unacceptable risks, and potential users of such products should be adequately warned of any remaining risks. Some guidance on what constitutes a safe product is contained in the directive. In general, the Product Safety Directive will not apply to those safety aspects of a product or category of products already covered under an EU directive. This directive may have some implications for suppliers regarding their quality systems. In the event of legal claims, suggests one legal opinion, ISO 9000 registration, combined with other, appropriate, technical documentation related to product safety and adequate product labeling/user instructions, could prove useful in a legal defense.[19] The same legal counsel also holds that "While ISO 9000 registration will not protect a company from being sued for a defective product, quality system documentation creates a technical record that could be useful in such prospective product liability suits."

Implementing an ISO 9000 Series Standard

Knowing Why the Company Should Embark on Such a Scheme

For successful implementation of an ISO 9000 standard, the first condition is to know why such a standard should be implemented. Many companies do it for the wrong reasons, such as "Everybody else is doing it," or "The CEO heard of it from a colleague on a plane flying to Chicago," or, even, "It is supposed to solve all our quality problems." A company should think of introducing an ISO 9000 type of quality system for one of the following three reasons.

1. To help achieve total quality. In the process of introducing total quality, TQM includes, as we have seen, activities devoted to both product quality assurance and total quality assurance, with the objective of preventing unquality products and services as well as the absence of total quality in general. Implementing an ISO 9000 standard is one such activity aimed at product quality assurance.

2. To satisfy a specific requirement from one or more customers.

3. To open up new domestic and foreign markets in cases where ISO 9000 is neither compulsory nor mandatory. Thus, the company would have a definite

advantage over the competition, assuring its potential customers of being supplied with quality products and services.

Setting up a quality system that complies with the ISO 9000 standards without trying to include this activity in a total quality orientation is possible, but it will yield negative results. It should be underlined that if full benefits are to be reaped, the TQM requisites must be met. It has to be understood that setting up an ISO 9000 quality system is an effort to increase the competitiveness of the company and its profitability, to improve the customers' satisfaction, and to enable the employees to enhance their quality of life.

Familiarizing Oneself with the ISO 9000 Series

It is important to get acquainted with the standards. Reading through the ISO 9000 series, including ISO 8402, gives a good idea of the standards, their philosophy, and the basic concepts and terminology they employ. At the same time, ISO 9001 to 9003 will usually come as a disappointment if one reads through them expecting to find a pat recipe for attaining quality. The standards are only intended to be a guide to implementing a quality system, not a detailed cookbook for quality or a systematic how-to manual. It indicates what the components of such a system should be rather than how to design it. This is where outside help is usually required. However, before deciding on the kind of help required, the company should appoint a coordinator for the project who can act as a scout, reconnoitering potential resources. Of course, if this process is part of the total quality project, the total quality coordinator should be assigned to this task.

ISO coordinators have the mission of gathering information from published material (books and articles, consultants' brochures, training courses, relevant association newsletters), attending conferences addressing the theory behind the standards, and analyzing case studies on real applications in general and those, in particular, in specific fields relevant to the type of industry or trade the company is in. Besides accumulating written information and attending conferences or courses on the subject, coordinators should arrange to visit companies that have implemented an ISO 9000 standard or, better yet, have been registered.

An ISO 9000 committee should be formed, with representatives from top management and various departments, such as marketing, purchasing, manufacturing and operations, engineering, research and development, and quality assurance.

Getting Outside Help

In a number of countries, government subsidies are available to businesses, especially small and medium-sized ones, that partially pay for an outside consultant when the businesses implement an ISO 9000 standard. However, before hiring such a consultant, research should be undertaken. Companies that have successfully implemented such a standard using one consulting firm or another should be contacted so that their experiences can be evaluated. The representatives of various consulting firms should be asked to submit their credentials and to meet the ISO 9000 committee of the business requiring consulting services. The consultants should present their approach, their proposed schedule and budget, and a list of firms for whom they have acted as consultants, specifying those that have subsequently qualified for registration. According a survey published in *Quality Progress,*

> 60% of companies seeking ISO 9000 registration fail to be immediately recommended for registration. Of these, half require more than six months of corrective action and reassessment before they are registered. This represents a significant number of companies that have to pay extra expenses for corrective actions and follow-up visits.[20]

As far as registrars' fees are concerned, the survey sampled the cost of assessment by asking registrars to submit a quote for two types of companies. One was a 250-employee company with a single manufacturing site, the second a 2000-employee company working in several buildings at a single site. The quotes varied from $7800 to $30,000 for the first and from $14,000 to $100,000 for the second!

Sensitizing Management and Nonmanagement

An ISO 9000 implementation project should be preceded by a sensitization effort—a campaign to mobilize management and nonmanagement. It must be made clear that standards do not improve quality of products and services—only people do. The objective is not to obtain registration or to implement a new quality system; it is to use the ISO 9000 project as an opportunity to improve competitiveness and profitability, customer satisfaction, and employee quality of life—the total quality triad. This project could be thought of as a first step toward a much larger goal: achieving and maintaining total quality.

Deciding Which ISO Standard to Implement

The committee has to choose between ISO 9001, 9002, or 9003. In general, ISO 9003 is for nonmanufacturing, distribution-type businesses, while ISO 9002 is chosen by most manufacturing companies, as well as a number of service organizations. ISO 9001, the most comprehensive of the three, is for manufacturing companies that develop their own products and thus wish their quality systems to cover design activities as well. A company that intends to go for registration should be aware that ISO 9003 is not considered by many as an indication of an adequate quality system. There is a common feeling that this standard will have to be eventually upgraded to be taken seriously. In cases in which the choice of the standard is based on a customer's requirement, satisfying that requirement is obviously the least that the company must aim for.

Among the factors considered when choosing a quality model[21] (or standard) are the customer requirements, the design process complexity, the maturity of the design, the production process complexity, the product or service characteristics and safety, and economic considerations.

Generally speaking, ISO 9001, 9002, and 9003 were designed to be used in contractual situations, as an agreement between a buyer and a supplier. They are the only standards to which a company can be registered. They represent *minimal requirements* to assure the buyer that the supplier is able to

- Design, produce, and service products with the right level of quality (9001)
- Produce and ship products with the right level of quality (9002)
- Ship products with the right level of quality (9003)

When a company wants to implement a quality system solely for its own use, ISO 9004-1 is a good guide to follow.

Auditing the Existing System[22]

Most companies, if not all, have some sort of quality system in place, be it formal or informal, complete or incomplete. However, the emphasis in the ISO 9000 standards, as well as in all of the other quality assurance systems, is on formalization through *documentation*. Nothing should be left to intuition and judgment calls. Besides, documentation results in traceability—being able to trace an effect back to its causes—and allows one to analyze any undesirable result on the basis of objective fact rather than subjective opinion, thus leaving no room for wild guesswork. This obviously creates a lot of paperwork, but that is the price you must pay if you want to increase the prevention of unquality or correct it promptly and ensure that it will not occur again.

Therefore, the first step toward setting up a complete quality system is to audit the existing system. Information is gathered on all existing quality-related documents and on the filing system of such documents, as well as on the working instructions. An evaluation grid is used to compare the existing documented activities with the required ones in the standard. In this way, one can evaluate the existing activities and identify those that are missing. An evaluation grid might consist of a three-column checklist that lists the requirements of the standard, the existing procedure, and the remarks of the evaluator on how they compare. Other grids may have more columns in order to indicate whether or not the activity exists and, if it does exist, whether it is satisfactory, to be improved, unsuitable and destined to be scrapped and replaced, or not applicable in the company being audited. An example of such a checklist is shown in Figure 12.3. For example, if the standard calls for a calibration system for all measuring instruments, whereas in actuality only 40 percent of the instruments are indeed calibrated, this activity would be indicated as *to be improved* and the situation explained in the comments column. It is evident that no two evaluators will evaluate a quality system exactly the same way. That is why quality systems should be evaluated by more than one auditor.

ISO ref.	Requirements	Mis	Rep	Imp	Sat	N/A	Comments
4.8 Product identification and traceability	Procedures have been established for identifying the product from applicable drawings, specifications, or other documents, during all stages of production, delivery, and installation. Where, and to the extent that, traceability is a specified requirement, individual products or batches have unique identification; this identification is recorded.		●				Existing procedure is to be replaced since it is ambiguous and unclear and results in confusion when identifying products.
4.9.2 Process control—special processes	Processes for which the results cannot be fully verified by subsequent inspection and testing of the product are subject to continuous monitoring and/or compliance with documented procedures.					●	No such processes exist in the company.

Key: Mis = missing; Rep = replace; Imp = improve; Sat = satisfactory.

Figure 12.3. ISO 9001 procedure evaluation checklist sample.

Undocumented existing activities have to be documented. In documenting these procedures and their instructions, one must at first document what is actually being done, not what is supposed to be done. Such documents must be prepared by, or with the intensive collaboration of, whoever performs those activities. As before, the resulting document should be evaluated with the grid in order to assess if the way the activity is carried out should be maintained, modified, or changed altogether. After this step, any activities that are missing but required by the standard should be initiated.

Setting Up the New Quality System

This stage consists of maintaining the suitable activities, modifying or replacing the unsuitable ones, and initiating the missing ones. Use of internal and external resources is essential. The utmost care must be taken to involve the personnel who will have an effect on or be affected by the quality system. Documenting existing informal procedures as well as writing new procedures to be followed should be done by the people who perform, or will perform, the activity in question. Of course, this is carried out with the help of others whose function is to make sure that the wording accurately reflects the reality of what is being done or what is supposed to be done. Some companies leave it to an internal or an external consultant to draw up these procedures and then train the employees who must follow the new procedures in their implementation.

Registering a Quality System

Companies may seek registration of their quality system for a number of reasons— to comply with a customer request, to obtain their own satisfaction and bolster their pride, to motivate their personnel, or to use the registration as a marketing tool.

The registration process starts with the choice of one of the three models, as indicated before, and then moves on to the system set-up, the choice of a registration organization, and the submission of an application and all documents relative to the system. The registration office evaluates the documents and informs the applicant if they are judged incomplete or inadequate. If the documents are judged satisfactory, the registration office sends a team of auditors to audit the system in detail. Any discrepancy is reported for correction. After the required corrections and modifications have been made, the auditors revisit the company. If the system is found to be adequate, a registration certificate is issued.

In appendix B of this book is reproduced the 1992 version of the procedures that the Canadian General Standards Board has recommended that companies follow for registration of a quality system in compliance with the ISO 9000 series.

Kymberly K. Hockman, Rita Grenville, and Susan Jackson describe another helpful guide to registration, entitled "Road Map to ISO 9000 Registration."[23] This working guide was developed by DuPont, a company that has had extensive experience with ISO 9000 as part of its registration effort. This company has achieved registration of 221 operations—90 in Europe, 106 in North America, 21 in Asia Pacific, and 4 in South America. This road map takes us through 9 steps over an 18-month time period.

1. Management decision commitment
   • Developing a strategic plan

2. Establishing and training management representatives, a steering group, and area coordinators
   - Communicating to the entire organization, defining and training audit teams

3. Beginning internal audits
   - Initiating the first round of internal audits; defining areas for upgrade and improvement; setting up documentation teams

4. Beginning documentation efforts
   - Analyzing work processes; writing/upgrading procedures and instructions; creating a first draft of the quality manual; implementing procedures and instructions; continuing internal audits and corrective actions

5. Choosing the registrar
   - Setting up the initial visit.

6. Documenting and implementing practices:
   - Revising and approving quality manual; continuing internal audits and corrective actions; management review

7. Pre-assessment
   - Correcting deficiencies; management review; practices documented and implemented

8. Registration assessment
   - Correcting deficiencies

9. Registration
   - Continuous improvement; continued internal audits; corrective actions; management reviews; and surveillance audits.

The ISO 9000 Series Standards and Total Quality

Many ask themselves what the relationship is between the ISO 9000 series and total quality. The EU's insistence on compliance with these standards as a condition of doing business within or with the EU has started a widespread movement in which companies all over the world are racing to apply these standards and, often, to obtain certification or registration by recognized national organizations. Many ads and much publicity are devoted to the fact that such and such company has made the grade and become ISO 9000 registered. Besides the fact that these standards are becoming a must for both world trade and for domestic business, many companies, having tried to implement TQM, find it much easier to aim for an ISO 9000 status.

TQM is a management philosophy that is defined differently from one author to the next, from one consultant to the next. This poses a problem for companies that embark on such a venture without being sure that it is actually in line with their goals. The ISO 9000 standards, however, do not change from one company to the other or from one consultant to the next. Quite the contrary, ISO 9000 is a guide that clearly specifies the characteristics of a quality system and thus provides a sense of security to its users. Besides, the fact that these standards have been developed by a prestigious, international standardization body with representatives from almost 100 countries and given the seal of approval by the mighty EU increases their credibility tremendously. They are not simply the work of one guru or the product of one expert's thinking.

These facts may seem as reassuring as a warm bath—in contrast with the cold shower of TQM. However, as James Corrigan puts it, "ISO 9000 doesn't have a sufficient customer focus, doesn't address how good a product or service is, . . . doesn't call for an ongoing evaluation and improvement of the quality system elements." TQM, of course, does. What it does not do, on the other hand, is provide a mechanism to ensure that the system is effective and is being followed. As Corrigan points out, TQM takes the existence of such a system, and the company's compliance to it, as a given. That, however, is not always the case; and this is precisely where ISO 9000 can prove so helpful—not as an alternative to TQM, but as a complement to it. He concludes that "Any organization starting a TQM effort should assess the adequacy of its underlying quality system. . . . Using an ISO 9000 standard for this assessment would provide excellent measurement criteria and a structured approach to periodic evaluation of the quality system."[24]

Although the ISO 9000 standards, or any other quality management and assurance standards for that matter, are important to the achievement of quality, they are not a guarantee that quality, let alone total quality, will indeed be achieved. This can be illustrated by using the analogy, albeit imperfect, of traffic regulations. Of course, with no traffic regulations, chaos would probably result. But, on the other hand, the fact that we have a well-thought-out code as well as a strong police force to back it up and to make sure it is applied does not mean that it is being followed as intended. Millions of traffic offense tickets bear witness to that, not to mention the flourishing radar detector industry. Some people (thankfully, a minority) even take pride in beating the system without being caught.

Another aspect to acknowledge is the fact that although ISO 9000 speaks of customer requirements, it really focuses almost exclusively on the quality of products and services produced, on the Q rather than on the VALITY. And even this is carried out in oblique fashion, for, although ISO 9000's ultimate aim may be product quality, it never examines the product or service itself, only the system that produces the product or service. This is not to minimize the importance of quality, which is of the utmost importance. However, it is also an area that generally leaves less room for improvement than other areas, because quality has taken great strides forward all over the world since the early 1970s, with the oil crises and subsequent economic recessions. Now, customers are demanding more than that: better delivery times; lower prices; less cumbersome relations with a company, its personnel, and its representatives; simplified terms and procedures of purchase (ordering, credit evaluation) and of payment; and better accessibility to product and services. Even if some of these aspects are indeed mentioned, no ISO 9000 standard goes so far as to spell out and integrate them.

If an ISO 9000 standard is to be used successfully, it has to be part of a more global approach. It cannot replace TQM, nor can it achieve total quality. It is a tool, and a good one at that, but still a tool among many others. While not an end in itself, an ISO 9000 standard nevertheless can be a motivating and mobilizing force to help a company implement a total quality effort.

Moreover, there are the other elements of the total quality triad that remain to be satisfied: profitability, training and quality of life for the workforce, protection of the environment, and the cooperation of the company's external partners. Within the context of that effort, adhering to an ISO 9000 standard can be viewed as an objective which, being very tangible and not too remote, may serve to unite the workforce and its management and give them an initial victory to encourage them along the longer road to total quality.

Conclusion

The attitude of the EU toward the ISO 9000 series standards, making it a condition of trade with and within its members, has created a worldwide movement and attention to this series. Registration is sought by an increasing number of organizations and, when obtained, is widely publicized. Registration becomes a motivating and mobilizing tool for the personnel as well as a marketing tool for luring new customers and keeping old ones loyal. Registration is becoming a sort of trademark of quality that companies exhibit to indicate that they produce quality products and services.

ISO 9000 standards do not replace TQM. They are an important part of it, however, and have to be treated as such. However, compliance with the standards, and even registration, do not guarantee that quality will be produced. That is why it is recommended that the ISO 9000 implementation effort be included in a wider, more global effort aiming at achieving total quality through TQM.

Review Questions

1. The EU member countries have made compliance with an ISO 9000 standard a condition for doing business with them. What triggered this decision, and what are its consequences?

2. Many suggest that ISO 9000 may serve as a replacement for TQM; others contend that ISO 9000 is the way to achieve total quality. Discuss.

3. Quality assurance standards have existed since World War II. How can the sudden interest in ISO 9000 be explained?

4. Standardization encourages technical development in local enterprises. International standardization bolsters trade relations between countries. Discuss.

5. What is the main objective of an ISO 9000 standard? What are its main components?

Notes

1. Unless otherwise indicated, information about ISO in this chapter was taken from informational publications produced and published by ISO, such as *International Organization for Standardization ISO* (Geneva, Switzerland: International Organization for Standardization, 1984).

2. Conformity assessment includes testing, inspection, laboratory accreditation, certification, quality system assessment, and other activities intended to ensure the conformity of products to a set of standards and/or technical specifications.

3. Reproduction of excerpts from ISO general information on ISO and its structure has been authorized by the Standards Council of Canada.

4. International Standard ISO 8402:1986.

5. Note that this definition is somewhat different from the ISO definition. ISO 9000:1987 defines a quality system as "the organization, structure, responsibilities, procedures, processes and resources for implementing quality management." The standard defines quality management as "that aspect of the overall management function that determines and implements quality policy." The standard defines quality policy as "the overall intentions and directions of an organization as regards quality, as formally expressed by top management." These ISO definitions also include several additional footnotes.

6. Stanley A. Marash and Donald W. Marquardt, "Quality, Standards, and Free Trade," *Quality Progress* 27, no. 5 (May 1994): 27–30.

7. Stephen D. Sawin and Spencer Hutchens Jr., "ISO 9000 in Operation," *1991 ASQC Quality Congress Transactions* (Milwaukee, Wis.: American Society for Quality Control, 1991): 915–16.

8. Mark Morrow, "Don't Ignore Japanese ISO 9000 Activity," *Quality Digest* 27, no. 5 (February 1993): 18.

9. "Registered Suppliers Must Meet New ISO 9000 Requirements," *Quality Progress* 27, no. 5 (May 1994): 20.

10. Pierre F. Caillibot and Denis Pronovost, "La normalisation internationale, pour gérer et assurer la qualité," *Qualité totale* 13, no. 2 (Summer 1992): 9–15.

11. CEN and CENELEC have issued a draft European standard, EN 46001—Specific Requirements for the Application for EN 2901 to Medical Devices. Medical device manufacturers doing business in the European Union will have to comply with the quality system requirements of EN 46001.

12. John T. Burr, "The Future Necessity," *Quality Progress* 23, no. 6 (June 1990): 19–23.

13. Y. N. Nuland, "Prerequisites to Implementation (ISO 9000)," *Quality Progress* 23, no. 6 (June 1990): 36–39; "The New Common Language for 12 Countries," 40–41.

14. Ian S. Kalinosky, "The Total Quality System—Going Beyond ISO 9000," *Quality Progress* 23, no. 6 (June 1990): 50–54.

15. J. J. Klock, "How to Manage 3500 (or Fewer) Suppliers," *Quality Progress* 23, no. 6 (June 1990): 43–47.

16. ISO/IEC Guide 48, the international document that governs the third-party assessment and registration process for quality systems, refers throughout to registration, not to certification, although many Europeans continue to use the term *certify. The Directory of Quality System Registration Bodies,* published by ISO, confirms the Guide 48 terminology.

17. Mark Morrow, "Establishing Common Interpretations," *Quality Digest* 13, no. 9 (September 1993): 22.

18. Morrow, "The Maturing of ISO 9000," *Quality Digest* 13, no. 1 (January 1993): 20.

19. Gregory G. Scott and Dr. James W. Kolka, *European Community Product Liability and Product Safety Directives* (Fairfax, Va.: CEEM, 1992).

20. "Survey Shows High Failure Rate for ISO 9000," *Quality Progress* 26, no. 7 (July 1993): 20.

21. ISO 9000 refers to the individual 9001, 9002, and 9003 standards as models.

22. Note that some people prefer the term *evaluation* to *auditing,* because auditing may have a pejorative connotation. I use both terms as synonyms.

23. Kymberly K. Hockman, Rita Grenville, and Susan Jackson "Road Map to ISO 9000 Registration," *Quality Progress* 27, no. 5 (May 1994): 39–42.

24. James P. Corrigan, "Is ISO 9000 the Path to TQM?" *Quality Progress* 27, no. 5 (May 1994): 33–36.

Chapter 13

Right the wrongs, better the rights, create the new . . .

Total Quality Management Practices

Total Quality Management Technology

As indicated many times in this book, a deep conviction that change is imperative—change in corporate culture, change in the way things are done—is the *sine qua non* for achieving and continually maintaining total quality. Everybody in the company, management and nonmanagement—as well as the upstream and downstream external partners—must share that same desire to change while, at the same time, demonstrating respect for the environment. We have also seen, however, that being convinced of having to seek total quality is not, in itself, enough because total quality is not a fortuitous occurrence; it does not happen by luck or accident. The logic behind it, as well as the technology (management practices, methods, tools, and techniques) needed to achieve it must be well understood and put into practice.

Among other things, a company must be able to identify all of its customers—past, present, potential, possible, and probable. It must know what their needs are, it must know what competitors are offering them, and it must measure the degree of satisfaction that the customers have with the products and services they receive. As we have see, satisfaction is best measured in terms of the seven total quality characteristics, QVALITY. The products and services must be made to rise above customer expectations (ACE), delighting them rather than merely satisfying them. Finally, total quality must then be managed—that is, planned, organized, controlled, and assured—and the organization members (or persons in the organization) mobilized, effectively empowered, recognized, and rewarded for their efforts and results.

In addition to knowing *what* to do to achieve and maintain total quality, an organization has to know *how* to do it. In other words, its members must be well versed in total quality management practices. This chapter presents an overview of the practices that make up what can be termed the TQM *technology*. People in the company should be trained to use the components of this technology because they will need them in their quest for continuous quality improvement as well as for innovation, that is, reengineering.

A number of these practices have been developed neither by total quality specialists nor for them, but, rather, by specialists in strategic planning, human resource management, accounting, production and operations management, computer systems design and management, and so on. At a meeting with university professors and practitioners from these various areas in both manufacturing and services organizations, we discussed the subjects that each of us was working on. We talked about the practices, techniques, and tools of interest to the participants, and the object of their readings, research, teaching, and projects, as well as the programs being implemented in their organizations. (These areas are summarized later in Table 13.2.) In the course of the discussion, I asked why they were working on those subjects or projects.

The objectives were the same in all cases, although not always spelled out in the same terms, arranged in the same order of importance, or stated explicitly: profitability, competitiveness in the new global economy, customer satisfaction, and employees' well-being. I suggested that all of the participants were working toward a common, triple goal of simultaneously satisfying the three stakeholders: the shareholders, the customers, and the company's people. They agreed unanimously.

Despite this ready admission, however, when I concluded by stating that, whatever particular name they chose to give it, they were all indeed working to achieve total quality, they were taken with surprise, a surprise that was all the greater for the participants who alleged that total quality was finished and done for. Nonetheless, total quality it was; and, while they may not have used that particular expression, all of the practices they were interested in or had developed ultimately sought to obtain a quality return for the shareholders, quality products and services for the customers (QVALITY + ACE), and a quality of life for the organization's members.

To return to the original point, the *how* represented by all of these specialized techniques and practices should be seen as being at the service of the *what* of total quality. As I observed earlier, a great number of organizations have failed in their attempt to achieve and/or maintain total quality precisely because they did not know how to do it.

The practices, techniques, and tools that help achieve and maintain total quality are presented here. They are not discussed in detail, for there are numerous, more specialized publications available for the interested reader, although none attempt—let alone succeed—to integrate all of these techniques. This is the challenge, because to be really effective, these practices, techniques, and tools have to be integrated in a common, global approach (whatever its name) such as the one presented in this book. I will first explain where and for what purpose these practices are used and then give a brief description of each.

A Prerequisite for Improving a Company's Performance

Total quality is achieved and maintained by improving a company's performance. This is done by linking the business process to the external stakeholders. Companies generally start with a diagnosis of the present situation and a prognosis for both the near and distant future. Problems identified must be solved, and opportunities to do better must be sought: preventing the undesirable, righting the wrongs, bettering the rights, and finding new ways to do what is being done or doing new things altogether, that is, creating, innovating, reengineering. This is all summarized by four words: *prevent* (the undesirable), *correct* (the wrong), *improve* (the right), *innovate* or *reengineer* (the old) (see Figure 13.1).

In extraversive management, a company *problem* is defined as being any reason for dissatisfaction among the two groups of its external stakeholders—shareholders and customers—and nothing else. Indeed, an organization is said to be practicing extraversive management precisely when it seeks to satisfy the external stakeholders.

All other difficulties encountered are either a cause or a consequence—but they must not be thought of as problems per se. Thus, any number of difficulties, such as poor or absent planning or control, a disorganized stockroom, absenteeism among the workforce, inadequate maintenance of production equipment, mismanagement of the company's assets, defective workshop lighting, or lack of office space (which, granted, are all correctly interpreted as problems if regarded

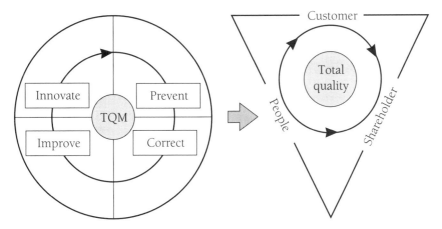

Figure 13.1. The prevent-correct-improve-innovate cycle, also known as the prevent-correct-improve-reengineer cycle.

from a traditional, introversive perspective) are all probable *causes* of problems such as late deliveries, unquality products, or inadequate return for the shareholders—because they directly or indirectly affect satisfaction (the seven QVALITY factors) or else increase costs, thus reducing the shareholder's return on their investments. By the same token, concerns such as customer complaints and the loss of market share stemming from disgruntled customers are symptomatic of the problem that is the source of customer dissatisfaction (see Table 13.1).

Note that the dissatisfaction of the organization's members, the people in the company, is not included in the definition of *problem*. When people to whom I am explaining this concept notice this apparent omission, they often react with surprise. After all, the organization's members are the third element in the total quality triad, are they not? Is their satisfaction not, as I have so often mentioned, an essential ingredient of this formula?

In answer to this, I should first of all stress that it is a given that an organization must satisfy its members. More to the point, the organization must satisfy its people because they *are* the organization. Furthermore, to say that people are the organization also means that they are not just resources to be exploited and that there is, or should be, no us/them, management/employee division. To be very specific, saying that an organization has to satisfy its people is tantamount to saying that an organization has to satisfy itself. This is true. It is also a tautology which, if pursued as a goal, leads nowhere.

This leads to a second point: that the dissatisfaction of the people in an organization should be regarded as a consequence of an external problem. If the problem of external stakeholder satisfaction is addressed successfully, profits will be gener-

Causes (Ms)	Problems	Consequences
• Machines	*Shareholders:*	*Shareholders:*
• Management	• Inadequate return on investment	• Loss of interest in company
• Manpower	• Unsatisfied other needs	• Decline in share values
• Materials		• Difficulty in financing further company projects
• Measure	*Customers:*	
• Memory	• Inadequate fulfillment of QVALITY	
• Methods	• ACE not achieved	*Customers:*
• Milieu		• Loss of market share
• Money		• Complaints
		• Product returns
		• Lawsuits

Table 13.1. Extraversive view of problems, their causes, and their consequences.

ated, which, in turn, will provide the organization's members with a quality of life (job stability, decent salary, challenges, recognition, rewards, and so on). In other words, solve the external problem and the internal symptoms—the dissatisfaction of the organization's members—will also clear up. Obviously, this does not apply to uncontrollable, external causes of problems; for example, an economic recession that reduces sales, revenues, profits, and dividends for the shareholders and, to the detriment of customers, increases production costs and, consequently, the product's price.

This point of view is a radical change from the traditional view wherein the people in the organization are divided along management and nonmanagement lines. This also means that they have to adapt to a new work style in which they work *with* each other rather than *for* each other. It means that all of the people in an organization must feel that they are members of the same team, the same family. They may have different functions, but they must all work toward the same goal. Cross-functional and cross-level teams and skill-based pay are ways to accomplish this. As with people working on a ship: If the ship sinks, everyone drowns, officers and crew alike; if it reaches its destination, everyone is safe and satisfied.

This new attitude is being seen in an increasing number of organizations that no longer refer to "our" employees (as if one could own an employee). Missions now use the term *us*—the people of the organization—often stating further, "We realize that we have to satisfy our customers and our shareholders in collaboration with our partners while protecting the environment and working for the well-being of our community."

But how can new ways of thinking be applied when employees suspect that increasing their effectiveness dooms them to losing their jobs? Let me just mention that this is changing because an increasing number of managers end up losing their jobs, too. We realize that the traditional antagonism between management and employees has to cease. On the other hand, we must not target only increased effectiveness; we must also plan for growth. In the past 10 to 15 years, many organizations have learned to produce more with less, as a result letting go as much as half of their workforce. However, by producing higher quality at lower costs and having succeeded in satisfying their customers in regard to most of the QVALITY factors, the demand for their products has increased and they have rehired most of their former people.

Taking dissatisfaction of the customer or shareholder as the starting point, we can trace a path backward through the entire business process and its environment, internal and external, in order to find the areas that are directly or indirectly responsible for the dissatisfaction. If, having already obtained the customers' or shareholders' satisfaction, we wish to improve the results and exceed their expectations, we use the same backtracking procedure to link the results to be improved with the appropriate areas in the business process. Mapping and backtracking may thus be used to identify the sources of the wrongs that must be righted and to locate the windows of opportunity for bettering (by improving) the rights or creating (by reengineering) the new.

The Business Process: A Black Box

To identify the causes for a problem as defined above, or to find the opportunities for improving the results and reengineering in order to increase the external stakeholders' satisfaction, one must understand how the organization works. For the customer and for many shareholders (as is the case in large organizations), an organization is like a black box. They do not know what goes inside it and, generally, do not care. They see only its outputs, which should, at all times, satisfy their needs and go beyond their expectations. However, external partners do, more and more, get acquainted with the functioning of the black boxes of their customers' and suppliers' organizations for better mutual results.

As indicated before, the company contains a *business process,* operated by people (the company's members) living in and sharing a certain organizational culture, in a certain structure, using information, materials, and equipment to satisfy themselves through the satisfaction of both the shareholders and the customers. Again, the business process consists of a (customer-driven) *mainstream process* and a number of *support processes* essential to the management and the operation of the mainstream process. We must also add that the *financial process* is shareholder oriented because it is clear that an organization can sometimes satisfy all its customers and still go bankrupt. Each of these processes can be broken down into a number of *work processes* consisting of activities or operations which, in turn, can be broken down into tasks.

Figure 13.2 is a simplified map of the business process. Although not indicated in this map, it should be noted that the financial process is shareholder driven. This process is concerned with the management of all of the financial resources—funds inputs as well as outputs. Inputs include shareholders' investments, sales and other revenues, subsidies, and long-term and short-term borrowings. Outputs include capital and interest on these debts, taxes, and the shareholders' dividends. Note that the shareholders' nonfinancial needs also have to be assessed and dealt with.

Last, but definitely not the least, is the *people process,* which is (obviously) people oriented. It has to do with people compensation, motivation, mobilization, recognition, health protection and safety, counseling, training, hiring, promoting, and so on. The mainstream financial and people processes are in line with the total quality triad philosophy and thinking.

Using this map allows us to trace back any problem to its causes within the business process and to identify within this process the areas that can be modified or reengineered to improve the satisfaction of the company's external stakeholders.

As mentioned before, many management practices should be used with TQM, although they were not created or developed for that purpose. Rather than describing each one of these practices, I will show how they can be integrated to help achieve total quality.

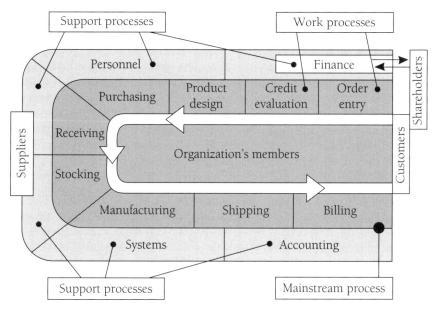

Figure 13.2. A business process map.

Source: J. N. Kelada, *Technologie de la qualité totale, reengineering et autres techniques* (Dollard-des-Ormeaux, Quebec, Canada: Quafec Publications, 1994), 2–4.

An Integrated Approach

In order to effectively implement the various practices, one should not yield to the temptation to use them haphazardly, as a stop-gap measure in one place or to put out a brush fire somewhere else. A practice used in the context of TQM should not be considered an objective; it has to be seen for what it really is, a means toward an end. Therefore, the use of these practices has to be oriented toward the organization's objectives and should be applied within a comprehensive scheme that is integrated into a global plan of action.

Framework for the Use of Practices

Some organizations do apply a management approach based on shareholder and customer needs. However, these needs are not validated on a systematic basis. Rather, they are more in the nature of impressions, founded upon a mixture of hearsay, scattered customer complaints, guesswork, gut feelings, and perhaps a bit of internal, objective data. What we have here, then, is not objectively measured facts about stakeholders' feelings toward the company and its outputs, but management's perceptions of and assumptions about these feelings. Acting upon, as it were, these *feelings about feelings,* management then designs a product or service and presents it to the customers in the hope that they will like it.

Recently, however, companies have increasingly begun to use a more objective approach because they can no longer afford to shoot in the dark and pray to hit their target, in a business environment that is so competitive and customer driven. Indeed, *customer/shareholder driven* is the way to describe this objective approach—a *backtracking–pull approach.* Were we to imagine the business process as being a cart, then in the more traditional push approach, that cart could be seen as being *pushed* by management. However, in the backtracking–pull approach, that cart would be pulled by the shareholder and the customer. Here, it is these two stakeholders' needs, objectively measured, that dictate the direction of the company's efforts—and when the company sets its sights and takes aim, it is no longer doing so in the dark, but in the full light of the facts.

The backtracking–pull approach to achieve total quality includes four steps: (1) diagnosing the problem, (2) setting objectives, (3) choosing a strategy to achieve these objectives, and (4) elaborating a detailed plan of action including corrections, improvements, and innovations. As indicated, this approach is based on objective information, actual results, facts, and opinions. These include

- The degree of satisfaction of the shareholders' financial and nonfinancial needs

- The needs of potential shareholders, if the organization wants to attract new ones

- The degree of satisfaction of the existing customers, as far as their needs and expectations are concerned

- The needs of potential customers who are either buying from the competitors or using substitute products for the ones produced by the organization

- The degree of satisfaction of the persons working in the company: the internal partners

- The degree of satisfaction of the external upstream and downstream partners

- The effects of the organization's operations on the socioeconomic environment (the community, the region, the country) and on the natural environment (air, water, noise, and so on).

One works backwards from these data, tracing problems back to their source or results that might be further improved back to the area where this change could be brought about. In this way, activities in the business process having a direct or indirect impact on these problem areas and results are identified and marked for corrective measures or else improvement or reengineering. This approach uses techniques that may be applied, for the most part, to services as well as products. These techniques are described in the following sections.

Total Quality Management Practices and Areas of Application

There are numerous practices that can be used to diagnose and assess the present situation. The Malcolm Baldrige National Quality Award organization suggests a number of criteria to be measured in order to evaluate an organization and its general management activities. It also publishes a self-assessment guide based on these criteria to help organizations identify their strengths and weaknesses. This practice will be discussed later in this chapter. Of a lesser scope, the ISO 9000 series standards, as we have seen, can be used to audit a quality system in an organization.

Identifying Customers' Needs and Evaluating Their Satisfaction

In order to identify the present and potential customers and their needs, and to evaluate the degree of satisfaction of actual customers with the organization's products and services, the marketing department uses mail, telephone surveys, and focus groups. The seven QVALITY factors should be used to identify the customers' needs or measure their satisfaction as well as their degree of delight, or ACE.

To reiterate, we have to consider not only the present customers but all potential customers as well. This includes past customers and noncustomers presently buying from the competition. The purpose of questioning the potential customers is to find out why they are not buying the company's products or using its services. Is it because the products or services do not meet their needs? Is it because they have never heard about the products or services? Is it because of the reputation of the company? The purpose of querying the existing customers is to assess their degree of satisfaction, as measured by the seven QVALITY characteristics and the ACE criteria. Remember that the QVLTY factors, if satisfied, are *turn-on* factors that exert an attraction and generally reflect the customers' requirements or expectations. On the other hand, the A–I factors are not the ones that would trigger the decision to buy a product or a service, but if they are unsatisfied they will have the effect of rebuffing the customers and dissuading them from buying. In other words, when absent, these can be *turn-off* factors that would not necessarily attract customers if they were met but would clearly discourage customers from buying.

This evaluation can be done through person-to-person interviews, telephone and mail surveys, toll-free telephone service, analyses of customer complaints, and focus groups.

Policy Deployment

In order to plan for total quality—that is, for the achievement of objectives regarding the shareholders, the customers, the organization members, the external partners, and the environment—companies are now applying the Japanese-inspired hoshin planning, also known as policy deployment. Global goals, which are the total quality objectives, are deployed to all sectors and departments within the company.

An annual policy (or objectives), based on the results of the previous year, is elaborated and then deployed to all departments for execution. Figure 13.3 shows the six steps of a policy deployment process at Komatsu, which is used in a number of companies (AT&T, for one). The results obtained and the policy or objectives set include the degree of satisfaction (or dissatisfaction) of all of the stakeholders.

The TQM components and principles are difficult to apply consistently without a common structure to reinforce their effective and coordinated application. The quality control story (QC story) method serves this function and may be a powerful tool in any employee's or company's toolbox.

The first documented formal application of a QC story was in Japan, by the Komatsu Corporation in 1960.[1] Developed initially as an approach for presenting and communicating quality improvement activities, its logic-based format lent itself to analysis as well. Incorporating statistical tools and graphics into the QC story strengthened the process because teams began to solve problems with facts instead of opinions. Management focus began to shift from the person responsible to the cause of the problem.

Audits by the president or the highest local manager give credibility to higher management involvement and participation in the process. Appendix C of this book gives a detailed example of an application of policy deployment at AT&T.

Benchmarking

Benchmarking is a tool by which standards of excellence are identified, established, and achieved—standards based on the realities of the marketplace. What successful companies do—whether or not they are competitors—is observed and, where it makes sense, their practices are adapted and built upon for the company's own use.

The benchmarking process consists of five phases: planning, analysis, integration, action, and maturity. As explained here, in each of the five phases are action items that need to be accomplished. These actions are the minimal prerequisite for successful implementation of the overall process (see Figure 13.4).

In the *planning* phase, there are three general questions that must be answered: What will be benchmarked? Who is the best competitor, and what other companies set the standard in a functional activity? How will the data be collected?

In the *analysis* phase, the data acquired has to be analyzed to understand the benchmarked organization's strengths and to assess those strengths against the company's own performance. This analysis should provide the dimensions of any gap—negative or positive—between the benchmarked organization and the company. The objective is to close a negative gap or extend a positive one.

The first initiative in the *integration* phase is to gain senior management's acceptance of the results of the competitive benchmarking analysis and its commit-

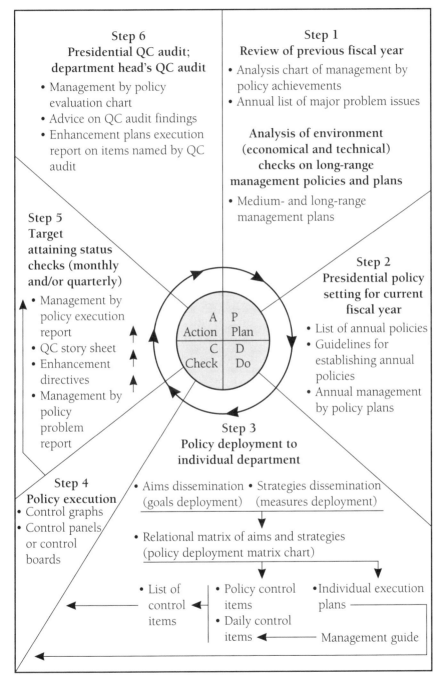

Figure 13.3. Policy deployment.

Source: Komatsu Corporation. Reprinted with permission.

ment to develop action plans. Finally, benchmarking needs to be clearly communicated, through formal action plans, down through the various organizational levels.

In the *action* phase, the action plans are implemented and progress in achieving them is periodically assessed and reported. Employees play an important role

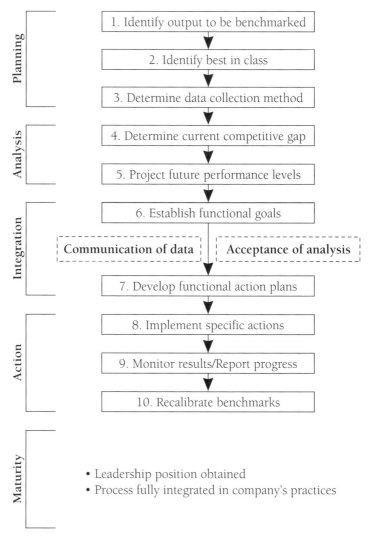

Figure 13.4. Key process phases of benchmarking.

Source: Xerox Corporation, "Leadership Through Quality, Implementing Competitive Benchmarking, Employee Involvement and Recognition," *Readings* (4), Part I, Section II, p. 12. Stamford, CT, 1987. Reprinted with permission.

during this phase as the creative talents of people are brought to bear on the problems and opportunities identified through benchmarking. Progress in achieving targets must be reported to all employees.

The *maturity* phase is reached when the company has attained a leadership position, and, secondly, when benchmarking has become an essential, ongoing element of the management process and an integral part of the overall management practices.

The benchmarking technique is very useful as it allows a company to compare a product with a competitor's and its processes with other processes known to be effective and efficient. According to Xerox, benchmarking, or, as they call it, *competitive benchmarking,* is the continuous process of measuring the company's products, services, and practices against their toughest competitors or those companies renowned as the leaders. Xerox has used the billing system at American Express (Japan) and the storing process of L. L. Bean as benchmarks to improve their own processes in these two fields.

Cross-Functional Teams

As I have emphasized, in traditional management, jobs and responsibilities are grouped by function or along departmental lines, whereas products are designed, produced, sold, and delivered through processes. These processes always cut across functional boundaries, such as marketing, engineering, purchasing, materials control, manufacturing, accounting, inventory control, and so on. Coordinators (project or product managers) have been traditionally used to integrate activities performed within a certain process. However, this presents some difficulties, because people working on a project or for a product have to answer to both a product manager and a functional manager.

Cross-functional teams, on the other hand, work with a team leader and are responsible for an entire process. Although this seems logical and easy to apply, it does represent a challenge, because people used to working within the confines of their function and area of expertise have to learn to work with people from different backgrounds and do so effectively while at the same time learning new ways of doing things. The team leader has the challenge of getting the most out of them without having any hierarchical authority over the team's members. For example, products and services development that would satisfy customers needs are examined by cross-functional teams composed of representatives from different departments, such as marketing, research and development, engineering, quality, production, and purchasing.

Quality Function Deployment

The objective of quality function deployment (QFD) is to translate the customer's requirements—known as the *customer's voice*—into appropriate, concrete company terms so that the requirements can be totally satisfied. The method's basic principle resides in the conviction that products must be designed to reflect the customer's desires and tastes; hence the importance of personnel from marketing, design, engineering, manufacturing, and purchasing working together right from the product's initial conception.

Traditionally, the process of designing, manufacturing, and marketing products has been done by separate groups within the company in a sequential fashion. After marketing has done the research and identified the customer needs, design does its job and hands the ball off to production, which produces it and flips it back out to sales and promotion, who sells it to the customer. The only people who directly hear the customer's voice are marketing and sales. As the message gets passed on from group to group, there is a natural distortion of information that takes place. With QFD, however, representatives of all groups get together, meet the customers, and listen to their needs as expressed in the customers' own terms. The activities of the various groups are carried out concurrently rather than sequentially.

Here is a brief and simplified description of the QFD method. It uses a diagram called the *house of quality* because of its shape. As shown in Figure 13.5, this diagram is based on the customer's needs, expressed by the customer *in his or her own words*. The relative importance of each of these needs for the customer is indicated in the first column, on a scale from 0 to 10. Needs are then translated by the company into precise terms describing the characteristics for the products and services that would meet those needs. The effect of each of these characteristics on any specific customer needs is indicated in a central matrix, where a value for this effect is given on a scale from 1 to 10. At the top of the diagram (the roof of the house), correlation between any two characteristics is estimated and expressed in a symbol, such as N for none, W for weak, and S for strong.

The customer's evaluation of the satisfaction of each of his or her needs by the company's product, as well as his or her perception of competitors' products, are also indicated. I use the word *perception* to indicate that the customers have not bought the competitor's products but, nevertheless, have certain ideas about their quality.

Finally, in the basement, measures for each of the product and service characteristics are identified. For example, we can see in Figure 13.5 that customer needs can be grouped into seven categories. The quality of the product required has values estimated by the customer as follows: the characteristic of a product that *does what it is supposed to do* (drill 1-inch holes, cut 2 inches of steel), as expressed by the customer, is termed *suitability* of the product. For the customer it has a value of 10—the highest possible. The customer would indicate the desire to acquire a product that *works when he or she needs it*. Again, for the customer, this aspect has a value of 7. It is expressed in the company's terms as the *reliability* of the product. The customer need for a *product that lasts* (value of 9) is translated by the term *durability*. A product that looks nice (value 4) is termed *appearance* by the company.

Suitability has an effect on the first need (does what it is supposed to do) of 10 (100 percent) and on the second need (product that lasts) of 5. Appearance affects 100 percent (value of 10) the way the product looks and it also affects its suitability (but only slightly—value of 2).

As far as the customer can see, the company's product works better than those of its two competitors (value of 9 against 7 and 4); lasts a shorter time than the second competitor's products (7 against 9), but longer than the first competitor's product (7 against 6); is less reliable than the first competitor's product (6 against 7) but more reliable than the second competitor's product (6 against 5); and does not look as nice as the products of the two competitors (5 against 7 and 8).

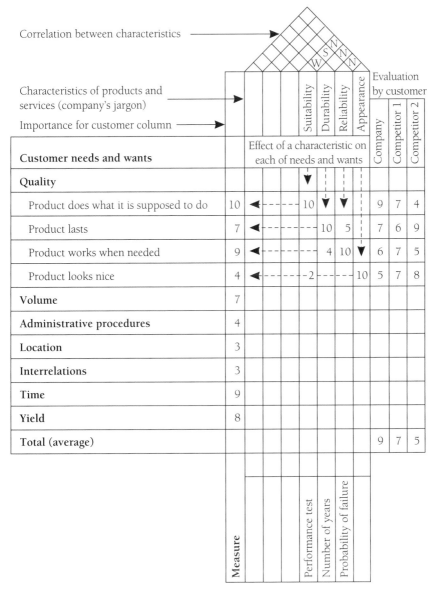

Figure 13.5. The house of quality.

The suitability is measured by testing the performance of the product, its durability by the number of years it can be used (tested by accelerated tests), and its reliability by the probability of failure over a given period of time (number of hours of use, a period of one year).

The overall customer satisfaction with the three products, the company's and the two competitors', is indicated in the total row as 9 for the company, 7 for the first competitor, and 5 for the second one. However, the chart also indicates precisely strengths and weaknesses of the company's product as compared to its competitors' and as perceived by the customer. Obviously, if this perception is proved to be wrong, it is not the product and services that have to be modified, it is the customer perception, and this can be accomplished through marketing activities (information brochures, advertising, and so on).

Just as this diagram translates customer needs into product and service characteristics, similarly, a second diagram will be used to depict the relationships between the product characteristics (replacing the customer needs in the first diagram) and the characteristics of its components (replacing the product's characteristics in the first diagram). A third diagram will represent the relationship between the components' characteristics and the characteristics of the process that will be used to manufacture them.

The participation in this exercise from representatives of different departments, generally with representatives of the customer as well, allows them firsthand access about information on what the customer really needs.

The Design of Experiments and Taguchi Methods

The Taguchi methods, which adapt and apply the design of experiments (DOE) technique in a unique manner, are used to produce *robust product design,* a design intended to enable products to withstand the effects of harmful, uncontrollable variables such as very high or very low temperature, humidity, rain, snow, wind pressure, and so on. They also allow the design of optimal production processes.

This technique helps identify the variable or variables that have the greatest effect on the product or process performance. This is then taken into consideration when designing the product or the process. For example, increasing the hardness of steel can be achieved either by changing one of the product ingredients or by introducing or by modifying a step in the process of producing it.

Failure Mode and Effect Analysis

Failure mode and effect analysis (FMEA) is used to identify all possible failures that could occur in a product, a component, a process, or an organization in general, as well as the most probable ones, the mode in which they occur (how they manifest themselves), and their effect. Therefore, it helps to identify anything that could go wrong (failure, F), the probability that it will go wrong (occurrence, O), its seriousness (S, which is its effect in the whole system—product, process, organization, and so on) and its detectability (the probability of not being detected, D).

Multiplying O by S by D gives what is called the *criticality factor* of such a possible failure.

For example, if we want to know if an action is required to eliminate errors in the bills that are sent to customers, we first identify the type of any possible error (failure), say, an error in the unit price of different items. We then estimate the probability that such an error occurs (is it 1 percent or 1 per 10,000?), the seriousness of such an error (would the customer just complain, or would he or she look for another supplier?), and the probability of not detecting such an error (is there a verification mechanism in the system to spot and eventually correct such an error, and how efficient and effective is it?). Each of these three aspects is evaluated on a scale from 1 to 10, and the three are multiplied by each other, giving a measure of the criticality (out of a possible 1000) of this type of error and the activities that can produce it in the billing process. The activities that could produce highly critical failures should then be analyzed, and action taken to eliminate them or at least reduce their criticality.

In order to apply the FMEA technique in the case of a service organization, such as a hotel, one identifies all of the steps of the process that a customer goes through. These include a potential customer looking for a hotel (yellow pages, brochures, travel agencies, recommendations of friends and acquaintances); calling for reservations; arriving at the hotel; registering at the reception desk; getting the key; entering the room; asking for room service; using the room facilities (telephone, fax, desk, bed, bathroom); using the dining room, the barbershop, the beauty parlor, the game room, or the gym; getting messages; reserving city tours; departing; paying the bill; and getting transportation to the airport.

At each of these steps, we ask, "What could go wrong?" We are looking for *types of possible failures*—the hotel is unknown because it is new or has changed its name; the reservation procedure is complex; there is error in registration; access to the hotel is difficult due to bad indications on maps, roads, highways, and so on; registration at the reception desk is complicated, lengthy, erroneous; the room is inadequate (too small, too big, noisy, smelly, not lit properly); the telephone is not working properly; the shower is too hot or too cold; the wake-up call is missed; the game room or pool is closed most of the time; there are long lines at checkout, errors in the bill, inadequate transportation to the airport, and so on.

We then estimate the *probability of occurrence* of each of these possible failures, based on past experience or on a what-if approach. This is when we consider the occurrence of a failure that never happened before. To this probability we attach a *degree of seriousness* (missing a plane is more damaging to the customer than finding the swimming pool water somewhat cold). Finally, we estimate the probability of not detecting such a failure, that is, we identify its detectability. For example, an error in a reservation can be detected by some control activity just after the reservation has been completed, say by reading back to the customer all of the information requested for validation purposes. So even if such a failure occurs, it is corrected immediately with no further damage to the customer. In the same way, controlling all of the information that goes on the customer's bill allows the detection and prompt correction of any possible error.

The criticality of each of these possible failures—or the activity causing it—is measured by multiplying, as before, O by S by D. The most critical ones will be analyzed in order to eliminate, or at least reduce, the risk of occurrence. Eliminating possible failures in products and in processes can be achieved by applying the poka-yoke concept.

The Poka-Yoke Concept

The poka-yoke concept is used in product and processes to eliminate or reduce human errors. For example, in some new cars the engine will not start unless the hand brake is off, the regular brake pedal is depressed, and the automatic transmission lever is on P (park). This eliminates unnecessary wear on the hand brake if it is left on while driving and the risk of an accident should the car move when the engine is started.

I once visited a coffee shop for a coffee and a croissant. As I touched the metal top of a cabinet near the cash register I almost burned my hand. The cabinet was heated to keep the croissants warm. I only then noticed a label warning patrons not to touch this top. Applying the poka-yoke concept would consist of placing a cover made of wood or any other insulating material on the hot top; then, nobody could get burned.

Concurrent Engineering

Concurrent engineering is applied to shorten the cycle time of new product development and production as well as to increase the quality of products. Members of a cross-functional team similar to the one described earlier in this chapter work *concurrently,* rather than in sequence, to develop the product and the process and to order materials and equipment required for the production. As the design specialists start presenting ideas on how the product would look and what it would consist of (that is to say, well before the design is completed), process engineers start working on possible processes to be developed to produce it; production personnel work on possible production strategies, schedules, and work methods; and purchasing people work on preparing possible suppliers for the materials and equipment that might be required for the manufacturing process.

The Horizontal Organization

In order to apply concurrent engineering, QFD, and many other practices, companies have to look beyond the traditional, pyramid-shaped organization and implement new forms of organization. The horizontal organization is being developed as a new trend in this field. Cross-functional teams are given the responsibility of developing new products, filling customers' orders, and so on. Rather than using a sequential approach in which representatives of each function perform some activities within a process and then pass the buck to another function, companies ensure that all functions involved are represented on a cross-functional team responsible for achieving an entire process.

Statistical Process Control

It has been observed that no process, however precise it is, can produce and maintain identical products or results. For any characteristic produced (weight, length, degree of temperature), there is always a range of variation around the desired (nominal) value. For example, it is impossible to produce steel bars with exactly 1-inch diameter. Bars produced will vary in diameter from, say, 1.01 to .99 inch. In order to limit these variations to a required minimum, designers indicate a maximum tolerable span for these variations, called *tolerances*. In the example of the steel bars, this span would be 1.01 − .99, or .02 inches.

During production, in order to monitor and control variations, statistical process control (SPC) is applied. It helps to identify the capability of the process to produce units within the tolerance span. This is done by comparing this span (S) to the range of variations (R) that the process produces. An index, or *coefficient of capability* (known as C_p), can be calculated by dividing S by R. C_p should obviously be greater than 1 for a process to be capable. Companies aim at a value of 1.3 or more.

SPC also allows monitoring of the variations as they are produced by a process (data on these variations are collected periodically, say, every hour or every two hours). These data are plotted on a *control chart,* which reveals if they are *under control* or *out of control.* In the latter case, an action is undertaken to correct the situation and avoid producing defective units.

Other TQM Practices

Activity-based costing (ABC), which will be described later, allows for identifying the value-added and the non–value-added activities in the organization. *Activity-based management* (ABM) helps identify the activities that should be closely managed and controlled for better results.

Henry Ford established mass production as the best way to produce a large number of similar products at a low cost. However, given worldwide competition and the existence of a wide variety of products on the market from which one can choose, the simple ability to produce rows upon rows of indistinguishably uniform whatnots will no longer cut the mustard. With the advent of new technologies, companies are now trying to produce large quantities of almost made-to-measure products. This is called *mass customization,* or *made-to-measure mass production.* In order to achieve this goal, three practices are used: just-in-time, flexible manufacturing, and skill-based pay systems.

Briefly, the just-in-time concept consists of eliminating the waste of time and money resulting from, among other things, accumulating costly inventories. Materials are delivered on time (no sooner, no later) for production; finished products are produced on time (no sooner, no later) and in the right quantity (no more, no less) for delivery as required. However, producing the right quantity, if small quantities are required, requires a substantial cut in set-up times, if it is to be done in a cost-effective manner.

As it stands, set-up times are lengthy and nonproductive. Thus, in order to reduce the unit production cost, long production runs that far exceed the required quantities are carried out, because the high cost of the set-up time can then be divided among a greater number of units produced. The excess production is stocked for later sales, which, however, might not materialize. Moreover, stocks take up valuable space, require supervision, and may become obsolete, be stolen, or deteriorate with time. Therefore, longer-than-required production runs, while reducing the unit production costs, have unduly increased the risks associated with them.

The *single-digit minute exchange die (SMED)* is a technique that cuts the machine or process set-up time to a bare minimum (from hours to less than 10 minutes) by simplifying the set-up or even automating it, thus making it possible and profitable to produce short runs. This, in turn, makes the practice of just-in-time feasible.

Flexible manufacturing consists of using computer-operated multifunction machines and computer-operated material-handling equipment, the whole system being controlled by a central computer. When a multifunction machine is idle after having completed a certain operation, the computer automatically directs a new part to this machine after having ascertained that the operation the part requires falls within the several functions that the machine is capable of performing.

As explained before, in skill-based pay systems people are paid not according to what they do—as is traditionally the case—but according to what they are capable of doing. The worker is paid according to his or her skills and is therefore encouraged to acquire more skills. This allows for personnel rotation, teamwork, and a more effective work allocation system which, with increased worker versatility, is now organized according to customer demand.

A concept called the *learning organization,* which was developed a few years ago, is now drawing a great deal of attention and interest. It provides a paradigm for collective learning within an organization. Traditional notions of the organization see it as a place where learning takes place atomistically and where individuals operating as individuals acquire new knowledge and/or experience. This concept, however, suggests that, in a successful company, it is the organization itself that learns. If an individual leaves the organization, the knowledge acquired remains in it. In a learning organization, teams develop knowledge by working as a whole. Over time, they enhance their capacity to create what they truly desire to create. The team members develop new skills and capabilities which alter what they can do and understand. They learn to learn together, and mechanisms are established to allow this type of learning to take place. The organization, besides being a place where activities and operations of all kinds are performed, becomes a giant laboratory where people at all levels are constantly experimenting with and testing new practices and techniques.

Peter Senge, the director of the Center for Organizational Learning at MIT's Sloan School of Management, states that

> One of the most powerful discoveries for us during the past several years has been seeing how closely our work on learning organizations dove-

tails with the "Total Quality" movement. Again and again we have found that organizations seriously committed to quality management are uniquely prepared to study the "learning disciplines."

These disciplines are the core of learning organization work: personal mastery, mental models, shared vision, team learning, and systems thinking.

None of the management practices and techniques mentioned above can be effectively applied without the constant collaboration of all persons in the organization. That is why successful organizations put a special emphasis on practices such as *empowerment, mobilization,* and *motivation* and make sure that they penetrate the entire workforce, from top management down to the operators on the assembly line or the office clerks. (These three practices were covered in chapter 7.)

Finally, *problem identification, solving, and prevention* (PISP) *techniques* include, among others, brainstorming, the nominal group technique, flowcharting, and the seven basic QC statistical tools: the cause-and-effect analysis, check sheets, control charts, graphs (bar, line, pie), histograms, Pareto diagrams, and scatter diagrams.

To these techniques I must add the seven *quality management tools.* These were proposed in 1977 by a committee for developing QC tools that was established in 1972 and chaired by Dr. Yoshinobu Nayatani at the Union of Japanese Scientists and Engineers (JUSE). They are the affinity diagram, the relations diagram, the tree diagram, the matrix diagram, the matrix-data analysis, the process decision program chart (PDPC), and the arrow diagram.

Table 13.2 presents a global view of the practices that can help achieve and maintain total quality. Although I have tried to indicate the area where each practice or technique is mainly used or the purpose of this use, it must be understood that they can be used—and are actually being used—in more than one area and for more than one purpose. For example, brainstorming can be used in all areas.

The Malcolm Baldrige Award Criteria for the Self-Assessment of a Management System

Introduction

The Malcolm Baldrige National Quality Award (sometimes called the Baldrige Award) is an annual award to recognize U.S. manufacturing companies, service companies, and small businesses for business excellence and quality achievement. It promotes the awareness of quality as an increasingly important element in competitiveness; the understanding of the requirements for performance excellence; and the sharing of information on successful performance strategies and the benefits derived from the implementation of these strategies.

The Baldrige Award examination is based upon performance excellence criteria created through a public–private partnership. The examination is designed

General sphere of activity	Specific activities targeted	Applicable practices and techniques
Planning	*Diagnosis* • Shareholders' satisfaction • Customers' satisfaction • Personal satisfaction • Existing management practices and operations evaluation • External partners interrelations • Environment	• Baldrige Award criteria • ISO 9000 audits • Failure mode and effect analysis (FMEA) • Benchmarking • Process mapping • Flowcharting • ABC/ABM (Activity-based costing/management) • Business process analysis
	Strategic planning	• Policy deployment (Hoshin) • Mass customization
	Operational planning	• Flexible production • Just-in-time (JIT)
	New product development	• Quality function deployment • Concurrent engineering • Design of experiments (DOE) • Taguchi methods
Quality control	Prevent and/or detect poor quality	• Statistical process control (SPC) • Acceptance sampling
Performance improvement	*Problem solving* Identification of problems and their possible and probable causes; evaluation and implementation of best solutions *Continuous quality improvement (CQI)* Incremental improvements	• Brainstorming • Pareto analysis • Cause-and-effect diagram • Scatter diagram • Control charts • Histograms • Graphs • Flowcharting • Process analysis • Methods • Automation
Reengineering	To radically increase efficiency and effectiveness	• Work process reengineering • Business process reengineering • Business reengineering • Total reengineering

Table 13.2.   Total quality management practices.

Source: Adapted from J. N. Kelada, *Technologie de la qualité totale, reengineering et autres techniques* (Dollard-des-Ormeaux, Quebec, Canada: Quafec Publications, 1994), 1–15.

General sphere of activity	Specific activities targeted	Applicable practices and techniques
Organization	To improve effectiveness of relations among groups and individuals	• Learning organization • Skill-based pay • Horizontal organization • Teams
Human aspects	To motivate and mobilize the workforce	• Empowerment • Reinforcement (rewards, recognition)
Quality management tools	To improve decision making	• Affinity diagram • Relations diagram • Tree diagram • Matrix diagram • Matrix-data analysis • Process decision program chart • Arrow diagram

Table 13.2. (continued)

not only to serve as a reliable basis for making awards, but also to permit a diagnosis of each applicant's overall management system.

The Award Criteria: Purpose and Goals

The Malcolm Baldrige National Quality Award criteria are the basis for making awards and for giving feedback to applicants. In addition, the criteria have three important roles.

1. To help improve performance practices and capabilities
2. To facilitate communication and sharing of best practices information among and within organizations of all types, based upon a common understanding of key performance requirements
3. To serve as a working tool for managing performance, planning, training, and assessment.

Figure 13.6 shows the dynamic relationships between the Baldrige Award criteria.

Core Values and Concepts

The award criteria are built upon the following set of core values and concepts, which integrate customer and company performance requirements.

• *Customer-driven quality.* The key focus of a company's management system must be on product and service characteristics that contribute value to customers and lead to customer satisfaction and preference.

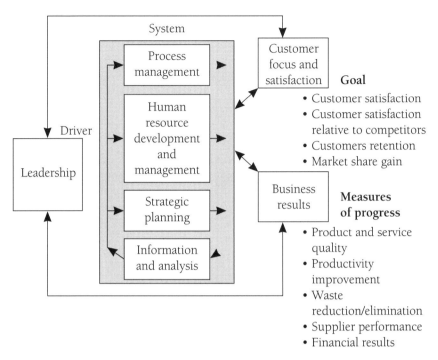

Figure 13.6. Dynamic relationships among the Baldrige Award criteria.

- *Leadership.* A company's senior leaders need to set directions and create a customer orientation, clear and visible values, and high expectations; this requires personal commitment and involvement.

- *Continuous improvement and learning.* Achieving the highest levels of performance requires a well-executed approach to continuous improvement. Continuous improvement refers here to both incremental and breakthrough improvement.

- *Employee participation and development.* A company's success in improving performance depends increasingly on the skills and motivation of its work force.

- *Fast response.* Success in competitive markets increasingly demands evershorter cycles for new or improved product and service introduction. Also, faster and more flexible response to customers is now a more critical requirement.

- *Design quality and prevention.* Business management should place strong emphasis on design quality—problem and waste prevention achieved through building quality into products and services and into production and delivery processes.

- *Long-range view of the future.* Pursuit of market leadership requires a strong future orientation and a willingness to make long-term commitments to all stakeholders—customers, employees, suppliers, stockholders, the public, and the community.

- *Management by fact.* A modern business management system needs to be built upon a framework of measurement, information, data, and analysis. This involves the creation and use of performance measures or indicators.

- *Partnership development.* Companies should seek to build internal and external partnerships to better accomplish their overall goals.

- *Corporate responsibility and citizenship.* A company's management should stress corporate responsibility and citizenship, including business ethics and protection of public health, safety, and the environment.

- *Results orientation.* A company's performance system needs to focus on results guided and balanced by the interests of all stakeholders—customers, employees, stockholders, suppliers and partners, the public, and the community. To meet the sometimes conflicting and changing aims that this balance implies, company strategy needs to explicitly address all stakeholder requirements to ensure that actions and plans meet the differing needs and avoid adverse impact on the stakeholders.

The MBNQA Criteria: A Part of a Diagnostic System

Table 13.3 lists the MBNQA examination criteria. These criteria, as well as their individual values, are constantly updated. (The criteria shown in the table are for 1995.) The National Institute of Standards and Technology publishes an annual booklet concerning these award criteria. (Individual copies can be ordered free of charge from NIST, fax 301-948-3716.)

The criteria and the scoring guidelines make up a two-part diagnostic (assessment) system. The 1995 criteria are a set of 24 basic, interrelated, results-oriented requirements. The scoring guidelines (see Table 13.4) spell out the three assessment dimensions—approach, deployment, and results—and the key factors used in assessment relative to each dimension. An assessment thus provides a profile of strengths and areas for improvement relative to the 24 requirements. In this way, the assessment directs attention to processes and actions that contribute to the performance of the company.

Comments on the Baldrige Award Criteria

In my opinion, the Baldrige Award diagnosis is an adequate general guide used to assess a management system. It is a tool whose usefulness resides in its fairly complete list of factors to be evaluated. However, I feel that there are several missing

Examination categories/criteria	Point values
1.0 Leadership	*90*
1 1.1 Senior executive leadership	45
2 1.2 Leadership system and organization	25
3 1.3 Public responsibility and corporate citizenship	20
2.0 Information and analysis	*75*
4 2.1 Management of information and data	20
5 2.2 Competitive comparisons and benchmarking	15
6 2.3 Analysis and use of company-level data	40
3.0 Strategic planning	*55*
7 3.1 Strategic development	35
8 3.2 Strategic deployment	20
4.0 Human resource development and management	*140*
9 4.1 Human resource planning and evaluation	20
10 4.2 High-performance work system	45
11 4.3 Employee education, training, and development	50
12 4.4 Employee well-being and satisfaction	25
5.0 Process management	*140*
13 5.1 Design and introduction of products and services	40
14 5.2 Process management: product and service production and delivery	40
15 5.3 Process management: support services	30
16 5.4 Management of supplier performance	30
6.0 Business results	*250*
17 6.1 Product and service quality results	75
18 6.2 Company operational and financial results	130
19 6.3 Supplier performance results	745
7.0 Customer focus and satisfaction	*250*
20 7.1 Customer and market knowledge	30
21 7.2 Customer relationship management	30
22 7.3 Customer satisfaction determination	30
23 7.4 Customer satisfaction results	100
24 7.5 Customer satisfaction comparison	60
Total points	*1000*

Table 13.3. The MBNQA seven categories and 24 requirements (1995).

Score	Approach/deployment	Score	Results
0%	• No systematic approach evident; anecdotal information	0%	• No results or poor results in areas reported
10% to 30%	• Beginning of a systematic approach to the primary purposes of the criterion • Early stages of a transition from reacting to problems to a general improvement orientation • No major gaps exist in deployment that would inhibit progress in achieving the primary purposes of the criterion	10% to 30%	• Early stages of developing trends; some improvements and/or early good performance levels in a few areas • Results not reported for many to most areas of importance to the applicant's key business requirements
40% to 60%	• A sound, systematic approach, responsive to the primary purposes of the criterion • A fact-based improvement process in place in key areas; more emphasis is placed on improvement than on reaction to problems • No major gaps in deployment, though some areas or work units may be in very early stages of deployment	40% to 60%	• Improvement trends and/or good performance levels reported for many to most areas of importance to the applicant's key business requirement • No pattern of adverse trends and/or poor performance levels in areas of importance to the applicant's key business requirements • Some trends and/or current performance levels—evaluated against relevant comparisons and/or benchmarks—show areas of strength and/or good to very good relative performance levels
70% to 90%	• A sound, systematic approach, responsive to the overall purposes of the criterion • A fact-based improvement process is a key management tool; clear evidence of refinement and improved integration as a result of improvement cycles and analysis • Approach is well deployed, with no major gaps; deployment may vary in some areas or work units	70% to 90%	• Current performance is good to excellent in most areas of importance to the applicant's key business requirements • Most improvement trends and/or performance levels are sustained • Many to most trends and/or current performance levels—evaluated against relevant comparisons and/or benchmarks—show areas of leadership and very good relative performance levels

Table 13.4. MBNQA scoring guidelines.

Score	Approach/deployment	Score	Results
100%	• A sound, systematic approach, fully responsive to all of the requirements of the criterion • A very strong, fact-based improvement process is a key management tool; strong refinement and integration—backed by excellent analysis • Approach is fully deployed without any significant weaknesses or gaps in any areas or work units	100%	• Current performance is excellent in most areas of importance to the applicant's key business requirements • Excellent improvement trends and/or sustained excellent performance levels in most areas • Strong evidence of industry and benchmark leadership demonstrated in many areas

Table 13.4. (continued)

elements. In point of fact, there is no precise definition of quality—let alone total quality—nor of customer satisfaction.

Although, recently, the satisfaction of all *stakeholders* is mentioned, little is done to concretely measure the shareholders' satisfaction. Financial results were optional in the 1992 version of the criteria and were included in the item *company operational results,* which accounted for 45 points out of the total of 1000. In 1993 and 1994, the value of this item has been raised to 50 points. In 1995, the item was renamed *company operational and financial results,* and its value has climbed to 130 points. Profitability of the organization is not directly measured.

According to the award criteria booklet,

> The Criteria do not require direct reporting of aggregate financial information such as quarterly or annual profits. The Criteria do encourage the use of financial information, including profit trends, in analyses and reporting of results derived from performance improvement strategies. That is, companies are encouraged to demonstrate the connection between quality, operational performance improvement, and financial performance.
>
> The exclusion of profit information that does not have a clear connection to quality and operational performance improvement is made for the following reasons—technical, fairness, and procedural:
>
> • Short-term profits may be affected by factors such as accounting practices, business decisions, write-offs, dividends, and investments.
> • Some industries historically have higher profit levels than others.
> • The time interval between quality improvement and overall financial improvement depends upon many factors. This interval is not likely to be the same from industry to industry or even for companies in the same industry.

- The Criteria measure performance relative to rigorous, customer-oriented, company-performance criteria. Though improved quality and productivity are likely to improve a company's overall financial performance, its financial performance depends also on the performance of competitors—which the Award process cannot measure directly.
- Financial performance depends upon many external factors, such as local, national, and international economic conditions and business cycles. Such conditions and cycles do not have the same impact on all types of businesses or on individual companies.
- Some companies would not participate in the Award process if required to provide financial information.[2]

This makes sense if we consider the use of these criteria for an evaluation leading to the award itself. However, for internal use and assessment of the management practices and the performance of an organization, financial information should be analyzed. Obviously, external, uncontrollable factors affecting the financial results of the organization must be taken into consideration. Because the main objective of any for-profit organization is profitability, the measuring of the shareholders' satisfaction is generally based on profitability. Of course, as I have indicated before, the nonfinancial needs of the shareholders should also be addressed.

Except for the item *customer and market knowledge* (30 points), where "expectations of customers and 'markets' are considered," there is no apparent consideration given to either former or potential customers. Interest appears to be limited to current clients. Moreover, it mixes objectives (company performance, customer satisfaction) and the means used to achieve them (business procedures, supplier assessment, workforce utilization, and so on).

Therefore, I suggest that, when these criteria are used, they be augmented to include all of the factors pertaining to customer total quality (QVALITY and ACE); that is, information concerning company profitability and its performance in *economic terms*, together with information on past and potential customers. In addition, when I use these criteria for a diagnosis, I start with category 8. Generally, my customers react promptly but politely to remind me that there are only seven categories, and wait for my apology with a light smile. I thank them and proceed to say that I always start with category 8; that is, I begin with shareholder satisfaction (which represents my additional category 8 and becomes my first category), followed by category 7 (customer satisfaction, my category 2) which is, indeed, the source of *quality of return* for the shareholders. The seven QVALITY factors are introduced and measured, and I then proceed to categories 6 to 1 (my categories 3 to 6).

Rather than evaluating both the extraversive objectives (7 and 8) and the introversive means (1 to 6) as part of one exercise, I separate the results of categories 7 and 8 (Part A) from the rest (Part B). Any strength or weakness in Part A is then traced back to strengths or weaknesses in Part B. Part A represents *what* is going right or wrong, Part B represents *why* it is going right or wrong.

The European Quality Award

In October 1990, the Governing Committee of the European Foundation for Quality Management (EFQM) decided that developing the European Quality Award should be the highest priority.

The European Quality award was launched during the 1991 European Quality Management Forum in Paris. The first award was presented the following year in Madrid, Spain, at the Fourth Forum. The award aims to recognize organizations paying exceptional attention to total quality, and to encourage others to follow by example. The European Quality Award was developed by EFQM in conjunction with the European Commission and the European Organization for Quality.

Nearly 300 people have been involved with the development of the criteria, including quality management practitioners, advocates, and professionals; academics, EFQM member company representatives; national award organizations; and quality associations. The European nature and values of the criteria aim to represent a model company, excelling in the European marketplace in the late twentieth century, irrespective of size and business.

Under the award assessment, a company is rated on its results and improved performance in customer satisfaction, employee satisfaction, business performance, and impact on society. The eight specific categories of criteria and their relevant values are shown in Table 13.5.

The relations between these criteria are illustrated in a general model (see Figure 13.7). Note that the priority here is given to the business results, which are of interest for the shareholders. Then we move to the customer, the people in the organization, and the impact of the company on society. The bottom section is termed *processes.* These are the means to achieve the four previous objectives: resources management, people management, policy and strategy, and leadership.

Note that customer satisfaction is given a 20 percent value, people satisfaction 18 percent, and business results 15 percent. In my opinion, for a for-profit organization, *business results* should be given the highest points and priority.

ABC/ABM and Its Relationship to Business Reengineering and Total Quality

In the accounting field, a new approach has been developed that modifies the traditional ways of accounting and of establishing the real cost of a product. This approach, known as ABC/ABM, or activity-based costing (ABC) and activity-based management (ABM), is a good tool for TQM. Ascertaining which activities contribute the most, the least, or, indeed, nothing at all to the achievement of customer and/or shareholder satisfaction helps identify the causes of problems and

Category	Value
• *Customer satisfaction.* The perceptions of external customers, direct and indirect, of the company and of its products and services.	20%
• *People.* The management of the company's people and the people's feelings about the company.	18%
• *Business results.* The company's achievement in relation to its planned business performance.	15%
• *Processes.* The management of all of the value-adding activities within the company.	14%
• *Leadership.* The behavior of all managers in transforming the company toward total quality.	10%

• *Resources.* The management, utilization, and preservation of
  • Financial resources
  • Information resources
  • Technological resources
	9%

• *Policy and strategy.* The company's vision, values, and direction, and the ways in which it achieves them.	8%
• *Impact on society.* The perceptions of the company on the part of the community at large. Views on the company's approach to quality of life, to the environment, and to the need for the preservation of global resources are included.	6%

Table 13.5. The European Quality Award criteria.

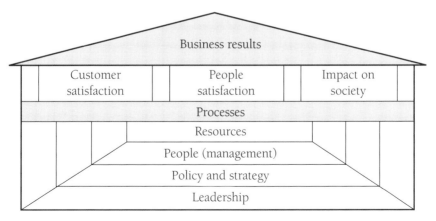

Figure 13.7. General model showing the relationships between the European Quality Award criteria.

constitutes an important step towards enhancing the results and eliminating total quality–related problems.

Conventional accounting considers a product from the point of view of the resources used to produce it (that is, costs). To calculate the cost of a product, direct costs (labor and materials) are easily calculated. All other costs (the president's and all managers' salaries, the rent, the insurance premiums, and so on) are lumped together in what are called *overhead costs*. At one time, direct costs were a significant proportion of the total costs of the product (see Figure 13.8a). Today, the reverse is true, and what is thrown indiscriminately into overhead accounts for much more than the direct costs (see Figure 13.8b).

Companies do attempt after the fact to calculate the individual product's overhead, but this calculation is based on a mechanical formula that is mistakenly applied to all products in a blanket fashion. The method of calculation assumes that each and every product has exactly the same proportional relationship between its direct costs and its overhead. (In other words, products' overheads are calculated based on their direct costs, using a certain fixed ratio.) This simply does not reflect reality, and as a result of this situation, companies are not able to divide up the overhead precisely and attribute it to specific products; and, therefore, they cannot determine the precise relationship between the total cost of a product and the price at which it is sold.

The size of the products' overheads relative to their direct costs is not all fixed and can vary enormously. Using the old accounting methods, companies may thus go through all the motions, but the truth is that they cannot evaluate exactly the cost of any specific product.

In the ABC concept, products do not use resources; they use activities which, in turn, use resources. This way, by identifying all of the activities that directly or indirectly contribute to a product, its cost can be more precisely calculated (see Figure 13.8c). For example, if the marketing manager spends 80 percent of his or her time on 10 percent of the products, these products should therefore be charged with 80 percent of his or her salary and expenses, while, in conventional accounting, 100 percent of his or her time would be incorrectly distributed among 100 percent of the products.

To go one step further, not all of the activities require the same attention. Among the activities required for a given product, a small proportion (say 15 percent) may have a much greater importance (say 80 percent) than all of the others (see Figure 13.8d). For instance, one activity out of nine required to manufacture a certain product could consume 75 percent of its manufacturing time. Management should therefore concern itself with these few activities of overriding importance rather than with all of them. This is the logic behind ABM.

After activities are formally linked to products with ABC and ABM, they should also be formally linked among themselves in a business process. If this linkage is not done in a formal fashion, processes get segmented among the various departments, which carry out their activities independently of one another. For example, let us take an order fulfillment process. An order would go through

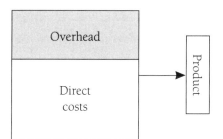

a. Traditional accounting:
former cost breakdown

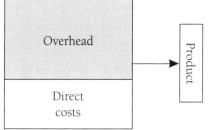

b. Traditional accounting:
today's cost breakdown

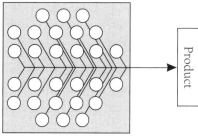

c. ABC
Circles represent activities

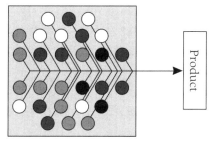

d. ABM
The shade of a circle indicates its
relative importance

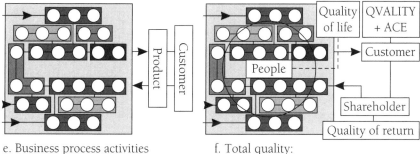

e. Business process activities
are grouped in processes

f. Total quality:
The business process is linked to the
total quality triad

Figure 13.8. From traditional accounting to ABC to ABM to process
management to total quality management.

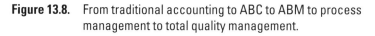

a whole circuit, at any point of which it might get lost, forgotten, or otherwise given short shrift. The order is taken by the salesperson, who then gives it to credit evaluation who, after ascertaining the client's good standing, passes it down to the stock room to see if the material is in stock. If the material is not in stock, the order is sent to manufacturing; when manufacturing finishes the product, they send it to shipping, who finally sends it to the customer.

The various departments operate almost as if they were contiguous, independent city-states, each with its own small territory and separate interests, each maintaining the thread of communication with its neighbors with occasional messages through emissaries. If at any point the customer calls to find out what becomes of the order, the chances are that no one will know where it is, because the various activities have not been unified in the seamless process they purport to serve. In short, the right hand knows not what the left hand is doing.

Activities can be linked, however, by cross-functional teams who work to make a process into a streamlined whole. Such a team would have the full responsibility for following order fulfillment through all of its steps from beginning to end. This results in a vastly reduced number of errors, easy follow-up, and better customer service. While cross-functional teams do not eradicate the departmental functional structure of an organization, they do mitigate it, as well as subordinate functions and departmental activities to a total process. This type of organization is called *management by processes.* Process management includes both management *by* processes and management *of* processes. In short, regrouping and linking all of a company's departments within a business process consisting of a mainstream process and support processes (see Figure 13.8e) allows these processes to be managed more effectively (see Figure 13.8f). Finally, in what constitutes the last step toward global integration, tying the business process to the total quality triad—shareholder, customer, organization members—allows the company to achieve and maintain total quality.

Apart from its indispensability for calculating the real costs to design, produce, and deliver a product, this approach is useful for backtracking a problem—shareholder or customer dissatisfaction—to its root cause or causes. This is rendered possible by tying each product, and the associated elements of QVALITY, to the activities that have contributed to produce it as well as to its contribution to the company's profitability, providing for a quality return for the shareholders. Appendix D shows how a plant has applied the QVALITY concept to elaborate its annual improvement plan. Each department has indicated the activities to be undertaken to improve one or more of these seven characteristics.

The Added Value Concept

Ideally speaking, each activity undertaken in an organization should add on some value to the product in process. Starting with the identification of the customer's needs, from the moment the product is being developed and designed, value is thus built up at every step along the way, and this process culminates when customers are presented with a *valuable* product (goods or service)—in other words, one that has a value for them because it is able to satisfy their needs. In manufacturing, value is added either by adding useful labor, useful materials, or both (useful in terms of the results for the customer). That an activity must add value and be useful might seem to be blatantly apparent; nevertheless, in reality, there are many activities that do not add any real value. An example of such superfluous activity would be *gold plating* (for example, using steel when cardboard would do, or gold when another material would do the job).

Activities can therefore be grouped into two categories: (1) value-adding activities, and (2) nonvalue-adding activities. The nonvalue-adding activities are of two types: (1) value-adding enablers, and (2) nonvalue-adding enablers.

The *value-adding enablers* comprise activities that, while they still do not add any value to the product in and of themselves, are essential to the creation of this value by enabling other value-adding activities to take place effectively. Thus, if this type of activity were not performed, there would either be a reduction in the value added to the product down the line or, in fact, no further value added to the product anywhere down the line. An example of such an activity is production planning. Obviously, products can be manufactured without any planning (a nonvalue-adding activity because, physically, it does add anything to the product), but there is a probability that what would then be produced might not be of the right type, nor in the right quantity, nor at the required time and at a minimum cost. Thus, the product would be of no value, or of reduced value, to the customer.

The *nonvalue-adding enablers* include those activities that neither add any value to the product in themselves nor have any usefulness by virtue of enabling other value-adding activities to be performed. The absence of these activities would therefore in no way affect the value of a product. For example, taking stock inventory is an activity that can be done away without being missed. If, as when just-in-time is put into practice, there is no inventory in the first place, then there is, of course, no inventory to be taken. The whole process has been knocked out in one blow, and the product goes on being produced and delivered all the same, without anybody being the wiser. The same goes for receiving. It can be eliminated, as is the case with just-in-time, by having suppliers bring materials directly to or near the workstations using them (see Table 13.6). To reiterate, because these activities neither add value nor enable other value-adding activities to take place, their elimination has no ill consequence and, indeed, serves to streamline processes and make them seamless. The basis of the business reengineering concept is indeed to eliminate such nonvalue, nonenabling activities and processes.

A *value analysis* consists of taking each activity or group of activities and measuring the relative value added by it, or else its contribution to the value added by other activities, and then making sure that its cost does not surpass the value added or its contribution to the value added. This contribution is measured by the difference in time, cost, and results when the contribution is not made. For

Activities			
Value-adding activities		**Nonvalue-adding activities**	
Customer value-adding activities	*Owner value-adding activities*	*Value-adding enablers*	*Nonvalue-adding enablers*
Designing	Credit assessing	Planning	Storing
Materials procurement	Collecting receivables	Scheduling	Materials handling
Cutting	Dividend payment	Organizing	Sorting
Shaping	Tax saving	Inspecting	Warehousing
Assembling	Subsidies research	Controlling	Inventories
Finishing	Insurance (value protection)	Assurance	Stock inventories
Painting		Packing	Shipping
Transportation		Documenting	Receiving
		Information systems	Order entry
		Marketing	Billing
		• Surveys	
		• Focus groups	
		Hiring	
		Training	
		Budgeting	

Table 13.6. Examples of the value-adding concept.

example, as Deming put it, inspection does not add (or contribute) quality (value) to a product being inspected, because quality is built into the product. Inspection is therefore being eliminated while workers are encouraged to do (build) things right the first time and all the time. On the other hand, the cost of planning activities is offset by their benefits, which allow the production of the right products, on time, in the right quantity, at a minimum cost. The contribution can be measured by the savings in possible penalties for late deliveries, in multiple shippings due to the production of a lesser quantity than required, or in unnecessary inventories resulting from producing more than the quantity ordered.

In the value analysis of a product, the relative value added by each of its components is analyzed. For example, in a lead pencil, the lead is the most valuable part. The wood serves only to protect the lead from breaking, to prevent the fingers holding the pencil from getting dirty, and to add to the appearance of the finished product. Consequently, one should use quality lead but not high-quality wood, given the limited importance and function of the latter.

Problem Identification, Solving, and Prevention (PISP)

Tracing back any dissatisfaction on the part of either the shareholders or the customers, or looking for ways to better these satisfactions, is done by finding the areas in the business process and its environment, external and internal, that cause these dissatisfactions or are means (opportunities) for increasing the satisfaction of either or both the shareholder and the customer.

Brainstorming

The intent behind brainstorming is to generate a wealth of ideas that may then be sorted and analyzed in order to choose the most pertinent. It is used, among other things, for identifying problems, causes, and solutions. This technique embodies two main, but distinct, activities, which often take place on separate occasions.

The first activity is brainstorming itself. While its goal, as the name itself suggests, is to unleash the creative energy of the group and spark a free flow of ideas, in order for this to take place, the discussion leader must nonetheless enforce strict adherence to the rules. One of the main rules is that all participants must refrain from commenting on, or criticizing, any idea suggested. No one can be allowed to act as a devil's advocate, show or express any hint of skepticism, discredit others' ideas by relating any similar experiences that have ended in failure, or offer any opinion on how pertinent the idea is to the given situation. Examples of the preceding strictures are often encountered in work groups and only serve to curb the enthusiasm of those who propose ideas; they then either withdraw and make no further suggestions or else dig in their heels to prove that they are right.

Because the aim of brainstorming is to give free rein to everybody's creativity, all ideas, even the most far-fetched, are not only accepted but even encouraged. Quantity, rather than quality, of ideas is the objective at this stage. For example, in one brainstorming session, a participant had proposed burning down the company's buildings! During the discussion period, this idea, originally meant as a joke, led the group to question whether the buildings were adequately protected against the risk of fire. They concluded that protection was inadequate and recommended that adequate fire protection be installed—and it was done. Humor is allowed, and even encouraged; it serves to put all of the participants at ease and creates a pleasant and relaxed atmosphere in the group. However, everyone must keep in mind that brainstorming is a serious activity. One has to avoid taking it lightly or reducing it to a laughing matter at all costs.

During a brainstorming session, the leader writes out all the ideas on flipchart sheets that are subsequently posted around the walls to serve as reference for the participants. The leader writes down the idea exactly as suggested, and offers no personal interpretation. If it is not clear, the leader asks the originator of the idea to explain. A discussion and analysis session follows the initial brainstorming session. However, between the two sessions, one notices a kind of *incubation* process taking place: people sleep on the ideas expressed in the brainstorming session, reviewing them as they take root in the subconscious. The seeds thus sown bear new fruit, either inspiring the emergence of new ideas or enabling a better assessment of the initial ideas to take place.

In the second session, participants discuss, revise, and analyze the ideas brought to the fore in the first session in light of their own knowledge, judgment, and expertise. Similar or complementary ideas are grouped together, the really outlandish ideas are eliminated, and the potentially workable ideas are culled from the lot and kept. Groups whose members lack all the knowledge required to make a well-informed decision often call in specialists from various domains to assist in their deliberations.

The brainstorming technique is used to identify a whole set of problems with a common theme—such as complaints from suppliers. It can also be used to determine the particular problems within that larger group. This technique is useful for tracing the probable causes of a given problem, in researching and evaluating possible solutions, and in determining the most appropriate solution.

The Nominal Group Technique

While this technique, like brainstorming, brings the group's creativity into play, it differs in several other respects. It entails six phases.

1. The group chooses a theme, problem, concern or subject to discuss. Their choice must be a specific topic—not a vague question, such as "How can we improve quality?"

2. Without consulting any other group members, each participant writes down his or her ideas on the subject.

3. The leader collects the ideas, one by one, from each member.

4. Similar ideas are grouped together and clarified if necessary.

5. Each idea collected is then numbered and written on a board, clearly visible to all. Next, each member establishes an order of priority for these ideas, using the following technique: Each participant chooses a number of ideas equal to half the total number plus one, which is to say that if they have compiled a list of 22 ideas, each member must choose 12 (11+1) ideas. The member gives a 0 to each idea he or she has not selected, then ranks the remaining ideas by giving 1 point to the one judged to be the least important, 2 to the next least important, and so on. In our example, the least important idea will get 1 point and the most important will get 12 points.

6. The leader asks each member how many points he or she has awarded to each idea and writes the number on the board. The leader also notes how many members selected each idea. For a team of eight people, a given idea might have a score of 12, 11, 9, 7, 5, 2, 0, 0, (6), meaning that six members chose it and gave it those particular points. The idea receiving the largest number of points and cho-

sen by the greatest number of people is considered to be the most important and, therefore, demands the highest priority.

Pareto Diagram and Analysis

This method of analysis can be used very effectively in a number of domains, quality not least among them, to see through a complex cluster of problems and pinpoint the worst offender among them. In this way, problem-solving efforts may be directed toward areas where they will make the most impact. There are two stages in this process: (1) gathering data related to the set of problems (see Figure 13.9), and (2) preparation of a Pareto chart (see Figure 13.10).

Pareto, an early twentieth-century econometrist, observed that 80 percent of a country's wealth belonged to about 20 percent of the population, that is to say, to a privileged few. This observation, known as the 80-20 rule, is what is called a natural law. We are familiar with other natural laws: Murphy's law, which claims that if anything can go wrong, it will; Parkinson's law, which, drawing an analogy with the variable density of gas, theorizes that work expands or compresses to fit precisely into whatever time is allotted for it; or the law of perversity, which decrees that every time we look for our keys in our left pocket, they invariably turn up in the right.

We see the Pareto phenomenon everywhere. Purchasing agents know that about 80 percent of the purchasing budget is spent on that privileged 20 percent of all items bought. They call this an ABC analysis, where class A represents roughly 20 percent of the items and B and C the other 80 percent.

Defect\Day	1	2	3	4	5	6	7	8	9	10	11	12	13	Total
Squareness						1								1
Hardness	4	6	3	4	1	3	6	7	2	3	14	3	2	58
Glue		1					1			1	2			5
Thickness	1				1	0					1			3
Identification	2		3	1	1	4		1	2		3		2	19
Packing		1									1			2
Appearance	1		1			1		1		1	2			7
Resistance			1											1
Durability		1		1	1						1			4
Total	8	9	8	6	4	9	7	9	4	5	24	3	4	100

Figure 13.9. Data collection for Pareto analysis.

Source: J. N. Kelada, *Comprendre et réaliser la qualité totale,* 2nd ed. (Dollard-des-Ormeaux, Quebec, Canada: Quafec Publications, 1992), 281. Reprinted with permission.

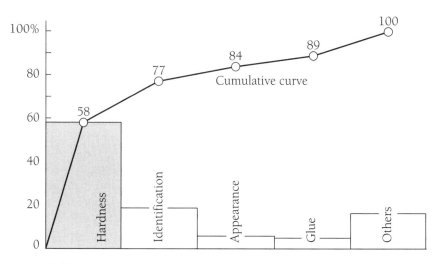

Figure 13.10. A Pareto chart.

Source: J. N. Kelada, *Comprendre et réaliser la qualité totale,* 2nd ed. (Dollard-des-Ormeaux, Quebec, Canada: Quafec Publications, 1992), 282. Reprinted with permission.

Sure enough, the 80-20 rule of thumb can also be counted on to pop up in the area of unquality—when we try, for instance, to examine a product in order to see which among its many characteristics are most liable to suffer from the occurrence of defects. Here too, we will find that 20 percent of product characteristics account for 80 percent of defects.

To give an example, in their quest for quality, officials in a factory specializing in the manufacture of floor tiles gathered data on the different types of defects that occurred. For each of the 13 lots of tiles manufactured (see Figure 13.9), they calculated the total numbers of each kind of defect and ranked these totals in decreasing order of importance. Then, they prepared a histogram showing these totals and highlighting the most serious defect (see Figure 13.10). Putting their energies where most needed, they would thus concentrate on eliminating this glaring defect first, instead of attacking all of the defects at the same time and spreading their efforts thin, to little effect.

Tracing the curve of the cumulative totals, one can see that 2 out of the 10 defects (20 percent) account for 77 out of 100 (77 percent) of all defects found. The type of defect appearing first on the left side of the chart calls for priority attention because it represents 58 percent of all defects found. Sometimes, when defects, errors, or failures are not of the same relative value, we can draw a *weighted Pareto diagram,* where each defect is multiplied by a weight factor. (For example, in an invoice, a spelling error has not the same effect—or value—as an error in price.) This could change the priority on the problem to handle shifting from the most frequent defect to the most important.

Ishikawa's Cause-and-Effect Diagram

One of the most frequently used techniques in problem-solving analysis is the cause-and-effect study. It involves producing a cause-and-effect diagram known as the Ishikawa diagram, after its Japanese inventor, Kaoru Ishikawa. Sometimes, because of its shape, it is referred to as the *fishbone diagram* (see Figure 13.11). The advantage of this technique is that it offers a way to categorize the causes underlying any type of problem, thus making it much easier to sift through the possible causes and determine the most probable ones. These categories, called the 4 Ms, are *manpower* (direct and indirect), *machinery* (production equipment, machines and tools), *materials* (raw materials, parts, subsets, and supplies), and *methods* (instructions, manuals, and procedures).

Other Ms can be added (see Figure 13.12), among them the following:

- *Milieu.* Physical work environment or setting and external environment (suppliers, market, governments).
- *Management.* Anything unrelated to the doer of a task—planning, organization, direction, control, assurance.
- *Money.* Operating budgets, investment policy.
- *Measure.* In order to monitor and control a process, measures have to be taken. Measures should be *precise, repeatable* (that is, the same result is obtained by the same person, using the same test or instrument, over and over again), *reproducible* (that is, the same result is obtained by another person using the same test or instrument), *documented,* and so on.
- *Memory.* A process memory consists of all data and information—managerial and operational—entering it, created by it, or outgoing (input, throughput, and output); its accuracy, precision, timing, and timeliness; and so on.

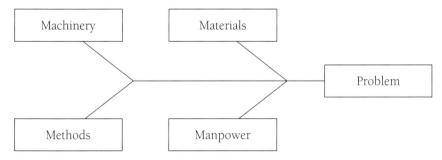

Figure 13.11. Ishikawa's fishbone diagram.

Source: J. N. Kelada, *Comprendre et réaliser la qualité totale,* 2nd ed. (Dollard-des-Ormeaux, Quebec, Canada: Quafec Publications, 1992), 283. Reprinted with permission.

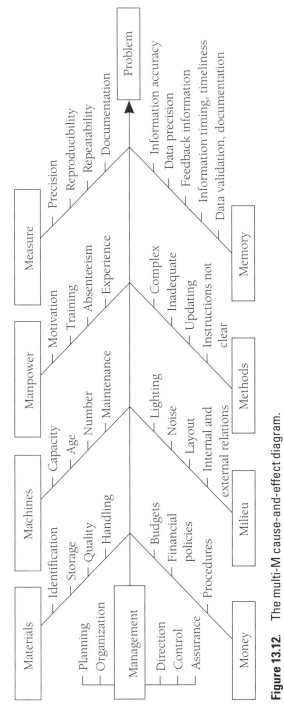

Figure 13.12. The multi-M cause-and-effect diagram.

Source: J. N. Kelada, *Comprendre et réaliser la qualité totale*, 2nd ed. (Dollard-des-Ormeaux, Quebec, Canada: Quafec Publications, 1992), 283. Reprinted with permission.

These multiple Ms assist the work team members to identify all the probable causes in the following way. When the group has determined the problem to be studied, the leader produces an Ishikawa diagram for them to complete as a group. They begin with a brainstorming session to identify all the possible causes of the given problem. The Ms on the diagram provide a mental focus for participants, directing their thoughts toward whatever aspect is under consideration, be it manpower or materials. To get good results and get them quickly, participants must be continually reminded to adhere to the basic rules of brainstorming.

We must keep in mind that the sole aim of thinking along the lines of categories is to stimulate the production of ideas. When people see the word *manpower,* they associate it with training, absenteeism, or experience. When the idea has been expressed, the purpose of categorization has been achieved; knowing exactly which category the idea should fall under is not important. We have seen groups waste precious time and almost bring the process to a standstill by trying to categorize a possible cause, such as production personnel receiving incomplete information. With so much energy being spent on deciding whether the problem should fall under manpower, work methods, or management, a casual observer could easily mistake pigeonholing to have been the purpose of the exercise.

Once the idea has been clearly expressed, the leader quickly puts it into the category which he or she deems to be the most appropriate. The group members then pass on to the next idea. By the end of this exercise, they will have identified a large number of possible causes. Next, they proceed to determine the most probable causes. These are the ones directly linked to the problem under study. Probable causes can be determined in three ways. The first, which is simple and democratic, is to vote. Each member of the group votes yes or no on each idea put forward. Members can abstain from voting on any given idea. The most probable causes are those that receive the largest number of votes. The advantage of this method lies in the speed with which the exercise can be accomplished. However, the majority obviously is not always right and may often be wrong.

The second method is to discuss each idea suggested. A cause is not considered probable until all of the members of the group have discussed and recognized it as such. Reaching consensus is therefore essential, no matter how much time it takes. This approach often proves to be long and arduous but generally yields better results than other approaches.

A third method, more rapid than the second, is a combination of the first two. A time limit is set to discuss the various arguments for and against each idea. At that point, if consensus is not reached, the group votes.

So which method should be chosen? That depends on the importance and complexity of the problem, the available time, and any number of other factors that have to be taken into account.

I would like to point out that the diagram of possible causes can be used in any number of cases to identify causes, because causes differ very little from one problem to the next and may usually be drawn from the fairly comprehensive range offered by the multi-Ms. At each session, the group will be able to fine-tune the diagram until, over a period of time, it becomes fully fleshed out.

When it comes to determining the most probable causes, a simple discussion period and vote are not generally enough. The group may have to do further research. If this is the case, the members would collect pertinent data, organize it, and analyze it before deciding whether the cause is one of the most probable ones or not. For example, one PISP team, after discussing the rejection of a product because it did not meet specifications, instigated a study on the capability of a process (determining whether it was capable of maintaining the required tolerances). The process proved to be incapable of doing so. Therefore, they calculated the probable percentage of items that would exceed those tolerances. This gave those in charge the choice of

- Negotiating the loosening of the strictness of the requirements (widening the tolerances)
- Replacing or modifying certain equipment
- Accepting the losses which would inevitably result from the calculated probable percentage of rejects caused by the lack of process capability

In order to evaluate a possible solution, a reverse fishbone diagram can be used (see Figure 13.13). Here the solution is the cause (while the problem was the effect in the regular cause-and-effect diagram), and its effects on each of the Ms are estimated or calculated. This is done by analyzing all of the possible positive benefits and negative effects of the given solution for each of the Ms. For example, installing a computer system to eliminate, or significantly reduce, existing billing errors would require an investment (negative effect on money) but would reduce the costs of correcting them (positive effect on this M). It would increase the skills of the employees (positive effect for manpower) when they are trained to use the new system, but could have some adverse effects on them, such as possible eye strain and back pains (negative effect for manpower). Each effect, positive or negative, is then given a numerical value, calculated or estimated. The sum of all these points (positive minus negative) for all the Ms for each solution is then compared with the sum of each of the other solutions. The one with the most points as the best solution.

PISP Step-by-Step Approach

This approach consists of two aspects: problem prevention and problem identification and solution. Problem prevention consists of identifying all possible cases that would cause dissatisfaction either to the shareholders or to the customers. The FMEA technique, explained earlier in this chapter, helps pinpoint these cases as well as their possible causes, effects, and the probability of detection. The poka-yoke concept can be applied to eliminate the most critical probable problems (failures).

Using the plan-do-check-act (PDCA) principle, problem identification and problem solving can be achieved through the step-by-step approach indicated in Table 13.7. Figure 13.14 shows the whole process of PISP.

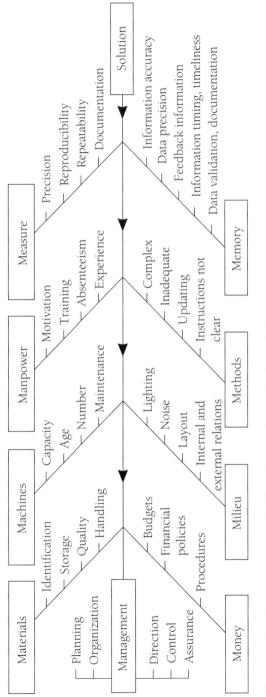

Figure 13.13. Reverse cause-and-effect diagram for evaluating solutions.

Source: Adapted from J. N. Kelada, *Comprendre et réaliser la qualité totale,* 2nd ed. (Dollard-des-Ormeaux, Quebec, Canada: Quafec Publications, 1992), 283. Reprinted with permission.

PDCA	Step	Activity	Technique(s)
Plan	1.	Choose a *theme* touching on either a shareholder's or a customer's dissatisfaction. Take, for example, the dissatisfaction of customers with the administrative procedures (A) that they have to go through.	• Data collected from surveys, focus groups • Pareto diagram to identify the most important theme or the most recurrent one • Brainstorming or NGT
	2.	Within this theme, identify an area problem, say billing.	Data gathering, representation, and analysis (histograms, graphs, control charts, scatter diagrams, checklists), brainstorming, NGT, Pareto diagrams
	3.	Within this area, identify all problems encountered, then the most important or most recurrent problem.	Data gathering, representation, and analysis (histograms, graphs, control charts, scatter diagrams, checklists), brainstorming, NGT, Pareto diagrams
	4.	Identify all of the possible causes of this problem.	Ishikawa fishbone cause-and-effect diagram, brainstorming
	5.	Identify the *most* probable cause or causes (one or two only).	Evaluate with data, proceed to a vote, NGT
	6.	Elaborate all possible solutions.	Brainstorming
	7.	Evaluate each solution.	Reverse fishbone, collect new data and/or use new data
	8.	Choose the best solution (either improving the existing process or reengineering it), and prepare a plan of action to implement it.	NGT, brainstorming, data from previous step
Do	9.	Implement the solution.	As per plan of action
Check	10.	Evaluate the results.	Monitor, collect data, draw conclusions
Act	11.	Standardize the solution.	Document, circulate, record

Table 13.7. The PISP step-by-step method.

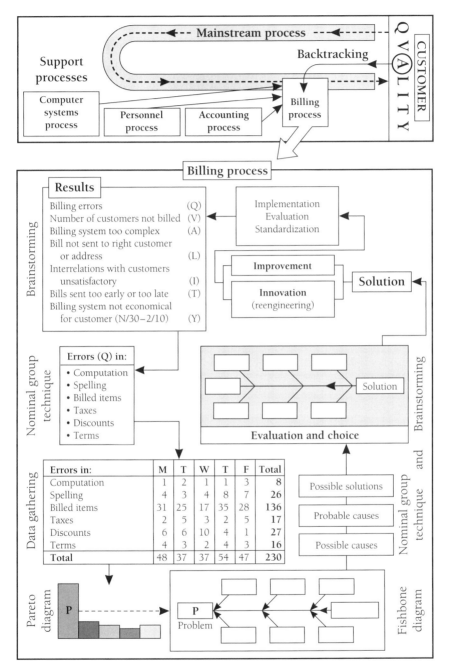

Figure 13.14. An example of an application of the PISP method.

Conclusion

In order to achieve and maintain total quality, people must use a number of practices that are now available and that I have grouped under the name *total quality technology*. These practices have been developed by specialists in all areas of management: total quality, personnel, accounting, computer science, production and operations management, and so on.

However, these practices should be integrated into a global approach aiming at the mutual satisfaction of people, customers, and shareholders. Traditional, introversive ways of thinking have to yield to extraversive ways. The very perception of the nature of a problem is totally different from the traditional one. A problem is anything that causes dissatisfaction for either the shareholder or the customer. Then, one has to go from there to prevent what may go wrong, to correct it if it does, to improve what is right, and to innovate and reengineer what can no more be improved. In order to do that, one has to be familiar with the practices that can help achieve such objectives.

Notes

1. *1995 Malcolm Baldrige National Quality Award Criteria* (Gaithersburg, Md.: National Institute of Standards and Technology, 1995).

2. Ibid.

Epilogue

The Path to Total Quality

According to Jacob,[1] "Total Quality Management was the elixir of the eighties. It was supposed to have all the answers; it was supposed to turn lead to gold. It didn't. Signs of disappointment are everywhere. Surveys show that up to two thirds of American managers think TQM has failed in their companies." The fact is, says Jacob, that "many TQM programs have been badly executed . . . but make no mistake: Thoughtfully applied and modified, total quality's principle still represents a sound way to run a company." He adds: "Indeed, many companies that have successfully adopted TQM don't even use the phrase total quality any more; it has simply become a way of doing business.

Many authors and consultants suggest that total quality—which they mistakenly equate with continuous improvement—is no answer to the revolution the business world is going through. They suggest that reengineering is the way to go and nothing else. Many companies, as well as a number of quality gurus, consultants, and experts, did indeed consider total quality as consisting of gradual, incremental, continuous improvement. As I have indicated, total quality is achieved through both continuous improvement and innovation, that is, reengineering.

As we read in a special section in *Fortune* magazine, under the title "Quality 2000: The Next Decade of Progress,"

> The future is not what it used to be. In the decade since 1985, thousands of organizations have adopted and applied the principles of total quality management (TQM). As a result, the worldwide standards for the quality of products and services have never been higher. TQM has proven to be a highly adaptive management tool that is here to stay. It has passed the fad test. TQM has delivered on its promise, but has not reached its potential. The challenge for the next decade is renewal. The global business community is in the midst of a revolution that is shaping how people and organizations will operate and work—well into the next century.[2]

The path to total quality—or, if one does not want to use this expression, the path to the mutual satisfaction of the shareholders, the customers, and the members of the organization—starts with understanding the five prerequisites to the success of the process leading to the achievement and the maintenance of total quality (see Figure E.1). One must grasp the meaning of the total quality triad, where the three stakeholders mutually satisfy each other. At FedEx, the CEO suggests that People–Service–Profits (PSP) is the way to do business. If he satisfies his people (P), they will satisfy his customers by offering them the services (S) required, and these, in turn will satisfy him by allowing his company to make the desired profits (P).

In order to put this triad into motion and achieve its triple objectives—quality return for the shareholders, QVALITY + ACE for the customers, and a quality of life for the organization members—a company must adopt TQM and collaborate with external upstream and downstream partners, while preserving and protecting the environment and contributing to the well-being of the community where it operates.

TQM is based on a five-point philosophy which is profit oriented, customer focused, people centered, partner assisted, and environmentally conscious. It consists of a human aspect, and follows a logic that indicates that total quality is not achieved or maintained by accident; it has to be managed. Finally, it is supported by a technology consisting of a number of practices, techniques, and tools, some of which have been developed by specialists in different fields, such as human resource management, compensation management, marketing, accounting, and so on.

The implementation of TQM in an organization must be done systematically, based on a rigorous plan of action. It must be evaluated periodically to correct any deviation or to improve on the plan of action. The implementation process consists of 10 steps and takes anywhere from 1 to 5 or even 10 years. However, that does not mean one has to wait 10 years to see any results or benefits. At AT&T, important results and savings have been achieved less than three years into the process.

Limiting total quality to incremental improvement is nonsense. It limits creativity and stops innovation. We must understand that when incremental improvement is no longer possible, effective, or profitable, we have to innovate, reengineer. However, reengineering as well as incremental improvement must be done in an extraversive fashion. They have to be directly linked to the satisfaction of the shareholders, who are the rightful owners of the organization, and the customers, who—by constantly purchasing the company's products and services—allow it to survive and progress. As far as the members of the organization are concerned, management and nonmanagement, white or blue collars, they are not a resource of the organization, as they are often considered to be. A resource is an available means, a computable wealth, an immediate and possible source of revenues. People are much more than that: They *are* the organization! When we say that an organization must satisfy its shareholders and customers, we must stress the fact that we mean that its members should do so in order to satisfy themselves.

Because total quality is an approach involving three stakeholders *mutually* satisfying themselves, these stakeholders must be educated to this philosophy. At

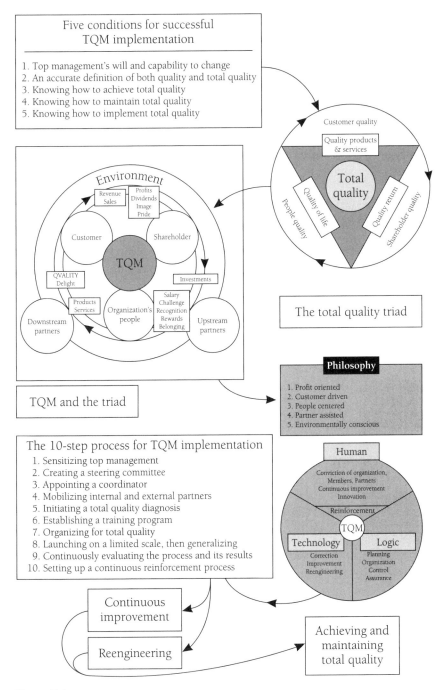

Five conditions for successful
TQM implementation

1. Top management's will and capability to change
2. An accurate definition of both quality and total quality
3. Knowing how to achieve total quality
4. Knowing how to maintain total quality
5. Knowing how to implement total quality

Customer quality

Quality products
& services

Total
quality

Quality of life

People quality

Quality return

Shareholder quality

The total quality triad

Environment

Revenue
Sales

Profits
Dividends
Image
Pride

Customer

Shareholder

TQM

QVALITY
Delight

Investments

Products
Services

Salary
Challenge
Recognition
Rewards
Belonging

Downstream
partners

Organization's
people

Upstream
partners

TQM and the triad

Philosophy

1. Profit oriented
2. Customer driven
3. People centered
4. Partner assisted
5. Environmentally conscious

The 10-step process for TQM implementation

1. Sensitizing top management
2. Creating a steering committee
3. Appointing a coordinator
4. Mobilizing internal and external partners
5. Initiating a total quality diagnosis
6. Establishing a training program
7. Organizing for total quality
8. Launching on a limited scale, then generalizing
9. Continuously evaluating the process and its results
10. Setting up a continuous reinforcement process

Human

Conviction of organization,
Members, Partners
Continuous improvement
Innovation

Reinforcement

TQM

Technology

Correction
Improvement
Reengineering

Logic

Planning
Organization
Control
Assurance

Continuous
improvement

Reengineering

Achieving and
maintaining
total quality

Figure E.1.

an introductory meeting aimed at launching a total quality effort in an organization, I noticed something very unusual. Management had invited the members of the organization, their spouses, some suppliers, a few important customers, a few important shareholders, and some members of the community. This was not done as a publicity stunt; it had been decided because the committee in charge of the event was convinced that, since they were embarking in a long-term process that would benefit all stakeholders, success was dependent on the collaboration and the joint efforts of them all.

In order to achieve and maintain total quality, traditional management approaches and practices are not enough. A new way of doing business and running it must be sought. Business leaders must learn to practice extraversive management. They should start managing by process rather than by function, and in order to do so, they must rely heavily on cross-functional teams. They must turn their organization into a *learning* one, where people not only learn to work together but also learn to learn together. People should be paid for what they *can* do rather than for what they do. Concepts such as skill-based pay increase the flexibility of production, allowing mass customization as well as increasing interest for work and challenges for all the members of the organization, regardless of their position in the hierarchy.

Managers must stop supervising and start coaching people, who do not work *for* them but rather *with* them as members of a team. Organization members have to train to identify and solve problems and learn to prevent them. They must be mobilized and understand how, by their work, they actually contribute to the challenge of satisfying themselves through satisfying the shareholders and customers. In return, they have a challenging job, decent pay, recognition and rewards for their efforts, and the joy of belonging to a winning team.

An organization cannot change unless it has the will and feels the urgency to change. It also must know how to change and have the power to do so. Ability to change is based on a number of factors and prerequisites, such as leadership and sponsorship, an adequate organizational structure and good communications, highly empowered employees with high morale, an ability for innovation, and open-minded managers who are willing to have everyone in the organization participate in decision making.

What about the loss of jobs resulting from improvement of the way an organization operates, eliminating all waste and focusing on the important processes? How can we expect people to work toward eliminating their jobs? The answer is not an easy one; a miracle solution has not been found yet. However, organizations are thinking about ways and means to alleviate this problem. Some are trying work-sharing or shorter work weeks. Others are helping their members to find other jobs or even start their own businesses. On the other hand, more and more organization members are taking over the responsibility of their job security by designing their own training, experience, and education programs. Rather than trying to require from the organization a guarantee for their job security, they convince their leaders of their possible contribution to the organization's survival and progress, based on their newly acquired training or education.

The more effective total quality processes include plans for the organization's growth. Rather than doing more with less, they are doing more with the same workforce, putting an emphasis on opening new markets and developing new opportunities.

Is all this utopia? It may seem so, but TQM is already a reality in an increasing number of successful organizations, in manufacturing as well as in services, in the private as well as in the public sector, in big organizations as well as in small businesses. Its principles are here to stay, as long as an organization's survival and progress depend on shareholders who want to invest in it, customers who buy its products and pay for its services, and the people in the organization who are deeply convinced of its win–win–win benefits for all.

Notes

1. Rahul Jacob, "TQM: More than a Dying Fad?" *Fortune*, 18 October 1993, 66–72.

2. "Quality 2000: The Next Decade of Progress," *Fortune*, 19 September 1994, 158.

APPENDICES

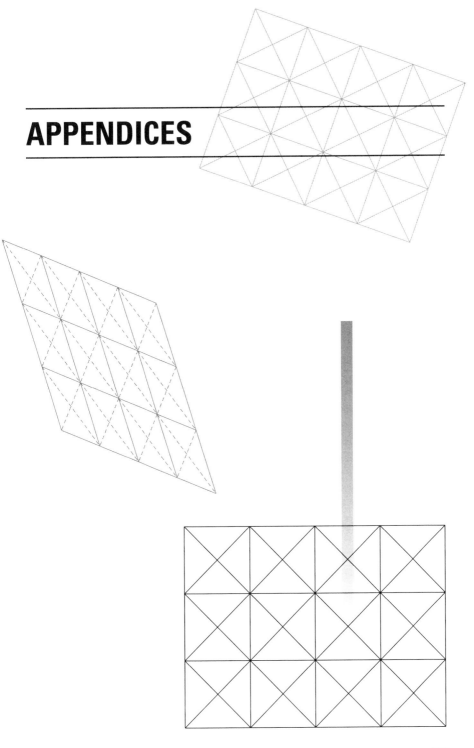

Appendix A

Implementing TQM at Stanford Inc.

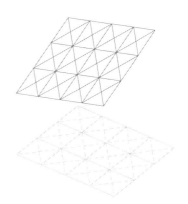

The year is 1990. On a sunny April morning, John Hall, president of Stanford Inc., is sitting at his desk on the thirtieth floor of the building where the company has its home office, which occupies three floors. From a small company that began manufacturing parts for the automotive industry 80 years ago, it has grown into a medium-sized one, with six plants located in three states. Among its customers are the big three, General Motors, Ford, and Chrysler, as well as some European car manufacturers.

Hall is reading an article on TQM. Sam Parkas appears. "You wanted to see me?" he asks. Parkas has been the corporate quality control manager for the past three years. Previously, he worked in manufacturing at one of the plants before moving to inspection and quality control.

"I have to make a decision, Sam," Hall replies. "I am contemplating starting a serious TQM effort at Stanford."

Hall often visits his customers, and notice that, for the past few years, they are all emphasizing quality, on-time deliveries, and TQM. Recently, visiting one of the big three, he notices a tremendous cultural change process working. Employee participation is more than a slogan. Innovative ideas are offered at all levels. Hall is very impressed.

Some time later, he receives an invitation from this customer to attend, with some people from his organization, a quality session that is being offered to its suppliers. The session's objective is to increase their awareness and to encourage them to introduce TQM.

"I want you to come with me to that session," Hall says. "I have asked all of the management team at the home office and two managers from the Cleveland plant to attend it."

Note: This case study is adapted from a true case. The names of companies, persons, and places were changed to preserve their identity. The original case was produced by the Houston-based American Productivity & Quality Center. I thank the Center for their permission to publish this adaptation.

This exposure to the TQM process sparks the interest of Stanford management to pursue a TQM effort. By this time, Hall is committed to leading the leap into an all-out TQM process. The question facing him and his management team is "How?"

Hall forms a Quality Steering Committee with his direct reports and names Sam Parkas the director of what he decides to call the Stanford Total Quality Challenge (STQC). Sam's initial assignment is to find a quality system that would work in the culture of Stanford. Hall also gives Parkas his personal vision of what he believes should be the focus of the company's quality efforts.

- Reduce the proportion of defective products.
- Reduce the cost of quality in the organization.
- Empower all employees in the company.

"Our customer has taken the 'Crosby approach' and tailored it to their own needs and devised an extremely organized way of approaching quality," says Hall.

So the decision is made for Stanford to pursue the Crosby method, and in the summer of 1990, 37 managers are sent to the Crosby College. The management team from the Cleveland plant—known for its desire to improve quality—also attends.

"It will only take a year!" is the phrase that rings in the ears of Sam and his new department from May 1990 to April 1991. But at the end of that year the process doesn't seem to be working in the Stanford environment.

Parkas characterizes the situation this way: "Top management haven't understood the depth of commitment and the time required for the quality effort. The managers haven't shared in developing John's vision for quality and don't understand why they went to the Crosby College. All through the organization people feel that our quality improvement effort is another book-of-the-month from the president. Besides, our employees believe that quality improvement is the responsibility of the STQC department."

But the news isn't all bad. The Cleveland plant has produced some encouraging results. They took the process and ran with it, significantly lowering defects per hundred units and opening up the lines of communication between managers and employees. Things have begun to change for the better in that plant, and employees are excited about participating in the change.

What to Do?

We are now in May 1991. A decision is needed. Stanford has three options, based on the mixed reviews of the first year of involvement.

1. The company can discontinue the process, because it has missed the mark with so many employees.
2. The company can continue the process with just the manufacturing facilities, because that's where there are victories.

3. The company can boldly continue to pursue quality improvement, believing that a shared vision and a different implementation strategy will provide different results.

Stanford's management opts to go forward with the company-wide STQC process. "If we focus on manufacturing, we would be limiting ourselves to improvements in product quality only," Parkas says. "We want to concentrate on improving everything we do, including services provided in our organization, because they all are critical." Parkas begins searching for alternative implementation strategies and realizes that any selected strategy will need to be tailored to fit the 80-year-old culture of Stanford.

An external consultant is brought in to help achieve the proper "fit." The result is the following Crosby-inspired Five Basic Principles, representing Stanford's fundamental beliefs about quality.

- The definition of quality is "conformance to requirements."
- Quality is the responsibility of every employee.
- The system for eliminating defects is the prevention method.
- The standard is zero defects.
- The measurement of quality is its cost in dollars.

The Nine Essentials of the STQC Process

In addition to the Five Basic Principles of Quality, a nine-point strategy for managing quality, the Nine Essentials, is developed—to be implemented by the Quality Teams (QTs). Each Essential is equal in value to the others. Also, each Essential relies on the others to move forward successfully. The Nine Essentials are

- Commitment
- Accountability
- Measurement
- Awareness
- Requirement setting
- Recognition
- Organization
- Problem solving
- Reinforcement

Hall and the Quality Steering Committee meet to discuss their commitment, with the goal of agreement on Hall's vision. They establish a strategy that says everybody will be trained—senior managers will become trainers—and management will become responsible for quality.

The Training Program

Armed with a "Stanford-ized" process, the STQC department focuses on the next phase of development, best described as "Training is the answer." There are some assumptions that accompany this phase.

- The sooner the organization is trained, the greater the results.

- Top management now understands the process, and everyone is committed.
- Culture is an issue, but management's commitment will overcome any obstacles that arise.

The execution of training goes just as planned—from the top down through the organization. Each of Hall's direct reports forms a quality team. A total of 118 plant and home office managers are trained between June of 1991 and April of 1992 to become quality team participants.

Awareness training for the department level problem-solving groups is developed by blending a number of quality gurus' teachings with Stanford's own quality philosophy. The training class is appropriately named "Basics of Quality." This training class is rolled out to all home office employees between December 1991 and May 1992. Department quality teams are set up to tackle problems in their own departments. And the first employee survey is conducted to determine employees' perceptions of management commitment.

Again, the results offer both reason to celebrate and reason to hesitate. On the good news side, the survey results indicate that employees approve of the process. However, the organization now seems appropriately structured to manage the quality improvement effort. Employees finally understand what it means to be a member of a quality team.

On the not-so-bright side, there is a mixed degree of commitment from top management. Some managers are more committed than others. And it shows. Also, it appears that no systems exist to manage accountability, organization, recognition, cost of quality, and problem resolution. The belief is still, "Those things will take care of themselves; don't worry about it."

Lastly, department quality teams are experiencing difficulty in their meetings. Joan Smith, quality education manager, sees the problem this way: "We gave employees a good awareness of quality, but not enough skills." The outcome is that teams are forever needing help with running meetings and accomplishing problem solving. The problems become more obvious and overwhelming than ever. Training has been conducted much too quickly, and top management still has no system in place to guide the process. A structure, yes, but a management system, no.

Problems, problems, problems. Was this to be the sad ending of Stanford's quality improvement drama? A curtain falling before the final scene? Hardly. While many companies might call it quits, Stanford does some intense self-examination and devises a new strategy.

A New, Slower Approach

The brakes are applied with the launching of the third phase. Stanford realizes how rushed the entire process has been and slows matters down to a sensible speed. The quality department and management agree on two major points: management is no longer confused about its role in the process; and a behavioral change on the part of management is mandatory if managers are to effectively facilitate the process.

Training is put on hold until the management plan is developed and implemented by top management. The Quality Education group uses this time to create a new generation of the "Basics of Quality" training that addresses the need for skills development. Nothing is left to chance when it comes time for the execution of this phase. Top management goes on site to initiate the Nine Essentials. Secondary plans are initiated by all of the quality teams. Department quality teams already underway receive additional training upon request. All education is brought in-house.

Once again it's time for a survey to determine how employees perceive management's commitment at this point. "Through the second survey, we wanted to know how our employees felt after they'd received the training," Parkas explains. This time, the report card shows something to feel good about; progress is being made.

Specifically, survey respondents are asked to rank several subjects according to their perceived importance to the company and to themselves. One of the most encouraging changes is that the percentage of employees ranking quality as number one in importance increases from 27 percent in 1992 to 40 percent in 1993. There is also a small increase in the number of employees who perceive quality as number one to the *company*, from 19 percent in 1992 to 21 percent in 1993. Parkas and his crew are particularly pleased with the response to one of the "agree or disagree" statements, which reads "Stanford management is held accountable for modeling and participating in the STQC." In 1993, 62 percent of the respondents agree with this statement.

"This was a big breakthrough for us, because we finally got the message across that management was being held accountable," says Parkas. More evidence of success emerges. The Nine Essentials plan is implemented; problem solving increases; a major, cross-functional, Corrective Action Team unravels a problem with contracting; and a training system for the field is completed.

The training area also enjoys success. The quality team participants who experience the new "Basics of Quality II" training are well prepared to practice the skills for effective meetings, problem solving, and requirement setting.

"Now we're hearing that the classroom practice is fabulous," says Kim Hudson, quality training specialist. "Commitment to the process is much improved; there is genuine confidence in the process. Making certain we tied everything we teach back to the Five Basic Principles and the Nine Essentials helped tremendously." Smith elaborates: "Returning to the 'Basics of Quality' skills training and making those skills applicable was a major win for us. We also established a forum for team building by having intact work groups attend the class together."

The Next Phase

The primary focus of the next phase is to further tailor the STQC process, clarify goals, and roll the process out to the rest of Stanford's 32,000 employees. With the training troubles alleviated, the management system in place, and employees boasting about the process, this next era should see the STQC fitting Stanford.

John Hall sees the following as important to the next phase of the STQC. "It is essential that our objectives are meaningful and understandable to everybody. And that there are real consequences that each one of us can feel personally if we don't reach our goals. Inevitably, behavior will direct itself to consequences. The reduction of our product cycle time is a critical, competitive battleground." he says. "In the next five years, I think response time will have an inverse relationship to success. Cycle time cannot be reduced unless everybody does it right the first time. There are no 'replays' available: execution must be perfect all the time. Commercial success and STQC are inseparable."

"The sunlight is finally beginning to shine through the trees," Parkas sums up. And perhaps attached to the trunks of those trees is the recognized Stanford label, which bears its more than 80-year-old slogan, "Quality First." Now the phrase relates not only to product quality, but to a way of life.

Epilogue

By early 1994, STQC is slowing down again. With the rumor that John Hall will be replaced as president of Stanford, some managers are questioning the relevance of the total quality effort started in 1990. No recognition process has been set up. By the end of 1994, John Hall leaves the company. The new president doesn't think much of the STQC effort. "What did it achieve?" he wonders, while the STQC process grinds to a halt.

Was it a failure? Was it worth the effort, time, and money spent?

According to Suzan Kelly, director of the information systems department, "Employees in my department were using conformance to requirements long before the STQC entered their lives." She explains, "Conformance to requirements has always been the way we look at work—business as usual, if you will. Where we were pretty much novices was in working together in teams to solve problems. For the most part, information systems employees were used to working independently, so working in teams in meetings was uncharted territory."

The ride was rough in the beginning. Employees weren't expressing themselves, and meetings were silent.

"Trust was an issue," Kelly says. "People weren't convinced that speaking freely was a safe thing to do. Our employees took a 'show me' attitude about it."

The information systems management team and the STQC department worked closely together to train more than 40 employees with a wide range of experience to work in groups. While the victories of the department's quality teams may sound less than major, Kelly considers all accomplishments, no matter how small, as successes—especially when groups not accustomed to working together achieve them. So when these teams solved problems with the photocopier, employee holiday schedules, and communications regarding departmental procedures, Kelly was even more convinced of the process's potential.

"The fact that they [the teams] can now run a decent meeting is a sensational step forward, in my opinion," she says. "The STQC process has helped change our environment for the better."

In the finance department, Tom Rich, director of planning, who at the beginning trained "a lot of blank faces" in the STQC process, says his area experienced the same roadblock as the other departments—lack of skills—but he stubbornly asked finance workers to address issues that directly affected them.

"The outcome was encouraging. Our area enjoys better awareness and better communication, and in my mind, if the process has accomplished that much, it's definitely done a lot," says Rich.

But finance deals in dollars, and the process also helped the company recover $200,000 in outstanding credit from vendors. "The reason we recovered that money is because of improved communication," he says. "Our people were no longer afraid to admit that they might not be doing something in the best possible way."

Rich's faith in the STQC effort extends beyond the finance department. He explains: "The distribution facilities have done a marvelous job with this process. I believe they should continue with it even if the rest of the organization calls it quits."

If the Detroit product and process design and review (PPDR) center receives a rush contract and doesn't communicate about its progress toward finishing the contract on time, then a production line in a plant could be left waiting. To guarantee that such a mistake does not occur, the PPDR department quality team identified its handling of rush contracts as a problem and set out to solve it using the tools of TQM.

A rush contract is a request for the PPDR to send instructions to a plant on how to manufacture a made-to-order part. The problem was that the PPDRs in other locations were not aware that they had to rush information back to Detroit. They also needed to set realistic due dates and to give notice if the original due date had to be changed.

"We were causing scheduling headaches for our internal customers, who are production and inventory control [PIC] and the plants," says Patricia Goulet, team member and manager of CAD-CAM Systems at the Detroit PPDR. "Changing dates was also hurting our credibility. It was like saying 'The check's in the mail' when it really wasn't."

To make the remote PPDRs aware of the problem and to track it, Goulet started to graph the department's performance on failures to communicate a due date, failure to communicate a changed due date, and missed due dates. She sent completed graphs to the remote PPDRs at least once a month.

Goulet credits the graphs, which are one of the tracking tools taught in STQC, with helping the department overcome the largest obstacle to solving the problem: convincing everyone that a genuine problem existed.

Once department members were convinced, the team then carefully set requirements for communicating among all PPDR locations. The department quality team began tracking the problem in April 1993. The first graphs went out in

June, and by September the graphs showed zero defects. All due dates were communicated, all revised dates were communicated, and no due dates were missed.

Goulet continued to produce the graphs for three more months, and each showed zero defects. She continues spot-checking the department's performance, and it continues to be flawless. "Solving the problem has really improved our credibility with our internal customers" says Goulet, "and we can do our job better. That makes life easier for the scheduler in PIC and the plants."

As we can see, the STQC process didn't revolutionize Stanford, but it did leave some tangible results.

Appendix B

Excerpt from Canadian General Standards Board Quality Assessment Program Manual

Phase One: Application and Undertaking

Manufacturers wishing to participate in the listing program submit to CGSB an Application and Undertaking form, together with a description of the facilities to be listed. This form is a legal document which, when signed by a senior official of the company, grants CGSB the authority to audit the firm's quality system. In signing the form, the applicant undertakes to

- Abide by the terms and conditions of the program.
- Maintain a system of quality assurance that will ensure the continuing quality of its products.
- Document the quality system.
- Assist CGSB staff, or their representatives, in conducting their on-site audits.
- Pay all applicable program fees.

The requirements for an adequate quality program are outlined in the publication *ISO 9004—Guidelines*. Manufacturers must include the application fee, as outlined in the costing section of this manual.

Please note: All documents and information submitted by an applicant to CGSB are treated in the strictest confidence and will not be released without the prior consent of the applicant.

Phase Two: Quality Model Selection

To participate in this program it is necessary to select one of the three quality models of the ISO 9000 series. The Guide for the Selection of a Quality Model in this manual will be a useful tool in this selection. You may also wish to review the ISO 9000 series completely to evaluate which model is best for you. The Procedure Evaluation Checklists included in this manual contain all of the elements of each of the ISO 9000 models.

In many cases your customer has already specified a quality level. In this case, selection is easy. However, you may still wish to use the selection guide and/or the Procedure Evaluation Checklists to evaluate your own system or to establish a different quality level. It must be stressed that ISO 9001 will not necessarily represent a higher level of quality than ISO 9003. The quality level must be selected on the basis of a real need.

To participate in the program, it is necessary for CGSB to review the logic behind the program selection. The Guide for the Selection of a Quality Model provides a satisfactory mechanism for this.

Phase Three: Quality Assurance System Evaluation/Procedure Compliance Audit

Upon receipt of a completed application form, together with all substantiating documents and the application fee, CGSB will evaluate the manufacturer's documented quality system against the applicable ISO 9000 quality system model. A guide to the use of the Procedure Evaluation Checklists is included in this manual. Should the documented system be insufficient, the supplier will be notified in writing of the problem areas. Assistance will be given to the manufacturer if required.

When the documented system is considered to be sufficient, a date for verification of compliance to the documented quality system will be arranged with the manufacturer.

An audit team will assess compliance to the documented quality system. Should major nonconformances be observed, the manufacturer will be notified verbally at the time of the audit, and later in writing. Corrective action will be assessed by CGSB to determine compliance to the ISO standard.

Phase Four: Program Listing and Licensing

All information provided by the manufacturer, together with the results of the audit, will be reviewed by CGSB. Upon technical review of the application and supporting documents, CGSB may accept or reject the application, or ask that additional information be provided. With successful application, CGSB identifies the manufacturer, the facility, the listing number, and the extent of recognition on the Registration List.

Firms qualifying for registration are required to enter into a license agreement with CGSB authorizing their use of the CGSB Certification Mark. The Certification Mark is a registered mark that is recognized nationwide as a symbol of quality and can be used on business stationery and promotional material. License agreements are renewable annually, provided that the program requirements continue to be met. Manufacturers on the Registration List are also identified with a unique CGSB listing number.

Phase Five: Ongoing Quality Assurance Audits

CGSB will monitor the manufacturer's quality assurance system a minimum of once per year. In this capacity, CGSB acts as an independent third party, ensuring impartiality and fairness, thereby maintaining the integrity of the program. In the event of repeated quality problems, complaints from users, or other evidence that indicates a lack of quality assurance within the manufacturing facility, CGSB may, at its discretion, conduct more frequent audits or delist the manufacturer.

Results of the ongoing quality assurance system audits are reviewed by CGSB. The manufacturer will be notified of any deficiencies identified and may be asked to comment or take corrective action. Participants who fail to demonstrate their ability or willingness to meet the program requirements within a specified time frame will be delisted.

Delisting, Appeals, and Reapplication

If a major noncompliance occurs, or a series of faults is identified, the manufacturer will be given the opportunity to offer an explanation and to voluntarily take corrective action within a specified time frame. Such action may include

- Improvement of the documented quality system
- Demonstrated compliance to the quality system (internal audit)

CGSB may also choose to increase the frequency of audit, or return to the facility to verify the effectiveness of the corrective action. Failure to comply with the program's requirements will result in delisting. Any decision made against the manufacturer by CGSB may be appealed. Details of the appeals process are available from CGSB. Manufacturers who wish to reapply to the program following delisting must repeat the entire listing process.

Preparing the Application: One Step at a Time

• *Step 1: Application and undertaking form.* This is a legal document certifying your company's commitment to quality and adherence to the appropriate quality model. The form must be signed by a senior company official in charge of quality assurance and by a responsible officer of the company (president, vice president, secretary, or treasurer).

• *Step 2: Quality model selection.* Select a Quality Model using the Guide for the Selection of a Quality Model.

• *Step 3: Procedure Evaluation Checklist.* Complete the relevant Procedure Evaluation Checklist, using the guide supplied, and submit all supporting documentation or present a matrix referencing where in your quality documentation conformance to the ISO 9000 model will be found.

• *Step 4: Send all documents and checks for the registration fee to:*

Quality Assessment Program
Qualification and Certification Listing Branch
Canadian General Standards Board
Ottawa, Canada K1A 1G6

APPLICATION

The

_____

(Legal Name of Applicant Company)

_____

_____

(Address of Applicant Company)

Hereinafter called the "applicant," hereby applies for listing for the manufacturing facilities listed on the attached "Facility Listing" form.

UNDERTAKING

The Applicant by and through its responsible officer states and undertakes:

That the applicable provisions of the international ISO 9000 series of quality assurance standards will be met;

That the attached list of manufacturing facilities meet the provisions of the applicable ISO 9000 quality model;

That all production of the above facility will be to the company's current specifications and will continue to meet the requirements of the applicable ISO 9000 document;

That the company management is familiar with, and accepts the conditions governing, this Listing as described in the Qualification and Certification Listing Branch Policies, November 1990.

That CGSB or its authorized representatives shall be permitted to inspect the manufacturing and quality assurance facilities at such times and in such a manner as CGSB shall decide;

To agree to abide by the applicable provisions of the program manual, a copy of which is acknowledged to have been received.

IN WITNESS WHEREOF this Application for Listing and Licensing has been executed by the Manufacturer this day of

_____ 19 _____

_____

(Signature) (Senior Manager in Charge of Quality Assurance)

_____

(Signature) (Responsible Officer of the Applicant Company)

NOTE:

The application must include:

1) A completed Application and Undertaking form.
2) A completed Guide for the Selection of a Quality Model.
3) A completed Procedure Evaluation Checklist and all relevant quality documentation.

Appendix C

Case Study: Theory and Application of TQM—TQM at AT&T Transmission Systems

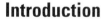

Introduction

As we have seen in chapter 13, achieving and maintaining total quality entails first understanding the total quality triad triple objective, where shareholders, customers, and people in the organization mutually satisfy each other's needs. Then, a number of management practices must be used in order to meet these objectives.

AT&T Transmission Systems successfully implemented this approach. This case study shows how the concepts and practices presented in this book in general, and in chapter 13 in particular, can be applied in real life.

According to Robert H. Seemer,[1] AT&T Transmission Systems entered the competition for the 1992 Malcolm Baldrige National Quality Award because it wanted to accelerate the integration of its total quality management system for its customers, employees, and shareholders. The successful two-and-one-half-year challenge put to rest arguments that achieving dramatic results through TQM is a five-year process.

In October 1992, AT&T Transmission Systems Business Unit (TBU) was awarded the hotly pursued Baldrige Award. To better understand the value of the TQM philosophy, let us accompany the AT&T TBU on its two-and-one-half-year odyssey toward this achievement. It was a journey that endured setbacks and leadership changes, a journey that demonstrated that a few key principles and shared values, coupled with proven management processes, can unite a large organization and enable it to achieve its vision.

A Total Quality Management System: The Theory

Seemer suggests that TQM is nothing more than an approach to running a business that is both comprehensive and natural because it depends on balancing the needs of business stakeholders—customers, employees, shareholders, suppliers, and communities.

Companies that find themselves in trouble often discover that they have concentrated too much on one stakeholder and placed insufficient emphasis on the others. For example, reducing expenses across the board to ensure satisfactory, short-term shareholder return on investment may negatively affect customer satisfaction or employees' attitudes. The TQM system is comprehensive because it depends on the effective—and efficient—use of all resources. It also incorporates all management tools espoused by the latest gurus. These tools, such as benchmarking, cycle time reduction, and just-in-time manufacturing, are of little practical value if not applied in a larger management framework. The framework is TQM.

To meet the needs of these stakeholder groups, all of which seem at times to have conflicting demands, the company must learn to optimize. The quest for balance and optimization drives the need to focus, prioritize, align scarce resources, manage with facts, and work as a team. Success in these areas enables the TQM system to meet its purpose: to achieve the organization's primary objective

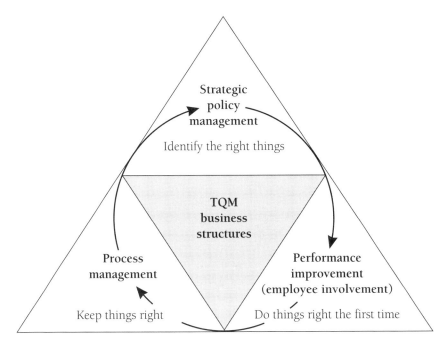

Figure C.1. TQM business structures.

by providing the greatest value of products and services to the customer at the lowest possible cost to society. To achieve this balance, shared business values must join proven business structures and TQM principles to drive the appropriate behaviors and action toward the achievement of the organization's vision. The TQM system is composed of three major business structures, or components (see Figure C.1). These three structures encourage the members of an organization to identify the right thing to do, to do it right the first time, and to keep it right.

Strategic policy management is the process that enables an organization to implement a results-oriented approach. It provides a focus on strategic and operational priorities and promotes resource alignment independent of organizational boundaries. It enhances management involvement because, through it, management's priorities receive attention. Through strategic policy management, the organization's vision is formulated and then broken down into its key components. Each component is translated into priorities and actions that are deployed into the business. Collectively, the successful performance of the activities throughout the organization enables the vision to be achieved. By identifying and directing attention to the right things, strategic policy management and deployment provides a systematic process for achieving the company's vision. Through it, the organization's focus is directed toward stakeholder-oriented operational improvements and strategic growth opportunities (see Figure C.2).

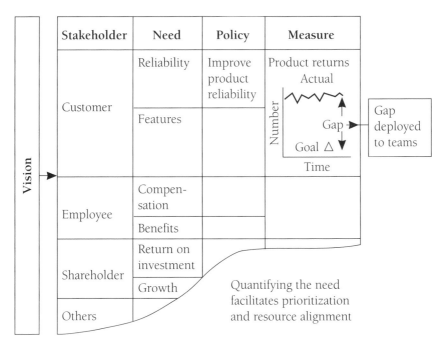

Figure C.2. Strategic policy management.

The performance improvement, or employee involvement, component is usually equated with quality circles or teams. However, this segment also includes employee suggestions and contributions from individual workers. Most companies begin their TQM implementation effort with quality improvement teams. This approach is often referred to as the *activity-based approach*—many teams working on activities important in each one's own context but collectively having no significant impact on the company's bottom line. Quality teams without policy-directed focus are much like nails without a hammer. Companies with a teams-only approach usually abandon TQM implementation, concluding that the process just isn't compatible with their corporate culture. To be effective, teams need direction, training, coaching, and feedback. Employees not trained to logically address issues or conduct root-cause analysis will probably have difficulty in doing their jobs right the first time. As Figure C.3 shows, one measure of team success is the impact a team has on its portion of the gap between actual performance and the team's goal.

Process management, or quality in daily work (QDW), is instrumental in involving all employees in TQM. Not all employees are involved in a policy-directed initiative, nor do they get involved in quality teams or turn in suggestions. However, every employee is linked to a superior's accountability and is a part of the process to fulfill that accountability. This is the realm of process management and a key to defect prevention and employee empowerment. Moreover, by standardizing improvement, process management establishes accountability to ensure that policy issues stay under control (see Figure C.4). Here are its other key objectives.

• It helps maintain the gains achieved through policy management and quality teams—it keeps things right.

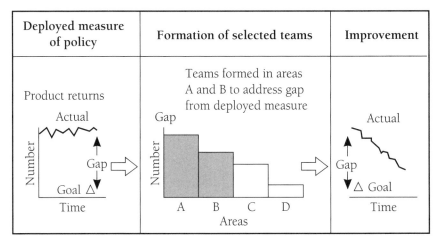

Figure C.3. Performance improvement through employee involvement.

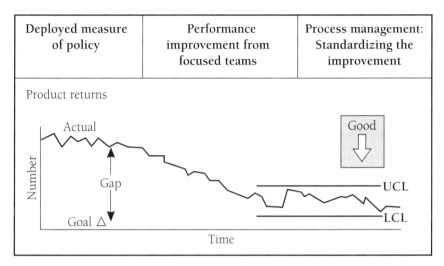

Figure C.4. Process management—maintaining the gains.

• It focuses attention on the core processes critical to the success of a company, such as new product introduction, the billing process, and customer service.

• It directs attention to the primary accountabilities of every supervisor and the process measures of success for these accountabilities.

• It facilitates the standardization and replication of best practices and helps prevent time wasted in "reinventing the wheel."

• It improves all processes in an organization by linking individual account-abilities to the core functions of the business. Core functions are processes that are critical to the organization's success and may be considered competitive strengths or weaknesses. Departments must understand how the successful fulfillment of their accountabilities contributes to competitive advantage.

As Figure C.5 shows, the manufacturing department would evaluate its key accountabilities and determine the impact each can have on the core functions. It must define the measures of success for each accountability's process and ensure that those processes meet the needs of the next customer (or partner) in line.

Applying TQM Principles

The three components of TQM are of little practical value unless some common principles are applied. The following principles are characteristic of companies that are successfully applying total quality management.

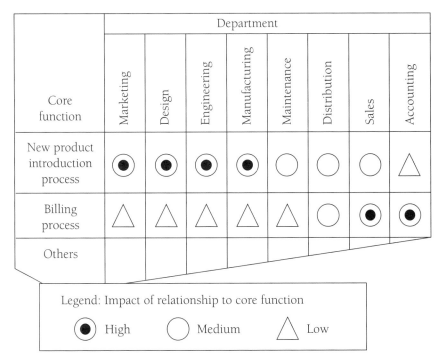

Figure C.5. Process management—engaging the entire organization.

• *Customer focus.* Without customer focus integrated with strategic thinking, policies have little meaning. By understanding its ability to meet the evolving needs of customers in changing markets, an organization can maintain a clear focus on what is important.

• *Managing with facts.* Understanding the customer's need is important, but only by quantifying the need in measurable terms can an organization know how it is doing in meeting the need. Measurements and data enable managers to prioritize and allocate scarce resources, verify root causes, develop appropriate plans, and measure the impact of their efforts to achieve performance improvements.

• *Respect for people.* Tapping and cultivating the limitless potential of people enables the management system to work. True performance improvement can be accomplished and sustained only through the effective use of people as individuals or as members of teams.

• *Plan-do-check-act.* PDCA is the model for continuous improvement. Plan your initiative with customer focused facts. Do—that is, implement—the plan, ensuring that the organization is trained and capable of achieving the plan's goals. Check, or measure, the success of the implementation in the same terms with which the plan was formulated. Act to standardize improvements, incorporate lessons learned into future plans, and provide appropriate coaching and recognition after documenting all results.

The three TQM components and the four principles are difficult to consistently apply without a common structure to reinforce their effective and coordinated application. The QC story method serves this function and may just be the most powerful tool in any employee's—or company's—toolbox. Recall the first documented formal application of a QC story: Japan's Komatsu Corporation, in 1960. Developed initially as an approach to present and communicate quality improvement activities, its logic-based format lent itself to analysis as well. Incorporating statistical tools and graphics into the QC story strengthened the process because teams began to replace opinions with facts in order to solve problems. Management focus began to shift from *who* was responsible to *what* was the cause of the problem. As employees and management began to speak with facts, employees felt less at risk in exposing problems. By 1962, Komatsu had embarked on a plan to train all employees in this approach to statistical problem solving and communication.

Figure C.6 outlines the steps in the QC story and the statistical tools used. The concepts of the QC story can be used to formulate corporate strategy and policy, reduce the gaps in operating performance indicators, and reduce special

The 7 basic QC statistical tools
Cause and effect analysis Checklists Control charts Graphs (bar, line, pie) Histograms Pareto charts Scatter diagrams

	QC story steps
Plan	1. Consider improvement needs (broad issues, stakeholders focused) 2. Select a specific issue (narrow the focus) 3. Analyze the problem (determine root causes) 4. Take corrective action (develop action plan)
Do	Implement plan
Check	5. Measure effects
Act	6. Control and replicate 7. Evaluate plan

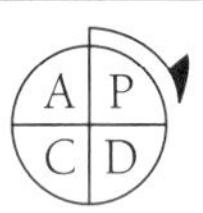

Figure C.6. The QC story: structured problem solving and logical thinking.

and common causes of process variation. The QC story method promotes the application of the four TQM principles by the following:

• Considering and selecting improvement needs by focusing on the customer or other key stakeholders.

• Ensuring that needs, as well as conclusions, are supported with data. Facts are the key to prioritizing and allocating scarce resources, as well as to knowing how well stakeholder needs are being satisfied.

• Providing employees with the capability to improve operations and to communicate in a common language to all levels of an organization. This is a key to empowerment. It is also a critical step to tapping unrealized organizational capability.

• Reinforcing the PDCA concept. If plans are driven by stakeholder needs data, gains are maintained; and if lessons learned are applied to future plans, continuous improvement will be promoted.

Critics usually attack structured problem-solving methods as restrictive to creative thought or too cumbersome to enable a team to solve a problem quickly. They fail to see the big picture. Organizations are composed of people with varying degrees of knowledge, skills, and capabilities. The QC story provides them all with a common thought and communication process.

TQM and Growth Strategies

The TQM system can become the process to improve operational performance or increase strategic capability. Most companies begin TQM implementation by focusing on problems, such as customer dissatisfaction or operating costs. This singular approach leads to at least one issue that must be confronted head-on: quality improvement increases productivity. Why would this be considered an issue? Because as Figure C.7 shows, applying quality management concepts only to reduce problems is a no-growth approach benefiting nobody in the long term. This is the single greatest argument by employee groups against TQM. Employee layoffs that can result from problem reduction also conflict with the TQM principle of respect for people. Therefore, management must incorporate growth strategies into its business system and increase revenues faster than productivity growth. This strategy will address the needs of all stakeholders—employees and shareholders alike. Focusing only on removing customer dissatisfaction will not

Figure C.7.   The quality improvement paradox.

		Total quality management structures							
		Principles			Business components				
		Customer focus	Respect people	Manage with facts	PDCA	Strategic policy management	Performance improvement	Process management	QC story
Baldrige categories	1) Leadership					✓			✓
	2) Information and analysis			✓					✓
	3) Strategic planning				✓	✓			✓
	4) Human resource management	✓					✓		✓
	5) Management of process quality				✓			✓	✓
	6) Quality and operation results				✓				✓
	7) Customer focus and satisfaction	✓							✓

Figure C.8. The relationship between the Baldrige Award criteria and TQM.

create satisfied or excited customers. Furthermore, focusing only on problem reduction does not help the business grow.

The criteria for the Malcolm Baldrige National Quality Award can be used to measure the degree of TQM system implementation. The criteria address the business components and principles discussed, and, of course, more that have not been discussed. Figure C.8 is a simplified matrix depicting the relationship between the seven Baldrige categories and the principles and components of TQM.

Because these criteria can be used to measure progress in implementing TQM, striving for the Baldrige Award can unite an organization toward a time-oriented goal. Winning an award is not a valid reason for implementing TQM, nor will it ensure profitability. Many critics fail to recognize the difference between the award—and its criteria—as a measuring tool and as a goal in itself. Many Baldrige Award and other quality award winners have also had the same problem.

AT&T Transmission Systems

In April 1989, AT&T announced that it was restructuring the company into 20 business units, one of which was the TBU. As a developer and manufacturer of systems for transporting voice and image data, it serves a global market and competes head-on with some of the best-known electronics manufacturers in the world. Emerging from a predivestiture, monopolistic environment, the new TBU leadership team, headed by Pete Fenner, president of the unit, realized that to retain and strengthen its position as an industry leader, it had to revamp its management system.

Winning an award is not a valid reason for implementing TQM, nor will it ensure profitability.

Although quality-related activities, such as teams, had been in place for some time in TBU's factories, these efforts were deemed insufficient to provide the results that were required in an increasingly competitive global market. The unit needed to develop a vision of its future and a management system to achieve it. Management wanted to build on the AT&T tradition of quality and its existing team activities. At a point at which many companies discard their quality programs, TBU examined its management system's gaps to determine causes and formulate actions for improvement. During 1989, TBU leadership formulated a vision of what they wanted the organization to become. This vision, however, was not just to be engraved on another nice plaque on the wall. It was going to become a dominant theme that could unite all employees toward a common goal. TBU's vision called for

- Being the best at everything it does, and exceeding customer expectations
- Expanding its business to increase in value to customers, employees, shareowners, and the communities in which TBU works
- Remaining integral with Network Systems in the achievement of AT&T's mission

Because many visions come and go, however, a process had to be found to enable the TBU to achieve its vision. During 1990, TBU management learned of a process for doing that that had worked for some companies. Called strategic policy management, or policy deployment, it was a lot like management by objectives (MBO) as practiced in many large corporations, but with a few key differences, which are outlined in Figure C.9. Basically, policy deployment differs from MBO in its emphasis on process improvement to achieve results and in its participative characteristics.

In May 1990, the TBU leadership team had its first policy deployment workshop. Armed with little more than its vision and plenty of skepticism, the group struggled for two days but came to some harsh realizations regarding

- *Customers.* Who are our customers, anyway, and what do they want?

Management by objectives (MBO)	Policy deployment (strategic policy management)
Focus on financial costs	Focus on customers, improving quality to improve financials
Focus on control	Emphasis on improvement
Top-down orientation, mostly one-way	Top-down but with "catchball" (negotiation with facts in a spirit of win–win) between organizational levels
Results achieved by managing the target	Results achieved by managing the process affecting the target

Figure C.9. Management by objectives vs. policy deployment.

- *Teams.* We have lots of quality teams already, but they're not able to give us the bottom-line impact we need.
- *Rabbits.* We already have too many rabbits to chase, and now we have to do this quality stuff.

The executive team began to address these critical issues one by one in the context of the TQM system.

Customers

Customer needs were known in the general sense, but not specifically in many cases. In addition, the customers' weighting of specific needs was not known and the TBU's performance in meeting the needs was not well understood or quantified. Many performance measures were internally focused and did not include the customers' viewpoint. This helped explain much of the discrepancy between performance indicators and customer feedback report cards.

To overcome this information shortcoming, the management team tentatively spoke for the customer by developing an initial list of specific needs and ranking their importance. Next, they developed indicators to determine existing TBU performance levels for each one. To prioritize their efforts, they used the approach depicted in Figure C.10, which determines priorities by considering the customer's rank of importance and the company's need to improve performance for each individual need.

At first glance, this approach appears to be in direct conflict with the TQM principle of management with facts. However, developing this information through formal market research would have taken at least nine months. More-

Customer need	Importance weight		Need to improve performance		Overall score
Reliability	4.8	×	5.0	=	24.0
Features	4.5		3.2		14.4
Price	4.4				
Others					

Priority →

Legend: 1 = Low   5 = High
Note: Highest scores are priorities

Figure C.10. Determining performance levels.

over, marketing and management already had a strong sense of the customers' needs and felt that they knew enough or could collect sufficient data to get started. Finally, because management was going to deploy more than one priority, there was a good chance that the right ones would be selected anyway; just the order of importance might be different. It was either start now or wait until next year. Management developed a list of deployment candidates and collected sufficient marketing and performance data to validate conclusions and make necessary adjustments to the list.

Teams

How can teams be used to get better results? Up to this point, employees had received training in team-building skills but little in the way of structured problem solving and root-cause analysis. Teams had used fishbone (cause-and-effect) diagrams before, but fishbones did not help verify root causes. Teams that did develop seemingly good recommendations often had difficulty communicating their ideas through multiple layers of management. A method for to thinking logically and analytically about issues and then communicating ideas in a common language throughout the entire organization was needed. The answer to this problem was the quality control story, or as known in TBU, the quality improvement story (QIS).

During the initial policy deployment workshop, one TBU executive said that if there was a way to prioritize vision-driven policy issues, then teams could be engaged to work on those issues using data to determine root causes and provide recommendations that would have impact; thus performance breakthroughs on corporate issues could be achieved. Management came up with the term *the Golden Thread* to identify the links between the customer-focused priority on the top floor and the employee working on a data-driven issue on the shop floor. These links improved the quality of the product or service to that customer. The management team members were now on a mission to create Golden Threads from their vision-driven stakeholder policies. They had a reason to be excited, for people working on teams would be addressing issues critical to the success of the company. In a sense, employees could influence their own futures.

A method to think logically and analytically about issues and then communicate ideas in a common language throughout the entire organization was needed.

Rabbits

During the workshop, enthusiasm to move forward was so great that priorities multiplied like rabbits. The management team knew that not all could receive priority treatment. Coordinating executives were assigned to each rabbit. Their mission was to use data to identify the fat rabbits. The management team would then use the resulting information to prioritize activities for incorporation into the business plan. The fat rabbits were selected for policy deployment, and accountability was established to ensure that Golden Threads were created. Benchmarking was used to establish world-class performance targets. By early July 1990, the management team had achieved some critical milestones established during the policy deployment workshop. For example, it finalized policy deployment priorities with which to engage the organization. The team also developed an education and training plan to enable the appropriate parts of the organization to competently address the priorities. The plan required that

- All policy deployment initiatives coordinating executives and their respective teams would receive policy management, quality improvement story, and quality control tools training.
- More than 700 middle-management employees would receive policy management overview, quality improvement story, and quality control tools training.
- More than 2000 employees at all levels, from the top floor to the shop floor, would receive quality improvement story and quality control tools training.
- Sixty-six team leaders with a vested interest in the policy deployment priorities would initially be trained in an intense, four-day, team leader skills workshop. They would be expected to coach their team members in the application of the quality improvement story process on Golden Thread issues. Reviews were

scheduled every 4 to 6 weeks to enable management to coach and advise the teams, thus facilitating progress. The 66 stories were to become the role models for hundreds of teams and stories to follow throughout the TBU and the rest of AT&T. As part of the training, an explanation of how initial TBU policy, shared values, vision, and purpose were developed was provided to the employees to help them understand the origins of the Golden Threads.

Management felt that committing the organization to a time line would spur it to rally behind the cause.

Putting the Model to Work

By the fall of 1990, the TBU had developed its vision, purpose, and shared values and was on the way toward incorporating them into the TQM model (see Figure C.11). By February 1991, some progress was being made in a few areas, but TQM system integration was not occurring. Anxious to accelerate the process, TBU executive management announced that it would submit an application for the 1991 Malcolm Baldrige Award. Management felt that committing the organization to a time line would spur it to rally behind the cause. To jump-start the process, the policy deployment training was rolled out to the 700 middle managers. Also, the 66 team leaders were trained to create the Golden Threads. Much progress was made; the self-assessment scores against the Baldrige examination items almost doubled in six months. Remarkably, the TBU did receive a Baldrige site visit, but was not given an award. Still, the challenge was considered a success because it raised the level of performance—and self-expectations—throughout the organization.

During the winter of 1991, two TBU manufacturing facilities continued to make progress in product and service quality. Return rates on one key product had decreased by over 50 percent in less than 9 months, and on-time delivery performance improved significantly. But staff groups were still not fully engaged. Without them, system integration and maximum gains could not be achieved.

Providing customers with maximum utility from hardware requires high-quality software. The TBU has an extensive software development organization of some 850 people. In February 1992, Mal Buchner, vice president of the TBU, determined that all senior-level managers and scientists would be trained in a customized version of the four-day team leader course. Departmental priorities linked to TBU policies were immediately selected, and the rest of the organization was trained in a customized version of the quality improvement story and quality control tools. Software quality began to improve.

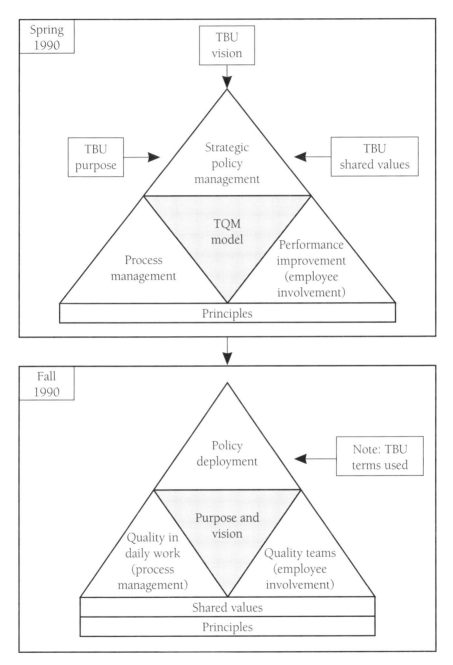

Figure C.11. Evolution of TBU management system.

At the same time, hardware designers and engineers began linking their goals to factory initiatives, and product quality continued to improve as designs became more robust. Not only were Golden Threads becoming more obvious, but more and more employees began to understand their roles in supporting them. Golden Threads were now extending from the customers to the employees on the shop floor, from the marketing specialists to the designers, from the factories to the parts suppliers. Integration was rapidly occurring. (For a closer look at how a Golden Thread can lead to improvement, see the section at the end of this appendix).

Bring on the Baldrige

By April 1992, it was clear that there was a renewed enthusiasm throughout the TBU. Operational indicators were improving significantly, and employee climate/attitude surveys had shown dramatic improvement in key areas. The momentum was building, and management, once again, announced the challenge for the Baldrige Award. On October 15, 1992, AT&T Transmission Systems was announced among the winners. It was evident to the examiners that the TBU management system was the process that had led to the many dramatic, operational performance improvements and the resulting increase in overall customer satisfaction.

A change of TBU presidents in June 1992 did not deter progress. Greg Hughes, the new president, had also been trained in the new management system and had been using it to manage another business unit. He simply continued the process. His commitment to stakeholder satisfaction through TQM and business growth assured all employees that this was not "just another program."

TBU is still short of achieving its vision for the next few years, but few now doubt that it will not be achieved. In a highly competitive and global business, one thing is certain: Determined employees with a process make their own conditions; they don't become victims of them. Only two-and-one-half years had passed between the first policy deployment workshop and the award announcement.

How a TBU Golden Thread Leads to Improvement

Golden Threads are created when the TQM business structures and principles are in harmony with the company's vision, purpose, and shared values. Effective application of TBU's quality improvement story process helps integrate these components to produce dramatic improvement. Figures C.12 and C.13 detail the improvements created when a Golden Thread links the TBU vision, customer, and employee with data.

In Section 1 of Figure C.12, the stakeholders' needs and the TBU's strategic intent are evaluated with respect to the vision, purpose, and shared values. Policy is formulated and fundamental objectives are developed. Fundamental objectives are measurable components of the vision.

In Section 2, the fundamental objectives are documented along with the corporate-level, detailed objectives and individual projects on the policy deployment matrix. The means by which the project will be measured and the goal also are included. The gap is analyzed through task teams with subject matter experts to determine where deployment, or the Golden Threads, should go to have the greatest impact. The circuit pack return rate is 145 per 10,000. The benchmarked goal for 1992 is 25 per 10,000 with a target of 1 per 10,000 by 1995.

In Section 3, the gap is stratified and more teams are formed to address the various bars on the Pareto charts—for example, components and transformers.

Section 4 shows how a team will evaluate the situation to identify a problem that is significant—for example, internal open circuits—and try to determine its root causes.

In Section 5, the team uses creative and subjective tools, such as brainstorming, consensus voting, and the fishbone diagram to determine potential causes. Other QC tools, such as histograms, scatter diagrams, and Pareto charts, help verify the root causes and assess the impact of each cause on the internal open circuit problem.

In Section 6, cost-effective countermeasures with an action plan are developed to attack the verified root causes. Accountability, schedule, and contingencies are also established to ensure success.

Section 7 measures results in the same terms as the root causes, and problems are quantified in the current situation and analysis sections (3, 4, and 5).

In Section 8, the impact on the policy deployment indicator is finally determined. In this case, just 1 team was able to reduce the circuit pack return rate from 145 per 10,000 to 126 per 10,000, or a 13 percent reduction.

In Section 9, improvements are standardized to prevent problem recurrence and then shared with other locations to prevent duplication of efforts.

In Section 10, remaining problems are addressed, and lessons learned are incorporated into future plans.

Section 11 shows that many teams improving operational performance in policy-focused areas can have a significant impact on customer satisfaction.

Finally, Figure C.13 shows the route of one Golden Thread from the customer to employees on teams.

By October 1992, the circuit pack return rate had been reduced from 145 per 10,000 to 29 per 10,000, well on the way to the interim goal of 25 per 10,000 by the end of 1992 and within reach of the previously unbelievable goal of 1 per 10,000 by 1995.

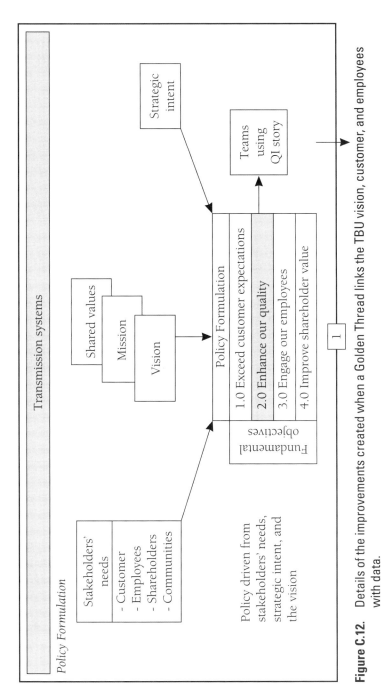

Figure C.12. Details of the improvements created when a Golden Thread links the TBU vision, customer, and employees with data.

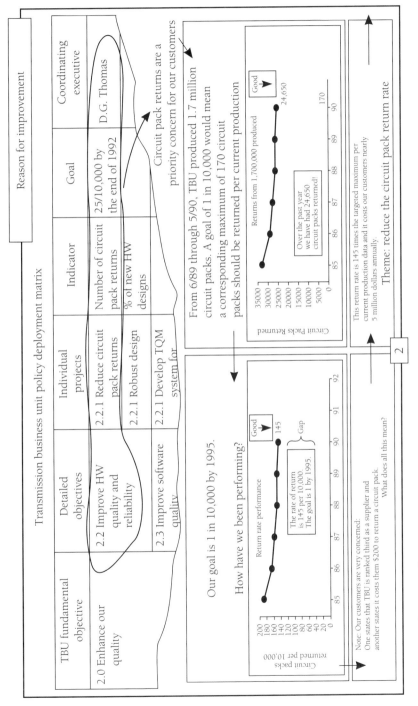

Reason for improvement

Transmission business unit policy deployment matrix

TBU fundamental objective	Detailed objectives	Individual projects	Indicator	Goal	Coordinating executive
2.0 Enhance our quality	2.2 Improve HW quality and reliability	2.2.1 Reduce circuit pack returns	Number of circuit pack returns	25/10,000 by the end of 1992	D.G. Thomas
		2.2.1 Robust design	% of new HW designs		
	2.3 Improve software quality	2.2.1 Develop TQM system for			

Circuit pack returns are a priority concern for our customers

From 6/89 through 5/90, TBU produced 1.7 million circuit packs. A goal of 1 in 10,000 would mean a corresponding maximum of 170 circuit packs should be returned per current production

Returns from 1,700,000 produced

Over the past year we have had 24,650 circuit packs returned!

Good →

24,650

170

Circuit Packs Returned
35000 30000 25000 20000 15000 10000 5000 0
85 86 87 88 89 90

Our goal is 1 in 10,000 by 1995.

How have we been performing?

Return rate performance

The rate of return is 145 per 10,000. The goal is 1 by 1995.

Good →

Gap

145

Circuit packs returned per 10,000
200 180 160 140 120 100 80 60 40 20 0
85 86 87 88 89 90 91 92

What does all this mean?

Note: Our customers are very concerned. One states that TBU is ranked third as a supplier and another states it costs them $200 to return a circuit pack.

This return rate is 145 times the targeted maximum per current production data and it costs our customers nearly 5 million dollars annually.

Theme: reduce the circuit pack return rate

2

Figure C.12. (continued)

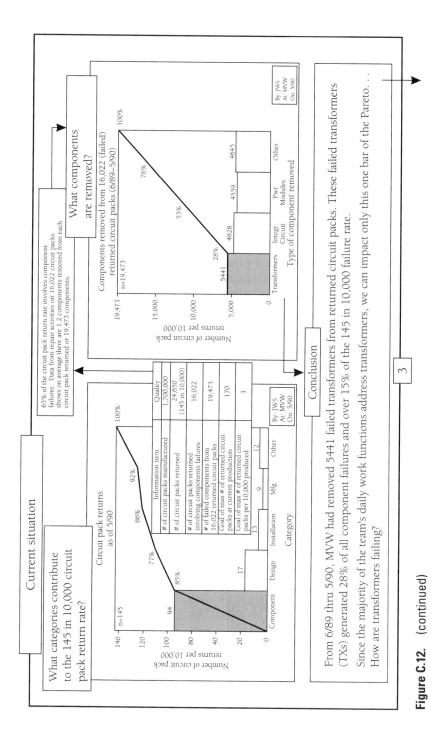

Figure C.12. (continued)

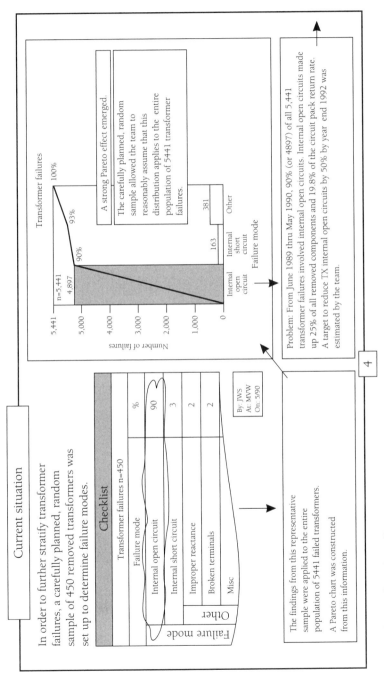

Current situation

In order to further stratify transformer failures, a carefully planned, random sample of 450 removed transformers was set up to determine failure modes.

Checklist

Transformer failures n=450		%
Failure mode		
Internal open circuit		90
Internal short circuit		3
Improper reactance		2
Broken terminals		2
Misc		2

By: JWS
At: MVW
On: 5/90

The findings from this representative sample were applied to the entire population of 5441 failed transformers.

A Pareto chart was constructed from this information.

Transformer failures

A strong Pareto effect emerged.

The carefully planned, random sample allowed the team to reasonably assume that this distribution applies to the entire population of 5441 transformer failures.

Pareto chart — Number of failures vs Failure mode:
- Internal open circuit: 4,897 (90%)
- Internal short circuit: 163 (93%)
- Other: 381 (100%)
- n=5,441

Problem: From June 1989 thru May 1990, 90% (or 4897) of all 5,441 transformer failures involved internal open circuits. Internal open circuits made up 25% of all removed components and 19.8% of the circuit pack return rate. A target to reduce TX internal open circuits by 50% by year end 1992 was estimated by the team.

4

Figure C.12. (continued)

435

Analysis

What causes transformer internal open circuits?

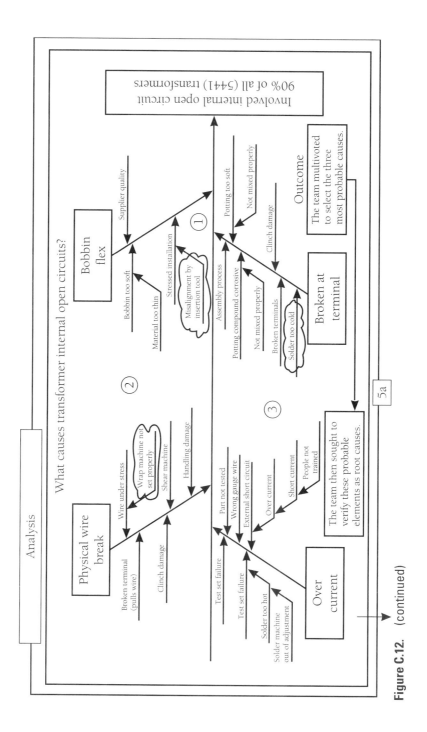

Involved internal open circuit
90% of all (5441) transformers

Bobbin flex

Supplier quality

Bobbin too soft

Material too thin

Stressed installation

Misalignment by insertion tool

①

Potting too soft

Not mixed properly

Assembly process

Potting compound corrosive

Not mixed properly

Broken terminals

Clinch damage

Solder too cold

Broken at terminal

Outcome

The team multivoted to select the three most probable causes.

Physical wire break

②

Wire under stress

Wrap machine not set properly

Shear machine

Handling damage

Broken terminal (pulls wire)

Clinch damage

③

Part not tested

Wrong gauge wire

External short circuit

Over current

Short current

People not trained

The team then sought to verify these probable elements as root causes.

Test set failure

Test set failure

Solder too hot

Solder machine out of adjustment

Over current

5a

Figure C.12. (continued)

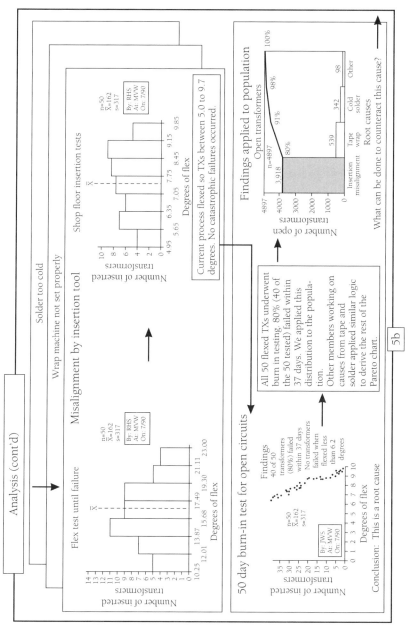

Figure C.12. (continued)

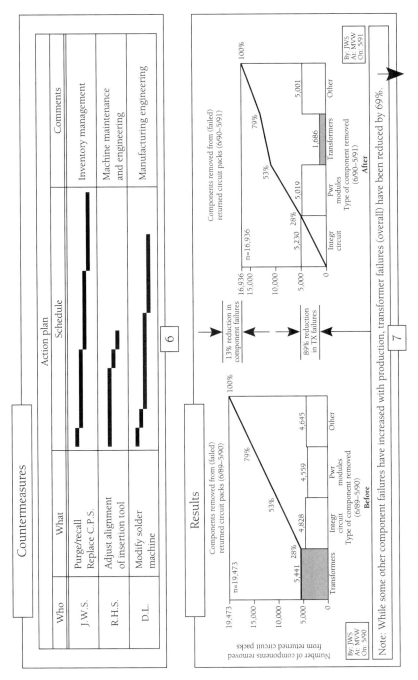

Countermeasures

Action plan

Who	What	Schedule	Comments
J.W.S.	Purge/recall Replace C.P.S.		Inventory management
R.H.S.	Adjust alignment of insertion tool		Machine maintenance and engineering
D.L.	Modify solder machine		Manufacturing engineering

6

Results

Components removed from (failed) returned circuit packs (6/89–5/90)

n=19,473

Before

By: JWS
At: MVW
On: 5/90

Components removed from (failed) returned circuit packs (6/90–5/91)

n=16,936

After

By: JWS
At: MVW
On: 5/91

13% reduction in component failures

89% reduction in TX failures

7

Note: While some other component failures have increased with production, transformer failures (overall) have been reduced by 69%.

Figure C.12. (continued)

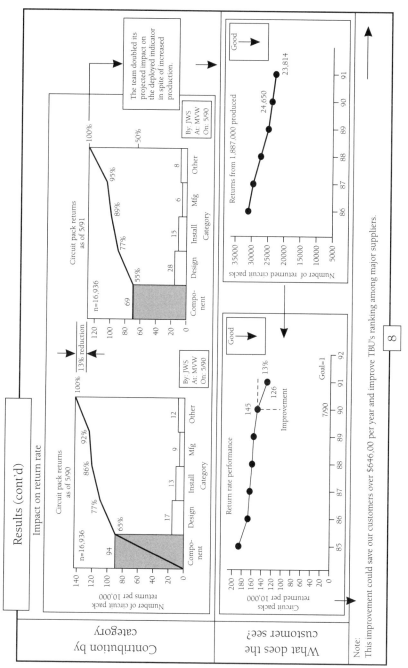

Figure C.12. (continued)

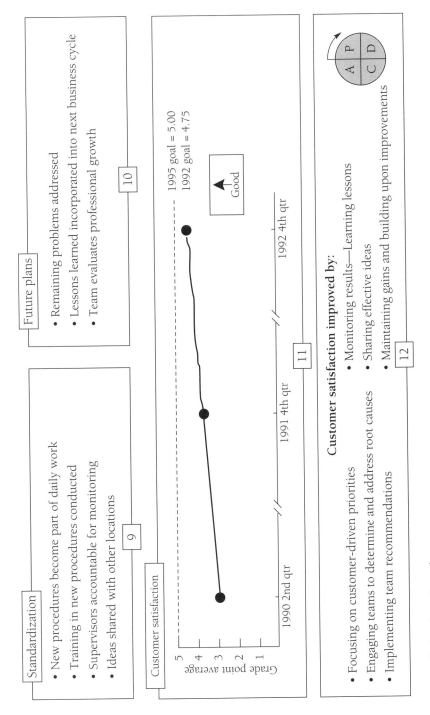

Figure C.12. (continued)

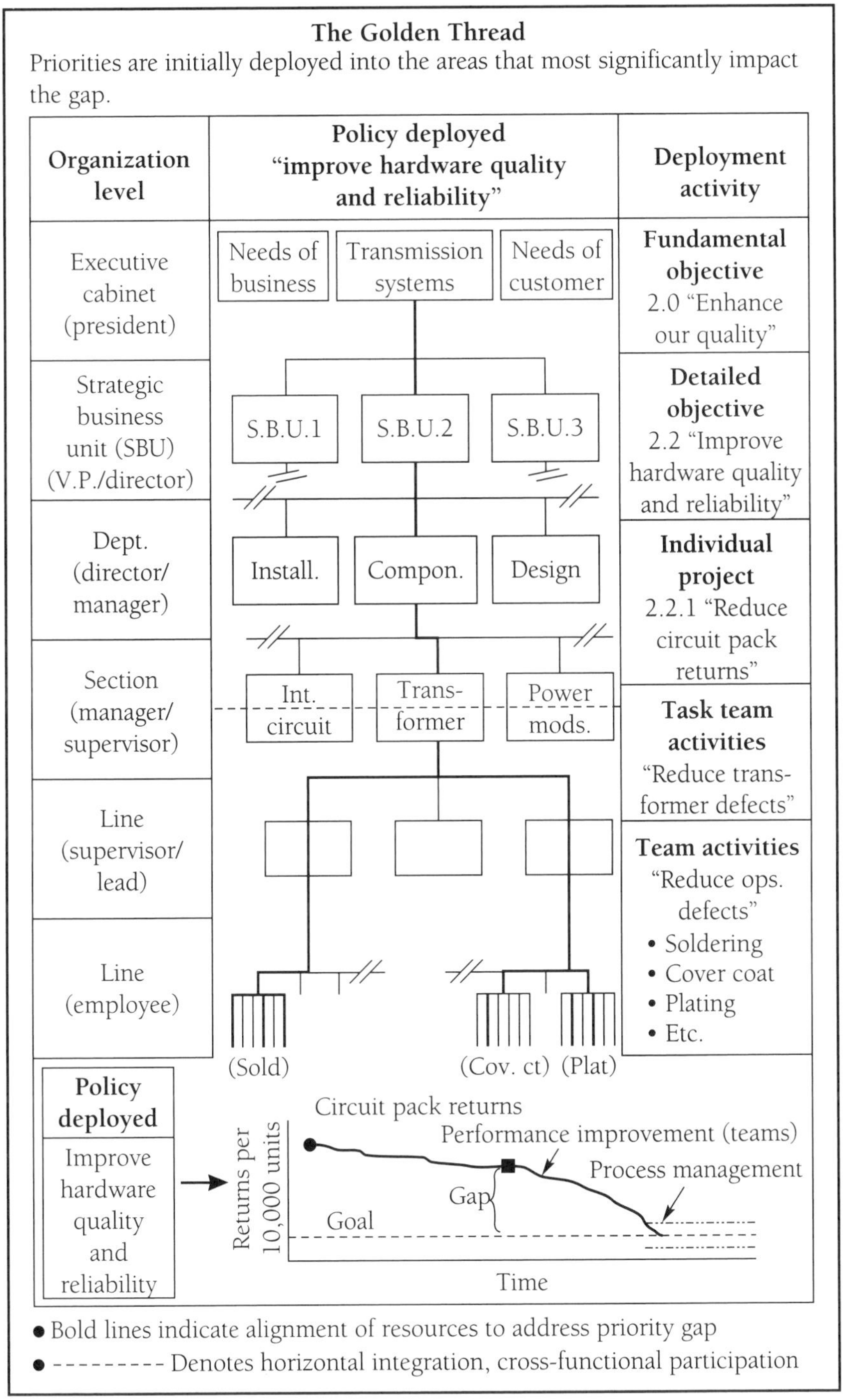

The Golden Thread
Priorities are initially deployed into the areas that most significantly impact the gap.
Organization level
Policy deployed "improve hardware quality and reliability"
Deployment activity
Executive cabinet (president)
Needs of business
Transmission systems
Needs of customer
Fundamental objective
2.0 "Enhance our quality"
Strategic business unit (SBU) (V.P./director)
S.B.U.1
S.B.U.2
S.B.U.3
Detailed objective
2.2 "Improve hardware quality and reliability"
Dept. (director/manager)
Install.
Compon.
Design
Individual project
2.2.1 "Reduce circuit pack returns"
Section (manager/supervisor)
Int. circuit
Trans-former
Power mods.
Task team activities
"Reduce trans-former defects"
Line (supervisor/lead)
Team activities
"Reduce ops. defects"
• Soldering
• Cover coat
• Plating
• Etc.
Line (employee)
(Sold)
(Cov. ct)
(Plat)
Policy deployed
Improve hardware quality and reliability
Circuit pack returns
Performance improvement (teams)
Process management
Returns per 10,000 units
Gap
Goal
Time
• Bold lines indicate alignment of resources to address priority gap
• --------- Denotes horizontal integration, cross-functional participation

Figure C.13. The route of one Golden Thread from the customer to employees on teams.

Note

1. Robert H. Seemer, "Winning More Than the Malcolm Baldrige National Quality Award at AT&T Transmission Systems," *National Productivity Review* (Spring 1993): 143–65.

Additional Resources

Competitive Technologies, Inc. *Policy Deployment Training Manual for AT&T Transmission Systems Business Unit.* Jupiter, Fla.: CTi Press, 1991.

Competitive Technologies, Inc. *Quality Improvement and Control Story.* Jupiter, Fla.: CTi Press, 1991.

Competitive Technologies, Inc. *Strategic Policy Management.* Jupiter, Fla.: CTi Press, 1991.

Kume, Hitoshi. *Statistical Methods for Quality Improvement.* Tokyo, Japan: AOTS Chosakai, Ltd., 1985.

Seemer, Robert. "Implementing TQM Through Policy Deployment." Presented for the National Engineering Consortium, New York, 1992.

Shingo, Shigeo. *Zero Quality Control.* Tokyo, Japan: Japan Management Association, 1985.

Appendix D

Case Study: QVALITY Improvement Program at Armstrong World Industries

The Improvement QVALITY Approach

In 1991, one of the plants of the multinational company, Armstrong World Industries, elaborated an improvement plan for 1992 based on the QVALITY customer satisfaction approach. It consisted of elaborating a plan of action for each of its seven departments, which culminated in a global plan for the plant. These departments were

1. Logistics
2. Quality control, and research and development
3. Maintenance and engineering.
4. Manufacturing "mineral"
5. Fiberglass
6. Human resources
7. Industrial engineering

To illustrate this, see the areas of improvement or blocks of improvement activities for the three departments 1, 2, 7, out of the seven, and the activities suggested within each block (see Figures D.1, D.2, and D.3).

In total, 50 blocks of improvement activities for the whole plant were identified (Figure D.4), and each of these blocks was related to one or more of the seven QVALITY characteristics which define the customers' needs (Figure D.5). Activities were aimed at improving each of the seven characteristics; however, the emphasis was on those most important for the customers. The cost–benefit relation of each suggested action was then considered.

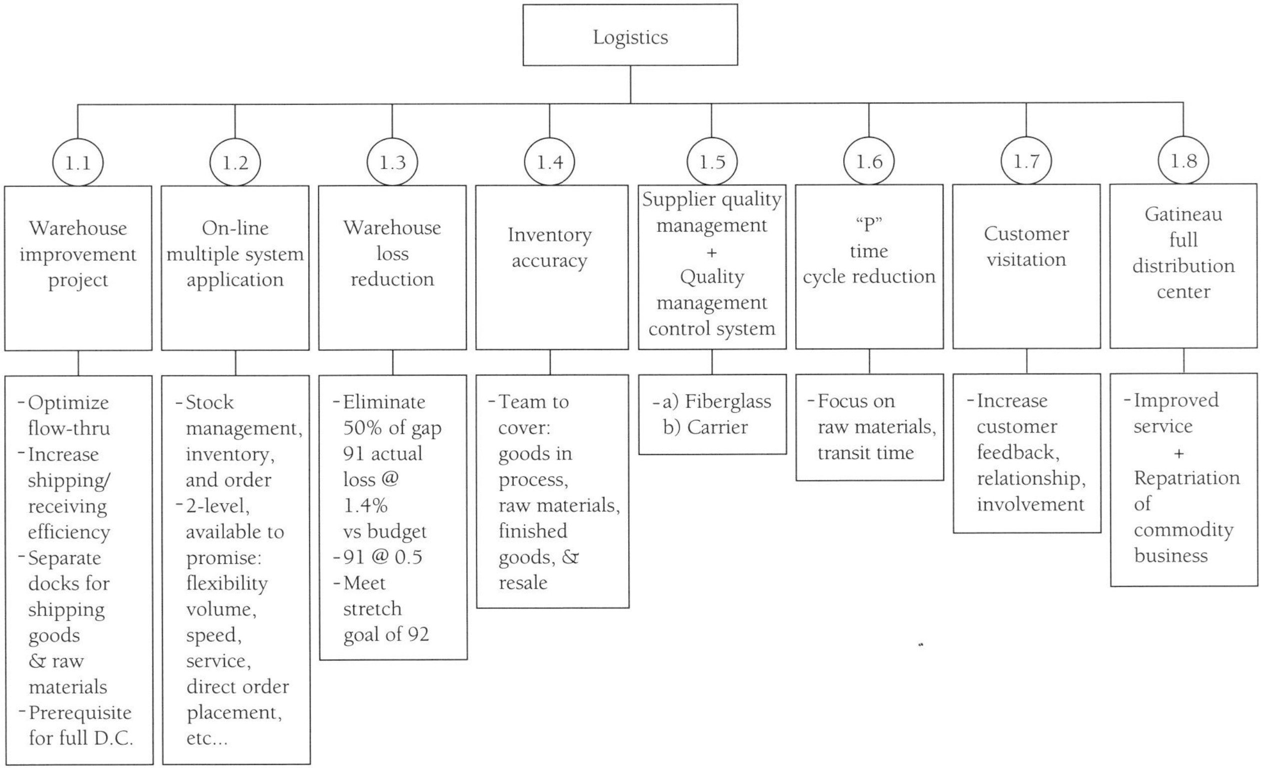

Figure D.1. The eight areas of improvement identified in the logistics department (department number 1) and the activities suggested to be undertaken in each area.

Figure D.2. The nine areas of improvement identified in the quality control and research and development department (department number 2) and the activities suggested to be undertaken in each area.

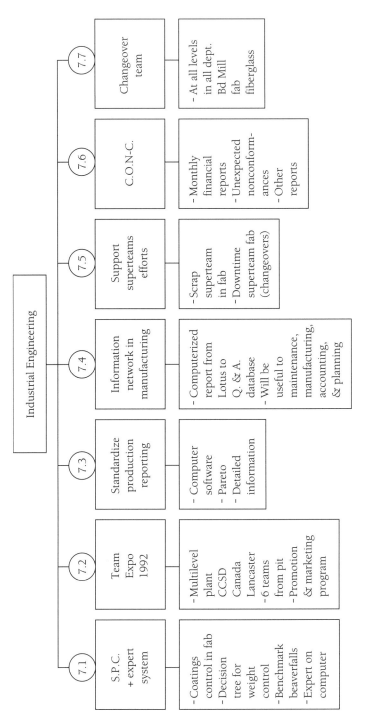

Figure D.3. The seven areas of improvement identified in the industrial engineering department (department number 7) and the activities suggested to be undertaken in each area.

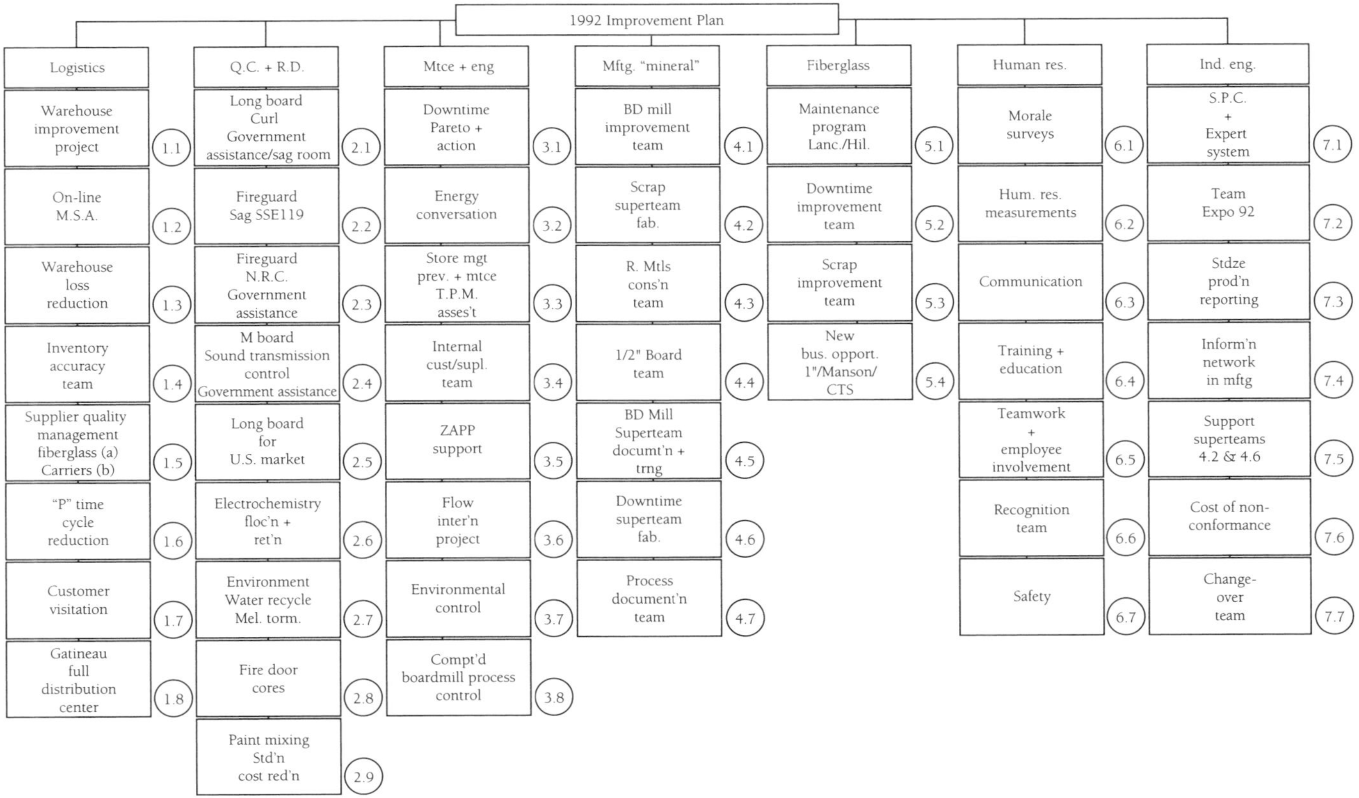

Figure D.4. The 50 areas of improvement identified for the whole plant, constituting its global improvement plan.

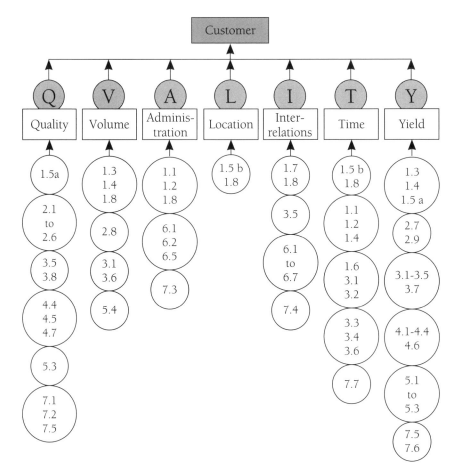

Figure D.5. Contribution of each of the 50 improvement activities blocks to one or more of the seven QVALITY factors.

Glossary

The definitions given to the following terms relate to their use in the management of organizations aiming at achieving their objectives. Therefore, they do not necessarily coincide with dictionary definitions.

Above customer expectations (ACE). Going beyond the mere satisfaction of a customer. Delighting the customer.

Absent turn-off factors (ATO). Factors that, when absent, repel customers and influence their decision not to buy a certain product from a certain vendor. These are the A and I factors in QVALITY. (see *QVALITY*)

Activity-based costing (ABC). A new approach to accounting in which the cost of any product in an organization is traced back to all activities contributing to its development, manufacturing, and delivery, including what—in traditional accounting—is termed overhead.

Activity-based management (ABM). The management of these activities in order to make sure they are done right, efficiently, and effectively. In the total quality extraversive approach, ABC/ABM can tie all activities in the organization to the satisfaction of shareholders' and customers' needs.

Customer. The person, persons, or organizations who decide or influence the decision to acquire a product. Some people advocate the use of the term *internal customer*. This expression has to be replaced by internal partner or teammate. Indeed, as explained before, the term internal customer can detract from the real end-customer, the only one. Besides, it tends to destroy the team spirit required to achieve total quality, as people work *for* a customer but *with* a partner. Moreover, the so-called internal customer may require actions or products that do not actually contribute to end-customer need satisfaction, but only to his or her personal needs. This results in a waste of a company's resources.

Extraversive management. Management in which the emphasis is *always* on the shareholders' and customers' needs. AT&T has developed the concept of Golden Threads which tie every activity or operation in an organization to these two stakeholders' needs (see appendix C). Individual managers' and their departments' evaluation is based on their contribution to these objectives.

Horizontal organization. Activities in an organization are carried out by cross-functional teams working on processes aimed at the satisfaction of shareholders, customers, and people in the organization.

Introversive management. This is the traditional way of management. Each manager is given departmental objectives that he or she has to achieve with the members of the group. For example, a personnel manager has to hire new employees, train the existing workforce, take care of health and safety of the employees, and so on. The buyer has to acquire goods and services as requested by other departments. The computer specialists develop and implement computer systems, and so on. There is no explicit mention in all these cases of the customers or the shareholders.

ISO 9000 series standards. This is an international series of quality management and quality assurance standards. Its purpose is to give buyers confidence in a supplier's quality system. What they standardize is not the quality of products but that of quality systems. Systems that comply with either of three of these standards (9001, 9002, 9003) can be registered by an accredited organization.

Kaizen, or continuing improvement. Kaizen is a strategy that maintains and improves the working standard through small, gradual improvements. It is continuing improvement, as opposed to radical improvement or innovation (as defined by Masaaki Imai, who coined the term *kaizen*).

Mass customization. Producing large quantities of almost made to measure products. This is the opposite of mass production where products are homogeneous if not of one type only. Henry Ford used to say he could manufacture cars in all colors as long as they were black.

Process. A process consists of a certain number of activities or operations which—acting on inputs in a given sequence—transform them to required outputs.

Process management. This includes the management of processes and management by processes. The management of a process means that all of the activities or operations of this process are required, are done correctly, at the right time, in the right place, by the right person.

Management by process (MBP), as opposed to management by function, is when work is organized and managed around a process (say order fulfillment or order to remittance) rather than around a function (marketing, production, purchasing, engineering), as is traditionally the case. MBP relies mainly on cross-functional teams.

Product. Any goods or services produced for a customer. We are not concerned here with internal products (introversive management).

Present turn-on factors (PTO). Factors that, when present, attract customers or influence their decision to buy a certain product from a certain vendor. These are the quality, the volume, the location, the time, and the yield, or QVLTY. (see *QVALITY*)

Quality. The totality of characteristics of a product (suitability, durability, reliability, dependability, and so on) and accompanying services (after-sales servicing, maintenance and repairs, warranties, and so on) that bear on its ability to satisfy a number of stated or implied customer needs.

Quality assurance. A number of systematic activities that provide a buyer the evidence needed to establish confidence that the quality function is being effectively performed. Contrary to quality control, quality assurance's objective is unquality prevention.

Quality control. This activity is aimed at unquality detection and correction. It relies on inspection, checks, and tests to make sure that what is done conforms to given specifications.

QVALITY. The seven factors that influence the decision of a person or organization to acquire or not acquire a certain product from a specific source or supplier: quality; volume; administrative procedures required to order, obtain credit, acquire, and pay for the product; location at which the product is available or can be shipped to, including the layout of the areas set up for the customers; interrelations between the customer and the organization's personnel or outside partners, and the image of an organization as perceived by its customers; timing and timeliness of the product availability and delivery; and yield of the product, which is the relation between the product's cost and benefits to the customer.

Reengineering. The radical change of a way of thinking or doing. It is synonymous with innovation and breakthrough.

Skill-based pay. A compensation system in which people are paid, not for what they do, but for what they can do. This results in people learning more skills and becoming more flexible and versatile.

Total quality. This is the raison d'être, the fundamental, triple objective of any organization: to provide a quality return for the shareholders, QVALITY + ACE for customers, and a quality of life for the people in the organization. Note that it is *not,* as many think or pretend, continuous improvement, zero defects, participative management, teamwork, the production of quality products at a minimum cost, doing things right the first time, and so on. It is also often mistaken for quality.

Total quality management. This is an extraversive management approach, essential for achieving and maintaining total quality. It is a profit-oriented, customer-focused, and people-centered approach in which people in a environmentally conscious organization constantly collaborate with outside upstream and downstream partners. It comprises a human aspect, is based on a logic, and uses a technology to achieve the total quality objectives.

Total quality triad. This triad consists of the three stakeholders of an organization who mutually satisfy each other's needs: the shareholder, the customer, and the people in the organization. It represents a win–win–win game.

Index

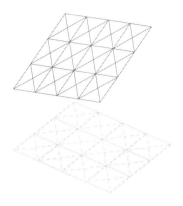